*Study Guide for*

LIPPINCOTT WILLIAMS AND WILKINS'

# CLINICAL

# Medical Assisting

5TH EDITION

*Study Guide for*
LIPPINCOTT WILLIAMS AND WILKINS'

# CLINICAL
# Medical Assisting

**Judy Kronenberger, PhD, RN, CMA(AAMA)**
Program Director, Medical Assisting Services
University of Cincinnati, Blue Ash College
Blue Ash, Ohio

Wolters Kluwer

Philadelphia • Baltimore • New York • London
Buenos Aires • Hong Kong • Sydney • Tokyo

*Acquisitions Editor:* Jay Campbell
*Senior Product Development Editor:* Amy Millholen
*Editorial Assistant:* Tish Rodgers
*Marketing Manager:* Shauna Kelley
*Production Project Manager:* David Saltzberg
*Design Coordinator:* Joan Wendt
*Manufacturing Coordinator:* Margie Orzech
*Prepress Vendor:* SPi Global

5th Edition

ISBN: 978-1-4963-1861-9

# Preface

Welcome to the *Study Guide for Lippincott Williams & Wilkins' Clinical Medical Assisting, Fifth Edition*. In this edition, I have aligned the exercises and activities with the most current (2015) Medical Assisting Education Review Board (MAERB) of the American Association of Medical Assistants (AAMA) curriculum standards. Program directors, instructors, and students will know which activities in this *Study Guide* support comprehension of knowledge from the textbook (cognitive domain), which support the practice and skills needed to become a competent entry-level medical assistant (psychomotor domain), and which exercises encourage critical thinking and professional behaviors in the medical office (affective domain). This *Study Guide* is unique in a number of ways and offers features that are not found in most Medical Assisting study guides.

The *Study Guide* is divided into sections that coincide with the textbook. Parts I and II include exercises that reinforce clinical and laboratory knowledge and skills. Part III includes activities to "put it all together" as a potential medical office employee. All chapters have been updated and revised and I believe the extensive revision of the Clinical Laboratory chapters will be especially helpful.

Each chapter includes the following:

- **Learning Outcomes**—Learning outcomes are listed at the beginning of the chapter and are divided into AAMA/CAAHEP categories (Cognitive, Psychomotor, Affective) and ABHES competencies.
- **A Variety of Question Formats**—To meet the needs of a variety of learning styles and to reinforce content and knowledge, each chapter of the *Study Guide* includes multiple choice, matching, short answer, completion, and where applicable, calculation-type questions. These formats will help you retain new information, reinforce previously learned content, and build confidence.
- **Case Studies for Critical Thinking**—These scenarios and questions are designed with real-world situations in mind and are intended to promote conversation about possible responses, not just one correct answer! These questions will be valuable to students who confront these types of situations during externship and graduates who encounter similar situations after employment.
- **Procedure Skill Sheets**—Every procedure in the textbook has a procedure skill sheet in the *Study Guide*. These procedures have been updated and revised in this edition and include steps on interacting with diverse patients, such as those who are visually or hearing impaired, those who do not speak English or who speak English as a second language (ESL), and patients who may have developmental challenges.
- **Putting It All Together**—Chapter 31 in the *Study Guide* gives students the opportunity to reinforce information learned throughout their program. This final *Study Guide* chapter includes documentation skills practice for a multitude of situations and active learning activities to engage students with previously learned knowledge.

This *Study Guide* has been developed in response to numerous requests from students and instructors for a concise, understandable, and interactive resource that covers the skills necessary to become a successful Medical Assistant. I hope you find the exercises and tools in this book productive and useful toward your goal of becoming the best Medical Assistant possible!

# Contents

*Study Guide for*
LIPPINCOTT WILLIAMS AND WILKINS'
# CLINICAL
## Medical Assisting

# The Clinical Medical Assistant

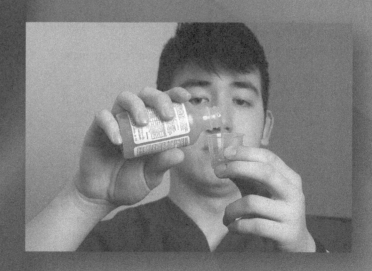

CHAPTER

# *1* Nutrition and Wellness

## Learning Outcomes

### COG Cognitive Domain

1. Spell and define the key terms
2. Identify body systems
3. List major organs in each body system
4. Identify the anatomical location of major organs in each body system
5. Describe the normal function of the digestive system
6. Analyze health care results as reported in graphs, and/or tables (BMI)
7. Describe dietary nutrients including carbohydrates, fat, protein, minerals, electrolytes, vitamins, fiber, and water.
8. Discuss the body's basal metabolic rate and its importance in weight management
9. Explain how to use the food pyramid and MyPlate guides to promote healthy food choices
10. Read and explain the information on food labels
11. Identify the special dietary needs for weight control, cardiovascular disease, and hypertension.
12. Define the function of dietary supplements
13. List the components of physical fitness
14. Discuss suggestions for a healthy lifestyle
15. Explain the importance of disease prevention
16. List and describe the effects of the substances most commonly abused
17. Recognize the dangers of substance abuse

### PSY Psychomotor Domain

1. Teach a patient how to read food labels (Procedure 1-1)
2. Document patient care accurately in the medical record
3. Develop a meal plan utilizing basic principles of nutrition (Procedure 1-2)
4. Instruct a patient according to patient's special dietary needs (Procedure 1-2)
5. Coach patients appropriately considering:
   a. cultural diversity
   b. developmental life stage
   c. communication barriers

### AFF Affective Domain

1. Incorporate critical thinking skills when performing patient assessment
2. Incorporate critical thinking skills when performing patient care
3. Show awareness of a patient's concerns regarding dietary changes

4. Protect the integrity of the medical record
5. Demonstrate:
   a. empathy
   b. active listening
   c. nonverbal communication
6. Demonstrate the principles of self-boundaries
7. Demonstrate respect for individual diversity including
   a. gender
   b. race
   c. religion
   d. age
   e. economic status
   f. appearance
8. Explain to a patient the rationale for performance of a procedure

### ABHES Competencies

1. Comprehend and explain to the patient the importance of diet and nutrition
2. Effectively convey and educate patients regarding the proper diet and nutrition guidelines
3. Identify categories of patients that require special diets or diet modifications
4. Document accurately

Name: _____    Date: _____    Grade: _____

## ⬡⬡G MULTIPLE CHOICE

Circle the letter preceding the correct answer.

1. The nutrient that cushions and protects body organs and sustains normal body temperature is:
   a. carbohydrate.
   b. fat.
   c. mineral.
   d. protein.
   e. vitamin.

2. The purpose of a therapeutic diet is to:
   a. treat an underlying condition or disease.
   b. enjoy foods that put a person in a good mood.
   c. experiment with foods not normally allowed on other diets.
   d. eat foods the person likes but only in moderation.
   e. replace medications.

3. Which of the following is true about the effects of drugs or alcohol on a developing fetus?
   a. They have no effect on the developing fetus.
   b. They could cause the baby to be addicted to the substance after birth.
   c. Drugs could cause the brain to stop developing, but alcohol has no effect.
   d. They can harm the fetus only if the mother harms herself while using them.
   e. They could make the fetus hyper in the womb but cause no long-term effects after birth.

4. Which of the following statements about cholesterol is true?
   a. A diet high in fat but low in cholesterol is healthy.
   b. Cholesterol is found only in animal products.
   c. Cholesterol is found in fresh fruits and vegetables.
   d. Since the body cannot produce cholesterol, it must be part of the diet.
   e. Adults should consume at least 350 mg of dietary cholesterol each day.

5. Which of the following would leave a person vulnerable to a disease?
   a. Keeping your immunizations up-to-date
   b. Washing your hands after using the bathroom
   c. Wearing insect repellent when outside in the summer
   d. Using someone else's antibiotics because he or she didn't finish them
   e. Washing cutting boards with soap and water after cutting uncooked chicken

6. Although alcohol intoxication may give a person a euphoric feeling, alcohol is a depressant. What does that mean?
   a. It gives the person a sad and gloomy feeling.
   b. It causes the person to suffer from depression.
   c. It causes increased heart rate and sleeplessness.
   d. It speeds up the functioning of the central nervous system.
   e. It causes a lack of coordination and impaired brain function.

7. The following statement about exercise is true:
   a. It induces stress.
   b. It suppresses the production of endorphins.
   c. It is effective if done for at least 40 minutes.
   d. It reduces the risk of developing certain diseases.
   e. Aerobic activities are most effective before target heart rate is reached.

8. Basal metabolic rate is:
   a. the constructive phase of metabolism.
   b. the destructive phase of metabolism.
   c. the baseline metabolic rate that is considered normal for the average adult.
   d. the amount of energy used in a unit of time to maintain vital functions by a fasting, resting person.
   e. the combination of the calories a person can consume and how long it takes to burn those calories.

9. A person who follows a lacto-ovo-vegetarian diet eats:
   a. vegetables only.
   b. vegetables and milk and cheese.
   c. vegetables and milk, eggs, and cheese.
   d. vegetables and milk, eggs, and poultry.
   e. vegetables and milk, eggs, and seafood.

10. Which of the following foods is a good source of fiber?
    a. Fish
    b. Milk
    c. Butter
    d. Chicken
    e. Vegetables

11. The five basic food groups include:
    a. dairy, vitamins, produce, meat, and grains.
    b. carbohydrates, fiber, vegetables, fruits, and meat.
    c. oils, lipids, refined sugars, whole grains, and dairy.
    d. grains, vegetables, milk, fruits, and meat and beans.
    e. proteins, carbohydrates, lipids, cholesterol, and minerals.

12. An overweight teenager asks you to suggest a cardiovascular exercise. Which of the following could you suggest?
    a. Yoga
    b. Sit-ups
    c. Stretching
    d. Lifting weights
    e. Jumping rope

13. Which vitamin is important for pregnant women because it reduces the risk of neural tube defects?
    a. Calcium
    b. Folate
    c. Mercury
    d. Potassium
    e. Zinc

14. To determine the correct number of daily servings from each food group, you need to know your:
    a. resting heart rate.
    b. height and weight.
    c. age and gender.
    d. waist measurement and target heart rate.
    e. level of physical activity and blood type.

15. How are refined grains different from whole grains?
    a. Refined grains are full of fiber.
    b. Whole grains lack fiber and iron.
    c. Whole grains are made with the entire grain kernel.
    d. Refined grains contain nutrients like carbohydrates and proteins.
    e. Refined grains are darker in color because they have more nutrients.

16. Water-soluble vitamins should be consumed:
    a. once a week.
    b. once a month.
    c. twice a week.
    d. daily.
    e. twice a month.

17. Pregnant women are advised to eat no more than one can of tuna per week because of the:
    a. iron content.
    b. lead content.
    c. mercury content.
    d. zinc content.
    e. calcium content.

18. How are substances such as cocaine and marijuana different from alcohol and nicotine?
    a. Alcohol and nicotine are legal; marijuana and cocaine are illegal.
    b. Cocaine and marijuana will not cause sudden death; alcohol and nicotine will cause sudden death.
    c. Alcohol and nicotine do not harm the body; marijuana and cocaine do harm the body.
    d. Cocaine and marijuana are used by people with health problems; alcohol and nicotine are not.
    e. Alcohol and nicotine are not addictive drugs; marijuana and cocaine are addictive drugs.

19. Which of the following drugs damages blood vessels, decreases heart strength, and causes several types of cancer?
    a. Caffeine
    b. Nicotine
    c. Hashish
    d. Mescaline
    e. Phencyclidine

20. Why does inhaling marijuana smoke cause more damage to a person's body than tobacco smoke?
    a. Marijuana smoke is inhaled as unfiltered smoke, so users take in more cancer-causing agents and do more damage to the respiratory system than with regular filtered tobacco smoke.
    b. Marijuana smoke is thicker and more odorous.
    c. Marijuana smoke is inhaled as filtered smoke, so users take in less cancer-causing agents and do more damage to the respiratory system than with regular filtered tobacco smoke.
    d. Marijuana smoke is inhaled more quickly than tobacco smoke.
    e. Marijuana plants are grown in more toxic environments than tobacco plants.

## ⬤⬤⬤ MATCHING

Match the essential nutrient with its description by placing the letter preceding the description of its function on the line next to the name of the nutrient.

**Nutrients**

21. _____ carbohydrates
22. _____ proteins
23. _____ fats
24. _____ vitamins
25. _____ minerals

**Description**

**a.** cushion and protect body organs and sustain normal body temperature
**b.** chemical substances that provide the body with energy
**c.** inorganic substances used in the formation of hard and soft body tissue
**d.** organic substances that enhance the breakdown of other nutrients in the body
**e.** substances that contain amino acids and help to build and repair tissue

## ⬤⬤⬤ MATCHING

Match the following terms to the correct definitions. Place the letter preceding the term on the line next to the sentence that best describes its definition.

**Key Terms**

26. _____ anabolism
27. _____ anencephaly
28. _____ basal metabolic rate
29. _____ body mass index
30. _____ calorie
31. _____ catabolism
32. _____ dental cavities
33. _____ endorphins
34. _____ essential amino acids
35. _____ euphoria
36. _____ homeostasis
37. _____ metabolism
38. _____ minerals
39. _____ spina bifida
40. _____ lipoprotein

**Definitions**

**a.** inorganic substances used in the formation of hard and soft body tissue
**b.** a process in which larger molecules break down into smaller molecules
**c.** a neural tube defect that causes an incomplete closure of a fetus' spine during early pregnancy
**d.** a neural tube defect that affects the fetus' brain during early pregnancy
**e.** a good feeling
**f.** maintaining a constant internal environment by balancing positive and negative feedback
**g.** a process in which smaller molecules are converted into larger molecules as food is absorbed into the bloodstream
**h.** the amount of energy used in a unit of time to maintain vital function by a fasting, resting subject
**i.** transports cholesterol between the liver and arterial walls
**j.** the sum of chemical processes that result in growth, energy production, elimination of waste, and body functions performed as digested nutrients are distributed
**k.** areas of decay in the teeth
**l.** pain-relieving substance released naturally from the brain
**m.** an individual's ratio of fat to lean body mass
**n.** proteins that come from your diet because the body does not produce them
**o.** the amount of energy used by the body

## ⬤⬤⬤ IDENTIFICATION

41. Indicate whether the following vitamins are fat soluble or water soluble by writing FS (fat soluble) or WS (water soluble) on the line preceding the name of the vitamin.

   **a.** _____ Vitamin A

   **b.** _____ Vitamin B complex

   **c.** _____ Vitamin C

   **d.** _____ Vitamin D

**e.** _____ Vitamin E

**f.** _____ Vitamin K

**g.** _____ Thiamin

**h.** _____ Riboflavin

**i.** _____ Niacin

**j.** _____ Folic acid

## **COG** COMPLETION

_____ Grade: _____

**42.** Calculate the maximum heart rate and target heart rate for the individuals below based on their ages and desired intensity.

| Person | Age | Maximum Heart Rate | Desired Intensity | Target Heart Rate |
|---|---|---|---|---|
| **a.** Tara | 25 | | 80% | |
| **b.** Yolanda | 45 | | 65% | |
| **c.** Hilel | 37 | | 75% | |
| **d.** Marco | 18 | | 90% | |

**43.** Review the food pyramid in your textbook and answer the following questions based on a 2,000-calorie diet.

**a.** How much food from the grains category should be eaten in a day? _____

**b.** How many vegetables should be eaten in a day? _____

**c.** How much fruit should be eaten in a day? _____

**d.** How much milk should be consumed in a day? _____

**e.** How much from the meat and beans category should be consumed in a day? _____

**44.** Answer the following questions based on the food label (Figure 1-4) in your textbook.

**a.** How many servings are in this can of vegetables? _____

**b.** What is the serving size? _____

**c.** How many calories are from fat per serving? _____

**d.** What is the least amount of sugar you would consume if you ate one cup of this vegetable? _____

**e.** What is the percentage of sodium in one serving? _____

**COG SHORT ANSWER**

Grade: _____

**45.** Explain what BMI stands for and describe how it is calculated.

_____

_____

_____

_____

**46.** Explain the three basic ways the body expends energy.

**a.** Basal metabolic rate:

_____

_____

_____

_____

**b.** Levels of physical activity:

_____

_____

_____

_____

**c.** Thermic effect of food:

_____

_____

_____

_____

**47.** What is the best defense against illness?

_____

_____

_____

_____

**48.** List three techniques that can help lessen stress.

_____

_____

_____

_____

**49.** Drugs can be classified as stimulants and/or depressants that cause various effects on the body. Read each symptom below and place a check in the appropriate column.

| Symptom | Depressant | Stimulant | Both |
|---|---|---|---|
| **a.** Poor fetal health | | | |
| **b.** Increased heart rate | | | |
| **c.** Psychological and physical dependence | | | |
| **d.** Increased pulse rate | | | |
| **e.** Slow respiratory rate | | | |
| **f.** Sleeplessness and anxiety | | | |
| **g.** Decreased activities of the central nervous system | | | |

**50.** There are two phases in the process of metabolism: anabolism and catabolism. Indicate on the line provided whether the statement about metabolism describes anabolism (A) or catabolism (C).

**a.** _____ Constructive phase.

**b.** _____ Amino acids are converted into proteins.

**c.** _____ Destructive phase.

**d.** _____ Smaller molecules are converted into larger molecules.

**e.** _____ Larger molecules are converted into smaller molecules.

**f.** _____ Breakdown fats to use for energy.

**g.** _____ Complex carbohydrates, such as starch, are converted into simple sugars.

**51.** Look at the list of foods and indicate on the line whether the food contains a good fat (G) or bad fat (B). Place the letter G on the line if the item is "good" and B if the item is "bad."

**a.** _____ Salmon

**b.** _____ Olive oil

**c.** _____ Hamburger

**d.** _____ Margarine

**e.** _____ Crackers

f. _____ Soybean oil

g. _____ Nuts

h. _____ Cookies

i. _____ Steak

j. _____ Sunflower oil

## COG AFF CASE STUDY FOR CRITICAL THINKING

_____ Grade: _____

1. While conducting a patient interview, your patient, a 20-year-old college student, is concerned about gaining weight. She says she eats the same foods as her roommate, but her roommate does not gain weight, and she has put on 25 pounds since starting school. The roommate has told your patient that she can eat more food because she has a "high" metabolism rate. The patient is not sure what this means. How will you answer your patient? Would you recommend a reduced fat and/or calorie diet? Why or why not?

_____

_____

_____

_____

2. When educating a patient on the difference between whole grains and refined grains, what would you tell your patient?

_____

_____

_____

_____

3. Mr. Consuelo is the president of a large manufacturing company. He is seeing Dr. Smith for frequent headaches. Dr. Smith has diagnosed the headaches as stress induced and has recommended that Mr. Consuelo develop some coping mechanisms to reduce the stress in his life. As Mr. Consuelo leaves the office, he asks you about ways he can comply with Dr. Smith's recommendation to decrease the stress in his life. What strategies can you offer this patient?

_____

_____

_____

_____

4. Marco is 53 years old and has been smoking since he was 13. He says he would like to try and quit smoking, but he doesn't think it's worth it because the damage is probably already done. What would you say to him?

_____

_____

_____

5. The physician asks you to explain the DASH diet to a patient with high blood pressure. How would you explain this diet including the basic dietary guidelines to a patient who speaks very little English?

_____

_____

_____

_____

6. Angelo, a 22-year-old man, comes to the office for a checkup. While interviewing him, he tells you that he drinks a lot on the weekends, but it's "no big deal." What three things could you say to Angelo that may help him understand that excessive alcohol is a big deal?

_____

_____

_____

7. Dr. Mercer has given Joe, an overweight patient, clearance to start exercising. He told him to include workouts that will target each of the components of physical fitness. Joe feels overwhelmed. When talking to Joe, describe how you would explain the three components of physical fitness and how each one will help his body and health.

_____

_____

_____

_____

8. Your patient Carolyn is working with a nutritionist to improve her health. The nutritionist told her it is okay to take vitamins C and B every day; however, she indicated that Carolyn should not take vitamin E every day. During her office visit, Carolyn asks you why she should not take vitamin E every day because she thought it was necessary to take all vitamins every day. What would you say to Carolyn?

_____

_____

_____

9. A patient is upset because he has been placed on a special therapeutic diet because of his high blood pressure. He doesn't understand why he needs to stop eating some of his favorite foods, and he is worried he will not be successful with changing his diet. How can you encourage him to follow the physicians order to improve his health?

_____

_____

_____

**10.** Your 17-year-old patient comes in to the physician's office because he has a bad cough. This is the second time this winter that he has seen the physician for respiratory problems. When you review the patient's chart, you see that he had asthma when he was younger. You ask the patient if he smokes and he says that he does occasionally with his friends but also indicates that he is "not a smoker" because he's not addicted to nicotine. He also notes that he would prefer that his parents not know that he smokes, even occasionally. What should you say to this patient about his breathing issues? Would it be appropriate to tell his parents? Why or why not?

_____

_____

_____

**PSY  PROCEDURE 1-1    Teach a Patient How to Read Food Labels**

Name: _____ Date: _____ Time: _____ Grade: _____

**EQUIPMENT/SUPPLIES:** Two boxes of the same item, one low calorie or "lite," the other regular; measuring cup; two bowls

**STANDARDS:** Given the needed equipment and a place to work, the student will perform this skill with _____ % accuracy in a total of _____ minutes. *(Your instructor will tell you what the percentage and time limits will be before you begin.)*

**KEY:**         4 = Satisfactory              0 = Unsatisfactory              NA = This step is not counted

| PROCEDURE STEPS | SELF | PARTNER | INSTRUCTOR |
|---|---|---|---|
| **1.** Identify the patient. | ❑ | ❑ | ❑ |
| **2.** Introduce yourself and explain the procedure including the rationale. | ❑ | ❑ | ❑ |
| **3.** Have the patient look at the labels comparing the two. | ❑ | ❑ | ❑ |
| **4.** Ask the patient to pour out a normal serving. | ❑ | ❑ | ❑ |
| **5.** Measure the exact serving size printed on the label. | ❑ | ❑ | ❑ |
| **6.** Compare the two. Discuss the difference, if any. | ❑ | ❑ | ❑ |
| **7.** Explain to the patient the sections of the label: serving size and servings per package. | ❑ | ❑ | ❑ |
| **8.** Explain column for amount in serving. | ❑ | ❑ | ❑ |
| **9.** Explain column for percent daily value (formerly RDA). | ❑ | ❑ | ❑ |
| **10.** Explain calories and calories from fat. | ❑ | ❑ | ❑ |
| **11.** Have the patient calculate the percentage of fat calories and compare with the label. | ❑ | ❑ | ❑ |
| **12.** Read down the label and discuss each nutrient, pointing out the amounts and percentages. | ❑ | ❑ | ❑ |
| **13.** Have the patient compare the two labels and tell you how many total carbohydrates are in each label, sugars, protein, etc. | ❑ | ❑ | ❑ |
| **14.** **AFF** Explain how to respond to a patient who has religious or personal beliefs against eating specific food groups, such as meats. | ❑ | ❑ | ❑ |

_____

_____

_____

_____

**PSY** PROCEDURE 1-1 **Teach a Patient How to Read Food Labels** (continued)

| | | | |
|---|---|---|---|
| **15.** Ask the patient if she has any questions. | ❏ | ❏ | ❏ |
| **16.** Log into the Electronic Medical Record (EMR) using your username and secure password OR obtain the paper medical record from a secure location and assure it is kept away from public access. | ❏ | ❏ | ❏ |
| **17.** Chart the verbal and written instructions given to the patient. When finished, log out of the EMR and/or replace the paper medical record in an appropriate and secure location. | ❏ | ❏ | ❏ |

**CALCULATION**

Total Possible Points: _____

Total Points Earned: _____ Multiplied by 100 = _____ Divided by Total Possible Points = _____ %

**PASS    FAIL    COMMENTS:**
❏         ❏

Student's signature _____ Date _____

Partner's signature _____ Date _____

Instructor's signature _____ Date _____

| **PSY**   PROCEDURE 1-2 | **Develop a Meal Plan Utilizing Basic Principles of Nutrition; Instruct a Patient according to Patient's Special Dietary Needs** |
|---|---|

Name: _____   Date: _____   Time: _____   Grade: _____

**EQUIPMENT/SUPPLIES:** Reference materials related to dietary choices that include nutritional components (i.e., calories and nutrient amounts such as protein, fat, and carbohydrates), a physician order, and the patient medical record.

**STANDARDS:** Given the needed equipment and a place to work, the student will perform this skill with _____ % accuracy in a total of _____ minutes. *(Your instructor will tell you what the percentage and time limits will be before you begin.)*

**KEY:**          4 = Satisfactory                    0 = Unsatisfactory                    NA = This step is not counted

| PROCEDURE STEPS | SELF | PARTNER | INSTRUCTOR |
|---|---|---|---|
| 1. Review the physician order to determine the specific nutritional information necessary for patient instruction. | ❑ | ❑ | ❑ |
| 2. Identify the patient. | ❑ | ❑ | ❑ |
| 3. Introduce yourself and explain the procedure including the rationale. | ❑ | ❑ | ❑ |
| 4. Develop a meal plan based on a regular (i.e., no special dietary needs) 2,000 calorie diet and include information on basic nutrition (nutrients, serving sizes, and calories). Printable materials may be used during instruction from the choosemyplate.gov website if approved by the physician. | ❑ | ❑ | ❑ |
| 5. Observe the patient during instruction for non-verbal signs such as confusion, interest or disinterest, emotions, etc. | ❑ | ❑ | ❑ |
| 6. Explain how to respond to a patient who verbalizes concern about the ability to purchase fresh fruits and vegetables due to lack of monetary resources and reliance on public transportation to shop for groceries. | ❑ | ❑ | ❑ |
| 7. Instruct a patient according to one of the following special dietary needs as ordered by the physician: <br> a. low sodium <br> b. low fat <br> c. low carbohydrate <br> d. high protein <br> e. restricted calorie (i.e., 500, 1,800, etc.) <br> f. lactose free <br> g. gluten free <br> h. high fiber | ❑ | ❑ | ❑ |
| 8. Ask the patient questions during instruction and allow the opportunity for them to ask questions during instruction and at the end. | ❑ | ❑ | ❑ |

**PSY** PROCEDURE 1-2 **Develop a Meal Plan Utilizing Basic Principles of Nutrition; Instruct a Patient according to Patient's Special Dietary Needs** (continued)

| | | | |
|---|---|---|---|
| **9.** Explain how to respond to a patient who has a religious or personal belief against specific food groups such as a vegetarian. | ❏ | ❏ | ❏ |
| **10.** Log into the Electronic Medical Record (EMR) using your username and secure password OR obtain the paper medical record from a secure location and assure it is kept away from public access. | ❏ | ❏ | ❏ |
| **11.** Chart the verbal and written instructions given to the patient. When finished, log out of the EMR and/or replace the paper medical record in an appropriate and secure location. | ❏ | ❏ | ❏ |

_____

_____

_____

_____

**CALCULATION**

Total Possible Points: _____

Total Points Earned: _____ Multiplied by 100 = _____ Divided by Total Possible Points = _____ %

**PASS   FAIL   COMMENTS:**
  ❏      ❏

Student's signature _____ Date _____

Partner's signature _____ Date _____

Instructor's signature _____ Date _____

# CHAPTER

# 2 Medical Asepsis and Infection Control

---

## Learning Outcomes

### **COG** Cognitive Domain

1. Spell and define key terms
2. Describe the infection cycle, including the infectious agent, reservoir, susceptible host, means of transmission, portals of entry, and portals of exit
3. List major types of infectious agents
4. Identify different methods of controlling the growth of microorganisms
5. Define the following as practiced within an ambulatory care setting: (a) medical asepsis; (b) surgical asepsis
6. List the various ways microbes are transmitted
7. Define the principles of standard precautions
8. Compare the effectiveness in reducing or destroying microorganisms using the various levels of infection control

9. Identify personal safety precautions as established by the Occupational Safety and Health Administration (OSHA)
10. Define personal protective equipment (PPE) for: (a) all body fluids, secretions, and excretions; (b) blood; (c) nonintact skin; (d) mucous membranes
11. Identify Center for Disease Control (CDC) regulations that impact health care practices
12. List the required components of an exposure control plan
13. Explain the facts pertaining to the transmission and prevention of the hepatitis B virus and the human immunodeficiency virus in the medical office

### **PSY** Psychomotor Domain

1. Perform a medical aseptic hand-washing procedure (Procedure 2-1)

2. Select appropriate PPE and remove contaminated gloves (Procedure 2-2)
3. Clean and decontaminate biohazardous spills (Procedure 2-3)
4. Participate in bloodborne pathogen training (Procedure 2-4)

### **AFF** Affective Domain

1. Incorporate critical thinking skills when performing patient care
2. Recognize the implications for failure to comply with the Center for Disease Control (CDC) regulations in health care settings.

### **ABHES Competencies**

1. Apply principles of aseptic techniques and infection control
2. Use standard precautions
3. Dispose of biohazardous materials

Name: _____  Date: _____  Grade: _____

## COG MULTIPLE CHOICE

Circle the letter preceding the correct answer.
*Scenario for Questions 1 through 3:* Susan enters the examination room, where a patient is being seen for flu-like symptoms. While Susan takes the patient's blood pressure, the patient suddenly coughs near her face. Three days later, Susan has the same signs and symptoms as the patient.

1. Which of the following terms best describes the patient in the infection cycle?
   **a.** Reservoir host
   **b.** Disease portal
   **c.** Pathogen portal
   **d.** Susceptible host
   **e.** Disease transmitter

2. Which of the following procedures could Susan have performed that might have helped to minimize contracting the patient's disease?
   **a.** Ask the patient to look the other way while coughing.
   **b.** Put on a facemask before entering the exam room.
   **c.** Run out of the room right after the patient coughed.
   **d.** Wash her face right after the coughing episode.
   **e.** Sterilize the examination room.

3. What type of transmission process occurred during Susan's contact with the patient?
   **a.** Direct
   **b.** Vector
   **c.** Viable
   **d.** Manual
   **e.** Indirect

4. *Clostridium tetani* causes tetanus. Because it does not require oxygen to survive, this microbe is an example of an:
   **a.** anoxic bacteria.
   **b.** aerobic bacteria.
   **c.** anaerobic bacteria.
   **d.** anaerolytic bacteria.
   **e.** aerosolized bacteria.

5. Which of the following groups of conditions best favors microbial growth?
   **a.** Cold, light, and dry
   **b.** Dry, dark, and warm
   **c.** Dark, moist, and cool
   **d.** Warm, moist, and light
   **e.** Moist, warm, and dark

6. *Escherichia coli* is normally found in the intestinal tract. *Escherichia coli* can be transmitted to the urinary tract, causing an infection. When in the urinary tract, *E. coli* is an example of:
   **a.** viral flora.
   **b.** normal flora.
   **c.** resident flora.
   **d.** resistant flora.
   **e.** transient flora.

7. Which of the following practices is most important for maintaining medical asepsis?
   **a.** Airing out examination rooms after each patient
   **b.** Receiving all available vaccinations on an annual basis
   **c.** Wearing gloves before and after handling medical tools
   **d.** Wearing a gown if you are concerned about bodily fluids
   **e.** Washing your hands before and after each patient contact

8. To minimize infection, an endoscope should be:
   **a.** rinsed.
   **b.** sanitized.
   **c.** sterilized.
   **d.** disinfected.
   **e.** germicided.

9. At which temperature do most pathogenic microorganisms thrive?
   **a.** Below 32°F
   **b.** Above 212°F
   **c.** Around body temperature
   **d.** Around room temperature
   **e.** At any temperature

10. What level of disinfection would be appropriate to use when cleaning a speculum?
    **a.** None
    **b.** Low
    **c.** Intermediate
    **d.** High
    **e.** Sterilization

11. Which of the following job responsibilities has the highest risk exposure in the group?
    **a.** Measuring a patient's body temperature
    **b.** Covering a urine-filled specimen jar
    **c.** Drawing blood for lab analysis
    **d.** Auscultating a blood pressure
    **e.** Irrigating a patient's ear for excess earwax.

**12.** OSHA is responsible for:
   **a.** certifying all medical doctors.
   **b.** vaccinating school-age children.
   **c.** ensuring the safety of all workers.
   **d.** analyzing medical laboratory samples.
   **e.** caring for people with contagious diseases.

**13.** Jeremy approaches you and says that he just accidentally stuck himself with a needle while drawing a blood sample from a patient. He points to his thumb, where you can see a puncture. There is no bleeding. Which of the following actions should you take *first*?
   **a.** Direct Jeremy to wash his hands with soap and water.
   **b.** Lance the puncture with a scalpel to induce bleeding.
   **c.** Help him complete an exposure report right away.
   **d.** Call the physician in the office to ask for advice.
   **e.** Drive him to an occupational health clinic.

**14.** One example of PPE includes:
   **a.** name tag.
   **b.** stethoscope.
   **c.** face shield.
   **d.** scrub pants.
   **e.** syringe.

**15.** A patient arrives at the urgent care center complaining of nausea. As you begin to assess her, she begins to vomit bright red blood. Which of the following sets of PPE would be *most* appropriate to wear in this circumstance?
   **a.** Gown, gloves, and booties
   **b.** Eyewear, gown, and uniform
   **c.** Face shield and safety glasses
   **d.** Gloves, face shield, and gown
   **e.** Face shield, gown, and booties

**16.** Which of the following statements is *true* regarding hepatitis B virus (HBV)?
   **a.** HBV dies quickly outside the host body.
   **b.** There are no effective treatments for HBV.
   **c.** There is no vaccine protection against HBV.
   **d.** HBV is transmitted through blood contact, such as a needle puncture.
   **e.** It is easier to contract human immunodeficiency virus (HIV) than HBV.

**17.** Which of the following is *not* part of the body's natural defenses against disease?
   **a.** Plasma in blood
   **b.** Mucus in the nose
   **c.** Lysozyme in tears
   **d.** Saliva in the mouth
   **e.** Acid in the stomach

**18.** A vial of blood fell on the floor, glass broke, and the contents spilled on the floor. Proper cleaning of this spill includes:
   **a.** depositing the blood-soaked towels into a biohazard container.
   **b.** pouring hot water carefully onto the spill to avoid any splash.
   **c.** notifying the physician.
   **d.** allowing the blood to dry before cleaning.
   **e.** trying to piece the vial back together.

**19.** If a biohazard container becomes contaminated on the outside, you should:
   **a.** fill out a biohazard report form.
   **b.** immediately wash the surface in a sink.
   **c.** dispose of the container in a trash facility outside.
   **d.** place the container inside another approved container.
   **e.** call the biohazard removal company as soon as possible.

**20.** You should change your gloves *after*:
   **a.** touching a patient's saliva.
   **b.** measuring a patient's weight.
   **c.** auscultating a blood pressure.
   **d.** palpating a patient's abdomen.
   **e.** taking a patient's temperature.

## COG MATCHING

Grade: _____

Match each key term with its description.

**Key Terms**

21. _____ aerobe
22. _____ asymptomatic
23. _____ disinfection
24. _____ germicide
25. _____ immunization
26. _____ microorganisms
27. _____ pathogens
28. _____ resistance
29. _____ spore
30. _____ sanitation
31. _____ standard precautions
32. _____ virulent

**Definitions**

a. the killing or rendering inert of most, but not all, pathogenic microorganisms
b. disease-causing microorganisms
c. bacterial life form that resists destruction by heat, drying, or chemicals
d. highly pathogenic and disease- producing; describes a microorganism
e. chemical that kills most pathogenic microorganisms; disinfectant
f. maintenance of a healthful, disease-free environment
g. microscopic living organisms
h. usual steps to prevent injury or disease
i. without any symptoms
j. body's immune response to prevent infections by invading pathogenic microorganisms
k. microorganism that requires oxygen to live and reproduce
l. act or process of rendering an individual immune to specific disease

## COG IDENTIFICATION

Grade: _____

33. Indicate whether the following microorganisms are resident or transient flora by writing RF (resident flora) or TF (transient flora) on the line preceding the name of the microbe and its location on or in the body.

a. _____ *Escherichia coli* (large intestine)

b. _____ *Staphylococcus aureus* (subcutaneous tissue)

c. _____ *Escherichia coli* (peritoneum)

d. _____ *Staphylococcus aureus* (epidermis; skin)

e. _____ *Helicobacter pylori* (digestive tract)

34. Indicate whether the following situations could be a direct or indirect mode of disease transmission by writing D (direct) or I (indirect) on the line preceding the situation.

a. _____ Shaking hands with someone

b. _____ Getting a mosquito bite

c. _____ Cleaning up a broken blood tube on the floor without gloves

d. _____ Sneezing

e. _____ Removing a tick from your leg

f. _____ Sharing a soda with a friend using the same straw

**35.** What type of PPE might be appropriate for a medical assistant to wear when facing specific types of bodily fluids? Place a check mark on the line under each of the types of PPE, if any, that you would use based on the patient's presentation in the exam room.

| Patient Presentation | Gloves | Protective Eyewear | Mask | Gown |
|---|---|---|---|---|
| **a.** Abdominal pain, vomiting | | | | |
| **b.** Abdominal pain | | | | |
| **c.** Headache, coughing | | | | |
| **d.** Confusion, nausea, diarrhea | | | | |
| **e.** Fever, nonproductive cough | | | | |
| **f.** Generalized weakness | | | | |

## COG SHORT ANSWER

Grade: _____

**36.** Your body is in a constant state of war—battling pathogens that are intent on getting into your body to grow and reproduce. Fortunately, your body has a variety of mechanisms to fight off pathogens. For each of the body structures below, explain how it fights the pathogens to protect the body.

**a.** Nose cilia: _____

**b.** Mucus: _____

**c.** Skin: _____

**d.** Urination: _____

**e.** Tears: _____

**f.** Saliva: _____

**g.** Stomach: _____

**37.** A nondisposable vaginal speculum has just been used by the physician on a patient. After the exam is over and the patient leaves, how do you prepare this equipment for the next patient?

_____

_____

_____

_____

**38.** Name four factors that affect the disinfection process.

_____

_____

_____

_____

**39.** You accidentally stick yourself with a bloody needle. After washing the site, describe what you should do next.

_____

_____

_____

_____

## **COG** TRUE OR FALSE?

Grade: _____

**40.** Indicate whether the statements are true or false by placing the letter T (true) or F (false) on the line preceding the statement.

**a.** _____ Adhering to "clean technique," or medical asepsis, ensures that an object or area is free from all microorganisms.

**b.** _____ Sterilization is the highest level of infection control.

**c.** _____ Low-level disinfection destroys bacteria, but not viruses.

**d.** _____ There are three levels of disinfection: minor, moderate, and severe.

**e.** _____ Handwashing is a form of surgical or sterile asepsis.

## **COG** **AFF** CASE STUDIES FOR CRITICAL THINKING

Grade: _____

**1.** Mei Lin is a clinical medical assistant who works in an outpatient clinic. Today she arrives at work with a minor cold. Over the course of an hour, she sees four patients. She draws a blood sample from one patient and retrieves a urine sample from another patient. During the hour, she sneezes three times. She is preparing to leave for her lunch break. How many times should she have washed her hands during this time period?

_____

_____

_____

_____

2. Your patient is a 24-year-old female who has been diagnosed with bacterial pneumonia. The physician has ordered antibiotic therapy and bedrest. When leaving the office, she tells you that she is concerned about the fact that she has a 7-month-old baby at home. What information could you give her to clearly explain what steps she can take to avoid transmitting her illness to her child?

_____

_____

_____

_____

3. An established patient in your office is a 38-year-old female with AIDS. One of your coworkers, Steve, is afraid of interacting with this patient and has made disparaging remarks about her in the back office. You worry that Steve's attitude will affect patient care and you decide to talk to him privately. What points will you make? Should you also talk with your supervisor about Steve? Why, or why not?

_____

_____

_____

_____

4. The test results for 15-year-old Ashley Lewis come in and show that she is positive for hepatitis C. Her mother phones and asks you for the results. Is it appropriate for you to give her mother the test results? Why, or why not? How would you handle this call?

_____

_____

_____

_____

5. A middle-aged male comes into the medical office with a low-grade fever and productive cough that has lasted several weeks. The physician orders a chest x-ray to aid in diagnosis. After the patient leaves to get his chest x-ray, you begin to clean the room for the next patient. What level of disinfection will you use? What product(s) will you use? Provide detailed information about your actions, including dilution instructions, if appropriate.

_____

_____

_____

_____

6. You work in a pediatrician's office and have been working extra hours to save for a new, more reliable vehicle. Between work and school, you are tired and rundown. This morning, you woke up with a sore throat and headache. The last thing you want to do is call in sick because you need the money and you want your supervisor to think you are reliable. What should you do? Explain your answer.

_____

_____

_____

**FSY** PROCEDURE 2-1 **Perform Medical Aseptic Handwashing Procedure**

Name: _____ Date: _____ Time: _____ Grade: _____

**EQUIPMENT/SUPPLIES:** Liquid soap, disposable paper towels, a waste can

**STANDARDS:** Given the needed equipment and a place to work, the student will perform this skill with _____ % accuracy in a total of _____ minutes. *(Your instructor will tell you what the percentage and time limits will be before you begin.)*

**KEY:** 4 = Satisfactory          0 = Unsatisfactory          NA = This step is not counted

| PROCEDURE STEPS | SELF | PARTNER | INSTRUCTOR |
|---|---|---|---|
| **1.** Remove all rings and wristwatch. | ❏ | ❏ | ❏ |
| **2.** Stand close to the sink without touching it. | ❏ | ❏ | ❏ |
| **3.** Turn on the faucet and adjust the temperature of the water to warm. | ❏ | ❏ | ❏ |
| **4.** Wet hands and wrists, apply soap, and work into a lather. | ❏ | ❏ | ❏ |
| **5.** Rub palms together and rub soap between your fingers at least 10 times. | ❏ | ❏ | ❏ |
| **6.** Scrub one palm with fingertips, work soap under nails, and then reverse hands. | ❏ | ❏ | ❏ |
| **7.** Rinse hands and wrists under warm running water. | ❏ | ❏ | ❏ |
| **8.** Hold hands lower than elbows and avoid touching the inside of the sink. | ❏ | ❏ | ❏ |
| **9.** Clean under the nails by scraping the fingernails of one hand against the soapy palm of the other hand for 10 seconds. Repeat with other hand. | ❏ | ❏ | ❏ |
| **10.** Reapply liquid soap and rewash hands and wrists. | ❏ | ❏ | ❏ |
| **11.** Rinse hands again while holding hands lower than the wrists and elbows. | ❏ | ❏ | ❏ |
| **12.** Use a dry paper towel to dry your hands and wrists gently. | ❏ | ❏ | ❏ |
| **13.** Use a dry paper towel to turn off the faucets and discard the paper towel. | ❏ | ❏ | ❏ |

_____

_____

_____

_____

**PSY**   PROCEDURE 2-1   **Perform Medical Aseptic Handwashing Procedure** (continued)

**CALCULATION**

Total Possible Points: _____

Total Points Earned: _____ Multiplied by 100 = _____ Divided by Total Possible Points = _____ %

**PASS**   **FAIL**    **COMMENTS:**
  ❑     ❑

Student's signature _____ Date _____

Partner's signature _____ Date _____

Instructor's signature _____ Date _____

**PSY** PROCEDURE 2-2 **Select Appropriate Personal Protective Equipment and Remove Contaminated Gloves**

Name: _____ Date: _____ Time: _____ Grade: _____

**EQUIPMENT/SUPPLIES:** PPE (Clean examination gloves; goggles or disposable masks with eye/splash guard; disposable masks; disposable gown); biohazard waste container

**STANDARDS:** Given the needed equipment and a place to work, the student will perform this skill with _____ % accuracy in a total of _____ minutes. *(Your instructor will tell you what the percentage and time limits will be before you begin.)*

**KEY:** 4 = Satisfactory 0 = Unsatisfactory NA =This step is not counted

| PROCEDURE STEPS | SELF | PARTNER | INSTRUCTOR |
|---|---|---|---|
| **1.** Given a potentially biohazardous situation, choose the correct PPE: <br> **a.** Cleaning up spilled urine <br> **b.** Irrigating a wound <br> **c.** Giving an injection <br> **d.** Disinfecting examination tables | ❏ | ❏ | ❏ |
| **2.** Apply appropriately chosen PPE. If a gown, mask, and goggles are necessary, apply the gown and mask/goggles first. Choose the appropriate size gloves for your hands and put them on last. | ❏ | ❏ | ❏ |
| **3.** Make sure clothing is protected if a gown is worn and no skin is showing. | ❏ | ❏ | ❏ |
| **4.** After the procedure is finished, appropriately remove PPE by removing the gloves first, next the gown, and last the goggles and mask or face shield. | ❏ | ❏ | ❏ |
| **5.** To remove gloves, grasp the glove of your nondominant hand at the palm and pull the glove away. | ❏ | ❏ | ❏ |
| **6.** Slide your hand out of the glove, rolling the glove into the palm of the gloved dominant hand. | ❏ | ❏ | ❏ |
| **7.** Holding the soiled glove in the palm of your gloved hand, slip your ungloved fingers under the cuff of the glove you are still wearing, being careful not to touch the outside of the glove. | ❏ | ❏ | ❏ |
| **8.** Stretch the glove of the dominant hand up and away from your hand while turning it inside out, with the already removed glove balled up inside. | ❏ | ❏ | ❏ |
| **9.** Both gloves should now be removed, with the first glove inside the second glove and the second glove inside out. | ❏ | ❏ | ❏ |
| **10.** Discard both gloves as one unit into a biohazard waste receptacle. | ❏ | ❏ | ❏ |

## PSY PROCEDURE 2-2 Select Appropriate Personal Protective Equipment and Remove Contaminated Gloves (continued)

| | | | |
|---|---|---|---|
| 11. If only gloves were worn as PPE, wash your hands. | ❏ | ❏ | ❏ |
| 12. If other PPE were worn (i.e., gown, mask, goggles), remove gloves following the procedure above and untie the gown carefully at the neck. Pull the neck strings of the gown toward the front of the body with the arms straight. Pull each arm out of the sleeve, making the sleeves inside out. Continue removing the gown, rolling it into a ball, touching only the uncontaminated inside of the gown with the hands. Drop the rolled gown in a biohazard waste container. | ❏ | ❏ | ❏ |
| 13. Remove the googles, face shield, and/or mask. Dispose of any disposable items appropriately. If goggles are nondisposable, place in a designated area for disinfecting. | ❏ | ❏ | ❏ |
| 14. Wash your hands. | ❏ | ❏ | ❏ |

_____

_____

_____

_____

_____

**CALCULATION**

Total Possible Points: _____

Total Points Earned: _____ Multiplied by 100 = _____ Divided by Total Possible Points = _____ %

**PASS   FAIL   COMMENTS:**
❏        ❏

Student's signature _____ Date _____

Partner's signature _____ Date _____

Instructor's signature _____ Date _____

## **PSY** PROCEDURE 2-3 **Cleaning Biohazardous Spills**

Name: _____ Date: _____ Time: _____ Grade: _____

**EQUIPMENT/SUPPLIES:** Commercially prepared germicide *or* 1:10 bleach solution, gloves, disposable towels, chemical absorbent, biohazardous waste bag, protective eye wear (goggles or mask and face shield), disposable shoe coverings, disposable gown or apron made of plastic or other material that is impervious to soaking up contaminated fluids

**STANDARDS:** Given the needed equipment and a place to work, the student will perform this skill with _____ % accuracy in a total of _____ minutes. *(Your instructor will tell you what the percentage and time limits will be before you begin.)*

**KEY:** 4 = Satisfactory 0 = Unsatisfactory NA = This step is not counted

| PROCEDURE STEPS | SELF | PARTNER | INSTRUCTOR |
|---|---|---|---|
| **1.** Put on gloves. Wear protective eyewear, gown or apron, and shoe coverings if you anticipate any splashing. | ❑ | ❑ | ❑ |
| **2.** Apply chemical absorbent material to the spill as indicated by office policy. Clean up the spill with disposable paper towels, being careful not to splash. | ❑ | ❑ | ❑ |
| **3.** Dispose of paper towels and absorbent material in a biohazard waste bag. | ❑ | ❑ | ❑ |
| **4.** Spray the area with commercial germicide or bleach solution and wipe with disposable paper towels. Discard towels in a biohazard bag. | ❑ | ❑ | ❑ |
| **5.** With your gloves on, remove the protective eyewear and discard or disinfect per office policy. Remove the gown or apron and shoe coverings and put in the biohazard bag if disposable or the biohazard laundry bag for reusable linens. | ❑ | ❑ | ❑ |
| **6.** Place the biohazard bag in an appropriate waste receptacle for removal according to your facility's policy. | ❑ | ❑ | ❑ |
| **7.** Remove your gloves and wash your hands thoroughly. | ❑ | ❑ | ❑ |

_____

_____

_____

_____

_____

**CALCULATION**

Total Possible Points: _____

Total Points Earned: _____ Multiplied by 100 = _____ Divided by Total Possible Points = _____ %

**PASS    FAIL    COMMENTS:**
   ❑        ❑

Student's signature _____ Date _____

Partner's signature _____ Date _____

Instructor's signature _____ Date _____

## PSY PROCEDURE 2-4 **Bloodborne Pathogen Training**

**Name:** _____ **Date:** _____ **Time:** _____ **Grade:** _____

**EQUIPMENT/SUPPLIES:** A commercial kit that includes presentation materials with current OSHA guidelines regarding bloodborne pathogen training; Participation log documenting training including date.

**STANDARDS:** Given the needed equipment and a place to work, the student will perform this skill with _____ % accuracy in a total of _____ minutes. *(Your instructor will tell you what the percentage and time limits will be before you begin.)*

**KEY:** 4 = Satisfactory 0 = Unsatisfactory NA = This step is not counted

| PROCEDURE STEPS | SELF | PARTNER | INSTRUCTOR |
|---|---|---|---|
| 1. Plan ahead to attend the training as scheduled by your facility. | ❏ | ❏ | ❏ |
| 2. Come to the training on time and prepared to take notes and ask questions. | ❏ | ❏ | ❏ |
| 3. The training includes information about the following: <br> a. Bloodborne pathogens and diseases <br> b. Exposure control plan <br> c. Postexposure evaluation and follow-up procedures | ❏ | ❏ | ❏ |
| 4. After participating in the training, you should be able to define bloodborne pathogens and the diseases that may affect humans from these pathogens. Procedures to follow in case of an accidental exposure, and engineering and workplace controls to reduce the likelihood of contamination. | ❏ | ❏ | ❏ |
| 5. Sign and date the Bloodborne Pathogen Training log to document your attendance. | ❏ | ❏ | ❏ |

_____

_____

_____

_____

**CALCULATION**

Total Possible Points: _____

Total Points Earned: _____ Multiplied by 100 = _____ Divided by Total Possible Points = _____ %

**PASS** **FAIL** **COMMENTS:**
❏ ❏

Student's signature _____ Date _____

Partner's signature _____ Date _____

Instructor's signature _____ Date _____

# 3 Medical History and Patient Assessment

## Learning Outcomes

### COG Cognitive Domain

1. Spell and define key terms
2. Recognize barriers to communication
3. Identify techniques for overcoming communication barriers
4. Give examples of the type of information included in each section of the patient history
5. Identify guidelines for conducting a patient interview using principles of verbal and nonverbal communication
6. Differentiate between subjective and objective information
7. Discuss open-ended and closed-ended questions and explain when to use each type during the patient interview

### PSY Psychomotor Domain

1. Use feedback techniques to obtain patient information including: (a) reflection, (b) restatement, and (c) clarification
2. Use medical terminology correctly and pronounced accurately to communicate information to providers and patients.
3. Respond to nonverbal communication.
4. Obtain and record a patient history (Procedure 3-1)
5. Accurately document a chief complaint and present illness (Procedure 3-2)

### AFF Affective Domain

1. Incorporate critical thinking skills when performing patient assessment

2. Demonstrate (a) empathy, (b) active listening, and (c) nonverbal communication
3. Demonstrate sensitivity to patient's rights
4. Demonstrate principles of self-boundaries
5. Demonstrate respect for individual diversity including (a) gender, (b) race, (c) religion, (d) age, (e) economic status, and (f) appearance

### ABHES Competencies

1. Be impartial and show empathy when dealing with patients
2. Interview effectively
3. Recognize and respond to verbal and nonverbal communication
4. Obtain chief complaint, recording patient history

Name: _____    Date: _____    Grade: _____

## COG MULTIPLE CHOICE

Circle the letter preceding the correct answer.

1. The best place to interview a patient is:
   a. over the phone.
   b. at the patient's home.
   c. in the reception area.
   d. in an examination room.
   e. in the physician's office.

2. Which of the following would appear in the past history (PH) section of a patient's medical history?
   a. Hospitalizations
   b. Chief complaint
   c. Insurance carrier
   d. Review of systems
   e. Deaths in immediate family

3. You are collecting the medical history of a patient. The patient discloses that her brother, sister, paternal grandfather, and paternal aunt are overweight. For this patient, obesity is considered to be:
   a. familial.
   b. historic.
   c. hereditary.
   d. homeopathic.
   e. demographic.

4. Under HIPAA, who may access a patient's medical records?
   a. Any health care provider
   b. The patient's family and friends
   c. Anyone who fills out the proper forms
   d. Only the patient's primary care physician
   e. Only health care providers directly involved in the patient's care

5. During an interview, your patient tells you that she drinks alcohol four to five times a week. This information should be included in the:
   a. chief complaint.
   b. past history.
   c. present illness.
   d. social history.
   e. family history.

6. Which of the following is included in the patient's present illness (PI)?
   a. Self-care activities
   b. Hereditary diseases
   c. Signs and symptoms
   d. Preventative medicine
   e. Name, address, and phone number

7. Who completes the patient's medical history form?
   a. The patient only
   b. The patient's insurance provider
   c. The patient's immediate family
   d. The patient, the medical assistant, and the physician
   e. The patient's former physician or primary care provider

8. A homeopathic remedy for a headache could be a(n):
   a. prescription painkiller.
   b. extended period of rest.
   c. 1,000 mg dose of acetaminophen.
   d. icepack on the forehead for 10 minutes.
   e. small dose of an agent that causes headache.

9. An open-ended question is one that:
   a. determines the patient's level of pain.
   b. determines where something happened.
   c. is rhetorical and does not require an answer.
   d. can be answered with a "yes" or a "no" response.
   e. requires the responder to answer using more than one word.

10. One sign of illness might be:
    a. coughing.
    b. headache.
    c. dizziness.
    d. nausea.
    e. muscle pain.

11. Which of the following is a closed-ended question?
    a. "What is the reason for your appointment today?"
    b. "Tell me what makes the pain worse?"
    c. "Does the pain leave and return throughout the day?"
    d. "How would you describe the pain you are feeling?"
    e. "What have you done to help eliminate the pain?"

12. At the beginning of an interview, you can establish a trusting, professional relationship with the patient by:
    a. thoroughly introducing yourself.
    b. listing the physician's credentials.
    c. observing the patient's signs of illness.
    d. conducting the review of systems (ROS).
    e. disclosing the patient's weight in private.

**13.** If you suspect that the patient you are assessing is the victim of abuse, you should:
   **a.** report your suspicions to the local police station.
   **b.** record your suspicion of abuse in the patient's chief complaint (CC).
   **c.** ask the patient if he or she is being abused with a closed-ended question.
   **d.** document the objective signs and notify the physician of your suspicions.
   **e.** review the patient's medical history for signs of an abusive spouse or parent.

**14.** Which of the following is included in the identifying database of a patient's medical history?
   **a.** The patient's emergency contact
   **b.** The patient's Social Security number
   **c.** The patient's reason for visiting the office
   **d.** The patient's signs and symptoms of illness
   **e.** The patient's family's addresses

**15.** One example of a symptom of an illness is:
   **a.** rash.
   **b.** cough.
   **c.** nausea.
   **d.** vomiting.
   **e.** wheezing.

**16.** The patient's PI includes which of the following:
   **a.** social history.
   **b.** family history.
   **c.** chronology of the illness.
   **d.** demographic information.
   **e.** history of hospitalizations.

**17.** Before you proceed with a patient interview, you should obtain:
   **a.** signs and symptoms.
   **b.** social and family history.
   **c.** the duration of pain and self-treatment information.
   **d.** the chief complaint and patient's present illness.
   **e.** the location of pain and self-treatment information.

**18.** Which of the following is a poor interview technique?
   **a.** Asking open-ended questions
   **b.** Noting observable information
   **c.** Suggesting expected symptoms
   **d.** Introducing yourself to the patient
   **e.** Reading through the patient's medical history beforehand

**19.** You think that a patient has a disease that was passed down from her parents. Where could you look to find information on the patient's parents?
   **a.** Medical history forms
   **b.** History of self-treatment
   **c.** Demographic information
   **d.** Notes during the patient interview
   **e.** Chief complaints from previous visits

**20.** While obtaining a patient's present illness, you need to find out:
   **a.** where she lives.
   **b.** the chief complaint.
   **c.** if she smokes tobacco.
   **d.** the severity of the pain.
   **e.** any hereditary disease(s) she has.

## COG MATCHING

Grade: _____

Match each key term with its definition.

**Key Terms**

21. _____ assessment
22. _____ chief complaint
23. _____ demographic
24. _____ familial
25. _____ hereditary
26. _____ homeopathic
27. _____ medical history
28. _____ over the counter
29. _____ signs
30. _____ symptoms

**Definitions**

**a.** relating to the statistical characteristics of populations
**b.** subjective indications of disease or bodily dysfunction as sensed by the patient
**c.** process of gathering information about a patient and the presenting condition
**d.** a record containing information about a patient's past and present health status
**e.** traits or disorders that are passed from parent to offspring
**f.** objective indications of disease or bodily dysfunction as observed or measured by the health care professional
**g.** the main reason for a patient's visit to the medical office
**h.** medications and natural drugs that are available without a prescription
**i.** traits that tend to occur often within a particular family
**j.** describing a type of alternative medicine in which patients are treated with small doses of substances that produce similar symptoms and use the body's own healing abilities

## ⬤⬤⬤ IDENTIFICATION

_____ Grade: _____

**31.** Indicate whether the following patient interview questions during a patient assessment are helpful or not helpful by writing H (helpful) or NH (not helpful) on the line preceding the question.

**a.** _____ "Do you feel pain?"

**b.** _____ "How often does the pain occur?"

**c.** _____ "What were you doing when the pain started?"

**d.** _____ "Have you taken ibuprofen for the pain?"

**e.** _____ "Does lying down lessen the pain you feel?"

**32.** Two types of home remedies are over-the-counter medications and homeopathic medications. Determine whether the items below are over-the-counter or homeopathic medications by writing OTC (over-the-counter) or H (homeopathic) on the line next to the item.

**a.** _____ 1,000 mg of acetaminophen to relieve the pain of a sprained ankle

**b.** _____ A small dose of mercury to treat symptoms similar to mercury poisoning

**c.** _____ Ingesting ipecacuanha, a root that causes vomiting, in order to treat vomiting

**d.** _____ A cooling topical ointment applied to skin afflicted by sunburn

**33.** As a medical assistant, you will have many responsibilities. Place a check mark on the line next to the actions that you may perform as a medical assistant.

**a.** _____ Documenting the patient's chief complaint (CC)

**b.** _____ Assessing the patient's present illness (PI) during a patient interview

**c.** _____ Going over the medical file to the patient's family and friends

**d.** _____ Reviewing the patient's medical history before interviewing the patient

**e.** _____ Recording judgments based on the patient's appearance in the patient's record

**f.** _____ Advising patient which over-the-counter or homeopathic treatments to use

## ⬤⬤⬤ COMPLETION

_____ Grade: _____

**34.** Using any available resources, find information about influenza. On the lines below, list three signs and three symptoms that a patient may have influenza (or the flu).

| Signs | Symptoms |
|-------|----------|
| **a.** | **a.** |
| **b.** | **b.** |
| **c.** | **c.** |

**35.** The section of the patient history that reviews each body system and invites the patient to share any information that he or she may have forgotten to mention earlier is called

_____ .

**36.** The _____ section covers the health status of the patient's immediate family members.

**37.** Information needed for administrative purposes, such as the patient's name, address, and telephone number, is included in the _____ section.

**38.** Important information about the patient's lifestyle is documented in the _____ section.

**39.** The section of the patient history that focuses on the patient's prior health status is called _____.

## COG SHORT ANSWER

_____ Grade: _____

**40.** What is the purpose of gathering a patient's social history?

_____

_____

_____

_____

**41.** When are closed-ended questions appropriate during a patient interview? Give one example of an appropriate closed-ended question.

_____

_____

_____

_____

**42.** During a patient interview, you learn that the patient is an extreme sports enthusiast and works in a coal mine. Where should you record this information in the patient's medical history forms?

_____

_____

_____

_____

**43.** Why is the reception area a poor place to interview a patient? What would be a better location for interviewing a patient?

_____

_____

_____

_____

**44.** What are two ways in which a patient's medical history is gathered in the medical office?

_____

_____

_____

_____

**45.** What should you say to the patient when introducing yourself? Why is a thorough introduction important?

_____

_____

_____

_____

## **COG** TRUE OR FALSE?                                         Grade: _____

Indicate whether the statements are true or false by placing the letter T (true) or F (false) on the line preceding the statement.

**46.** _____ Unlike OTC medications, homeopathic medications are only available by prescription.

**47.** _____ Nausea is a sign of food poisoning.

**48.** _____ It is always the patient's responsibility to fill out his medical history completely and accurately.

**49.** _____ The chief complaint is always a description of a patient's signs and symptoms.

**50.** _____ Obtaining a urine specimen from the patient may be part of the chief complaint.

**51.** _____ It is appropriate to assist an older adult who cannot hold a pen due to arthritis with filling out the medical history form.

**52.** _____ Entries made in the patient record should be signed and dated.

**53.** _____ It is the responsibility of the receptionist to make sure the demographic information is complete.

## **COG** **AFF** CASE STUDIES FOR CRITICAL THINKING          Grade: _____

**1.** You are interviewing a patient, Mr. Gibson. You learn that Mr. Gibson is a 55-year-old male. He is starting a new job as a childcare provider and needs to submit a physical examination to his new place of employment. Mr. Gibson's father died of colon cancer when he was 60 years old, and Mr. Gibson's wife is a smoker. Mr. Gibson says he feels healthy and has not had any health-related problems in the last few years. What should you record as the chief complaint in Mr. Gibson's medical record?

_____

_____

_____

_____

2. Mrs. Frank is a returning patient at Dr. Mohammad's office. She is 89 years old and needs the assistance of a wheelchair. What are some important considerations that you should make when showing Mrs. Frank to an exam room, gathering her medical history, and performing a patient assessment? How would those considerations change if the patient was a 2-year-old child?

_____

_____

_____

_____

3. Your patient is a 49-year-old female who speaks very little English. She is a returning patient, so her medical history is already on file at the office. You have called a coworker who can act as a translator, but he will not arrive at the office for an hour. Meanwhile, the patient is clearly uncomfortable. She appears sweaty and lethargic. She leans on you as you escort her to an examination room. Describe how you can determine the patient's chief complaint and present illness so that you and the physician can begin to help her.

_____

_____

_____

_____

4. Alicia, a medical assistant in Dr. Howard's office, has recorded the following in a patient assessment:
"CC: Pt. c/o fatigue, depressed mood, and inability to stay asleep at night. He has taken Tylenol PM for two nights with "no effect" on sleep and has not eaten for 2 days because of lack of appetite, which is likely caused by his depression. His face is pale and his skin clammy."
Was there anything in this documentation that should not have been recorded? Explain your answer.

5. Giles is a medical assistant in Dr. Yardley's office. Giles enters the examination room to interview a patient. Giles notices that the patient is lying on the examination table, holding his abdomen. He is holding a black trash bin that contains a small amount of his vomit. The patient is flushed and sweating. Before even speaking to the patient, Giles has realized some of the patient's signs and symptoms of illness. Explain the significance of signs and symptoms and then fill in this patient's signs and symptoms in the chart below.

| Signs | Symptoms |
|---|---|
| a. | a. |
| b. | b. |
| c. | c. |

**6.** There are two patients waiting in examination rooms to see the physician. Patient A is a new patient, and Patient B is coming into the office for a complete physical examination. When sorting these patients to determine who should be taken back to the exam room first, what factors should be considered?

_____

_____

_____

_____

**7.** What are your ethical and legal responsibilities as a medical assistant concerning a patient's medical history records?

_____

_____

_____

_____

**8.** Your patient is a 17-year-old male. His symptoms are shortness of breath and fatigue. During the interview, you learn that his father and older brother are obese. You also learn that both of his grandfathers died of complications resulting from heart disease. Although this patient is not overweight, he tells you that he does not have time to exercise but would like to avoid gaining weight, especially when he enters college this fall. What changes does the patient needs to make in his lifestyle in order to improve his health and avoid obesity and heart disease? Should you make suggestions for the members of his family who are obese? Why or why not?

_____

_____

_____

_____

**9.** Ms. Butler, 20 years old, received a pregnancy test during a visit to the physician's office. A week later, Mr. Gordon, a 25-year-old male, comes into the office demanding to see the results of Ms. Butler's test. He tells you that he is her boyfriend and that if Ms. Butler is pregnant, he deserves to know. What would you say to Mr. Gordon?

_____

_____

_____

_____

**10.** On your way to the exam room, you notice a coworker weighing another patient on the scales located in the hallway. As the patient steps onto the scale, your coworker moves the weights on the scale and then reads the patient's weight out loud. The patient appears embarrassed. What would you say, if anything, to your coworker? Why or why not?

_____

_____

_____

## PSY  PROCEDURE 3-1  Obtain and Record a Patient History

Name: _____  Date: _____  Time: _____  Grade: _____

**EQUIPMENT/SUPPLIES:** Paper medical history form or questionnaire, black or blue pen

**STANDARDS:** Given the needed equipment and a place to work, the student will perform this skill with _____ % accuracy in a total of _____ minutes. *(Your instructor will tell you what the percentage and time limits will be before you begin.)*

**KEY:**        4 = Satisfactory         0 = Unsatisfactory         NA = This step is not counted

| PROCEDURE STEPS | SELF | PARTNER | INSTRUCTOR |
|---|---|---|---|
| **1.** Gather the supplies. | ❏ | ❏ | ❏ |
| **2.** Review the medical history form for completeness. | ❏ | ❏ | ❏ |
| **3.** Take the patient to a private area or the examination room and assist him or her with completing the form. | ❏ | ❏ | ❏ |
| **4.** Sit across from the patient at eye level and maintain eye contact. | ❏ | ❏ | ❏ |
| **5.** Introduce yourself and explain the purpose of the interview. | ❏ | ❏ | ❏ |
| **6.** Using language the patient can understand, ask the appropriate questions, and document the patient's responses. Be sure to determine the patient's CC and PI. | ❏ | ❏ | ❏ |
| **7.** Use feedback techniques including:<br>**a.** Reflection.<br>**b.** Restatement.<br>**c.** Clarification. | ❏ | ❏ | ❏ |
| **8.** Regardless of the confidences shared by the patient, avoid projecting a judgmental attitude with words or actions. | ❏ | ❏ | ❏ |
| **9.** **AFF** Explain how to respond to a patient who does not speak English. | ❏ | ❏ | ❏ |
| **10.** **AFF** Explain to the patient what to expect during examinations or procedures at that visit. | ❏ | ❏ | ❏ |
| **11.** Review the history form for completion and accuracy. | ❏ | ❏ | ❏ |
| **12.** Thank the patient for cooperating during the interview, and offer to answer any questions. | ❏ | ❏ | ❏ |
| **13.** Describe examples of applying local, state, and federal health care legislation and regulation in the medical office. | ❏ | ❏ | ❏ |

_____

_____

_____

_____

## FSY PROCEDURE 3-1 Obtain and Record a Patient History (continued)

**CALCULATION**

Total Possible Points: _____

Total Points Earned: _____ Multiplied by 100 = _____ Divided by Total Possible Points = _____ %

**PASS   FAIL   COMMENTS:**
  ❏       ❏

Student's signature _____ Date _____

Partner's signature _____ Date _____

Instructor's signature _____ Date _____

**PSY** PROCEDURE 3-2  **Document a Chief Complaint and Present Illness**

Name: _____ Date: _____ Time: _____ Grade: _____

**EQUIPMENT/SUPPLIES:** A paper or electronic medical record including a cumulative problem list or progress notes form, black or blue ink pen

**STANDARDS:** Given the needed equipment and a place to work, the student will perform this skill with _____ % accuracy in a total of _____ minutes. *(Your instructor will tell you what the percentage and time limits will be before you begin.)*

**KEY:**          4 = Satisfactory          0 = Unsatisfactory          NA =This step is not counted

| PROCEDURE STEPS | SELF | PARTNER | INSTRUCTOR |
|---|---|---|---|
| **1.** Gather the supplies including the medical record containing the cumulative problem list or progress note form. | ❏ | ❏ | ❏ |
| **2.** Review the new or established patient's medical history form. | ❏ | ❏ | ❏ |
| **3.** Greet and identify the patient while escorting him or her to the examination room. Close the door. | ❏ | ❏ | ❏ |
| **4.** Use open-ended questions to find out why the patient is seeking medical care; maintain eye contact. | ❏ | ❏ | ❏ |
| **5.** When reviewing medical history including medications with patient, pronounce all terms and medications accurately. | ❏ | ❏ | ❏ |
| **6.** **AFF** Explain how to respond to a patient who has dementia and whose facial expression shows confusion. | ❏ | ❏ | ❏ |
| **7.** Determine the PI using open-ended and closed-ended questions. | ❏ | ❏ | ❏ |
| **8.** Document the CC and PI correctly on the cumulative problem list or progress report form. | ❏ | ❏ | ❏ |
| _____ | | | |
| _____ | | | |
| _____ | | | |
| _____ | | | |
| **9.** How would you respond to a patient who is moving to another town and asks about having his or her medical records transferred to a physician in another town? | ❏ | ❏ | ❏ |
| **10.** Thank the patient for cooperating, and explain that the physician will soon be in to examine the patient. | ❏ | ❏ | ❏ |

## PROCEDURE 3-2 Document a Chief Complaint and Present Illness (continued)

**CALCULATION**

Total Possible Points: _____

Total Points Earned: _____ Multiplied by 100 = _____ Divided by Total Possible Points = _____ %

**PASS  FAIL  COMMENTS:**
❏      ❏

Student's signature _____ Date _____

Partner's signature _____ Date _____

Instructor's signature _____ Date _____

# CHAPTER

# 4 Anthropometric Measurements and Vital Signs

## Learning Outcomes

### COG Cognitive Domain

1. Spell and define key terms
2. Explain the procedures for measuring a patient's height and weight
3. Identify and describe the types of thermometers
4. Compare the procedures for measuring a patient's temperature using the oral, rectal, axillary, and tympanic methods
5. List the fever process, including the stages of fever
6. Describe the procedure for measuring a patient's pulse and respiratory rates
7. Identify the various sites on the body used for palpating a pulse
8. Define Korotkoff sounds and the five phases of blood pressure
9. Identify factors that may influence the blood pressure
10. Explain the factors to consider when choosing the correct blood pressure cuff size

### PSY Psychomotor Domain

1. Measure and record a patient's weight (Procedure 4-1)

2. Measure and record a patient's height (Procedure 4-2)
3. Measure and record a patient's rectal temperature (Procedure 4-3)
4. Measure and record a patient's axillary temperature (Procedure 4-4)
5. Measure and record a patient's temperature using an electronic thermometer (Procedure 4-5)
6. Measure and record a patient's temperature using a tympanic thermometer (Procedure 4-6)
7. Measure and record a patient's temperature using a temporal artery thermometer (Procedure 4-7)
8. Measure and record a patient's radial pulse (Procedure 4-8)
9. Measure and record a patient's respirations (Procedure 4-9)
10. Measure and record a patient's blood pressure (Procedure 4-10)
11. Instruct and prepare a patient for a procedure or a treatment
12. Document patient care accurately in the medical record

13. Coach patients appropriately considering cultural diversity, developmental life stage, and communication barriers

### AFF Affective Domain

1. Incorporate critical thinking skills when performing patient assessment
2. Demonstrate respect for individual diversity including gender, race, religion, age, economic status, and appearance
3. Explain to a patient the rationale for performance of a procedure
4. Demonstrate empathy, active listening, and nonverbal communication
5. Demonstrate the principles of self-boundaries
6. Show awareness of a patient's concerns related to the procedure being performed

### ABHES Competencies

1. Take vital signs
2. Document accurately

Name: _____    Date: _____    Grade: _____

## cog MULTIPLE CHOICE

Circle the letter preceding the correct answer.

1. Anthropometric measurements:
   a. include vital signs.
   b. include height and weight.
   c. don't include height in adults.
   d. are taken only at the first visit.
   e. are used only as baseline information.

2. What are the cardinal signs?
   a. Height and weight
   b. Baseline measurements
   c. Pulse, respiration, and blood pressure
   d. Pulse, respiration, blood pressure, and temperature
   e. Temperature, pulse, blood pressure, respiration, and cardiac output

3. When you greet a patient, what should you always do before taking any measurements?
   a. Put on gloves.
   b. Identify the patient.
   c. Get a family history.
   d. Get a medical history.
   e. Determine whether the patient speaks English.

4. After getting an accurate weight measurement, what is the next thing you should do?
   a. Remove the paper towel.
   b. Write down the measurement.
   c. Assist the patient off the scale.
   d. Tell the patient his or her weight.
   e. Convert the measurement to kilograms.

5. If the balance bar of a balance beam scale points to the midpoint when the large counterweight is at 100, and the small counterweight is 2 lines to the right of the mark for 30, what is the patient's weight?
   a. 32 pounds
   b. 73 pounds
   c. 128 pounds
   d. 132 pounds
   e. 264 pounds

6. To get an accurate height measurement, you should:
   a. wash your hands and put down a paper towel.
   b. have the patient stand barefoot with heels together.
   c. have the patient face the ruler and look straight ahead.
   d. put the measuring bar on the patient's hair and deduct an inch.
   e. record the measurement before helping the patient off the scale.

7. An axillary temperature would be a good measurement to take when:
   a. the patient is very talkative.
   b. there are no more disposable plastic sheaths.
   c. the office is so full that there is little privacy.
   d. the patient is wearing many layers of clothing.
   e. you need to know the temperature as quickly as possible.

8. One difference between using electronic thermometers and using glass thermometers is the:
   a. use of gloves for rectal measurements.
   b. use of a disposable cover for the thermometer.
   c. color code for oral and rectal measurements.
   d. wait time before the thermometer is removed.
   e. receptacle for disposable covers after measurements.

9. The three stages of fever are:
   a. abrupt onset, course, and lysis.
   b. onset, various course, and lysis.
   c. onset, sustained fever, and crisis.
   d. abrupt or gradual onset, course, and resolution.
   e. onset, fluctuating course, and abrupt resolution.

10. Which method would you use to take a brachial pulse?
    a. Palpation alone
    b. Auscultation alone
    c. Palpation and/or auscultation
    d. Palpation and/or use of a Doppler unit
    e. Auscultation and/or use of a Doppler unit

11. Which method would you use to take an apical pulse?
    a. Palpation alone
    b. Auscultation alone
    c. Palpation and/or auscultation
    d. Palpation and/or use of a Doppler unit
    e. Auscultation and/or use of a Doppler unit

12. Which statement is true of a respiratory rate?
    a. It increases when a patient is lying down.
    b. It is the number of expirations in 60 seconds.
    c. It is the number of complete inspirations per minute.
    d. It should be taken while the patient is not aware of it.
    e. It is the number of inspirations and expirations in 30 seconds.

13. Abnormal breathing may be characterized by:
    a. inhalations that are medium and rhythmic.
    b. inhalations and exhalations that are regular and consistent.
    c. air moving in and out heard with a stethoscope.
    d. breathing that is shallow or wheezing.
    e. a rate of 16 to 20.

14. Hyperpnea is:
    a. no respiration.
    b. shallow respirations.
    c. abnormally deep, gasping breaths.
    d. inability to breathe while lying down.
    e. a respiratory rate that is too high for oxygen demand.

15. The Korotkoff sound that signals systolic blood pressure is:
    a. faint tapping.
    b. soft swishing.
    c. soft tapping that becomes faint.
    d. rhythmic, sharp, distinct tapping.
    e. sharp tapping that becomes soft swishing.

16. Which group of factors is likely to affect blood pressure?
    a. Age, exercise, occupation
    b. Activity, stress, tobacco use
    c. Alcohol, education, prescriptions
    d. Body position, height, history of heart conditions
    e. Dietary habits, wealth, family history of heart disease

17. Which blood pressure cuff is the correct size?
    a. One that has the Velcro in places that match up
    b. One with a length that wraps three times around the arm
    c. One with a width that goes halfway around the upper arm
    d. One with a width that wraps all the way around the lower arm
    e. One with a length that wraps one and a half times around the arm

18. Which measurement is a normal axillary temperature?
    a. 36.4°C
    b. 37.0°C
    c. 37.6°C
    d. 98.6°F
    e. 99.6°F

19. A tympanic thermometer measures temperature:
    a. in the ear.
    b. in the mouth.
    c. under the armpit.
    d. on the temple.
    e. in the rectum.

20. Diaphoresis is:
    a. sweating.
    b. constant fever.
    c. elevated blood pressure.
    d. needing to sit upright to breathe.
    e. blood pressure that drops upon standing.

## COG MATCHING

Grade: _____

Match each key term with its definition.

**Key Terms**

21. _____ afebrile
22. _____ anthropometric
23. _____ apnea
24. _____ baseline
25. _____ calibrated
26. _____ cardiac cycle
27. _____ cardinal signs
28. _____ diastole
29. _____ diaphoresis
30. _____ dyspnea
31. _____ febrile
32. _____ hyperpnea
33. _____ hyperpyrexia
34. _____ hypertension
35. _____ hyperventilation
36. _____ hypopnea
37. _____ intermittent

**Definitions**

a. profuse sweating
b. fever that is fluctuating
c. no respiration
d. fever that is constant
e. shallow respirations
f. occurring at intervals
g. elevated blood pressure
h. pertaining to measurements of the human body
i. difficult or labored breathing
j. device used to measure blood pressure
k. abnormally deep, gasping breaths
l. phase in which the heart contracts
m. having a temperature above normal
n. original or initial measure with which other measurements will be compared
o. having a temperature within normal limits
p. extremely high temperature, from 105° to 106°F

| Key Terms | Definitions |
|---|---|
| **38.** _____ orthopnea | **q.** marked in units of measurement |
| **39.** _____ palpation | **r.** phase in which the heart pauses briefly to rest and refill |
| **40.** _____ postural hypotension | **s.** fever of 102°F or higher rectally or 101°F or higher orally |
| **41.** _____ pyrexia | **t.** act of pressing an artery against an underlying firm surface |
| **42.** _____ relapsing fever | **u.** sudden drop in blood pressure upon standing |
| **43.** _____ remittent fever | **v.** fever returning after an extended period of normal readings |
| **44.** _____ sphygmomanometer | **w.** respiratory rate that greatly exceeds the body's oxygen demand |
| **45.** _____ sustained fever | **x.** period from the beginning of one heartbeat to the beginning of the next |
| **46.** _____ systole | **y.** inability to breathe lying down |
| | **z.** measurements of vital signs |

## COG IDENTIFICATION

_____ Grade: _____

**47.** Place a check mark on the line next to each factor that can affect blood pressure.

a. _____ Activity

b. _____ Age

c. _____ Alcohol use

d. _____ Arteriosclerosis

e. _____ Atherosclerosis

f. _____ Body position

g. _____ Dietary habits

h. _____ Economic status

i. _____ Education

j. _____ Exercise

k. _____ Family history of heart conditions

l. _____ General health of the patient

m. _____ Height

n. _____ History of heart conditions

o. _____ Medications

p. _____ Occupation

q. _____ Stress

r. _____ Tobacco use

## COG COMPLETION

Grade: _____

**48.** Indicate whether the following measurements are anthropometric, cardinal signs, performed at the first office visit (baseline), or performed at every office visit. Place a check mark in the appropriate column. Measurements may have more than one check mark.

| | Anthropometric | Baseline (First Time) | Every Time | Cardinal Sign |
|---|---|---|---|---|
| **a.** Blood pressure | | | | |
| **b.** Cardiac output | | | | |
| **c.** Height | | | | |
| **d.** Pulse rate | | | | |
| **e.** Respiratory rate | | | | |
| **f.** Temperature | | | | |
| **g.** Weight | | | | |

**49.** The steps for weighing a patient with a balance beam scale are listed below, but they are not in the correct order. Starting with the number one (1), number the steps in the correct order.

_____ Record the weight.

_____ Memorize the weight.

_____ Help the patient off the scale.

_____ Help the patient onto the scale.

_____ Be sure the counterweights are both at zero.

_____ Be sure the counterweights are both at zero.

_____ Slide the larger counterweight toward zero until it rests securely in a notch.

_____ Slide the smaller counterweight toward zero until the balance bar is exactly at the midpoint.

_____ Slide the larger counterweight away from zero until the balance bar moves below the midpoint.

_____ Slide the smaller counterweight away from zero until the balance bar moves below the midpoint.

_____ Add the readings from the two counterweight bars, counting each line after the smaller counterweight as 1/4 pound.

**50.** For each step listed in measuring a patient's height, circle the correct word or phrase from the two options given in parentheses.

**a.** Wash your hands if the height is measured at (a different time from/the same time as) the weight.

**b.** The patient should (remove/wear) shoes.

**c.** The patient should stand straight with heels (a hand's width apart/together).

**d.** The patient's eyes should be looking (at the floor/straight ahead).

**e.** A better measurement is usually taken with the patient's (back/front) to the ruler.

**f.** Position the measuring bar perpendicular to the (ruler/top of the head).

**g.** Slowly lower the measuring bar until it touches the patient's (hair/head).

**h.** Measure at the (point of movement/top of the ruler).

**i.** A measurement of 66 inches should be recorded as (5 feet, 6 inches/66 inches).

## **COG** SHORT ANSWER

Grade: _____

**51.** What does the hypothalamus do when it senses that the body is too warm?

_____

_____

_____

_____

**52.** What happens when the body temperature is too cool?

_____

_____

_____

_____

**53.** What factors aside from illness affect body temperature?

_____

_____

_____

_____

_____

**54.** List and describe the three stages of fever. Include the variations in the time and their related terms.

_____

_____

_____

_____

**55.** If the patient has 19 full inspirations and 18 full expirations in 1 minute, what is the patient's respiratory rate?

_____

_____

_____

_____

**56.** At which sound is the systolic blood pressure recorded?

_____

_____

_____

_____

**57.** At which sound is the diastolic blood pressure recorded?

_____

_____

_____

_____

## OOG TRUE OR FALSE? _____ Grade: _____

**58.** Indicate whether the statements are true or false by placing the letter T (true) or F (false) on the line preceding the statement.

**a.** _____ The weight scale should be kept in the waiting room for ease of access.

**b.** _____ An axillary temperature can be taken with either an oral or a rectal thermometer.

**c.** _____ In pediatric offices, temperatures are almost always taken rectally.

**d.** _____ If a glass mercury thermometer breaks, you should soak up the mercury immediately with tissues and put them in the trash before the mercury sinks into any surfaces.

## AFF CASE STUDIES FOR CRITICAL THINKING _____ Grade: _____

**1.** Ms. Green arrived at the office late for her appointment, frantic and explaining that her alarm clock had not gone off. She discovered that her car was almost out of gas, and she had to stop to refuel. Once she got to the clinic, she could not find a parking place in the lot and she had to park two blocks away. How would you expect this to affect her vital signs? Explain why.

_____

_____

_____

_____

2. A patient comes into the office complaining of fever and chills. While taking her vital signs, you notice that her skin feels very warm. When you take her temperature, you find that her oral temperature is 105°F. What should you do?

_____

_____

_____

_____

3. Mr. Juarez, the father of a 6-month-old baby and a 4-year-old child, would like to purchase a thermometer. He is not sure which one to buy and isn't familiar with how to use the different kinds of thermometers. He also isn't aware of the possible variations that may occur in readings. How would you explain the various types of thermometers and temperature readings to him? What would you recommend and why?

_____

_____

_____

_____

4. Mrs. Chin has come into the office complaining of pain in her right foot. You take her vital signs, which are normal, and you help her remove her shoes so that the doctor can examine both feet. You notice a difference in appearance between her two feet, and it occurs to you to check her femoral, popliteal, posterior tibial, and dorsalis pedis pulses. What are you looking for, and what should you look for next?

_____

_____

_____

_____

5. You've noticed that whenever you try to take Mr. Kimble's respiration rate, he always breathes in when you do and breathes out when you do. You're concerned that you're not assessing Mr. Kimble's breathing accurately, and you know that he has had asthma on occasion. What can you do to get an accurate reading?

_____

_____

_____

_____

**PSY** PROCEDURE 4-1 **Measure and Record a Patient's Weight**

Name: _____ Date: _____ Time: _____ Grade: _____

**EQUIPMENT/SUPPLIES:** Calibrated balance beam scale, digital scale or dial scale; paper towel

**STANDARDS:** Given the needed equipment and a place to work, the student will perform this skill with _____ % accuracy in a total of _____ minutes. *(Your instructor will tell you what the percentage and time limits will be before you begin.)*

**KEY:**     4 = Satisfactory     0 = Unsatisfactory     NA =This step is not counted

| PROCEDURE STEPS | SELF | PARTNER | INSTRUCTOR |
|---|---|---|---|
| **1.** Wash your hands. | ❏ | ❏ | ❏ |
| **2.** Ensure that the scale is properly balanced at zero. | ❏ | ❏ | ❏ |
| **3.** Greet and identify the patient. Explain the procedure. | ❏ | ❏ | ❏ |
| **4.** Escort the patient to the scale and place a paper towel on the scale. | ❏ | ❏ | ❏ |
| **5.** Have the patient remove shoes and heavy outerwear and put down purse. | ❏ | ❏ | ❏ |
| **6.** Assist patient onto the scale facing forward and standing on paper towel without touching or holding on to anything if possible, while watching for difficulties with balance. | ❏ | ❏ | ❏ |
| **7.** Weigh the patient:<br>**A.** Balance beam scale: Slide counterweights on bottom and top bars (start with heavier bars) from zero to approximate weight. Each counterweight should rest securely in the notch with indicator mark at proper calibration. To obtain measurement, balance bar must hang freely at exact midpoint. To calculate weight, add top reading to bottom one. (Example: If bottom counterweight reads 100 and lighter one reads 16 plus three small lines, record weight as 116 3/4 pounds).<br>**B.** Digital scale: Read and record weight displayed on digital screen.<br>**C.** Dial scale: Indicator arrow rests at patient's weight. Read this number directly above the dial. | ❏ | ❏ | ❏ |
| **8.** Return the bars on the top and bottom to zero. | ❏ | ❏ | ❏ |
| **9.** Assist the patient from the scale if necessary and discard the paper towel. | ❏ | ❏ | ❏ |
| **10.** Record the patient's weight. | ❏ | ❏ | ❏ |
| **11.** **AFF** Explain how to respond to a patient who is visually impaired. | ❏ | ❏ | ❏ |

_____

_____

_____

_____

**FSY** PROCEDURE 4-1 **Measure and Record a Patient's Weight**
(continued)

**CALCULATION**

Total Possible Points: _____

Total Points Earned: _____ Multiplied by 100 = _____ Divided by Total Possible Points = _____ %

**PASS** **FAIL** **COMMENTS:**
❑ ❑

Student's signature _____ Date _____

Partner's signature _____ Date _____

Instructor's signature _____ Date _____

**PSY** PROCEDURE 4-2 **Measure and Record a Patient's Height**

**Name:** _____ **Date:** _____ **Time:** _____ **Grade:** _____

**EQUIPMENT/SUPPLIES:** A scale with a ruler

**STANDARDS:** Given the needed equipment and a place to work, the student will perform this skill with _____ % accuracy in a total of _____ minutes. *(Your instructor will tell you what the percentage and time limits will be before you begin.)*

**KEY:** 4 = Satisfactory 0 = Unsatisfactory NA = This step is not counted

| PROCEDURE STEPS | SELF | PARTNER | INSTRUCTOR |
|---|---|---|---|
| **1.** Wash your hands if this procedure is not done at the same time as the weight. | ❏ | ❏ | ❏ |
| **2.** Have the patient remove shoes and stand straight and erect on the scale, with heels together and eyes straight ahead. (Patient may face the ruler, but a better measurement is made with the patient's back to the ruler.) | ❏ | ❏ | ❏ |
| **3.** With the measuring bar perpendicular to the ruler, slowly lower it until it firmly touches the patient's head. Press lightly if the hair is full or high | ❏ | ❏ | ❏ |
| **4.** Read the measurement at the point of movement on the ruler. If measurements are in inches, convert to feet and inches (e.g., if the bar reads 65 plus two smaller lines, read it at 65 1/2. Remember that 12 inches equals 1 foot; therefore, the patient is 5 feet, 5 1/2 inches tall). | ❏ | ❏ | ❏ |
| **5.** Assist the patient from the scale if necessary; watch for signs of difficulty with balance. | ❏ | ❏ | ❏ |
| **6.** Record the weight and height measurements in the medical record. | ❏ | ❏ | ❏ |
| **7.** **AFF** Explain how to respond to a patient who has dementia. | ❏ | ❏ | ❏ |

_____

_____

_____

_____

**CALCULATION**

Total Possible Points: _____

Total Points Earned: _____ Multiplied by 100 = _____ Divided by Total Possible Points = _____ %

**PASS FAIL COMMENTS:**
❏ ❏

Student's signature _____ Date _____

Partner's signature _____ Date _____

Instructor's signature _____ Date _____

## FSY PROCEDURE 4-3  Measure and Record a Rectal Temperature

Name: _____ Date: _____ Time: _____ Grade: _____

**EQUIPMENT/SUPPLIES:** Electronic thermometer with rectal probe; tissues or cotton balls; disposable plastic sheaths; surgical lubricant; biohazard waste container; gloves.

**STANDARDS:** Given the needed equipment and a place to work, the student will perform this skill with _____ % accuracy in a total of _____ minutes. *(Your instructor will tell you what the percentage and time limits will be before you begin.)*

**KEY:**       4 = Satisfactory       0 = Unsatisfactory       NA =This step is not counted

| PROCEDURE STEPS | SELF | PARTNER | INSTRUCTOR |
|---|---|---|---|
| **1.** Wash your hands and assemble the necessary supplies. | ❑ | ❑ | ❑ |
| **2.** Insert the thermometer into a plastic sheath. | ❑ | ❑ | ❑ |
| **3.** Spread lubricant onto a tissue and then from the tissue onto the sheath of the thermometer. | ❑ | ❑ | ❑ |
| **4.** Greet and identify the patient and explain the procedure. | ❑ | ❑ | ❑ |
| **5.** Ensure the patient's privacy by placing the patient in a side-lying position facing the examination room door and draping appropriately. | ❑ | ❑ | ❑ |
| **6.** Apply gloves and visualize the anus by lifting the top buttock with your nondominant hand. | ❑ | ❑ | ❑ |
| **7.** Gently insert the thermometer past the sphincter muscle about 1 1/2 inches for an adult, 1 inch for a child, and 1/2 inch for an infant. | ❑ | ❑ | ❑ |
| **8.** Release the upper buttock and hold the thermometer in place with your dominant hand for 3 minutes. Replace the drape without moving the dominant hand. | ❑ | ❑ | ❑ |
| **9.** The electronic thermometer will signal when the reading is obtained. Discard the sheath into an appropriate waste container and note the reading. | ❑ | ❑ | ❑ |
| **10.** Replace the electronic thermometer into the charger as necessary. | ❑ | ❑ | ❑ |
| **11.** Remove your gloves and wash your hands. | ❑ | ❑ | ❑ |
| **12.** Record the procedure and mark the letter R next to the reading, indicating that the temperature was taken rectally. | ❑ | ❑ | ❑ |
| **13.** AFF Explain how to respond to a patient who is developmentally challenged. | ❑ | ❑ | ❑ |

_____

_____

_____

_____

**PSY** PROCEDURE 4-3 **Measure and Record a Rectal Temperature** (continued)

**CALCULATION**

Total Possible Points: _____

Total Points Earned: _____ Multiplied by 100 = _____ Divided by Total Possible Points = _____ %

**PASS**   **FAIL**   **COMMENTS:**
  ❏         ❏

Student's signature _____ Date _____

Partner's signature _____ Date _____

Instructor's signature _____ Date _____

## **FSY** PROCEDURE 4-4   Measure and Record an Axillary Temperature

Name: _____ Date: _____ Time: _____ Grade: _____

**EQUIPMENT/SUPPLIES:** Electronic thermometer (oral or rectal); tissues or cotton balls; disposable plastic sheaths; biohazard waste container.

**STANDARDS:** Given the needed equipment and a place to work, the student will perform this skill with _____ % accuracy in a total of _____ minutes. *(Your instructor will tell you what the percentage and time limits will be before you begin.)*

**KEY:**          4 = Satisfactory                    0 = Unsatisfactory               NA =This step is not counted

| PROCEDURE STEPS | SELF | PARTNER | INSTRUCTOR |
|---|---|---|---|
| **1.** Wash your hands and assemble the necessary supplies. | ❑ | ❑ | ❑ |
| **2.** Insert the electronic thermometer probe into a plastic sheath. | ❑ | ❑ | ❑ |
| **3.** Expose the patient's axilla without exposing more of the chest or upper body than is necessary. | ❑ | ❑ | ❑ |
| **4.** Place the tip of the thermometer deep in the axilla and bring the patient's arm down, crossing the forearm over the chest. Drape the patient as appropriate for privacy. | ❑ | ❑ | ❑ |
| **5.** The electronic thermometer will signal when the reading is obtained. Discard the sheath into an appropriate waste container and note the reading. | ❑ | ❑ | ❑ |
| **6.** Replace the electronic thermometer into the charger as necessary. | ❑ | ❑ | ❑ |
| **7.** Wash your hands. | ❑ | ❑ | ❑ |
| **8.** Record the procedure and mark a letter A next to the reading, indicating that the reading is axillary. | ❑ | ❑ | ❑ |
| **9.** **AFF** Explain how to respond to a patient who is from a different generation. | ❑ | ❑ | ❑ |

_____

_____

_____

_____

**PSY** PROCEDURE 4-4 **Measure and Record an Axillary Temperature** (continued)

**CALCULATION**

Total Possible Points: _____

Total Points Earned: _____ Multiplied by 100 = _____ Divided by Total Possible Points = _____ %

**PASS   FAIL   COMMENTS:**
❑        ❑

Student's signature _____ Date _____

Partner's signature _____ Date _____

Instructor's signature _____ Date _____

---

**PSY**   PROCEDURE 4-5    **Measure and Record a Patient's Oral Temperature Using an Electronic Thermometer**

**Name:** _____ **Date:** _____ **Time:** _____ **Grade:** _____

**EQUIPMENT/SUPPLIES:** Electronic thermometer with oral or rectal probe, disposable probe covers, biohazard waste container, gloves for taking an oral temperature

**STANDARDS:** Given the needed equipment and a place to work, the student will perform this skill with _____ % accuracy in a total of _____ minutes. *(Your instructor will tell you what the percentage and time limits will be before you begin.)*

**KEY:**         4 = Satisfactory         0 = Unsatisfactory         NA =This step is not counted

| PROCEDURE STEPS | SELF | PARTNER | INSTRUCTOR |
|---|---|---|---|
| **1.** Wash your hands and assemble the necessary supplies. | ❏ | ❏ | ❏ |
| **2.** Greet and identify the patient and explain the procedure. | ❏ | ❏ | ❏ |
| **3.** Attach the appropriate probe to the battery-powered unit. | ❏ | ❏ | ❏ |
| **4.** Insert the probe into a probe cover. | ❏ | ❏ | ❏ |
| **5.** Position the thermometer appropriately for the method. To take an oral temperature, place the end of the thermometer under the patient's tongue to either side of the frenulum. | ❏ | ❏ | ❏ |
| **6.** Wait for the electronic thermometer unit to "beep" when it senses no signs of the temperature rising further. This usually occurs within 20 to 30 seconds. | ❏ | ❏ | ❏ |
| **7.** After the beep, remove the probe and note the reading on the digital display screen on the unit before replacing the probe into the unit. | ❏ | ❏ | ❏ |
| **8.** Discard the probe cover by pressing a button, usually on the end of the probe, while holding the probe over a biohazard container. After noting the temperature, replace the probe into the unit. | ❏ | ❏ | ❏ |
| **9.** Remove your gloves, if used, wash your hands, and record the procedure | ❏ | ❏ | ❏ |
| **10.** Return the unit and probe to the charging base. | ❏ | ❏ | ❏ |
| **11. AFF** Explain how to respond to a patient who is hearing impaired. | ❏ | ❏ | ❏ |

_____

_____

_____

_____

**PSY** PROCEDURE 4-5 **Measure and Record a Patient's Oral Temperature Using an Electronic Thermometer** (continued)

**CALCULATION**

Total Possible Points: _____

Total Points Earned: _____ Multiplied by 100 = _____ Divided by Total Possible Points = _____ %

**PASS    FAIL    COMMENTS:**
  ❏        ❏

Student's signature _____ Date _____

Partner's signature _____ Date _____

Instructor's signature _____ Date _____

## FSY PROCEDURE 4-6 Measure and Record a Patient's Temperature Using a Tympanic Thermometer

Name: _____ Date: _____ Time: _____ Grade: _____

**EQUIPMENT/SUPPLIES:** Tympanic thermometer, disposable probe covers, biohazard waste container

**STANDARDS:** Given the needed equipment and a place to work, the student will perform this skill with _____ % accuracy in a total of _____ minutes. *(Your instructor will tell you what the percentage and time limits will be before you begin.)*

**KEY:**        4 = Satisfactory        0 = Unsatisfactory        NA = This step is not counted

| PROCEDURE STEPS | SELF | PARTNER | INSTRUCTOR |
|---|---|---|---|
| **1.** Wash your hands and assemble the necessary supplies. | ❑ | ❑ | ❑ |
| **2.** Greet and identify the patient and explain the procedure. | ❑ | ❑ | ❑ |
| **3.** Insert the ear probe into a probe cover. | ❑ | ❑ | ❑ |
| **4.** Place the end of the ear probe into the patient's ear canal with your dominant hand while straightening out the ear canal with your nondominant hand. | ❑ | ❑ | ❑ |
| **5.** With the ear probe properly placed in the ear canal, press the button on the thermometer. The reading is displayed on the digital display screen in about 2 seconds. | ❑ | ❑ | ❑ |
| **6.** Remove the probe and note the reading. Discard the probe cover into an appropriate waste container. | ❑ | ❑ | ❑ |
| **7.** Wash your hands and record the procedure. | ❑ | ❑ | ❑ |
| **8.** Return the unit to the charging base. | ❑ | ❑ | ❑ |
| **9.** **AFF** Explain how to respond to a patient who is deaf. | ❑ | ❑ | ❑ |

_____

_____

_____

_____

**CALCULATION**

Total Possible Points: _____

Total Points Earned: _____ Multiplied by 100 = _____ Divided by Total Possible Points = _____ %

**PASS    FAIL    COMMENTS:**
  ❑         ❑

Student's signature _____ Date _____

Partner's signature _____ Date _____

Instructor's signature _____ Date _____

**FSY** PROCEDURE 4-7 **Measure and Record a Patient's Temperature Using a Temporal Artery Thermometer**

Name: _____ Date: _____ Time: _____ Grade: _____

**EQUIPMENT/SUPPLIES:** Temporal artery thermometer, antiseptic wipes

**STANDARDS:** Given the needed equipment and a place to work, the student will perform this skill with _____ % accuracy in a total of _____ minutes. *(Your instructor will tell you what the percentage and time limits will be before you begin.)*

**KEY:** 4 = Satisfactory 0 = Unsatisfactory NA = This step is not counted

| PROCEDURE STEPS | SELF | PARTNER | INSTRUCTOR |
|---|---|---|---|
| **1.** Wash your hands and assemble the necessary supplies. | ❑ | ❑ | ❑ |
| **2.** Greet and identify the patient and explain the procedure. | ❑ | ❑ | ❑ |
| **3.** Place the probe end of the hand-held unit on the forehead of the patient. Make sure the patient's skin is dry. | ❑ | ❑ | ❑ |
| **4.** With the thermometer against the forehead, depress the on/off button, move the thermometer across and down the forehead, and release the on/off button with the unit over the temporal artery. | ❑ | ❑ | ❑ |
| **5.** The reading is displayed on the digital display screen in 1 to 2 seconds. | ❑ | ❑ | ❑ |
| **6.** Properly disinfect the end of the thermometer according to manufacturer instructions | ❑ | ❑ | ❑ |
| **7.** Wash your hands and record the procedure. | ❑ | ❑ | ❑ |
| **8.** Return the unit to the charging base. | ❑ | ❑ | ❑ |
| **9.** **AFF** Explain how to respond to a patient who is visually impaired. | ❑ | ❑ | ❑ |

_____

_____

_____

_____

**CALCULATION**

Total Possible Points: _____

Total Points Earned: _____ Multiplied by 100 = _____ Divided by Total Possible Points = _____ %

**PASS   FAIL   COMMENTS:**
❑        ❑

Student's signature _____ Date _____

Partner's signature _____ Date _____

Instructor's signature _____ Date _____

| **PSY** PROCEDURE 4-8 | **Measure and Record a Patient's Radial Pulse** |
|---|---|

**Name:** _____ **Date:** _____ **Time:** _____ **Grade:** _____

**EQUIPMENT/SUPPLIES:** A watch with a sweeping second hand

**STANDARDS:** Given the needed equipment and a place to work, the student will perform this skill with _____ % accuracy in a total of _____ minutes. *(Your instructor will tell you what the percentage and time limits will be before you begin.)*

**KEY:**          4 = Satisfactory          0 = Unsatisfactory          NA =This step is not counted

| PROCEDURE STEPS | SELF | PARTNER | INSTRUCTOR |
|---|---|---|---|
| **1.** Wash your hands. | ❏ | ❏ | ❏ |
| **2.** Greet and identify the patient and explain the procedure. | ❏ | ❏ | ❏ |
| **3.** Position the patient with the arm relaxed and supported either on the lap of the patient or on a table. | ❏ | ❏ | ❏ |
| **4.** With the index, middle, and ring fingers of your dominant hand, press with your fingertips firmly enough to feel the pulse but gently enough not to obliterate it | ❏ | ❏ | ❏ |
| **5.** If the pulse is regular, count it for 30 seconds, watching the second hand of your watch. Multiply the number of pulsations by 2 since the pulse is always recorded as beats per minute. If the pulse is irregular, count it for a full 60 seconds. | ❏ | ❏ | ❏ |
| **6.** Record the rate in the medical record with the other vital signs. Also note the rhythm if irregular and the volume if thready or bounding. | ❏ | ❏ | ❏ |
| **7.** **AFF** Explain how to respond to a patient who is developmentally challenged. | ❏ | ❏ | ❏ |

_____

_____

_____

_____

**CALCULATION**

Total Possible Points: _____

Total Points Earned: _____ Multiplied by 100 = _____ Divided by Total Possible Points = _____ %

**PASS   FAIL   COMMENTS:**
 ❏         ❏

Student's signature _____ Date _____

Partner's signature _____ Date _____

Instructor's signature _____ Date _____

**PSY** PROCEDURE 4-9 **Measure and Record a Patient's Respirations**

**Name:** _____ **Date:** _____ **Time:** _____ **Grade:** _____

**EQUIPMENT/SUPPLIES:** A watch with a sweeping second hand

**STANDARDS:** Given the needed equipment and a place to work, the student will perform this skill with _____ % accuracy in a total of _____ minutes. *(Your instructor will tell you what the percentage and time limits will be before you begin.)*

**KEY:**      4 = Satisfactory      0 = Unsatisfactory      NA = This step is not counted

| PROCEDURE STEPS | SELF | PARTNER | INSTRUCTOR |
|---|---|---|---|
| **1.** Wash your hands. | ❏ | ❏ | ❏ |
| **2.** Greet and identify the patient and explain the procedure. | ❏ | ❏ | ❏ |
| **3.** After counting the radial pulse and still watching your second hand, count a complete rise and fall of the chest as one respiration. Note: Some patients have abdominal movement rather than chest movement during respirations. Observe carefully for the easiest area to assess for the most accurate reading | ❏ | ❏ | ❏ |
| **4.** If the breathing pattern is regular, count the respiratory rate for 30 seconds and multiply by 2. If the pattern is irregular, count for a full 60 seconds. | ❏ | ❏ | ❏ |
| **5.** Record the respiratory rate in the medical record with the other vital signs. Also, note whether the rhythm is irregular, along with any unusual or abnormal sounds such as wheezing. | ❏ | ❏ | ❏ |
| **6.** **AFF** Explain how to respond to a patient who has dementia. | ❏ | ❏ | ❏ |

_____

_____

_____

_____

**CALCULATION**

Total Possible Points: _____

Total Points Earned: _____ Multiplied by 100 = _____ Divided by Total Possible Points = _____ %

**PASS   FAIL   COMMENTS:**
  ❏       ❏

Student's signature _____ Date _____

Partner's signature _____ Date _____

Instructor's signature _____ Date _____

## PSY PROCEDURE 4-10 Measure and Record a Patient's Blood Pressure

Name: _____ Date: _____ Time: _____ Grade: _____

**EQUIPMENT/SUPPLIES:** Sphygmomanometer, stethoscope

**STANDARDS:** Given the needed equipment and a place to work, the student will perform this skill with _____ % accuracy in a total of _____ minutes. *(Your instructor will tell you what the percentage and time limits will be before you begin.)*

**KEY:**        4 = Satisfactory          0 = Unsatisfactory          NA = This step is not counted

| PROCEDURE STEPS | SELF | PARTNER | INSTRUCTOR |
|---|---|---|---|
| **1.** Wash your hands. | ❏ | ❏ | ❏ |
| **2.** Greet and identify the patient and explain the procedure. | ❏ | ❏ | ❏ |
| **3.** Position the patient with the arm to be used supported with the forearm on the lap or a table and slightly flexed, with the palm upward. The upper arm should be level with the patient's heart. | ❏ | ❏ | ❏ |
| **4.** Expose the patient's upper arm. | ❏ | ❏ | ❏ |
| **5.** Palpate the brachial pulse in the antecubital area and center the deflated cuff directly over the brachial artery. The lower edge of the cuff should be 1 to 2 inches above the antecubital area. | ❏ | ❏ | ❏ |
| **6.** Wrap the cuff smoothly and snugly around the arm and secure it with the Velcro edges. | ❏ | ❏ | ❏ |
| **7.** With the air pump in your dominant hand and the valve between your thumb and the forefinger, turn the screw clockwise to tighten. Do not tighten it to the point that it will be difficult to release. | ❏ | ❏ | ❏ |
| **8.** While palpating the brachial pulse with your nondominant hand, inflate the cuff and note the point or number on the dial or mercury column at which you no longer feel the brachial pulse | ❏ | ❏ | ❏ |
| **9.** Deflate the cuff by turning the valve counterclockwise. Wait at least 30 seconds before reinflating the cuff. | ❏ | ❏ | ❏ |
| **10.** Place the stethoscope earpieces in your ears with the openings pointed slightly forward. Stand about 3 feet from the manometer with the gauge at eye level. Your stethoscope tubing should hang freely without touching or rubbing against any part of the cuff. | ❏ | ❏ | ❏ |
| **11.** Place the diaphragm of the stethoscope against the brachial artery and hold it in place with the nondominant hand without pressing too hard. | ❏ | ❏ | ❏ |
| **12.** With your dominant hand, turn the screw on the valve just enough to close the valve; inflate the cuff. Pump the valve bulb to about 30 mm Hg above the number felt during Step 8. | ❏ | ❏ | ❏ |

**PSY** PROCEDURE 4-10 **Measure and Record a Patient's Blood Pressure** (continued)

| | | | |
|---|---|---|---|
| **13.** Once the cuff is appropriately inflated, turn the valve counter-clockwise to release air at about 2 to 4 mm Hg per second. | ❏ | ❏ | ❏ |
| **14.** Listening carefully, note the point on the gauge at which you hear the first clear tapping sound. This is the systolic sound, or Korotkoff I | ❏ | ❏ | ❏ |
| **15.** Maintaining control of the valve screw, continue to listen and deflate the cuff. When you hear the last sound, note the reading and quickly deflate the cuff. Note: Never immediately reinflate the cuff if you are unsure of the reading. Totally deflate the cuff and wait 1 to 2 minutes before repeating the procedure. | ❏ | ❏ | ❏ |
| **16.** Remove the cuff and press the air from the bladder of the cuff. | ❏ | ❏ | ❏ |
| **17.** If this is the first recording or a new patient, the physician may also want a reading in the other arm or in another position. | ❏ | ❏ | ❏ |
| **18.** Put the equipment away and wash your hands. | ❏ | ❏ | ❏ |
| **19.** Record the reading with the systolic over the diastolic pressure, noting which arm was used (120/80 LA). Also, record the patient's position if other than sitting. | ❏ | ❏ | ❏ |
| **20.** **AFF** Explain how to respond to a patient who is from a different culture. | ❏ | ❏ | ❏ |

_____

_____

_____

_____

**CALCULATION**

Total Possible Points: _____

Total Points Earned: _____ Multiplied by 100 = _____ Divided by Total Possible Points = _____ %

**PASS   FAIL   COMMENTS:**
  ❏        ❏

Student's signature _____ Date _____

Partner's signature _____ Date _____

Instructor's signature _____ Date _____

CHAPTER

# 5

# Assisting with the Physical Examination

## Learning Outcomes

### COG Cognitive Domain

1. Spell and define the key terms
2. Identify and state the use of the basic and specialized instruments and supplies used in the physical examination
3. Describe the four methods used to examine the patient
4. State your responsibilities before, during, and after the physical examination
5. List the basic sequence of the physical examination
6. Describe the normal function of each body system

### PSY Psychomotor Domain

1. Assist with the adult physical examination (Procedure 5-1)

2. Assist provider with a patient exam
3. Coach patients appropriately considering cultural diversity, developmental life stages, and communication barriers
4. Document accurately in the medical record

### AFF Affective Domain

1. Incorporate critical thinking skills when performing patient assessment
2. Show awareness of a patient's concerns related to the procedure being performed
3. Explain to a patient the rationale for performance of a procedure

4. Demonstrate empathy, active listening, and nonverbal communication
5. Demonstrate respect for individual diversity including gender, race, religion, age, economic status, and appearance
6. Protect the integrity of the medical record

### ABHES Competencies

1. Prepare and maintain examination and treatment area
2. Prepare patient for examinations and treatments
3. Assist physician with routine and specialty examinations and treatments

Name: _____     Date: _____     Grade: _____

## COG MULTIPLE CHOICE

Circle the letter preceding the correct answer.

**1.** Which of these instruments would a physician use to examine a patient's throat?
   **a.** Stethoscope
   **b.** Laryngeal mirror
   **c.** Percussion hammer
   **d.** Ayre spatula
   **e.** Tuning fork

**2.** The purpose of a regular physical examination is to:
   **a.** identify a disease or condition based on patient symptoms.
   **b.** compare symptoms of several diseases that the patient may exhibit.
   **c.** look for late warning signs of disease.
   **d.** maintain the patient's health and prevent disease.
   **e.** ensure the patient is maintaining a healthy diet and exercise regime.

**3.** Which of the following tasks would be performed by a medical assistant?
   **a.** Collecting specimens for diagnostic testing
   **b.** Diagnosing a patient
   **c.** Prescribing treatment for a patient
   **d.** Performing a physical examination
   **e.** Testing a patient's reflexes

**4.** Which of the following statements is true about physical examinations?
   **a.** Patients aged 20 to 40 years should have a physical examination every year.
   **b.** It is not necessary to have a physical examination until you are over age 40 years.
   **c.** Women should have physical examinations more frequently than men.
   **d.** Patients ages 20 to 40 years should have a physical examination every 1 to 3 years.
   **e.** Patients over the age 60 years should have a physical examination every 6 months.

**5.** In which information-gathering technique might a physician use his or her sense of smell?
   **a.** Palpation
   **b.** Percussion
   **c.** Inspection
   **d.** Auscultation
   **e.** Visualization

**6.** If a physician notices asymmetry in a patient's features, it means that the patient:
   **a.** is normal and has nothing wrong.
   **b.** has features that are of unequal size or shape.
   **c.** has features that are abnormally large.
   **d.** will need immediate surgery.
   **e.** has perfectly even features.

**7.** Which part of the body can be auscultated?
   **a.** Lungs
   **b.** Legs
   **c.** Spine
   **d.** Feet
   **e.** Ears

**8.** The best position in which to place a female patient for a genital and rectum examination is the:
   **a.** Sims position.
   **b.** Fowler position.
   **c.** lithotomy position.
   **d.** Trendelenburg position.
   **e.** prone position.

**9.** A patient may be asked to walk around during a physical examination in order to:
   **a.** raise the pulse rate.
   **b.** observe gait and coordination.
   **c.** loosen the muscles in the legs.
   **d.** assess posture.
   **e.** demonstrate balance.

**10.** Women over age 40 years should receive mammograms every:
   **a.** 6 months.
   **b.** 2 years.
   **c.** 5 years.
   **d.** 1 year.
   **e.** 3 months.

**11.** How would a physician use a tuning fork to test a patient's hearing?
   **a.** By striking the prongs against the patient's leg and holding the handle in front of the patient's ear
   **b.** By holding the prongs behind the patient's ear and tapping the handle against their head
   **c.** By striking the prongs against the hand and holding the handle against the skull near the patient's ear
   **d.** By repeatedly tapping the prongs against the skull near the patient's ear
   **e.** By tapping the prongs on the table and inserting the handle into the patient's ear

**12.** Which of these may be an early warning sign of cancer?
  **a.** Obvious change in a wart or mole
  **b.** Dizziness or fainting spells
  **c.** Loss of appetite
  **d.** Inability to focus attention
  **e.** Sudden weight gain

**13.** How would a physician most likely be able to diagnose a hernia?
  **a.** Inspection
  **b.** Percussion
  **c.** Auscultation
  **d.** Palpation
  **e.** Visualization

*Scenario for questions 14–16:* A patient arrives for her physical checkup. While you are obtaining the patient's history, she mentions to you that she is taking several over-the-counter medications.

**14.** What is the correct procedure?
  **a.** Tell the physician immediately.
  **b.** Tell the patient that it will not affect her physical examination.
  **c.** Make a note of the medications the patient is taking in her medical record.
  **d.** Ask the patient to reschedule the physical examination when she has stopped taking the medications for at least a week.
  **e.** Prepare the necessary materials for a blood test.

**15.** During the patient's physical examination, the physician asks you to hand her the instruments needed to examine the patient's eyes. You should give her a(n):
  **a.** otoscope and penlight.
  **b.** stethoscope and speculum.
  **c.** ophthalmoscope and penlight.
  **d.** laryngoscope and gloves.
  **e.** anoscope and speculum.

**16.** Once the examination is over, you escort the patient to the front desk. After she has left the office, what do you do with her medical record?
  **a.** Check that the data have been accurately documented and release it to the billing department.
  **b.** Check that the data have been accurately documented and file the medical report under the patient's name.
  **c.** Pass the medical report on to the physician to check for any errors.
  **d.** Give the medical report directly to the billing department to maintain confidentiality.
  **e.** File the medical report under the patient's name for easy retrieval.

**17.** What is the difference between an otoscope and an audioscope?
  **a.** An otoscope is used to screen patients for hearing loss, whereas an audioscope is used to assess the internal structures of the ear.
  **b.** An audioscope is used to screen patients for hearing loss, whereas an otoscope is used to assess the internal structures of the ear.
  **c.** An otoscope is made of stainless steel, whereas an audioscope is made of plastic.
  **d.** An audioscope is made of plastic, whereas an otoscope is made of stainless steel.
  **e.** An otoscope is an older version of an audioscope and is not used much anymore.

**18.** A baseline examination is a(n):
  **a.** examination to determine the cause of an illness.
  **b.** full medical examination for people over age 50 years.
  **c.** initial examination to give physicians information about the patient.
  **d.** examination based on the patient's symptoms.
  **e.** examination of the abdominal regions of the patient.

**19.** Which of the following materials should be stored in a room away from the examination room?
  **a.** Gloves
  **b.** Tongue depressors
  **c.** Tape measure
  **d.** Cotton tipped applicators
  **e.** Syringes

**20.** What does the "P" stand for in PERRLA?
  **a.** Position
  **b.** Protrusion
  **c.** Posture
  **d.** Pupil
  **e.** Perception

## **COG MATCHING**

Grade: _____

Match each key term with its definition.

**Key Terms**

21. _____ auscultation
22. _____ Babinski reflex
23. _____ bimanual
24. _____ bruit
25. _____ cerumen
26. _____ extraocular
27. _____ hernia
28. _____ occult
29. _____ Papanicolaou (Pap) test
30. _____ PERRLA
31. _____ range of motion (ROM)
32. _____ sclera
33. _____ speculum
34. _____ transillumination
35. _____ tympanic membrane
36. _____ clinical diagnosis
37. _____ differential diagnosis
38. _____ gait
39. _____ lubricant
40. _____ manipulation
41. _____ nasal septum
42. _____ rectovaginal
43. _____ peripheral
44. _____ applicator
45. _____ symmetry
46. _____ asymmetry

**Definitions**

**a.** an instrument used for examining body cavities
**b.** thin, semitransparent membrane in the middle ear that transmits vibrations
**c.** a reflex noted by the extension of the great toe and abduction of the other toes
**d.** a test in which cells from the cervix are examined microscopically for abnormalities
**e.** an examination performed with both hands
**f.** the extent of movement in the joints
**g.** abnormal sound or murmur in the blood vessels
**h.** white fibrous tissue covering the eye
**i.** passage of light through body tissues for the purpose of examination
**j.** blood present in stool that is not visibly apparent
**k.** a diagnosis based only on a patient's symptoms
**l.** act of listening to the sounds within the body to evaluate the heart, lungs, intestines, or fetal heart tones
**m.** an acronym that means pupils are equal, round, and reactive to light and accommodation
**n.** earwax
**o.** a protrusion of an organ through a weakened muscle wall
**p.** outside of the eye
**q.** a diagnosis made by comparing symptoms of several diseases
**r.** the passive movement of the joints to determine the extent of movement
**s.** pertaining to the rectum and vagina
**t.** equality in size and shape or position of parts on opposite sides of the body
**u.** a water-soluble agent that reduces friction
**v.** device for applying local treatments and tests
**w.** inequality in size and shape on opposite sides of the body
**x.** pertaining to or situated away from the center
**y.** partition dividing the nostrils
**z.** a manner of walking

## **COG MATCHING**

Grade: _____

Match each physical examination technique with its description by placing the letter preceding the definition on the line next to the correct basic examination technique.

**Techniques**

47. _____ inspection
48. _____ palpation
49. _____ percussion
50. _____ auscultation

**Descriptions**

**a.** touching or moving body areas with fingers or hands
**b.** looking at areas of the body to observe physical features
**c.** listening to the sounds of the body
**d.** tapping the body with the hand or an instrument to produce sounds

## **COG** MATCHING

Grade: _____

Match each medical instrument with its description by placing the letter preceding the definition on the line next to the correct instrument.

**Instruments**

**51.** _____ tuning fork
**52.** _____ ophthalmoscope
**53.** _____ anoscope
**54.** _____ stethoscope
**55.** _____ laryngeal mirror
**56.** _____ headlight

**Descriptions**

**a.** an instrument used for listening to body sounds and taking blood pressure
**b.** an instrument used to examine the interior structures of the eyes
**c.** an instrument with two prongs used to test hearing
**d.** a light attached to a headband that provides direct light on the area being examined
**e.** an instrument used to examine areas of the patient's throat and larynx
**f.** a short stainless steel or plastic speculum used to inspect the anal canal

## **COG** IDENTIFICATION

Grade: _____

Anticipating what the physician will need during a patient examination is a skill that the competent medical assistant must develop. Indicate which of the following instruments would the physician most likely ask for to examine the patient in each situation. Place a check mark on the line next to the possible instrument (more than one instrument may apply).

**57.** A patient comes into the physician's office complaining of ringing in her ears.

**a.** _____ percussion hammer

**b.** _____ tuning fork

**c.** _____ laryngeal mirror

**d.** _____ otoscope

**e.** _____ ophthalmoscope

**58.** A male patient complains of weakness in his legs.

**a.** _____ percussion hammer

**b.** _____ tuning fork

**c.** _____ laryngeal mirror

**d.** _____ otoscope

**e.** _____ ophthalmoscope

**59.** A young female patient complains of a headache and fever.

**a.** _____ percussion hammer

**b.** _____ tuning fork

**c.** _____ laryngeal mirror

**d.** _____ otoscope

**e.** _____ ophthalmoscope

**60.** Listed below are the body areas inspected by the physician during a physical examination, but they are not in the correct order. Starting with the number one (1), number the body areas in the correct order in which they are examined.

_____ Eyes and ears

_____ Legs

_____ Head and neck

_____ Chest, breasts, and abdomen

_____ Nose and sinuses

_____ Reflexes

_____ Posture, gait, balance, and strength

_____ Mouth and throat

_____ Genitalia and rectum

**61.** Place a check mark on the line next to each factor that may be a warning sign for cancer. Check all that apply.

_____ an itchy rash on the arms and legs

_____ a nagging cough or hoarse voice

_____ unusual bleeding or discharge

_____ stiffness in joints

_____ a sore that will not heal

_____ frequent upper respiratory infections

_____ pain in any body area

**62.** As a medical assistant, you will be required to assist the physician before, during, and after physical examinations. Read the list of tasks below and place a letter on the line preceding the task indicating whether you would perform the task before (B), during (D), or after (A) the examination.

**a.** _____ Escort the patient to the front desk.

**b.** _____ Obtain a urine specimen from the patient, if required.

**c.** _____ Adjust the drape on the patient to expose the necessary body part.

**d.** _____ Ask the patient about medication used on a regular basis.

**e.** _____ Check the patient's medical record to ensure all the information has been accurately documented.

**f.** _____ Place the patient's chart outside the examining room door.

**g.** _____ Offer reassurance to the patient and check for signs of anxiety.

_____ Grade: _____

**63.** A patient calls the physician's office and explains that her daughter cries continuously, has been vomiting regularly, and stumbles a lot. Which of these do you recommend and why?

**a.** Tell her that it is probably a bug and to keep her child home from school for a couple of days.

_____

_____

_____

_____

**b.** Advise that she keep an eye on the child and inform the physician if there is any change.

_____

_____

_____

_____

**c.** Tell her to have the child examined immediately.

_____

_____

_____

_____

**64.** A patient comes into the physician's office with an open wound. When obtaining the patient's medical records, you discover that he last had a tetanus booster 4 years ago. What is the correct procedure and why?

**a.** Recommend the patient has another tetanus booster.

_____

_____

_____

**b.** Tell the patient he does not need immunizing for another 6 years.

_____

_____

_____

**c.** Tell the patient he should have a booster if he is traveling abroad.

_____

_____

_____

**65.** Dr. O'Brien tells you that a patient's eardrum is infected. What are the symptoms that could have led Dr. O'Brien to this diagnosis?

_____

_____

_____

_____

**66.** As a medical assistant, you are responsible for checking each examination room at the beginning of the day to make sure that it is ready for patients. List three things that need to be done to ensure that a room is ready.

_____

_____

_____

_____

## COG TRUE OR FALSE?

Grade: _____

Indicate whether the statements are true or false by placing the letter T (true) or F (false) on the line preceding the statement.

**67.** _____ A normal tympanic membrane will be light pink and curve slightly outward.

**68.** _____ Patients should have a baseline electrocardiogram (ECG) when they turn age 60 years.

**69.** _____ The instruments used to examine the rectum and colon are all one standard size.

**70.** _____ The medical assistant is responsible for preparing the examination room, preparing the patient, assisting the physician, and cleaning the equipment and examination room.

## COG AFF CASE STUDY FOR CRITICAL THINKING

Grade: _____

**1.** A 19-year-old patient has never had a Pap smear before and does not understand what the test is for, or what is going to happen during the procedure. The physician asks you to explain the process to her in simple terms. List some key aspects of a Pap smear and explain the purpose of the procedure to this patient in a way that she will understand.

_____

_____

_____

_____

2. Alicia is assisting a male physician with performing a gynecological examination. Midway through the examination, she is paged to assist another medical procedure. Explain what she should do and why.

_____

_____

_____

_____

3. Your patient is a 35-year-old male who has a long family history of cancer. The patient is terrified of developing cancer and has been to see the physician several times for minor false alarms. Prepare an information sheet for the patient, explaining the early warning signs of cancer. What else can you do to alleviate the fear in this patient?

_____

_____

_____

_____

4. You are assisting with the physical examination of a 55-year-old male. When the physician begins to prepare for the rectal examination, the patient refuses and says that it is unnecessary and that he is fine. What would be the most appropriate thing to do at this point?

_____

_____

_____

_____

5. At the beginning of the day, you are preparing the examination rooms with a fellow medical assistant. You are both in a hurry because the first patients are arriving and the physicians are waiting for you to finish. Your fellow medical assistant suggests that you don't need to check the batteries in the equipment because everything worked well yesterday. What would you do or say?

_____

_____

_____

_____

6. While you are escorting a patient to the front desk, the patient asks you whether an over-the-counter medication will affect her prescribed treatment. You are familiar with both drugs. What is the correct response?

_____

_____

_____

_____

**7.** You are assisting a physician during a genital and pelvic examination on a female disabled patient who cannot be placed into the lithotomy position. What is the correct course of action?

_____

_____

_____

_____

## PSY PROCEDURE 5-1 Assisting with the Adult Physical Examination

**Name:** _____ **Date:** _____ **Time:** _____ **Grade:** _____

**EQUIPMENT/SUPPLIES:** A variety of instruments and supplies, including the stethoscope, ophthalmoscope, otoscope, penlight, tuning fork, nasal speculum, tongue blade, percussion hammer, gloves, water-soluble lubricant, an examinations light, and patient gown and draping supplies

**STANDARDS:** Given the needed equipment and a place to work, the student will perform this skill with _____ % accuracy in a total of _____ minutes. *(Your instructor will tell you what the percentage and time limits will be before you begin.)*

**KEY:**     4 = Satisfactory          0 = Unsatisfactory          NA =This step is not counted

| PROCEDURE STEPS | SELF | PARTNER | INSTRUCTOR |
|---|---|---|---|
| **1.** Wash your hands. | ❏ | ❏ | ❏ |
| **2.** Prepare the examination room and assemble the equipment. | ❏ | ❏ | ❏ |
| **3.** Greet the patient by name and escort him or her to the examining room. | ❏ | ❏ | ❏ |
| **4.** Explain the procedure. | ❏ | ❏ | ❏ |
| **5.** Obtain and record the medical history and chief complaint. | ❏ | ❏ | ❏ |
| **6.** Take and record the vital signs, height, weight, and visual acuity. | ❏ | ❏ | ❏ |
| **7.** If anticipated, instruct the patient to obtain a urine specimen and escort him or her to the bathroom. | ❏ | ❏ | ❏ |
| **8.** Once inside the examination room, instruct the patient in disrobing including directions on how to put the gown on (open in the front or back). Leave the room unless the patient needs assistance. | ❏ | ❏ | ❏ |
| **9.** **AFF** Explain how to respond to a patient who has cultural or religious beliefs and is uncomfortable about disrobing. | ❏ | ❏ | ❏ |
| **10.** Assist patient into a sitting position on the edge of the examination table. Cover the lap and legs with a drape. | ❏ | ❏ | ❏ |
| **11.** **AFF** Place the medical record outside the examination room and notify the physician that the patient is ready. If your office uses an electronic medical record, assure you have entered and updated all information necessary and log off the computer before leaving the room. | ❏ | ❏ | ❏ |
| **12.** Assist the physician by handing him or her the instruments as needed and positioning the patient appropriately. | ❏ | ❏ | ❏ |
| **13.** Help the patient return to a sitting position. | ❏ | ❏ | ❏ |

| PSY PROCEDURE 5-1 **Assisting with the Adult Physical Examination** (continued) | | | |
|---|:---:|:---:|:---:|
| **14.** Perform any follow-up procedures or treatments. | ❏ | ❏ | ❏ |
| **15.** Leave the room while the patient dresses unless assistance is needed. | ❏ | ❏ | ❏ |
| **16.** Return to the examination room after the patient has dressed to:<br>**a.** answer questions.<br>**b.** reinforce instructions.<br>**c.** provide patient education. | ❏ | ❏ | ❏ |
| **17.** Escort the patient to the front desk. | ❏ | ❏ | ❏ |
| **18.** Properly clean or dispose of all used equipment and supplies. | ❏ | ❏ | ❏ |
| **19.** Clean the room with a disinfectant and prepare for the next patient. | ❏ | ❏ | ❏ |
| **20.** Wash your hands.<br>**a.** Record any instructions that were ordered for the patient.<br>**b.** Note if any specimens were obtained.<br>**c.** Indicate the results of the test or note the laboratory where the specimens are being sent for testing. | ❏ | ❏ | ❏ |

_____

_____

_____

_____

**CALCULATION**

Total Possible Points: _____

Total Points Earned: _____ Multiplied by 100 = _____ Divided by Total Possible Points = _____ %

**PASS**   **FAIL**   **COMMENTS**:
  ❏    ❏

Student's signature _____ Date _____

Partner's signature _____ Date _____

Instructor's signature _____ Date _____

# 6 Sterilization and Surgical Instruments

## Learning Outcomes

### COG Cognitive Domain

1. Spell and define the key terms
2. Define the following as practiced within an ambulatory care setting: surgical asepsis
3. Identify quality assurance practices in health care.
4. Describe several methods of sterilization
5. Categorize surgical instruments based on use and identify each by its characteristics
6. Identify surgical instruments specific to designated specialties

7. State the difference between reusable and disposable instruments
8. Explain how to handle and store instruments, equipment, and supplies
9. Describe the necessity and steps for maintaining documents and records of maintenance for instruments and equipment

### PSY Psychomotor Domain

1. Sanitize equipment and instruments (Procedure 6-1)
2. Prepare items for autoclaving

3. Properly wrap instruments for autoclaving (Procedure 6-2)
4. Perform sterilization procedures
5. Perform sterilization technique and operate an autoclave (Procedure 6-3)
6. Perform a quality control measure

### ABHES Competencies

1. Wrap items for autoclaving
2. Practice quality control
3. Use standard precautions
4. Perform sterilization techniques

Name: _____ Date: _____ Grade: _____

## [COG] MULTIPLE CHOICE

Circle the letter preceding the correct answer:

**1.** A sterile field is defined as an area:
   **a.** where the autoclave is kept.
   **b.** that is free of all microorganisms.
   **c.** where sterilized instruments are stored.
   **d.** that has been cleaned with a chemical disinfectant.
   **e.** in which only sanitized equipment can be used.

**2.** Instruments that are sterilized in the autoclave maintain their sterility for:
   **a.** 15 days.
   **b.** 20 days.
   **c.** 25 days.
   **d.** 30 days.
   **e.** 35 days.

**3.** Autoclave tape indicates that an object:
   **a.** has not been sterilized.
   **b.** contains a specific type of microorganism.
   **c.** has been exposed to steam in the autoclave.
   **d.** needs to be placed on its side in the autoclave.
   **e.** did not reach the proper pressure and temperature in the autoclave.

**4.** Material used to wrap items that are being sterilized in the autoclave must be:
   **a.** permeable to steam but not contaminants.
   **b.** permeable to distilled water but not tap water.
   **c.** permeable to heat but not formaldehyde.
   **d.** permeable to ethylene oxide but not pathogens.
   **e.** permeable to contaminants but not microorganisms.

**5.** Which of the following should be included in an equipment record?
   **a.** Expiration date
   **b.** Date of purchase
   **c.** Physician's name
   **d.** The office's address
   **e.** Date of last sterilization

**6.** Which of the following should be included in a sterilization record?
   **a.** Location of the item
   **b.** Number of items in the load
   **c.** Method of sterilization used
   **d.** Reason for the service request
   **e.** Results of the sterilization indicator

**7.** One instrument commonly used in urology is a(n):
   **a.** curet.
   **b.** tonometer.
   **c.** urethral sound.
   **d.** sigmoidoscope.
   **e.** uterine dilator.

**8.** Forceps are used to:
   **a.** cut sutures.
   **b.** dissect tissue.
   **c.** make incisions.
   **d.** guide instruments.
   **e.** compress or join tissue.

**9.** All packs containing bowls or containers should be placed in the autoclave:
   **a.** upright.
   **b.** under a cloth.
   **c.** on their sides.
   **d.** stacked on top of each other.
   **e.** with their sterilization indicators facing up.

**10.** Consult the material safety data sheet (MSDS) before:
   **a.** handling a chemical spill.
   **b.** reading a sterilization indicator.
   **c.** sterilizing an instrument in the autoclave.
   **d.** requesting service for a piece of equipment.
   **e.** disposing of a disposable scalpel handle and blade.

**11.** Why does the autoclave use pressure in the sterilization process?
   **a.** Pathogens and microorganisms thrive in low-pressure environments.
   **b.** High pressure makes the wrapping permeable to steam and not contaminants.
   **c.** Pressure must be applied to distilled water in order to release sterilizing agents.
   **d.** High pressure prevents microorganisms from penetrating the objects being sterilized.
   **e.** High pressure allows the steam to reach the high temperatures needed for sterilization.

**12.** Which of the following instruments are used to hold sterile drapes in place during surgical procedures?
   **a.** Directors
   **b.** Serrations
   **c.** Towel clamps
   **d.** Curved scissors
   **e.** Alligator biopsies

**13.** Notched mechanisms that hold the tips of the forceps together tightly are called:
   **a.** springs.
   **b.** sutures.
   **c.** ratchets.
   **d.** serrations.
   **e.** clamps.

**14.** After use, scalpel blades should be:
   **a.** sterilized in the autoclave.
   **b.** discarded in a sharps container.
   **c.** reattached to a scalpel handle.
   **d.** processed in a laboratory.
   **e.** wrapped in cotton muslin.

**15.** The instrument used to hold open layers of tissue to expose the areas underneath during a surgical procedure is a:
   **a.** retractor.
   **b.** scalpel.
   **c.** director.
   **d.** clamp.
   **e.** forceps.

**16.** Ratcheted instruments should be stored:
   **a.** open.
   **b.** closed.
   **c.** hanging.
   **d.** standing.
   **e.** upside down.

**17.** Medical asepsis is intended to prevent the spread of microbes from:
   **a.** one patient to another.
   **b.** the autoclave to the patient.
   **c.** the instruments to the physician.
   **d.** the inside to the outside of the body.
   **e.** the physician to the medical assistant.

**18.** A punch biopsy is used to:
   **a.** diagnose glaucoma.
   **b.** dissect delicate tissues.
   **c.** explore bladder depths.
   **d.** remove tissue for microscopic study.
   **e.** guide an instrument during a procedure.

**19.** The best way to test the effectiveness of an autoclave is to use:
   **a.** thermometers.
   **b.** wax pellets.
   **c.** autoclave tape.
   **d.** color indicators.
   **e.** strips with heat-resistant spores.

**20.** Which is a step in operating the autoclave?
   **a.** Stacking items on top of each other
   **b.** Filling the reservoir tank with tap water
   **c.** Filling the reservoir a little past the fill line
   **d.** Removing items from the autoclave the moment they are done
   **e.** Setting the timer after the correct temperature has been reached

# COG MATCHING

_____ Grade: _____

Match each key term with its definition.

**Key Terms**

21. _____ autoclave
22. _____ disinfection
23. _____ ethylene oxide
24. _____ forceps
25. _____ hemostat
26. _____ needle holder
27. _____ obturator
28. _____ ratchet
29. _____ sanitation
30. _____ sanitize
31. _____ scalpel
32. _____ scissors
33. _____ serration
34. _____ sound
35. _____ sterilization

**Definitions**

**a.** surgical instrument used to grasp, hold, compress, pull, or join tissue, equipment, or supplies

**b.** a long instrument used to explore or dilate body cavities

**c.** a gas used to sterilize surgical instruments and other supplies

**d.** appliance used to sterilize medical instruments with steam under pressure

**e.** a surgical instrument with slender jaws that is used to grasp blood vessels

**f.** groove, either straight or crisscross, etched or cut into the blade or tip of an instrument to improve its bite or grasp

**g.** a notched mechanism that clicks into position to maintain tension on the opposing blades or tips of the instrument

**h.** killing or rendering inert most but not all pathogenic microorganisms

**i.** to reduce the number of microorganisms on a surface by use of low-level disinfectant practices

**j.** a sharp instrument composed of two opposing cutting blades, held together by a central pin on which the blades pivot

**k.** a type of forceps that is used to hold and pass suture through tissue

**l.** a small pointed knife with a convex edge for surgical procedures

**Key Terms**

**Definitions**

**m.** a process, act, or technique for destroying microorganisms using heat, water, chemicals, or gases

**n.** the maintenance of a healthful, disease-free environment

**o.** a smooth, rounded, removable inner portion of a hollow tube that allows for easier insertion

## COG MATCHING

Grade: _____

Match each instrument with its description.

**Instruments**

36. _____ forceps
37. _____ scissors
38. _____ scalpels
39. _____ clamps
40. _____ retractors

**Descriptions**

**a.** dissect delicate tissue
**b.** hold sterile drapes in place
**c.** grasp tissue for dissection
**d.** make an incision
**e.** transfer sterile supplies
**f.** cut off a bandage
**g.** excise tissue
**h.** hold open layers of tissue

## COG IDENTIFICATION

Grade: _____

41. Complete this table, which identifies four types of scissors and their use.

| Type | Use |
| --- | --- |
| bandage scissors | **a.** |
| **b.** | dissect superficial and delicate tissues |
| straight scissors | **c.** |
| **d.** | remove sutures |

42. Complete the chart below by identifying one instrument used in each specialty.

| Specialty | Instrument |
| --- | --- |
| Obstetrics, gynecology | **a.** |
| Orthopedics | **b.** |
| Urology | **c.** |
| Proctology | **d.** |
| Otology, rhinology | **e.** |
| Ophthalmology | **f.** |
| Dermatology | **g.** |

**43.** Complete this table, which describes the most effective method of sterilizing various instruments and materials.

| Method of Sterilization | Most Effective for |
|---|---|
| a. | minor surgical instruments<br>surgical storage trays and containers<br>bowls for holding sterile equipment |
| b. | instruments or equipment subject to water damage |
| c. | instruments or equipment subject to heat damage |

## COG SHORT ANSWER

_____ Grade: _____

**44.** Describe the process by which an autoclave sterilizes instruments.

_____

_____

_____

_____

**45.** What is the purpose of sterilization indicators? What factors may alter the results of a sterilization indicator?

_____

_____

_____

_____

**46.** What components must be properly set in order for the autoclave to work effectively?

_____

_____

_____

_____

**47.** List the guidelines that you should follow when handling and storing sharp instruments.

_____

_____

_____

_____

**48.** What is the purpose of autoclave tape?

_____

_____

_____

**49.** Which method of sterilization is more effective: boiling water or the autoclave? Why?

_____

_____

_____

_____

**50.** Compare the qualities of medical asepsis and surgical asepsis.

_____

_____

_____

_____

## OOG TRUE OR FALSE?     Grade: _____

Indicate whether the statements are true or false by placing the letter T (true) or F (false) on the line preceding the statement.

**51.** _____ Equipment must be sanitized before it is sterilized.

**52.** _____ Autoclave indicator tape is 100% effective in indicating whether a package is sterile.

**53.** _____ It is the medical assistant's responsibility to maintain complete and accurate records of sterilized equipment.

**54.** _____ The handle and blade of a reusable steel scalpel may be reused after being properly sterilized.

## OOG AFF CASE STUDIES FOR CRITICAL THINKING     Grade: _____

**1.** You are one of two medical assistants working in a small office that specializes in ophthalmology. There is one examination room. The office sees about 50 patients a week, with an average of 3 patients a week needing minor ophthalmologic procedures. The physician has asked you to order new instruments for the office for the next month. What are two of the instruments that you will order? What factors will you need to consider when placing the order?

_____

_____

_____

_____

2. Your medical office has one autoclave along with two pairs of sterilized suture scissors and adequate numbers of other instruments. In the morning, the physician uses one pair of suture scissors to perform a minor procedure. He tosses the scissors into a sink when he is finished, damaging the instrument. At noon, the autoclave suddenly malfunctions, and you put in a service request to repair it. In the afternoon, a patient comes into the office complaining that her sutures are painful. The physician decides that he must remove them right away. Right before the procedure begins, the physician drops the only sterile pair of suture scissors in the office before he can use them. Describe two possible plans of action you can take to help the patient who is still in pain.

_____

_____

_____

_____

3. The physician has just completed a procedure in which he used a disposable scalpel. How should you dispose of this instrument and why? Would it be appropriate to autoclave this scalpel to save money? Why or why not?

_____

_____

_____

4. Your patient is about to undergo a minor office surgery and is concerned because she once received a facial piercing that led to a massive infection due to improperly sterilized instruments. Now, she is worried about the cleanliness of your office. How would you explain the precautions your office takes to ensure that all instruments and equipment are safe and sterile in a language that the patient can understand?

_____

_____

_____

5. A package arrives at your office and you and your coworker are unable to open it. After looking around the immediate area, your coworker leaves the room and comes back with a pair of sterile operating scissors to open the package. Should you allow your coworker to use the scissors to open the package? What reason would you give your coworker for allowing or not allowing him or her to use the scissors?

_____

_____

_____

_____

**6.** Your office uses formaldehyde to sterilize some instruments. While transporting the instruments soaking in formaldehyde, you accidentally spill the formaldehyde. You are in a hurry and consider leaving the small amount of chemical on the floor until later. Would this be an appropriate action to take? Why or why not? How would you clean up this spill?

_____

_____

_____

_____

## PSY PROCEDURE 6-1 Sanitize Equipment and Instruments

Name: _____ Date: _____ Time: _____ Grade: _____

**EQUIPMENT/SUPPLIES:** Instruments or equipment to be sanitized, gloves, eye protection, impervious gown, soap and water, small hand-held scrub brush

**STANDARDS:** Given the needed equipment and a place to work, the student will perform this skill with _____ % accuracy in a total of _____ minutes. *(Your instructor will tell you what the percentage and time limits will be before you begin.)*

**KEY:** 4 = Satisfactory 0 = Unsatisfactory NA =This step is not counted

| PROCEDURE STEPS | SELF | PARTNER | INSTRUCTOR |
|---|---|---|---|
| **1.** Put on gloves, gown, and eye protection. | ❑ | ❑ | ❑ |
| **2.** For equipment that requires assembly, take removable sections apart. | ❑ | ❑ | ❑ |
| **3.** Check the operation and integrity of the equipment. | ❑ | ❑ | ❑ |
| **4.** Rinse the instrument with cool water. | ❑ | ❑ | ❑ |
| **5.** Force streams of soapy water through any tubular or grooved instruments. | ❑ | ❑ | ❑ |
| **6.** Use a hot, soapy solution to dissolve fats or lubricants left on the surface. | ❑ | ❑ | ❑ |
| **7.** Soak 5 to 10 minutes. <br> **a.** Use friction (brush or gauze) to wipe down the instruments. <br> **b.** Check jaws or scissors/forceps to ensure that all debris has been removed. | ❑ | ❑ | ❑ |
| **8.** Rinse well. | ❑ | ❑ | ❑ |
| **9.** Dry well before autoclaving if sterilizing or soaking in disinfecting solution. | ❑ | ❑ | ❑ |
| **10.** Items (brushes, gauze, solution) used in sanitation process must be disinfected or discarded. | ❑ | ❑ | ❑ |

**CALCULATION**

Total Possible Points: _____

Total Points Earned: _____ Multiplied by 100 = _____ Divided by Total Possible Points = _____ %

**PASS FAIL COMMENTS:**
❑ ❑

Student's signature _____ Date _____

Partner's signature _____ Date _____

Instructor's signature _____ Date _____

**PSY** PROCEDURE 6-2 **Properly Wrap Instruments for Autoclaving**

Name: _____ Date: _____ Time: _____ Grade: _____

**EQUIPMENT/SUPPLIES:** Sanitized and wrapped instruments or equipment, distilled water, autoclave operating manual

**STANDARDS:** Given the needed equipment and a place to work, the student will perform this skill with _____ % accuracy in a total of _____ minutes. *(Your instructor will tell you what the percentage and time limits will be before you begin.)*

**KEY:** 4 = Satisfactory  0 = Unsatisfactory  NA =This step is not counted

| PROCEDURE STEPS | SELF | PARTNER | INSTRUCTOR |
|---|---|---|---|
| **1.** Assemble the equipment and supplies. | ❑ | ❑ | ❑ |
| **2.** Check the instruments being wrapped for working order. Explain what to do if an instrument is found not to be in good working order. | ❑ | ❑ | ❑ |
| **3.** Obtain correct material for wrapping instruments to be autoclaved. | ❑ | ❑ | ❑ |
| **4.** Tear off 1 to 2 pieces of autoclave tape. On one piece, label the contents of the pack, the date, and your initials. | ❑ | ❑ | ❑ |
| **5.** Lay the wrap diagonally on a flat, clean, dry surface. **a.** Place the instrument in the center, with ratchets or handles in open position. **b.** Include a sterilization indicator. | ❑ | ❑ | ❑ |
| **6.** Fold the first flap up at the bottom of the diagonal wrap. Fold back the corner to make a tab. | ❑ | ❑ | ❑ |
| **7.** Fold left corner of the wrap toward the center. Fold back the corner to make a tab. | ❑ | ❑ | ❑ |
| **8.** Fold right corner of the wrap toward the center. Fold back the corner to make a tab. | ❑ | ❑ | ❑ |
| **9.** Fold the top corner down, making the tab tuck under the material. | ❑ | ❑ | ❑ |
| **10.** Secure the package with labeled autoclave tape. | ❑ | ❑ | ❑ |

**CALCULATION**

Total Possible Points: _____

Total Points Earned: _____ Multiplied by 100 = _____ Divided by Total Possible Points = _____ %

**PASS  FAIL  COMMENTS:**
  ❑      ❑

Student's signature _____ Date _____

Partner's signature _____ Date _____

Instructor's signature _____ Date _____

## PSY PROCEDURE 6-3 Perform Sterilization Technique and Operate an Autoclave

Name: _____ Date: _____ Time: _____ Grade: _____

**EQUIPMENT/SUPPLIES:** Sanitized and wrapped instruments or equipment, distilled water, autoclave, autoclave operating manual

**STANDARDS:** Given the needed equipment and a place to work, the student will perform this skill with _____ % accuracy in a total of _____ minutes. *(Your instructor will tell you what the percentage and time limits will be before you begin.)*

**KEY:** 4 = Satisfactory  0 = Unsatisfactory  NA = This step is not counted

| PROCEDURE STEPS | SELF | PARTNER | INSTRUCTOR |
|---|---|---|---|
| **1.** Assemble the equipment, including the wrapped articles with a sterilization indicator in each package according to office policy. | ❑ | ❑ | ❑ |
| **2.** Check the water level of the autoclave reservoir and add more if needed. | ❑ | ❑ | ❑ |
| **3.** Add water to the internal chamber of the autoclave to the fill line. | ❑ | ❑ | ❑ |
| **4.** Properly load the autoclave. | ❑ | ❑ | ❑ |
| **5.** Read the instructions, close the door, and secure or lock it. Turn the machine on. | ❑ | ❑ | ❑ |
| **6.** Set the timer at the appropriate time and for the proper length of time. | ❑ | ❑ | ❑ |
| **7.** When the timer indicates that the cycle is over, vent the chamber. | ❑ | ❑ | ❑ |
| **8.** When the load has cooled, remove the items. Check the separately wrapped sterilization indicator, if used, for proper sterilization. | ❑ | ❑ | ❑ |
| **9.** Store the items in a clean, dry, dust-free area. | ❑ | ❑ | ❑ |
| **10.** Explain how to clean the autoclave. | ❑ | ❑ | ❑ |

**CALCULATION**

Total Possible Points: _____

Total Points Earned: _____ Multiplied by 100 = _____ Divided by Total Possible Points = _____ %

**PASS   FAIL   COMMENTS:**
❑       ❑

Student's signature _____ Date _____

Partner's signature _____ Date _____

Instructor's signature _____ Date _____

# CHAPTER

# 7 Assisting with Minor Office Surgery

## Learning Outcomes

### COG Cognitive Domain

1. Spell and define key terms
2. List your responsibilities before, during, and after minor office surgery
3. Identify the guidelines for preparing and maintaining sterility of the field and surgical equipment during a minor office procedure
4. State your responsibility in relation to informed consent and patient preparation
5. Explain the purpose of local anesthetics and list three commonly used in the medical office
6. Describe the types of needles and sutures and the uses of each
7. Describe the various methods of skin closure used in the medical office
8. Explain your responsibility during surgical specimen collection
9. List the types of laser surgery and electrosurgery used in the medical office and explain the precautions for each
10. Describe the guidelines for applying a sterile dressing

### PSY Psychomotor Domain

1. Open sterile surgical packs (Procedure 7-1)
2. Use sterile transfer forceps (Procedure 7-2)
3. Add sterile solution to a sterile field (Procedure 7-3)
4. Perform skin preparation and hair removal (Procedure 7-4)
5. Apply sterile gloves (Procedure 7-5)
6. Apply a sterile dressing (Procedure 7-6)
7. Change an existing sterile dressing (Procedure 7-7)
8. Assist with excisional surgery (Procedure 7-8)
9. Assist with incision and drainage (Procedure 7-9)
10. Remove sutures (Procedure 7-10)
11. Remove staples (Procedure 7-11)

### AFF Affective Domain

1. Incorporate critical thinking skills when performing patient care
2. Demonstrate empathy, active listening, nonverbal communication
3. Explain to a patient the rationale for performance of a procedure
4. Show awareness of a patient's concerns related to the procedure being performed
5. Protect the integrity of the medical record

### ABHES Competencies

1. Prepare patients for examinations and treatments
2. Assist physician with minor office surgical procedures
3. Dispose of biohazardous materials
4. Use standard precautions
5. Document accurately

87

Name: _____   Date: _____   Grade: _____

## OOG MULTIPLE CHOICE

Circle the letter preceding the correct answer.

1. Which of the following statements is true about working in a sterile field?
   a. Sterile packages should be kept damp.
   b. Your back must be kept to the sterile field at all times.
   c. A 3-inch border around the field is considered contaminated.
   d. All sterile items should be held above waist level.
   e. Cover your mouth when coughing near the sterile field.

2. Why is a fenestrated drape helpful during surgery?
   a. It is made of lightweight fabric.
   b. It has an opening to expose the operative site.
   c. It can be used as a blanket to keep the patient warm.
   d. It does not need to be sterilized before surgery.
   e. It allows for easy cleanup after the surgery.

3. Epinephrine is added to local anesthetics during surgery to:
   a. ensure sterilization.
   b. protect the tips of the fingers.
   c. lengthen the anesthetic's effectiveness.
   d. prevent vasoconstriction.
   e. create rapid absorption.

4. Which needles are used most frequently in the medical office?
   a. Curved swaged needles
   b. Traumatic needles
   c. Straight needles
   d. Domestic needles
   e. Keith needles

5. A preservative is added to specimen containers to be sent to a pathologist to:
   a. help the pathologist see the specimen.
   b. delay decomposition.
   c. identify the patient.
   d. make the specimen grow.
   e. prevent contamination.

6. Which type of electrosurgery destroys tissue with controlled electric sparks?
   a. Electrocautery
   b. Electrodesiccation
   c. Electrosection
   d. Fulguration
   e. Electrophysiology

7. Why is it important to know if a patient has a pacemaker before performing electrosurgery?
   a. Metal implants can become very hot and malfunction during the procedure.
   b. The electrical charge can cause the electrosurgical device to malfunction.
   c. The patient needs to sign a separate consent form if he has any heart problems.
   d. The patient can receive an electrical shock from the equipment.
   e. The implants may counteract the electrosurgery results.

*Scenario for questions 8 and 9:* A female patient returns to the office to have sutures removed from her forearm. When you remove the dressing, you notice that there is a small amount of clear drainage.

8. The patient's drainage is:
   a. purulent.
   b. sanguineous.
   c. serous.
   d. copious.
   e. serosanguineous.

9. Before you remove the patient's sutures, you should:
   a. apply a local anesthetic to numb the area.
   b. offer the patient pain medication to reduce discomfort.
   c. place an ice pack on the patient's forearm.
   d. advise the patient that she should feel pulling sensation but not pain.
   e. gently tug on the ends of the suture to make sure they are secure.

10. Which of the following is characteristic of healing by primary intention?
    a. Clean incision
    b. Gaping, irregular wound
    c. Increased granulation
    d. Wide scar
    e. Indirect edge joining

11. What happens during phase II of wound healing?
    a. Fibroblasts build scar tissue to guard the area.
    b. The scab dries and pulls the edges of the wound together.
    c. Circulation increases and brings white blood cells to the area.
    d. Serum and red blood cells form a fibrin to plug the wound.
    e. An antiseptic sterilizes the area from possible contamination.

12. How must the physician care for an abscess in order for it to heal properly?
    a. Drain the infected material from the site.
    b. Suture the site closed.
    c. Cover the site with a sterile dressing.
    d. Perform cryosurgery to remove the site.
    e. Perform a skin graft to cover the site.

13. Which of the following items should be added to the label on a specimen container?
    a. The contents of the container
    b. The office number
    c. The patient's age
    d. The patient's gender
    e. The date

14. Which of the following is true about laser surgery?
    a. The Argon laser is the only laser used for coagulation.
    b. Colored filters allow the physician to see the path of the laser.
    c. Most lasers are used simply as markers for surgery.
    d. Laser incisions generally bleed more than regular incisions.
    e. Everyone in the room must wear goggles to protect his or her eyes.

15. What is the best way to prepare a patient for surgery?
    a. Remind the patient of procedures by calling a few days before the surgery.
    b. Tell the patient all the instructions on the visit before the surgery.
    c. Send the patient home with written instructions on what to do.
    d. Instruct the patient to call the day of the procedure for instructions.
    e. Have the patient tell a second person about what she needs to do.

16. Which of the following supplies must be added at the time of setup for a surgery?
    a. Liquids in open containers
    b. Sterile transfer forceps
    c. Peel-back envelopes
    d. Sterile gloves
    e. Fenestrated drape

17. Absorbable sutures are most frequently used:
    a. in medical offices for wound sutures.
    b. in hospitals for deep-tissue surgery.
    c. in hospitals for surface-tissue surgery.
    d. when patients are young and heal easily.
    e. whenever a wound needs to be sutured.

18. Which of the following might contaminate a sterile dressing?
    a. A patient accidentally bumps into another person.
    b. The wound still has sutures underneath.
    c. The weather outside has been rainy and damp.
    d. The patient adjusted the dressing at home.
    e. The patient has had a cold for the past week.

19. A child came in with a slight cut on his leg, but there is little tension on the skin, and the cut is clean. The physician believes the wound will heal on its own, with time, and wants to approximate the edges of the wound so that it will heal with minimum scarring. Which of the following would be best used to close the child's wound?
    a. Adhesive skin closures
    b. Fine absorptive sutures
    c. Traumatic sutures
    d. Staples
    e. Nothing

20. The last step in any surgical procedure is to:
    a. assist the patient to leave.
    b. instruct the patient on postoperative procedures.
    c. remove all biohazardous materials.
    d. wash your hands.
    e. record the procedure.

## COG MATCHING

Grade: _____

Place the letter preceding the definition on the line next to the term.

**Key Terms**

21. _____ approximate
22. _____ atraumatic
23. _____ bandage
24. _____ cautery
25. _____ coagulate
26. _____ cryosurgery
27. _____ dehiscence
28. _____ dressing
29. _____ electrode
30. _____ fulgurate
31. _____ keratosis
32. _____ lentigines
33. _____ preservative
34. _____ purulent
35. _____ swaged needle
36. _____ traumatic

**Definitions**

a. separation or opening of the edges of a wound
b. a medium for conducting or detecting electrical current
c. tissue surfaces that are as close together as possible
d. a covering applied directly to a wound to apply pressure, support, absorb secretions, protect from trauma, slow or stop bleeding, or hide disfigurement
e. a means or device that destroys tissue using an electric current, freezing, or burning
f. causing or relating to tissue damage
g. a swaged type of needle that does not require threading
h. to destroy tissue by electrodesiccation
i. a soft material applied to a body part to immobilize the body part or control bleeding
j. to change from a liquid to a solid or semisolid mass
k. brown skin macules occurring after exposure to the sun; freckles
l. drainage from a wound that is white, green, or yellow, signaling an infection
m. a metal needle fused to suture material
n. a skin condition characterized by overgrowth and thickening
o. a substance that delays decomposition
p. surgery in which abnormal tissue is removed by freezing

## COG MATCHING

Grade: _____

Place the letter preceding the description on the line next to the procedure.

**Procedures**

37. _____ electrocautery
38. _____ electrodesiccation
39. _____ electrosection
40. _____ fulguration

**Descriptions**

a. destroys tissue with controlled electric sparks
b. causes quick coagulation of small blood vessels with the heat created by the electric current
c. is used for incision or excision of tissue
d. dries and separates tissue with an electric current

## COG IDENTIFICATION

Grade: _____

41. As a medical assistant, you may be called on to assist a physician with minor office surgery. Review the list of tasks below and determine which tasks you are responsible for as a medical assistant. Place a check in the "Yes" column for those duties you will assist with as a medical assistant, and place a check in the "No" column for those tasks that you would not be able to perform.

| Task | Yes | No |
| --- | --- | --- |
| **a.** Remind the patient of the physician's presurgery instructions, such as fasting. | | |
| **b.** Prepare the treatment room, including the supplies and equipment. | | |
| **c.** Obtain the informed consent document from the patient. | | |
| **d.** Inject the patient with local anesthesia if necessary. | | |
| **e.** Choose the size of the suture to be used to close the wound. | | |
| **f.** Apply a dressing or bandage to the wound. | | |
| **g.** Instruct the patient about postoperative wound care. | | |
| **h.** Prescribe pain medication for the patient to take at home. | | |
| **i.** Prepare lab paperwork for any specimens that must be sent out to the lab. | | |
| **j.** Patient materials | | |
| **k.** Clean and sterilize the room for the next patient. | | |

42. A patient comes into the physician's office with a large wound on his leg. The physician asks you to assist with minor surgery to care for the wound. Because you must help maintain a sterile field before and during the procedure, review the list of actions below and indicate whether sterility (S) was maintained or if there has been any possible contamination (C).

**a.** _____ The sterile package was moist before the surgery started.

**b.** _____ The physician spills a few drops of sterile water onto the sterile field.

**c.** _____ You hold the sterile items for the physician above waist level.

**d.** _____ The physician rests the sterile items in the middle of the sterile field.

**e.** _____ You ask the physician a question over the sterile field.

**f.** _____ The physician leaves the room and places a drape over the field.

**g.** _____ The physician passes soiled gauze over the sterile field and asks you to dispose of them properly.

43. As a medical assistant, you may be responsible for preparing and maintaining sterile packs. Determine if the packs listed below are appropriately sterilized (S) or if they need to be repackaged (R) and sterilized again.

**a.** _____ No moisture is present on the pack.

**b.** _____ The package was sterilized onsite 15 days ago.

**c.** _____ The wrapper is ripped down one side.

**d.** _____ The sterilization indicator has changed color.

**e.** _____ An item from the package fell out onto the floor when you picked it up.

**44.** Which of the following information must be stated on the informed consent document? Circle the letter preceding all items that apply.

**a.** The name of the procedure

**b.** The tools used in the procedure

**c.** The purpose of the procedure

**d.** The expected results

**e.** The patient's Social Security number

**f.** Possible side effects

**g.** The length of the procedure

**h.** Potential risks and complications

**i.** The date of the follow-up appointment

**45.** Listed below are the steps that a medical assistant should take to clean the examination room and prepare it for the next patient after a minor office surgical procedure. However, the steps below are not listed in the correct order. Review the steps and then place a number on the line next to each step to show the correct order in which they should occur with number 1 being the first step taken.

**a.** _____ Put on gloves.

**b.** _____ Remove papers and sheets from the table and discard properly.

**c.** _____ Replace the table sheet paper for the next patient.

**d.** _____ Wipe down the examination table, surgical stand, sink, counter, and other surfaces used during the procedure with a disinfectant and allow them to dry.

## COG SHORT ANSWER

_____ Grade: _____

**46.** List the three ways in which you may add the contents of peel-back packages to a sterile field.

**a.** _____

**b.** _____

**c.** _____

**47.** Name four anesthetics that are commonly used in a medical office.

**a.** _____

**b.** _____

**c.** _____

**48.** Name three ways in which needles can be classified.

**a.** _____

**b.** _____

**c.** _____

## 🔲 TRUE OR FALSE?

Grade: _____

Indicate whether the statements are true or false by placing the letter T (true) or F (false) on the line preceding the statement.

**49.** _____ Anesthesia with epinephrine is approved for use on the tips of the fingers, toes, nose, and penis.

**50.** _____ Atraumatic needles need to be threaded by the physician before they can be used.

**51.** _____ Nonabsorbable sutures must be removed after healing.

**52.** _____ All metal must be removed from a patient before electrosurgery.

## 🔲 🔲 CASE STUDIES FOR CRITICAL THINKING

Grade: _____

**1.** The physician asks you to position a patient for surgery in the lithotomy position. You know that the physician has to meet with another patient before he will come into the room to perform the surgery. What can you do to keep the patient comfortable before the physician is ready to begin? List three things you can do, and explain why they are important.

_____

_____

_____

_____

**2.** There is a delay in the office, and all of the appointments are running 30 minutes late. The patients are becoming upset, and the office manager said that you should work quickly to try to get back on schedule. You assist the physician with the removal of a small wart from a patient's neck. After the surgery is completed, you need to meet with a new patient to go over the new patient interview and paperwork. But it's also your job to label the specimen and complete the paperwork to send it to the lab. It's almost lunchtime, and you know the lab won't get to it right away. Which task should you complete first—meeting with the patient or preparing the specimen for the lab? Explain your answer.

_____

_____

_____

_____

**3.** Dante is a clinical medical assistant who is assisting a physician with minor office surgery. Dr. Yan asks him to prepare the local anesthesia. Dante chooses the anesthetic and draws the medication into a syringe. Next, he places the filled syringe on the sterile tray. Were these actions appropriate? Why or why not? Should Dr. Yan put on sterile gloves before or after she administers the anesthesia? Explain your answer.

_____

_____

_____

_____

**4.** A homeless patient comes into the urgent care office with a cut on his chin. Which size suture would the physician likely want for this procedure in order to reduce the size of the scar—a size 3 suture or a size 23-0 suture? The patient seems confused and smells of alcohol. How would you handle this situation before, during, and after the procedure?

_____

_____

_____

_____

**5.** Ghani is a clinical medical assistant. On Monday, he assisted the physician while she sutured a deep wound on a 7-year-old boy's leg. A few hours after the surgery, the mother brings the boy back to the office because she is concerned the site is infected. When Ghani inspects the sterile dressing, he notes that there is a moderate amount of pink drainage. What does this drainage indicate about the healing process? Is the mother's concern legitimate? How would you respond to her?

_____

_____

_____

_____

**6.** Your patient is a 79-year-old female who has had a large mole excised from her forearm. The cyst is being sent out for pathology to rule out skin cancer. You give her extra bandages so she can change the dressing herself and explain that the physician wants to see her back in the office in 1 week. She is very hard of hearing and lives alone. What instructions would you need to explain to the patient about caring for the wound? How would you handle this situation?

_____

_____

_____

_____

**7.** Your patient is a 13-year-old boy who received staples for a wound he got in a biking accident. While you are removing the staples, he asks why staples are being used, and not stitches. Explain the difference between sutures and staples, and when it is more appropriate to use each.

_____

_____

_____

_____

8. A 15-year-old patient has a mole on her face that needs to be removed. She feels anxious about having to wear a large dressing to cover the wound on her face while it heals. In addition, she is nervous about the possibilities of scarring, and she is worried that the mole is cancerous. How would you handle this situation? What would you say to her to ease her mind before and after the procedure?

_____

_____

_____

_____

9. You are working with another medical assistant to prepare a sterile field for surgery. You are almost finished setting up the sterile field when your coworker sneezes over the sterile field. She says that it's only allergies and that she's not contagious, so the field isn't contaminated. She assures you that you don't need to start your work over again. How would you handle this situation? What would you say to your coworker? What should you do next?

_____

_____

_____

_____

## PSY PROCEDURE 7-1   **Opening Sterile Surgical Packs**

Name: _____ Date: _____ Time: _____ Grade: _____

**EQUIPMENT/SUPPLIES:** Surgical pack, surgical or Mayo stand

**STANDARDS:** Given the needed equipment and a place to work, the student will perform this skill with _____ % accuracy in a total of _____ minutes. *(Your instructor will tell you what the percentage and time limits will be before you begin.)*

**KEY:**          4 = Satisfactory              0 = Unsatisfactory            NA =This step is not counted

| PROCEDURE STEPS | SELF | PARTNER | INSTRUCTOR |
|---|---|---|---|
| **1.** Wash your hands. | ❏ | ❏ | ❏ |
| **2.** Verify the procedure to be performed and remove the appropriate tray or item from the storage area. Check the label for contents and expiration date. Check the package for tears and moisture. | ❏ | ❏ | ❏ |
| **3.** Place the package, with the label facing up, on a clean, dry, flat surface such as a Mayo or surgical stand. | ❏ | ❏ | ❏ |
| **4.** Without tearing the wrapper, carefully remove the sealing tape. With commercial packages, carefully remove the outer protective wrapper. | ❏ | ❏ | ❏ |
| **5.** Loosen the first flap of the folded wrapper by pulling it up, out, and away; let it fall over the far side of the table or stand. | ❏ | ❏ | ❏ |
| **6.** Open the side flaps in a similar manner, using your left hand for the left flap and your right hand for the right flap. Touch only the unsterile outer surface; do not touch the sterile inner surface. | ❏ | ❏ | ❏ |
| **7.** Pull the remaining flap down and toward you by grasping the outside surface only. The outer surface of the wrapper is now against the surgical stand; the sterile inside of the wrapper forms the sterile field. | ❏ | ❏ | ❏ |
| **8.** Open the side flaps in a similar manner. Do not touch the sterile inner surface. | ❏ | ❏ | ❏ |
| **9.** Pull the remaining flap down and toward you. | ❏ | ❏ | ❏ |
| **10.** Repeat steps 4 through 6 for packages with a second or inside wrapper. | ❏ | ❏ | ❏ |
| **11.** If you must leave the area after opening the field, cover the tray with a sterile drape. | ❏ | ❏ | ❏ |

**PSY** PROCEDURE 7-1 **Opening Sterile Surgical Packs** (continued)

**CALCULATION**

Total Possible Points: _____

Total Points Earned: _____ Multiplied by 100 = _____ Divided by Total Possible Points = _____ %

**PASS   FAIL   COMMENTS:**
❏       ❏

Student's signature _____ Date _____

Partner's signature _____ Date _____

Instructor's signature _____ Date _____

**PSY** PROCEDURE 7-2 **Using Sterile Transfer Forceps**

Name: _____ Date: _____ Time: _____ Grade: _____

**EQUIPMENT/SUPPLIES:** Sterile transfer forceps in a container with sterilization solution, sterile field, sterile items to be transferred

**STANDARDS:** Given the needed equipment and a place to work, the student will perform this skill with _____ % accuracy in a total of _____ minutes. *(Your instructor will tell you what the percentage and time limits will be before you begin.)*

**KEY:** 4 = Satisfactory 0 = Unsatisfactory NA =This step is not counted

| PROCEDURE STEPS | SELF | PARTNER | INSTRUCTOR |
|---|---|---|---|
| **1.** Slowly lift the forceps straight up and out of the container without touching the inside above the level of the solution or outside of the container. | ❏ | ❏ | ❏ |
| **2.** Hold the forceps with the tips down at all times. | ❏ | ❏ | ❏ |
| **3.** Keep the forceps above waist level. | ❏ | ❏ | ❏ |
| **4.** With the forceps, pick up the articles to be transferred and drop them onto the sterile field, but do not let the forceps come into contact with the sterile field. | ❏ | ❏ | ❏ |
| **5.** Carefully place the forceps back into the sterilization solution. | ❏ | ❏ | ❏ |

**CALCULATION**

Total Possible Points: _____

Total Points Earned: _____ Multiplied by 100 = _____ Divided by Total Possible Points = _____ %

**PASS   FAIL   COMMENTS:**
❏       ❏

Student's signature _____ Date _____

Partner's signature _____ Date _____

Instructor's signature _____ Date _____

## FSY PROCEDURE 7-3 Adding Sterile Solution to a Sterile Field

Name: _____ Date: _____ Time: _____ Grade: _____

**EQUIPMENT/SUPPLIES:** Sterile setup, container of sterile solution, sterile bowl or cup

**STANDARDS:** Given the needed equipment and a place to work, the student will perform this skill with _____ % accuracy in a total of _____ minutes. *(Your instructor will tell you what the percentage and time limits will be before you begin.)*

**KEY:** 4 = Satisfactory 0 = Unsatisfactory NA =This step is not counted

| PROCEDURE STEPS | SELF | PARTNER | INSTRUCTOR |
|---|---|---|---|
| **1.** Identify the correct solution by carefully reading the label. | ❏ | ❏ | ❏ |
| **2.** Check the expiration date on the label. | ❏ | ❏ | ❏ |
| **3.** If adding medications into the solution, show medication label to the physician. | ❏ | ❏ | ❏ |
| **4.** Remove the cap or stopper; avoid contamination of the inside of the cap. | ❏ | ❏ | ❏ |
| **5.** If it is necessary to put the cap down, place on side table with opened end facing up. | ❏ | ❏ | ❏ |
| **6.** Retain bottle to track amount added to field. | ❏ | ❏ | ❏ |
| **7.** Grasp container with label against the palm of your hand. | ❏ | ❏ | ❏ |
| **8.** Pour a small amount of the solution into a separate container or waste receptacle. | ❏ | ❏ | ❏ |
| **9.** Slowly pour the desired amount of solution into the sterile container. | ❏ | ❏ | ❏ |
| **10.** Recheck the label for the contents and expiration date and replace the cap. | ❏ | ❏ | ❏ |
| **11.** Return the solution to its proper storage area or discard the container after rechecking the label again. | ❏ | ❏ | ❏ |

**CALCULATION**

Total Possible Points: _____

Total Points Earned: _____ Multiplied by 100 = _____ Divided by Total Possible Points = _____ %

**PASS  FAIL  COMMENTS:**
❏      ❏

Student's signature _____ Date _____

Partner's signature _____ Date _____

Instructor's signature _____ Date _____

**PSY** PROCEDURE 7-4 **Performing Skin Preparation and Hair Removal**

Name: _____ Date: _____ Time: _____ Grade: _____

**EQUIPMENT/SUPPLIES:** Nonsterile gloves; shave cream, lotion, or soap; new disposable razor; gauze or cotton balls; warm water; antiseptic; sponge forceps

**STANDARDS:** Given the needed equipment and a place to work, the student will perform this skill with _____ % accuracy in a total of _____ minutes. *(Your instructor will tell you what the percentage and time limits will be before you begin.)*

**KEY:** 4 = Satisfactory 0 = Unsatisfactory NA = This step is not counted

| PROCEDURE STEPS | SELF | PARTNER | INSTRUCTOR |
| --- | --- | --- | --- |
| **1.** Wash your hands. | ❑ | ❑ | ❑ |
| **2.** Assemble the equipment. | ❑ | ❑ | ❑ |
| **3.** Greet and identify the patient; explain the procedure and answer any questions. | ❑ | ❑ | ❑ |
| **4.** Put on gloves. | ❑ | ❑ | ❑ |
| **5.** Prepare the patient's skin. | ❑ | ❑ | ❑ |
| **6.** If the patient's skin is to be shaved, apply shaving cream or soapy lather.<br>**a.** Pull the skin taut and shave in the direction of hair growth.<br>**b.** Rinse and pat the shaved area thoroughly dry using a gauze square. | ❑ | ❑ | ❑ |
| **7.** If the patient's skin is not to be shaved, wash with soap and water; rinse well and pat the area thoroughly dry using a gauze square. | ❑ | ❑ | ❑ |
| **8.** Apply antiseptic solution to the operative area using sterile gauze sponges.<br>**a.** Wipe skin in circular motions starting at the operative site and working outward.<br>**b.** Discard each sponge after a complete sweep has been made.<br>**c.** If circles are not appropriate, the sponge may be wiped straight outward from the operative site and discarded.<br>**d.** Repeat the procedure until the entire area has been thoroughly cleaned. | ❑ | ❑ | ❑ |
| **9.** Instruct the patient not to touch or cover the prepared area. | ❑ | ❑ | ❑ |
| **10.** Explain how to respond to a patient who is developmentally challenged. | ❑ | ❑ | ❑ |

**PSY** PROCEDURE 7-4 **Performing Skin Preparation and Hair Removal** (continued)

_____

_____

_____

_____

_____

| | | | |
|---|---|---|---|
| **11.** Remove your gloves and wash your hands. | ❏ | ❏ | ❏ |
| **12.** Inform the physician that the patient is ready for the surgical procedure. | ❏ | ❏ | ❏ |
| **13.** Drape the prepared area with a sterile drape if the physician will be delayed more than 10 or 15 minutes. | ❏ | ❏ | ❏ |

**CALCULATION**

Total Possible Points: _____

Total Points Earned: _____ Multiplied by 100 = _____ Divided by Total Possible Points = _____ %

**PASS  FAIL  COMMENTS:**
❏      ❏

Student's signature _____ Date _____

Partner's signature _____ Date _____

Instructor's signature _____ Date _____

**FSY**  PROCEDURE 7-5   **Applying Sterile Gloves**

Name: _____  Date: _____  Time: _____  Grade: _____

**EQUIPMENT/SUPPLIES:** One package of sterile gloves in the appropriate size

**STANDARDS:** Given the needed equipment and a place to work, the student will perform this skill with _____ % accuracy in a total of _____ minutes. *(Your instructor will tell you what the percentage and time limits will be before you begin.)*

**KEY:**          4 = Satisfactory                0 = Unsatisfactory               NA =This step is not counted

| PROCEDURE STEPS | SELF | PARTNER | INSTRUCTOR |
|---|---|---|---|
| **1.** Remove rings and other jewelry. | ❑ | ❑ | ❑ |
| **2.** Wash your hands. | ❑ | ❑ | ❑ |
| **3.** Place prepackaged gloves on a clean, dry, flat surface with the cuffed end toward you.<br>**a.** Pull the outer wrapping apart to expose the sterile inner wrap.<br>**b.** With the cuffs toward you, fold back the inner wrap to expose the gloves. | ❑ | ❑ | ❑ |
| **4.** Grasping the edges of the outer paper, open the package out to its fullest. | ❑ | ❑ | ❑ |
| **5.** Use your nondominant hand to pick up the dominant hand glove.<br>**a.** Grasp the folded edge of the cuff and lift it up and away from the paper.<br>**b.** Curl your fingers and thumb together and insert them into the glove.<br>**c.** Straighten your fingers and pull the glove on with your nondominant hand still grasping the cuff. | ❑ | ❑ | ❑ |
| **6.** Unfold the cuff by pinching the inside surface and pull it toward your wrist. | ❑ | ❑ | ❑ |
| **7.** Place the fingers of your gloved hand under the cuff of the remaining glove.<br>**a.** Lift the glove up and away from the wrapper.<br>**b.** Slide your ungloved hand carefully into the glove with your fingers and thumb curled together.<br>**c.** Straighten your fingers and pull the glove up and over your wrist by carefully unfolding the cuff. | ❑ | ❑ | ❑ |
| **8.** Settle the gloves comfortably onto your fingers by lacing your fingers together. | ❑ | ❑ | ❑ |
| **9.** Remove contaminated sterile gloves and discard them appropriately. Wash your hands. | ❑ | ❑ | ❑ |

**FSY** P R O C E D U R E 7 - 5 **Applying Sterile Gloves** (continued)

**CALCULATION**

Total Possible Points: _____

Total Points Earned: _____ Multiplied by 100 = _____ Divided by Total Possible Points = _____ %

**PASS    FAIL    COMMENTS:**
  ❑         ❑

Student's signature _____ Date _____

Partner's signature _____ Date _____

Instructor's signature _____ Date _____

## PSY PROCEDURE 7-6 Applying a Sterile Dressing

Name: _____ Date: _____ Time: _____ Grade: _____

**EQUIPMENT/SUPPLIES:** Sterile gloves, sterile gauze dressings, scissors, bandage tape, any medication to be applied to the dressing if ordered by the physician

**STANDARDS:** Given the needed equipment and a place to work, the student will perform this skill with _____ % accuracy in a total of _____ minutes. *(Your instructor will tell you what the percentage and time limits will be before you begin.)*

**KEY:** 4 = Satisfactory 0 = Unsatisfactory NA =This step is not counted

| PROCEDURE STEPS | SELF | PARTNER | INSTRUCTOR |
|---|---|---|---|
| **1.** Wash your hands. | ❏ | ❏ | ❏ |
| **2.** Assemble the equipment and supplies. | ❏ | ❏ | ❏ |
| **3.** Greet and identify the patient. | ❏ | ❏ | ❏ |
| **4.** Ask about any tape allergies before deciding on what type of tape to use. | ❏ | ❏ | ❏ |
| **5.** Cut or tear lengths of tape to secure the dressing. | ❏ | ❏ | ❏ |
| **6.** Explain the procedure and instruct the patient to remain still; avoid coughing, sneezing, or talking until the procedure is complete. | ❏ | ❏ | ❏ |
| **7.** Open the dressing pack to create a sterile field, maintaining sterile asepsis. **a.** If sterile gloves are to be used, open and place near dressing pack. **b.** If using a sterile transfer forceps, place it near the other supplies. | ❏ | ❏ | ❏ |
| **8.** Apply topical medication to the sterile dressing that will cover the wound. | ❏ | ❏ | ❏ |
| **9.** Apply the number of dressings necessary to properly cover and protect the wound. | ❏ | ❏ | ❏ |
| **10.** Apply sufficient cut lengths of tape over the dressing to secure. | ❏ | ❏ | ❏ |
| **11.** Remove contaminated gloves and discard in the proper receptacle. Wash your hands. | ❏ | ❏ | ❏ |
| **12.** Provide patient education and supplies as appropriate. | ❏ | ❏ | ❏ |
| **13.** AFF Explain how to respond to a patient who is visually impaired. | ❏ | ❏ | ❏ |

**PSY** PROCEDURE 7-6 **Applying a Sterile Dressing** (continued)

| | | | |
|---|---|---|---|
| | | | |
| **14.** Clean and sanitize the room and equipment. | ❏ | ❏ | ❏ |
| **15.** Record the procedure. | ❏ | ❏ | ❏ |

**CALCULATION**

Total Possible Points: _____

Total Points Earned: _____ Multiplied by 100 = _____ Divided by Total Possible Points = _____ %

**PASS    FAIL    COMMENTS:**
  ❏     ❏

Student's signature _____ Date _____

Partner's signature _____ Date _____

Instructor's signature _____ Date _____

**FSY** P R O C E D U R E  7 - 7  **Changing an Existing Sterile Dressing**

Name: _____ Date: _____ Time: _____ Grade: _____

**EQUIPMENT/SUPPLIES:** Sterile gloves, nonsterile gloves, sterile dressing, prepackaged skin antiseptic swabs (or sterile antiseptic solution poured into a sterile basin and sterile cotton balls or gauze), tape, approved biohazard containers

**STANDARDS:** Given the needed equipment and a place to work, the student will perform this skill with _____ % accuracy in a total of _____ minutes. *(Your instructor will tell you what the percentage and time limits will be before you begin.)*

**KEY:** 4 = Satisfactory  0 = Unsatisfactory  NA = This step is not counted

| PROCEDURE STEPS | SELF | PARTNER | INSTRUCTOR |
|---|---|---|---|
| **1.** Wash your hands. | ❏ | ❏ | ❏ |
| **2.** Assemble the equipment and supplies. | ❏ | ❏ | ❏ |
| **3.** Greet and identify the patient; explain the procedure and answer any questions. | ❏ | ❏ | ❏ |
| **4.** Prepare a sterile field including opening sterile dressings. | ❏ | ❏ | ❏ |
| **5.** Open a sterile basin and use the inside of the wrapper as the sterile field.<br>**a.** Flip the sterile gauze or cotton balls into the basin.<br>**b.** Pour antiseptic solution appropriately into the basin.<br>**c.** If using prepackaged antiseptic swabs, carefully open an adequate number.<br>**d.** Set swabs aside without contaminating them. | ❏ | ❏ | ❏ |
| **6.** Instruct the patient not to talk, cough, sneeze, laugh, or move during the procedure. | ❏ | ❏ | ❏ |
| **7.** **AFF** Explain how to respond to a patient who has dementia. | ❏ | ❏ | ❏ |
| _____<br>_____<br>_____<br>_____ | | | |
| **8.** Wear clean gloves and carefully remove tape from the wound dressing by pulling it toward the wound.<br>**a.** Remove the old dressing.<br>**b.** Discard the soiled dressing into a biohazard container. | ❏ | ❏ | ❏ |
| **9.** Inspect wound for the degree of healing, amount and type of drainage, and appearance of wound edges. | ❏ | ❏ | ❏ |

## PROCEDURE 7-7  Changing an Existing Sterile Dressing
(continued)

| | | | |
|---|---|---|---|
| **10.** Observing medical asepsis, remove and discard your gloves. | ❏ | ❏ | ❏ |
| **11.** Using proper technique, apply sterile gloves. | ❏ | ❏ | ❏ |
| **12.** Clean the wound with the antiseptic solution ordered by the physician. | ❏ | ❏ | ❏ |
| **13.** Clean in a straight motion with the cotton or gauze or the prepackaged antiseptic swab. Discard the wipe (cotton ball, swab) after each use. | ❏ | ❏ | ❏ |
| **14.** Remove your gloves and wash your hands. | ❏ | ❏ | ❏ |
| **15.** Change the dressing using the procedure for sterile dressing application (Procedure 7-6) and using sterile gloves (Procedure 7-5) or sterile transfer forceps (Procedure 7-2). | ❏ | ❏ | ❏ |
| **16.** Record the procedure. | ❏ | ❏ | ❏ |

**CALCULATION**

Total Possible Points: _____

Total Points Earned: _____ Multiplied by 100 = _____ Divided by Total Possible Points = _____ %

**PASS  FAIL  COMMENTS:**
❏        ❏

Student's signature _____ Date _____

Partner's signature _____ Date _____

Instructor's signature _____ Date _____

## PSY PROCEDURE 7-8 Assisting with Excisional Surgery

Name: _____ Date: _____ Time: _____ Grade: _____

**EQUIPMENT/SUPPLIES:** Sterile gloves, local anesthetic, antiseptic wipes, adhesive tape, specimen container with completed laboratory request; *On the field:* basin for solutions, gauze sponges and cotton balls, antiseptic solution, sterile drape, dissecting scissors, disposable scalpel, blade of physician's choice, mosquito forceps, tissue forceps, needle holder, suture and needle of physician's choice

**STANDARDS:** Given the needed equipment and a place to work, the student will perform this skill with _____ % accuracy in a total of _____ minutes. *(Your instructor will tell you what the percentage and time limits will be before you begin.)*

**KEY:**          4 = Satisfactory          0 = Unsatisfactory          NA = This step is not counted

| PROCEDURE STEPS | SELF | PARTNER | INSTRUCTOR |
|---|---|---|---|
| **1.** Wash your hands. | ❑ | ❑ | ❑ |
| **2.** Assemble the equipment appropriate for the procedure and according to physician preference. | ❑ | ❑ | ❑ |
| **3.** Greet and identify the patient; explain the procedure and answer any questions. | ❑ | ❑ | ❑ |
| **4.** Set up a sterile field on a surgical stand with additional equipment close at hand. | ❑ | ❑ | ❑ |
| **5.** Cover the field with a sterile drape until the physician arrives. | ❑ | ❑ | ❑ |
| **6.** Position the patient appropriately. | ❑ | ❑ | ❑ |
| **7.** Put on sterile gloves (Procedure 7-5) or use sterile transfer forceps (Procedure 7-2) and cleanse the patient's skin (Procedure 7-4). | ❑ | ❑ | ❑ |
| **8.** Be ready to assist during the procedure: adding supplies as needed, assisting the physician, and comforting the patient. | ❑ | ❑ | ❑ |
| **9.** Assist with collecting tissue specimen in an appropriate container. | ❑ | ❑ | ❑ |
| **10.** At the end of the procedure, wash your hands and dress the wound using sterile technique (Procedure 7-6). | ❑ | ❑ | ❑ |
| **11.** Thank the patient and give appropriate instructions. | ❑ | ❑ | ❑ |
| **12.** AFF Explain how to respond to a patient who is hearing impaired. | ❑ | ❑ | ❑ |

**PSY** PROCEDURE 7-8 **Assisting with Excisional Surgery** (continued)

| | | | |
|---|---|---|---|
| **13.** Sanitize the examining room in preparation for the next patient. | ❏ | ❏ | ❏ |
| **14.** Discard all disposables in the appropriate biohazard containers. | ❏ | ❏ | ❏ |
| **15.** Record the procedure. | ❏ | ❏ | ❏ |

**CALCULATION**

Total Possible Points: _____

Total Points Earned: _____ Multiplied by 100 = _____ Divided by Total Possible Points = _____ %

**PASS    FAIL    COMMENTS:**
   ❏         ❏

Student's signature _____ Date _____

Partner's signature _____ Date _____

Instructor's signature _____ Date _____

## PSY PROCEDURE 7-9   Assisting with Incision and Drainage

Name: _____ Date: _____ Time: _____ Grade: _____

**EQUIPMENT/SUPPLIES:** Sterile gloves, local anesthetic, antiseptic wipes, adhesive tape, sterile dressings, packing gauze, a culture tube if the wound may be cultured; *On the field:* basin for solutions, gauze sponges and cotton balls, antiseptic solution, sterile drape, syringes and needles for local anesthetic, commercial I&D sterile setup *or* scalpel, dissecting scissors, hemostats, tissue forceps, 4 × 4 gauze sponges, probe (optional)

**STANDARDS:** Given the needed equipment and a place to work, the student will perform this skill with _____ % accuracy in a total of _____ minutes. *(Your instructor will tell you what the percentage and time limits will be before you begin.)*

**KEY:**          4 = Satisfactory              0 = Unsatisfactory              NA = This step is not counted

| PROCEDURE STEPS | SELF | PARTNER | INSTRUCTOR |
|---|---|---|---|
| 1. Wash your hands. | ❏ | ❏ | ❏ |
| 2. Assemble the equipment appropriate for the procedure and according to physician preference. | ❏ | ❏ | ❏ |
| 3. Greet and identify the patient. Explain the procedure and answer any questions. | ❏ | ❏ | ❏ |
| 4. Set up a sterile field on a surgical stand with additional equipment close at hand | ❏ | ❏ | ❏ |
| 5. Cover the field with a sterile drape until the physician arrives. | ❏ | ❏ | ❏ |
| 6. Position the patient appropriately. | ❏ | ❏ | ❏ |
| 7. Put on sterile gloves (Procedure 7-5) or use sterile transfer forceps (Procedure 7-2) and cleanse the patient's skin (Procedure 7-4). | ❏ | ❏ | ❏ |
| 8. Be ready to assist during the procedure: adding supplies as needed, assisting the physician, comforting the patient. | ❏ | ❏ | ❏ |
| 9. Assist with collecting culturette specimen for culture and sensitivity. | ❏ | ❏ | ❏ |
| 10. At the end of procedure, remove gloves, wash your hands, and dress the wound using sterile technique (Procedure 7-6). | ❏ | ❏ | ❏ |
| 11. Thank the patient and give appropriate instructions. | ❏ | ❏ | ❏ |
| 12. Sanitize the examining room in preparation for the next patient. | ❏ | ❏ | ❏ |
| 13. Discard all disposables in appropriate biohazard containers. | ❏ | ❏ | ❏ |
| 14. Record the procedure. | ❏ | ❏ | ❏ |

**PSY** PROCEDURE 7-9   **Assisting with Incision and Drainage**
(continued)

**CALCULATION**

Total Possible Points: _____

Total Points Earned: _____ Multiplied by 100 = _____ Divided by Total Possible Points = _____ %

**PASS   FAIL   COMMENTS:**
❏         ❏

Student's signature _____ Date _____

Partner's signature _____ Date _____

Instructor's signature _____ Date _____

## PROCEDURE 7-10    **Removing Sutures**

Name: _____  Date: _____  Time: _____  Grade: _____

**EQUIPMENT/SUPPLIES:** Skin antiseptic, sterile gloves, prepackaged suture removal kit or thumb forceps, suture scissors, gauze

**STANDARDS:** Given the needed equipment and a place to work, the student will perform this skill with _____ % accuracy in a total of _____ minutes. *(Your instructor will tell you what the percentage and time limits will be before you begin.)*

**KEY:**         4 = Satisfactory          0 = Unsatisfactory          NA = This step is not counted

| PROCEDURE STEPS | SELF | PARTNER | INSTRUCTOR |
|---|---|---|---|
| **1.** Wash your hands and apply clean examination gloves. | ❏ | ❏ | ❏ |
| **2.** Assemble the equipment. | ❏ | ❏ | ❏ |
| **3.** Greet and identify the patient; explain the procedure and answer any questions. | ❏ | ❏ | ❏ |
| **4.** If dressings have not been removed previously, remove them from the wound area.<br>**a.** Properly dispose of the soiled dressings in the biohazard trash container.<br>**b.** Remove your gloves and wash your hands. | ❏ | ❏ | ❏ |
| **5.** Cover the field with a sterile drape until the physician arrives. | ❏ | ❏ | ❏ |
| **6.** Open suture removal packet using sterile asepsis. | ❏ | ❏ | ❏ |
| **7.** Put on sterile gloves.<br>**a.** With the thumb forceps, grasp the end of the knot closest to the skin surface and lift it slightly and gently up from the skin.<br>**b.** Cut the suture below the knot as close to the skin as possible.<br>**c.** Use the thumb forceps to pull the suture out of the skin with a smooth motion. | ❏ | ❏ | ❏ |
| **8.** Place the suture on the gauze sponge; repeat the procedure for each suture to be removed. | ❏ | ❏ | ❏ |
| **9.** Clean the site with an antiseptic solution and cover it with a sterile dressing. | ❏ | ❏ | ❏ |
| **10.** Thank the patient. | ❏ | ❏ | ❏ |
| **11.** **AFF** Explain how to respond to a patient who is developmentally challenged. | ❏ | ❏ | ❏ |

**PSY** PROCEDURE 7-10    **Removing Sutures** (continued)

| | | | |
|---|---|---|---|
| _____ | | | |
| _____ | | | |
| _____ | | | |
| _____ | | | |
| _____ | | | |
| **12.** Properly dispose of the equipment and supplies. | ❏ | ❏ | ❏ |
| **13.** Clean the work area, remove your gloves, and wash your hands. | ❏ | ❏ | ❏ |
| **14.** Record the procedure, including the time, location of sutures, the number removed, and the condition of the wound. | ❏ | ❏ | ❏ |

**CALCULATION**

Total Possible Points: _____

Total Points Earned: _____ Multiplied by 100 = _____ Divided by Total Possible Points = _____ %

**PASS    FAIL    COMMENTS:**
 ❏        ❏

Student's signature _____ Date _____

Partner's signature _____ Date _____

Instructor's signature _____ Date _____

## PSY PROCEDURE 7-11 Removing Staples

Name: _____ Date: _____ Time: _____ Grade: _____

**EQUIPMENT/SUPPLIES:** Antiseptic solution or wipes, gauze squares, sponge forceps, prepackaged sterile staple removal instrument, examination gloves, sterile gloves

**STANDARDS:** Given the needed equipment and a place to work, the student will perform this skill with _____ % accuracy in a total of _____ minutes. *(Your instructor will tell you what the percentage and time limits will be before you begin.)*

**KEY:** 4 = Satisfactory 0 = Unsatisfactory NA =This step is not counted

| PROCEDURE STEPS | SELF | PARTNER | INSTRUCTOR |
|---|---|---|---|
| **1.** Wash your hands. | ❏ | ❏ | ❏ |
| **2.** Assemble the equipment. | ❏ | ❏ | ❏ |
| **3.** Greet and identify the patient; explain the procedure and answer any questions. | ❏ | ❏ | ❏ |
| **4.** If the dressing has not been removed, put on clean examination gloves and do so. | ❏ | ❏ | ❏ |
| **5.** Dispose of the dressing properly in a biohazard container. | ❏ | ❏ | ❏ |
| **6.** Clean the incision with antiseptic solution. | ❏ | ❏ | ❏ |
| **7.** Pat dry using dry sterile gauze sponges. | ❏ | ❏ | ❏ |
| **8.** Put on sterile gloves. | ❏ | ❏ | ❏ |
| **9.** Gently slide the end of the staple remover under each staple to be removed; press the handles together to lift the ends of the staple out of the skin and remove the staple. | ❏ | ❏ | ❏ |
| **10.** Place each staple on a gauze square as it is removed. | ❏ | ❏ | ❏ |
| **11.** When all staples are removed, clean the incision as instructed for all procedures. | ❏ | ❏ | ❏ |
| **12.** Pat dry and dress the site if ordered to do so by the physician. | ❏ | ❏ | ❏ |
| **13.** Thank the patient and properly care for, or dispose of, all equipment and supplies. | ❏ | ❏ | ❏ |
| **14.** AFF Explain how to respond to a patient who is visually impaired. | ❏ | ❏ | ❏ |

| | | | |
|---|---|---|---|
| | _____ | | |
| | _____ | | |
| | _____ | | |
| | _____ | | |
| | _____ | | |
| **15.** Clean the work area, remove your gloves, and wash your hands. | ❏ | ❏ | ❏ |
| **16.** Record the procedure. | ❏ | ❏ | ❏ |

**CALCULATION**

Total Possible Points: _____

Total Points Earned: _____ Multiplied by 100 = _____ Divided by Total Possible Points = _____ %

**PASS   FAIL   COMMENTS:**
  ❏       ❏

Student's signature _____ Date _____

Partner's signature _____ Date _____

Instructor's signature _____ Date _____

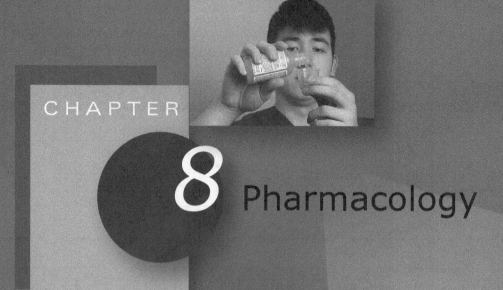

# CHAPTER

# 8 Pharmacology

## Learning Outcomes

Name: _____    Date: _____    Grade: _____

## cog MULTIPLE CHOICE

Circle the letter preceding the correct answer.

**1.** A physician needs to register with the U.S. Attorney General:
 **a.** every 3 years.
 **b.** every 2 years.
 **c.** every 4 years.
 **d.** only once; registration is for life.
 **e.** every year.

**2.** When a drug is contraindicated, it:
 **a.** is not properly eliminated.
 **b.** is distributed throughout the bloodstream.
 **c.** should not be used.
 **d.** is detected in urine excretion.
 **e.** should be retested for accuracy.

**3.** Emetics are used to:
 **a.** dilate bronchi.
 **b.** prevent symptoms of menopause.
 **c.** control diabetes.
 **d.** dissolve blood clots.
 **e.** promote vomiting.

**4.** Which substance is an example of a Schedule I controlled substance?
 **a.** Morphine
 **b.** Ritalin
 **c.** Amphetamines
 **d.** Opium
 **e.** Tylenol with codeine

**5.** Which drug below is an example of an antipyretic?
 **a.** Aspirin
 **b.** Dramamine
 **c.** Lanoxin
 **d.** Zantac
 **e.** Benylin

**6.** A symptom of an allergic reaction is:
 **a.** nausea.
 **b.** drowsiness.
 **c.** dryness of mouth.
 **d.** hives.
 **e.** fever.

**7.** Two drugs when taken together that can create synergism are:
 **a.** sedatives and barbiturates.
 **b.** antacids and antibiotics.
 **c.** diuretics and decongestants.
 **d.** antibiotics and antifungals.
 **e.** antihypertensives and expectorants.

**8.** The DEA is a branch of the:
 **a.** BNDD.
 **b.** DOJ.
 **c.** FDA.
 **d.** AMA.
 **e.** AHFS.

**9.** All drugs cause:
 **a.** cellular and physiological change.
 **b.** cellular and psychological change.
 **c.** physiological and psychological change.
 **d.** physiological changes.
 **e.** cellular, physiological, and psychological change.

**10.** Green leafy vegetables can sometimes interact with:
 **a.** coumadin.
 **b.** verapamil.
 **c.** ibuprofen.
 **d.** amoxicillin.
 **e.** phenobarbital.

**11.** Drugs with a potential for abuse and currently accepted for medicinal use are:
 **a.** Schedule I drugs.
 **b.** Schedule II drugs.
 **c.** Schedule III drugs.
 **d.** Schedule IV drugs.
 **e.** Schedules I and IV drugs.

**12.** A drug is given a brand name when it:
 **a.** is first developed in laboratories.
 **b.** is used in field testing and studies.
 **c.** is assigned a sponsor for the research.
 **d.** is approved by the FDA.
 **e.** is available for commercial use.

*Scenario for questions 13 and 14:* A teenaged patient has called in saying that the pharmacy will not refill her painkiller prescription. It has been just over a month since she last refilled her prescription.

**13.** What is the first step you should take?
 **a.** Check her records to see how many more refills she has left.
 **b.** Inform the physician about the situation for directions.
 **c.** Call the pharmacy to find out how many refills she has gotten.
 **d.** Write out another prescription and fax it to the pharmacy.
 **e.** Inform the patient that she has no more refills remaining.

14. The patient still has three remaining refills on her prescription. After you call the pharmacy, however, you are informed that the patient has been purchasing over-the-counter painkillers along with her prescription. There is suspicion that the patient might be selling her medication and taking over-the-counter drugs. What do you do?
   a. Call the patient and confront her about the purchases.
   b. Discuss the possibility of drug abuse with the physician.
   c. Call the police immediately and report the patient.
   d. Tell the pharmacy to give her the prescriptions anyway.
   e. Gather information and report your findings.

15. The study of how drugs act on the body, including cells, tissues, and organs, is:
   a. pharmacokinetics.
   b. pharmacodynamics.
   c. synergism.
   d. antagonism.
   e. potentiation.

16. What kind of drug is used to increase the size of arterial blood vessels?
   a. Anticonvulsants
   b. Emetics
   c. Cholinergics
   d. Antihypertensives
   e. Immunologic agents

17. Which of the following is a trait of a Schedule I drug?
   a. No accepted safety standards
   b. Cannot be prescribed by a physician
   c. Lowest potential for abuse
   d. May be filled up to five times in 6 months
   e. Requires a handwritten prescription

18. When you are administering a controlled substance in a medical office, you must include:
   a. a drug schedule.
   b. the time of administration.
   c. patient allergies.
   d. your name.
   e. location.

19. If a patient is receiving a medication that has a high incidence of allergic reactions, how long should the patient wait before leaving the office?
   a. No wait time necessary
   b. 5 to 10 minutes
   c. 20 to 30 minutes
   d. 30 minutes to an hour
   e. Overnight observation

20. The chemical name of a drug is the:
   a. last name a drug is given before it is put on the market.
   b. description of the chemical compounds found in the drug.
   c. name given to the drug during research and development.
   d. name given to the drug by the FDA and AMA.
   e. name of the chemical the drug supplements in the body.

## COG MATCHING

_____ Grade: _____

Match each key term with its definition.

**Key Terms**

21. _____ allergy
22. _____ anaphylaxis
23. _____ antagonism
24. _____ chemical name
25. _____ contraindication
26. _____ drug
27. _____ generic name
28. _____ interaction
29. _____ pharmacodynamics
30. _____ pharmacokinetics
31. _____ pharmacology
32. _____ potentiation
33. _____ synergism
34. _____ trade name

**Definitions**

a. effects, positive and negative, of two or more drugs taken by a patient
b. situation or condition that prohibits the prescribing or administering of a drug or medication
c. any substance that may modify one or more of the functions of an organism
d. study of drugs and their origin, nature, properties, and effects upon living organisms
e. exact chemical descriptor of a drug
f. official name given to a drug whose patent has expired
g. name given to a medication by the company that owns the patent
h. study of the effects and reactions of drugs within the body
i. study of the action of drugs within the body from administration to excretion
j. harmonious action of two agents, such as drugs or organs, producing an effect that neither could produce alone or that is greater than the total effects of each agent operating by itself

**Key Terms**

**Definitions**

k. mutual opposition or contrary action with something else; opposite of synergism

l. describes the action of two drugs taken together in which the combined effects are greater than the sum of the independent effects

m. acquired abnormal response to a substance (allergen) that does not ordinarily cause a reaction

n. severe allergic reaction that may result in death

## MATCHING

Grade: _____

Match each drug term with its description.

**Drug Terms**

35. _____ therapeutic classification
36. _____ idiosyncratic reaction
37. _____ indications
38. _____ teratogenic category
39. _____ hypersensitivity
40. _____ contraindications
41. _____ adverse reactions

**Descriptions**

a. relates the level of risk to fetal or maternal health (These rank from Category A through D, with increasing danger at each level. Category X indicates that the particular drug should never be given during pregnancy.)

b. refers to an excessive reaction to a particular drug; also known as a *drug allergy* (The body must build this response; the first exposures may or may not indicate that a problem is developing.)

c. indicates conditions or instances for which the particular drug should not be used

d. states the purpose for the drug's use (e.g., cardiotonic, anti-infective, antiarrhythmic)

e. refers to an abnormal or unexpected reaction to a drug peculiar to the individual patient; not technically an allergy

f. gives diseases for which the particular drug would be prescribed

g. refers to undesirable side effects of a particular drug

## IDENTIFICATION

Grade: _____

42. Identify whether the following descriptions describe the chemical, generic, or trade name of a drug by writing C (chemical), G (generic), or T (trade) on the line preceding the description.

a. _____ The name of a drug that begins with a lowercase letter

b. _____ The name assigned to a drug during research and development

c. _____ The name given to a drug when it is available for commercial use

d. _____ The first name given to any medication

e. _____ The name that is registered by the U.S. patent office

f. _____ The name that identifies the chemical components of the drug

43. Determine if the information below can be found in the *Physicians' Desk Reference (PDR)* or the *United States Pharmacopeia Dispensing Information (USPDI)*. Place a check mark in the appropriate box below.

| | Physicians' Desk Reference | United States Pharmacopeia Dispensing Information |
|---|---|---|
| **a.** Drug sources | | |
| **b.** Indications | | |
| **c.** Dosages | | |
| **d.** Pictures | | |
| **e.** Chemistry | | |
| **f.** Physical properties | | |
| **g.** Side effects | | |
| **h.** Tests for identity | | |
| **i.** Storage | | |
| **j.** Contraindications | | |

**44.** Indicate where the following elements of a prescription go in sequential order.

Patient's name and address      Line 1: _____

Date      Line 2. _____

Inscription      Line 3. _____

Superscription      Line 4. _____

Subscription      Line 5. _____

Physician's signature      Line 6. _____

Signature      Line 7. _____

Generic      Line 8. _____

Refills      Line 9. _____

**45.** Indicate each drug's controlled substance category by writing I, II, III, IV, or V on the line preceding the drug name.

     **a.** _____ morphine

     **b.** _____ Tylenol with codeine

     **c.** _____ cocaine

     **d.** _____ codeine in cough medications

     **e.** _____ marijuana

     **f.** _____ Valium

     **g.** _____ LSD

     **h.** _____ Ritalin

     **i.** _____ Librium

## COG COMPLETION

Grade: _____

**46.** Each of the following statements about inventory of controlled substances is incorrect or incomplete. Rewrite each statement to make it correct or complete.

**a.** List only category III controlled substances on the appropriate inventory form.

_____

**b.** When you receive controlled substances, make sure that only the physician signs the receipt.

_____

**c.** Keep all controlled substance inventory forms for 10 years.

_____

**d.** When a controlled substance leaves the medical office inventory, record the following information: drug name and patient.

_____

**e.** Notify the office manager immediately if these drugs are lost or stolen.

_____

**f.** Store controlled substances in the same cabinet as other medications and supplies.

_____

## COG SHORT ANSWER

Grade: _____

**47.** What are pharmacodynamics and pharmacokinetics? Explain the relationship between these two processes.

_____

_____

_____

_____

**48.** What four processes are connected to pharmacokinetics?

_____

_____

_____

_____

**49.** Why is it important for patients to know about food–drug interactions?

_____

_____

_____

_____

**50.** Explain the difference between drug side effects and allergic reactions.

_____

_____

_____

_____

**51.** List three common and predictable drug side effects.

_____

_____

_____

_____

**52.** Compare and contrast the different types of drug interactions, including synergism, antagonism, and potentiation.

_____

_____

_____

_____

**53.** Compare the effect or action of the following therapeutic classifications: stimulants, diuretics, emetics, and immunologic agents.

_____

_____

_____

_____

## COG TRUE OR FALSE?

Grade: _____

Indicate whether the statements are true or false by placing the letter T (true) or F (false) in the blank preceding the statement.

**54.** _____ The DEA is concerned with controlled substances only.

**55.** _____ Drugs are derived from natural and synthetic sources.

**56.** _____ Children have a slower response to drug intakes.

**57.** _____ Allergic reactions are always immediate.

**58.** _____ Side effects from drugs are often life threatening.

**59.** _____ A drug is a chemical substance that affects body function or functions.

**60.** _____ A drug administered for a systemic effect is applied topically.

**61.** _____ Women may react differently to certain drugs than men.

**62.** _____ Medications should always be taken on a full stomach.

## COG AFF CASE STUDIES FOR CRITICAL THINKING

Grade: _____

1. You are doing an inventory of the controlled substances in your office and notice that the office's supply of morphine is off count. You double-check all written records of medications given for administration and still cannot account for the missing morphine. After realizing this, you immediately tell the physician. The physician tells you not to worry about it. Three weeks later you notice that more morphine is missing. What do you do?

_____

_____

_____

_____

2. A patient just received a shot of penicillin. Before the shot was administered, you advised the patient that she needs to remain in the physician's office for 30 minutes before leaving. However, the patient just remembers that she must pick her mother up for an appointment that her mother needs to attend. The patient is adamant that she must leave right away so as not to be late. How would you respond to this patient?

_____

_____

_____

_____

3. You have an elderly patient who is taking Lasix for his high blood pressure. This patient has recently called in to the office complaining of muscle weakness. What classification is the drug Lasix? What is possibly causing the patients' muscle weakness? How would you respond to this patient?

_____

_____

_____

_____

4. You have a patient with hepatic disease. After she consults with the physician, she asks you some general questions to clarify how her body processes medication. Think about the pharmacokinetic effects of drugs on her body. What processes would you discuss with her about her condition and medications?

_____

_____

_____

_____

**5.** Your patient tells you that she feels like she is coming down with a cold and has had a sore throat since yesterday. She also tells you that her friend gave her some leftover antibiotics that she did not finish when she had strep throat last month. How would you respond to this patient? Is this important information for the physician to know? Why or why not?

_____

_____

_____

_____

**6.** Louise asks Mr. Fujiwara about his medical history and if he has any allergies to any medications. Mr. Fujiwara says that he has an allergy to aspirin. Louise marks Mr. Fujiwara's drug allergy prominently on the front of his medication record before giving the record to the physician. What else should the medical assistant do?

_____

_____

_____

_____

# CHAPTER

# 9 Preparing and Administering Medications

## Learning Outcomes

### COG Cognitive Domain

1. Spell and define the key terms
2. Demonstrate knowledge of basic math computations
3. Apply mathematical computations to solve equations
4. Define basic units of measurement in metric and household systems
5. Convert among measurement systems
6. Identify abbreviations and symbols used in calculating medication dosages
7. List the safety guidelines for medication administration
8. Explain the differences between various parenteral and nonparenteral routes of medication administration
9. Describe the parts of a syringe and needle and name those parts that must be kept sterile
10. List the various needle lengths, gauges, and preferred site for each type of injection
11. Compare the types of injections and locate the sites where each may be administered safely
12. Describe principles of intravenous therapy

### PSY Psychomotor Domain

1. Administer oral medications (Procedure 9-1)
2. Prepare injections (Procedure 9-2)
3. Administer an intradermal injection (Procedure 9-3)
4. Administer a subcutaneous injection (Procedure 9-4)
5. Administer an intramuscular injection (Procedure 9-5)
6. Administer an intramuscular injection using the Z-track method (Procedure 9-6)
7. Apply transdermal medications (Procedure 9-7)
8. Complete an incident report related to an error in patient care (Procedure 9-8)

### AFF Affective Domain

1. Incorporate critical thinking skills when performing patient care
2. Verify ordered doses/dosages prior to administration
3. Show awareness of patient's concerns related to the procedure being performed
4. Demonstrate empathy, active listening, nonverbal communication
5. Demonstrate respect for individual diversity including gender, race, religion, age, economic status, and appearance
6. Explain to a patient the rationale for performance of a procedure.
7. Protect the integrity of the medical record.

### ABHES Competencies

1. Demonstrate accurate occupational math and metric conversions for proper medication administration
2. Apply principles of aseptic techniques and infection control
3. Maintain medication and immunization records
4. Use standard precautions
5. Prepare and administer oral and parenteral medications as directed by physician
6. Document accurately
7. Dispose of biohazardous materials

Name: _____    Date: _____    Grade: _____

## OG MULTIPLE CHOICE

Circle the letter preceding the correct answer.

1. When administering an unfamiliar drug, you should look up information on:
   a. alternate formulations.
   b. the chemical name.
   c. generic alternatives.
   d. how the medication is stored.
   e. the route of administration.

2. When preparing medications you should:
   a. use previous medications and dosages listed on the patient's chart as a safety check.
   b. use a resource like the Internet to cross reference generic and brand names for medications.
   c. work in a quiet, well-lighted area.
   d. crush tablets so patients can swallow them easily.
   e. recap used needles to protect against accidental jabs.

3. Patient safety is protected by ensuring:
   a. a nurse prepares the medication for you to administer.
   b. you are administering the right drug to the right patient.
   c. medications are delivered to the right room for administration by the nurse.
   d. you are using the right type of syringe.
   e. you write down and document medications before you give them.

4. When dispensing drugs, make sure you convert the dosage ordered to the:
   a. apothecary system.
   b. household system.
   c. imperial units.
   d. system and units noted on the medication label.
   e. metric units.

5. The basic unit of weight in the metric system is the:
   a. grain.
   b. gram.
   c. liter.
   d. newton.
   e. pound.

6. What number do you multiply the base metric unit if the prefix is "milli"?
   a. 1,000
   b. 1,000,000
   c. 0.000001
   d. 0.001
   e. 0.01

7. Which of these measurements equals 2 cc?
   a. 2 mg
   b. 20 mg
   c. 2 mL
   d. 30 g
   e. 120 mg

8. Which of these measurements equals 45 mL?
   a. 0.75 fl oz
   b. 1.5 fl oz
   c. 3.0 fl oz
   d. 4.5 fl oz
   e. 20.5 fl oz

9. The physician orders chloroquine syrup 100 mg oral for a 20-kg child. The concentration of the syrup is 50 mg/mL. How much medication do you give the child?
   a. 0.5 mL
   b. 2 mL
   c. 10 mL
   d. 40 mL
   e. 250 mL

10. Which method is the most accurate means of calculating pediatric dosages?
    a. Body weight method
    b. The Clarke rule
    c. The Fried rule
    d. BSA method
    e. The Young rule

11. Medicine administered under the tongue follows the:
    a. buccal route.
    b. dental route.
    c. dermal route.
    d. oral route.
    e. sublingual route.

12. Which item below could be a multiple-dose dispenser?
    a. Ampule
    b. Cartridge
    c. Carpuject
    d. Tubex
    e. Vial

13. How large is a tuberculin syringe?
    a. 10 U
    b. 5 mL
    c. 3 mL
    d. 1 mL
    e. 0.1 mL

**14.** A possible site for an intradermal injection is the:
a. antecubital fossa.
b. anterior forearm.
c. upper arm.
d. deltoid.
e. vastus lateralis.

*Scenario for questions 15 and 16:* You are directed to set up an IV line delivering RL 30 mL/hour TKO with a 10-gtt/mL system.

**15.** How many drips per minute should the IV deliver?
a. 1 gtt/minute
b. 3 gtt/minute
c. 5 gtt/minute
d. 10 gtt/minute
e. 20 gtt/minute

**16.** A good site for the angiocatheter would be the:
a. antecubital fossa.
b. anterior forearm.
c. upper arm.
d. deltoid.
e. vastus lateralis.

**17.** A good place to administer a 0.25-mL IM injection on a child is the:
a. antecubital fossa.
b. anterior forearm.
c. upper arm.
d. deltoid.
e. vastus lateralis.

**18.** The physician orders Demerol 150 mg IM for a patient. The vial label indicates a total of 20 mL of medication with 100 mg/mL. Find the dosage.
a. 0.67 mL
b. 1.5 mL
c. 2.5 mL
d. 7.5 mL
e. 30 mL

**19.** A good site to inject a medication ordered SC would be the:
a. antecubital fossa.
b. anterior forearm.
c. upper arm.
d. deltoid.
e. vastus lateralis.

**20.** You are told to administer a medicine by the otic route. This medicine should be administered into:
a. the ears.
b. inhaler.
c. the eyes
d. the mouth.
e. the nose.

## **COG MATCHING**

Grade: _____

Match each key term with its definition.

**Key Terms**

**21.** _____ ampule
**22.** _____ apothecary system of measurement
**23.** _____ buccal
**24.** _____ diluent
**25.** _____ gauge
**26.** _____ induration
**27.** _____ infiltration
**28.** _____ Mantoux
**29.** _____ metric system
**30.** _____ nebulizer
**31.** _____ ophthalmic
**32.** _____ otic
**33.** _____ parenteral
**34.** _____ sublingual
**35.** _____ topical
**36.** _____ vial

**Definitions**

a. leakage of intravenous fluids into surrounding tissues
b. administration of medication between the cheek and gum of the mouth
c. all systemic administration routes excluding the gastrointestinal tract
d. a system of measurement that uses grams, liters, and meters
e. diameter of a needle lumen
f. device for administering respiratory medications as a fine inhaled spray
g. a tuberculosis screening test
h. small glass container that must be broken at the neck so that the solution can be aspirated into the syringe
i. administration route to a local spot on the outside of the body
j. administration route to the eyes
k. a system of measures based on drops, minims, grains, drams, and ounces
l. administration route to or by way of the ears
m. hardened area at the injection site after an intradermal screening test for tuberculosis
n. administration beneath the tongue
o. glass or plastic container sealed at the top by a rubber stopper
p. specified liquid used to reconstitute powder medications for injection

## **COG** MATCHING

Grade: _____

Match the injection route to the proper location for administration. There may be more than one location for each injection.

**Injection Routes**

**37.** _____ intradermal (ID)
**38.** _____ adult intramuscular (IM)
**39.** _____ juvenile (<2 years old) intramuscular (IM)
**40.** _____ Z-track intramuscular (IM)
**41.** _____ subcutaneous (SC)

**Locations**

**a.** abdomen
**b.** anterior forearm
**c.** back
**d.** deltoid
**e.** dorsogluteal
**f.** rectus femoris
**g.** thigh
**h.** upper arm
**i.** vastus lateralis
**j.** ventrogluteal

## **COG** IDENTIFICATION

Grade: _____

**42.** When preparing medications, the patient's safety relies on good communication between the physician and yourself. Identify the safety rules you should use to prevent communication errors by placing a check mark on the line under "Yes" if the statement is a safety rule and check "No" if the rule does not apply.

| Rule | Yes | No |
|------|-----|-----|
| **a.** Confirm all medications verbally. Do not try to interpret the physician's handwriting. | | |
| **b.** Use previous medications and dosages listed on the patient's chart as a safety check. | | |
| **c.** Check with the physician if you have any doubt about a medication or an order. | | |

**43.** Once you have correctly interpreted the medication order from the physician, you must locate and identify the correct drugs to dispense or administer. Choose the rules that prevent errors with identifying the correct medications by placing a check mark on the line under "Yes" if the statement is a safety rule and check "No" if the rule does not apply.

| Rule | Yes | No |
|------|-----|-----|
| **a.** Check the label when taking the medication from the shelf, when preparing it, and again when replacing it on the shelf or disposing of the empty container. | | |
| **b.** Peel off the label from the medication and place it in the patient's record. | | |
| **c.** Place the order and the medication side by side to compare for accuracy. | | |
| **d.** Only fill prescriptions written using brand names. | | |
| **e.** Read labels carefully. Do not scan labels or medication orders. | | |
| **f.** Use a resource like the Internet to cross-reference generic and brand names for medications. | | |
| **g.** It is always safer to give a medication poured or drawn up by someone more experienced. | | |

**44.** Once you have correctly interpreted the medication order from the physician and identified the correct medication, you must safely dispense and/or administer the medication. Identify which rules prevent mistakes in dispensing and administering medications by placing a check mark on the line under "Yes" if the statement is a safety rule and check "No" if the rule does not apply.

| Rule | Yes | No |
|---|---|---|
| **a.** Know the policies of your office regarding the administration of medications. | | |
| **b.** Never question the physician's written orders. | | |
| **c.** Prepare medications in the presence of the patient so you can discuss what you are doing and answer the patient's questions. | | |
| **d.** Check the strength of the medication (e.g., 250 vs. 500 mg) and the route of administration. | | |
| **e.** If you are interrupted, return the medicine to its original container so you can correctly identify it when you come back and finish. | | |
| **f.** Work in a quiet, well-lit area. | | |
| **g.** Check the patient's medical record for allergies to the actual medication or its components before administering. | | |
| **h.** Check the patient's medical record for allergies to the actual medication or its components before administering. | | |
| **i.** Check the patient's medical record for allergies to the actual medication or its components before administering. | | |
| **j.** Check the patient's medical record for allergies to the actual medication or its components before administering. | | |
| **k.** Check the patient's medical record for allergies to the actual medication or its components before administering. | | |

**45.** Indicate whether the following are parenteral or enteral by writing P (parenteral) or E (enteral) on the line preceding the route.

**a.** _____ buccal

**b.** _____ inhalation

**c.** _____ intramuscular

**d.** _____ intravenous

**e.** _____ oral

**f.** _____ rectal

**g.** _____ subcutaneous

**h.** _____ sublingual

**i.** _____ transdermal

**46.** Identify the medical term for the route for administration by placing the term on the line next to the administration method.

**a.** ear drops _____

**b.** eye drops _____

**c.** nitroglycerine patch _____

**d.** lotion _____

**e.** TB test _____

**f.** nebulizer _____

**g.** suppositories _____

**h.** cough syrup _____

## COG COMPLETION

Grade: _____

For each of the dosage calculations, show your work and circle your answer.

**47.** The physician orders enoxaparin 40 mg SC. The label on the package reads 150 mg/mL. Find the correct dosage for this patient.

_____

_____

_____

_____

**48.** You are directed to give a heroin addict 30 mg of methadone PO. The medication comes in tablets labeled 20 mg/tablet. How many tablets would you give the patient?

_____

_____

_____

_____

**49.** As ordered by the physician, your patient needs 300,000 units of penicillin G IM. The label on the medication vial reads "Penicillin G 1 million units/2 mL." How many mL would you need to give?

_____

_____

_____

_____

**50.** The physician has written an order for you to give 40 mg of prednisone PO now before the patient leaves the office. You have on hand two strengths of prednisone: 10 mg/tablet and 5 mg/tablet. Choose the appropriate strength and calculate the number of tablets you would give to the patient.

_____

_____

_____

_____

51. Your patient has been ordered by the physician to receive 40 mg of furosemide IM. The ampule states "Furosemide 20 mg/mL." How much medication should you draw up to administer?

_____

_____

_____

_____

52. The patient seen in your office today is ordered by the physician to receive 750 mg of Rocephin™ deep IM. The label on the vial states "Rocephin 1 g/2 cc." How much would you give?

_____

_____

_____

_____

53. The physician has ordered your patient to take doxycycline 100 mg BID for 7 days. She would like the patient to have a dose before leaving the office. The medication label on the doxycycline in your office reads "Doxycycline 50 mg/capsule." How many would you give to the patient?

_____

_____

_____

_____

54. Your patient arrives at the office with nausea and vomiting. The physician orders you to give 12.5 mg of Phenergan™ IM. The vial states "Phenergan 25 mg/mL." How much would you give to the patient?

_____

_____

_____

_____

55. An order has been written by the physician for you to administer 7 mg of warfarin PO to your patient. You have three bottles of warfarin available: 2 mg/tablet; 2.5 mg/tablet; and 5 mg/tablet. Which tablet strength would you choose and how many tablets would you give the patient to ensure 7 mg were taken?

_____

_____

_____

_____

## **COG** SHORT ANSWER _____ Grade: _____

**56.** What are the primary differences between enteral, parenteral, and topical medications?

_____

_____

_____

_____

**57.** List the four parts of a syringe that must be kept sterile.

_____

_____

_____

_____

**58.** What size needle (gauge and length) would you use for the following administration routes?

| Route | Gauge | Length |
|-------|-------|--------|
| **a.** IM | | |
| **b.** SC | | |
| **c.** ID | | |

## **COG** TRUE OR FALSE? _____ Grade: _____

Indicate whether the statements are true or false by placing the letter T (true) or F (false) on the line preceding the statement.

**59.** _____ It is normal for frightened patients to have trouble breathing after taking a medication.

**60.** _____ A sip of water will help a patient take nitroglycerine sublingually.

**61.** _____ During SC and IM injections, a small amount of blood appears in the syringe when there is good penetration.

**62.** _____ Redness, swelling, pain, and discomfort are normal complications of IV therapy.

**63.** _____ Check the medication's expiration date, and use outdated medications first.

**64.** _____ Be alert for color changes, precipitation, odor, or any indication that the medication's properties have changed and discard appropriately.

**65.** _____ Keep narcotics on your person so others do not have access to them.

**66.** _____ Do not leave the medication cabinet unlocked when it is not in use.

**67.** _____ Never give keys for the medication cabinet to an unauthorized person.

## COG AFF CASE STUDIES FOR CRITICAL THINKING

Grade: _____

1. The parent of an 18-month old insists that you give the IM immunization in the child's "hip." How would you respond to the parent's request?

_____

_____

_____

_____

2. The patient you are monitoring is receiving intravenous fluids for rehydration. Unfortunately, the insertion site in the left anterior forearm has developed complications and must be removed. How would you respond to the patient who does not understand why the IV must be removed?

_____

_____

_____

_____

3. One of the physicians in your medical office would like to change office policy so that no abbreviations are used in the patients' medical charts for fear of potentially harmful errors. The office is divided on the issue. What is your opinion and why?

_____

_____

_____

_____

4. You are directed to give a Z-track IM injection to a patient. The patient's spouse observes you deliberately draw a bubble into the syringe and panics because you are about to inject air into the patient. How do you address the spouse's concerns?

_____

_____

_____

## PSY PROCEDURE 9-1 Administer Oral Medications

**Name:** _____ **Date:** _____ **Time:** _____ **Grade:** _____

**EQUIPMENT/SUPPLIES:** Physician's order, oral medication, disposable calibrated cup, glass of water, patient's medical record

**STANDARDS:** Given the needed equipment and a place to work, the student will perform this skill with _____ % accuracy in a total of _____ minutes. *(Your instructor will tell you what the percentage and time limits will be before you begin.)*

**KEY:**          4 = Satisfactory          0 = Unsatisfactory          NA = This step is not counted

| PROCEDURE STEPS | SELF | PARTNER | INSTRUCTOR |
|---|---|---|---|
| **1.** Wash your hands. | ❑ | ❑ | ❑ |
| **2.** Review the physician's medication order and select the correct oral medication. <br> **a.** Compare the label with the physician's instructions. <br> **b.** Note the expiration date. <br> **c.** Check the label three times: when taking it from the shelf, while pouring, and when returning to the shelf. | ❑ | ❑ | ❑ |
| **3.** Calculate the correct dosage to be given if necessary. | ❑ | ❑ | ❑ |
| **4.** If using a multidose container, remove cap from container. For single-dose medications, obtain the correct amount of medication. | ❑ | ❑ | ❑ |
| **5.** Remove the correct dose of medication. <br> **a.** For solid medications: <br> **(1)** Pour the capsule/tablet into the bottle cap. <br> **(2)** Transfer the medication to a disposable cup. <br> **b.** For liquid medications: <br> **(1)** Open the bottle lid: place it on a flat surface with open end up. <br> **(2)** Palm the label to prevent liquids from dripping onto the label. <br> **(3)** With opposite hand, place the thumbnail at the correct calibration. <br> **(4)** Pour the medication until the proper amount is in the cup. | ❑ | ❑ | ❑ |
| **6.** Greet and identify the patient. Explain the procedure. | ❑ | ❑ | ❑ |
| **7.** Ask the patient about medication allergies that might not be noted on the chart. | ❑ | ❑ | ❑ |
| **8.** Give the patient a glass of water, unless contraindicated. Hand the patient the disposable cup containing the medication or pour the tablets or capsules into the patient's hand. | ❑ | ❑ | ❑ |
| **9.** Remain with the patient to be sure that all of the medication is swallowed. <br> **a.** Observe any unusual reactions and report them to the physician. | ❑ | ❑ | ❑ |
| **10.** Thank the patient and give any appropriate instructions. | ❑ | ❑ | ❑ |

| **PSY** PROCEDURE 9-1 **Administer Oral Medications** (continued) | | | |
|---|---|---|---|
| **11.** **AFF** Explain how to respond to a patient who is hearing impaired. | ❑ | ❑ | ❑ |
| | | | |
| **12.** Wash your hands. | ❑ | ❑ | ❑ |
| **13.** **AFF** Log into the Electronic Medical Record (EMR) using your username and secure password OR obtain the paper medical record from a secure location and assure it is kept away from public access. Record the procedure noting the date, time, name of medication, dose administered, route of administration, and your name. | ❑ | ❑ | ❑ |
| **14.** When finished, log out of the EMR and/or replace the paper medical record in an appropriate and secure location. | ❑ | ❑ | ❑ |

**CALCULATION**

Total Possible Points: _____

Total Points Earned: _____ Multiplied by 100 = _____ Divided by Total Possible Points = _____ %

**PASS    FAIL    COMMENTS:**
   ❑         ❑

Student's signature _____ Date _____

Partner's signature _____ Date _____

Instructor's signature _____ Date _____

## PSY   PROCEDURE 9-2   **Prepare Injections**

**Name:** _____ **Date:** _____ **Time:** _____ **Grade:** _____

**EQUIPMENT/SUPPLIES:** Physician's order, medication for injection in ampule or vial, antiseptic wipes, gloves, appropriate-size needle and syringe, small gauze pad, biohazard sharps container, patient's medical record

**STANDARDS:** Given the needed equipment and a place to work, the student will perform this skill with _____ % accuracy in a total of _____ minutes. *(Your instructor will tell you what the percentage and time limits will be before you begin.)*

**KEY:**      4 = Satisfactory      0 = Unsatisfactory      NA =This step is not counted

| PROCEDURE STEPS | SELF | PARTNER | INSTRUCTOR |
|---|:---:|:---:|:---:|
| **1.** Wash your hands. | ❑ | ❑ | ❑ |
| **2.** Review the physician's medication order and select the correct medication.<br>  **a.** Compare the label with the physician's instructions. Note the expiration date.<br>  **b.** Check the label three times: when taking it from the shelf, while drawing it up into the syringe, and when returning to the shelf. | ❑ | ❑ | ❑ |
| **3.** Calculate the correct dosage to be given, if necessary. | ❑ | ❑ | ❑ |
| **4.** Choose the needle and syringe according to the route of administration, type of medication, and size of the patient. | ❑ | ❑ | ❑ |
| **5.** Open the needle and syringe package. Assemble if necessary. Secure the needle to the syringe. | ❑ | ❑ | ❑ |
| **6.** Withdraw the correct amount of medication:<br>  **a.** From an ampule:<br>    **(1)** Tap the stem of the ampule lightly.<br>    **(2)** Place a piece of gauze around the ampule neck.<br>    **(3)** Grasp the gauze and ampule firmly. Snap the stem off the ampule.<br>    **(4)** Dispose of the ampule top in a biohazard sharps container.<br>    **(5)** Insert the needle lumen below the level of the medication.<br>    **(6)** Withdraw the medication.<br>    **(7)** Dispose of the ampule in a biohazard sharps container.<br>    **(8)** Remove any air bubbles in the syringe.<br>    **(9)** Draw back on the plunger to add a small amount of air; then gently push the plunger forward to eject the air out of the syringe. | ❑ | ❑ | ❑ |

## PSY PROCEDURE 9-2 **Prepare Injections** (continued)

| | | | |
|---|---|---|---|
| **b.** From a vial:<br>  **(1)** Using the antiseptic wipe, cleanse the rubber stopper of the vial.<br>  **(2)** Pull air into the syringe with the amount equivalent to the amount of medication to be removed from the vial.<br>  **(3)** Insert the needle into the vial top. Inject the air from the syringe.<br>  **(4)** With the needle inside the vial, invert the vial.<br>  **(5)** Hold the syringe at eye level.<br>  **(6)** Aspirate the desired amount of medication into the syringe.<br>  **(7)** Displace any air bubbles in the syringe by gently tapping the barrel.<br>  **(8)** Remove the air by pushing the plunger slowly and forcing the air into the vial. | ❏ | ❏ | ❏ |
| **7.** Carefully recap the needle using one-hand technique. | ❏ | ❏ | ❏ |

_____

_____

_____

_____

_____

**CALCULATION**

Total Possible Points: _____

Total Points Earned: _____ Multiplied by 100 = _____ Divided by Total Possible Points = _____ %

**PASS**   **FAIL**   **COMMENTS:**
❏     ❏

Student's signature _____ Date _____

Partner's signature _____ Date _____

Instructor's signature _____ Date _____

## PSY PROCEDURE 9-3 Administer an Intradermal Injection

Name: _____ Date: _____ Time: _____ Grade: _____

**EQUIPMENT/SUPPLIES:** Physician's order, medication for injection in ampule or vial, antiseptic wipes, gloves, appropriate-size needle and syringe, small gauze pad, biohazard sharps container, patient's medical record

**STANDARDS:** Given the needed equipment and a place to work, the student will perform this skill with _____ % accuracy in a total of _____ minutes. *(Your instructor will tell you what the percentage and time limits will be before you begin.)*

**KEY:**          4 = Satisfactory          0 = Unsatisfactory          NA = This step is not counted

| PROCEDURE STEPS | SELF | PARTNER | INSTRUCTOR |
|---|---|---|---|
| **1.** Wash your hands.<br>   **a.** Review the physician's medication order and select the correct medication.<br>   **b.** Compare the label with the physician's instructions. Note the expiration date.<br>   **c.** Check the label three times: when taking it from the shelf, while drawing it up into the syringe, and when returning it to the shelf. | ❑ | ❑ | ❑ |
| **2.** Prepare the injection according to the steps in Procedure 9-2. | ❑ | ❑ | ❑ |
| **3.** Greet and identify the patient. Explain the procedure. | ❑ | ❑ | ❑ |
| **4.** Ask patient about medication allergies. | ❑ | ❑ | ❑ |
| **5.** Select the appropriate site for the injection. | ❑ | ❑ | ❑ |
| **6.** Prepare the site by cleansing with an antiseptic wipe. | ❑ | ❑ | ❑ |
| **7.** Put on gloves. Remove the needle guard. | ❑ | ❑ | ❑ |
| **8.** Using your nondominant hand, pull the patient's skin taut. | ❑ | ❑ | ❑ |
| **9.** With the bevel of the needle facing upward, insert needle at a 10- to 15-degree angle into the upper layer of the skin.<br>   **a.** When the bevel of the needle is under the skin, stop inserting the needle.<br>   **b.** The needle will be slightly visible below the surface of the skin.<br>   **c.** It is not necessary to aspirate when performing an intradermal injection. | ❑ | ❑ | ❑ |
| **10.** Inject the medication slowly by depressing the plunger.<br>   **a.** A wheal will form as the medication enters the dermal layer of the skin.<br>   **b.** Hold the syringe steady for proper administration. | ❑ | ❑ | ❑ |
| **11.** Remove the needle from the skin at the same angle at which it was inserted.<br>   **a.** Do not use an antiseptic wipe or gauze pad over the site.<br>   **b.** Do not press or massage the site. Do not apply an adhesive bandage. | ❑ | ❑ | ❑ |

| **PSY** PROCEDURE 9-3    **Administer an Intradermal Injection** (continued) | | | |
|---|:---:|:---:|:---:|
| **12.** Do not recap the needle. | ❏ | ❏ | ❏ |
| **13.** Dispose of the needle and syringe in an approved biohazard sharps container. | ❏ | ❏ | ❏ |
| **14.** **AFF** Explain how to respond to a patient with dementia. | ❏ | ❏ | ❏ |
| _____<br><br>_____<br><br>_____<br><br>_____ | | | |
| **15.** Remove your gloves, and wash your hands. | ❏ | ❏ | ❏ |
| **16.** Depending upon the type of skin test administered, the length of time required for the body tissues to react, and the policies of the medical office, perform one of the following:<br>**a.** Read the test results. Inspect and palpate the site for the presence and amount of induration.<br>**b.** Tell the patient when to return (date and time) to the office to have the results read.<br>**c.** Instruct the patient to read the results at home.<br>**d.** Make sure the patient understands the instructions. | ❏ | ❏ | ❏ |
| **17.** **AFF** Log into the Electronic Medical Record (EMR) using your username and secure password OR obtain the paper medical record from a secure location and assure it is kept away from public access. Record the procedure noting the date, time, name of medication, dose administered, route of administration, patient instructions, and your name. | ❏ | ❏ | ❏ |
| **18.** When finished, log out of the EMR and/or replace the paper medical record in an appropriate and secure location. | ❏ | ❏ | ❏ |

**CALCULATION**

Total Possible Points: _____

Total Points Earned: _____ Multiplied by 100 = _____ Divided by Total Possible Points = _____ %

**PASS**    **FAIL**    **COMMENTS:**
  ❏      ❏

Student's signature _____ Date _____

Partner's signature _____ Date _____

Instructor's signature _____ Date _____

## PROCEDURE 9-4    Administer a Subcutaneous Injection

**Name:** _____    **Date:** _____    **Time:** _____    **Grade:** _____

**EQUIPMENT/SUPPLIES:** Physician's order, medication for injection in ampule or vial, antiseptic wipes, gloves, appropriate-size needle and syringe, small gauze pad, biohazard sharps container, patient's medical record

**STANDARDS:** Given the needed equipment and a place to work, the student will perform this skill with _____ % accuracy in a total of _____ minutes. *(Your instructor will tell you what the percentage and time limits will be before you begin.)*

**KEY:**         4 = Satisfactory              0 = Unsatisfactory              NA = This step is not counted

| PROCEDURE STEPS | SELF | PARTNER | INSTRUCTOR |
|---|---|---|---|
| **1.** Wash your hands.<br>  **a.** Review the physician's medication order and select the correct medication.<br>  **b.** Compare the label with the physician's instructions. Note the expiration date.<br>  **c.** Check the label three times: when taking it from the shelf, while drawing it up into the syringe, and when returning it to the shelf. | ❏ | ❏ | ❏ |
| **2.** Prepare the injection according to the steps in Procedure 9-2. | ❏ | ❏ | ❏ |
| **3.** Greet and identify the patient. Explain the procedure. | ❏ | ❏ | ❏ |
| **4.** Ask the patient about medication allergies. | ❏ | ❏ | ❏ |
| **5.** Select the appropriate site for the injection. | ❏ | ❏ | ❏ |
| **6.** Prepare the site by cleansing with an antiseptic. | ❏ | ❏ | ❏ |
| **7.** Put on gloves. | ❏ | ❏ | ❏ |
| **8.** Using your nondominant hand, hold the skin surrounding the injection site. | ❏ | ❏ | ❏ |
| **9.** With a firm motion, insert the needle into the tissue at a 45-degree angle to the skin surface. | ❏ | ❏ | ❏ |
| **10.** Hold the barrel between the thumb and the index finger of your dominant hand. | ❏ | ❏ | ❏ |
| **11.** Insert the needle completely to the hub. | ❏ | ❏ | ❏ |
| **12.** Remove your nondominant hand from the skin. | ❏ | ❏ | ❏ |
| **13.** Holding the syringe steady, pull back on the syringe gently. If blood appears in the hub or the syringe, do not inject the medication; remove the needle and prepare a new injection. | ❏ | ❏ | ❏ |
| **14.** Inject the medication slowly by depressing the plunger. | ❏ | ❏ | ❏ |

**PSY** PROCEDURE 9-4 **Administer a Subcutaneous Injection**
(continued)

| | | | |
|---|---|---|---|
| **15.** Place a gauze pad over the injection site and remove the needle.<br>**a.** Gently massage the injection site with the gauze pad.<br>**b.** Do not recap the used needle; place it in the biohazard sharps container.<br>**c.** Apply an adhesive bandage if needed. | ❏ | ❏ | ❏ |
| **16.** Remove your gloves and wash your hands. | ❏ | ❏ | ❏ |
| **17.** **AFF** Explain how to respond to a patient who is deaf. | ❏ | ❏ | ❏ |
| **18.** An injection given for allergy desensitization requires:<br>**a.** Keeping the patient in the office for at least 30 minutes for observation.<br>**b.** Notifying the doctor of any reaction. (Be alert, anaphylaxis is possible.) | ❏ | ❏ | ❏ |
| **19.** **AFF** Log into the Electronic Medical Record (EMR) using your username and secure password OR obtain the paper medical record from a secure location and assure it is kept away from public access. Record the procedure noting the date, time, name of medication, dose administered, route of administration, and your name. | ❏ | ❏ | ❏ |
| **20.** When finished, log out of the EMR and/or replace the paper medical record in an appropriate and secure location. | ❏ | ❏ | ❏ |

**CALCULATION**

Total Possible Points: _____

Total Points Earned: _____ Multiplied by 100 = _____ Divided by Total Possible Points = _____ %

**PASS   FAIL   COMMENTS:**
  ❏       ❏

Student's signature _____ Date _____

Partner's signature _____ Date _____

Instructor's signature _____ Date _____

## PROCEDURE 9-5   Administer an Intramuscular Injection

**PSY**

Name: _____ Date: _____ Time: _____ Grade: _____

**EQUIPMENT/SUPPLIES:** Physician's order, medication for injection in ampule or vial, antiseptic wipes, gloves, appropriate-size needle and syringe, small gauze pad, biohazard sharps container, patient's medical record

**STANDARDS:** Given the needed equipment and a place to work, the student will perform this skill with _____ % accuracy in a total of _____ minutes. *(Your instructor will tell you what the percentage and time limits will be before you begin.)*

**KEY:**          4 = Satisfactory          0 = Unsatisfactory          NA =This step is not counted

| PROCEDURE STEPS | SELF | PARTNER | INSTRUCTOR |
|---|---|---|---|
| **1.** Wash your hands.<br> **a.** Review the physician's order and select the correct medication.<br> **b.** Compare the label with the physician's instructions. Note the expiration date.<br> **c.** Check the label three times: when taking it from the shelf, while drawing it up into the syringe, and when returning to the shelf. | ❏ | ❏ | ❏ |
| **2.** Prepare the injection according to the steps in Procedure 9-2. | ❏ | ❏ | ❏ |
| **3.** Greet and identify the patient. Explain the procedure. | ❏ | ❏ | ❏ |
| **4.** Ask the patient about medication allergies. | ❏ | ❏ | ❏ |
| **5.** Select the appropriate site for the injection. | ❏ | ❏ | ❏ |
| **6.** Prepare the site by cleansing with an antiseptic wipe. | ❏ | ❏ | ❏ |
| **7.** Put on gloves. | ❏ | ❏ | ❏ |
| **8.** Using your nondominant hand, hold the skin surrounding the injection site. | ❏ | ❏ | ❏ |
| **9.** While holding the syringe like a dart, use a quick, firm motion to insert the needle at a 90-degree angle to the skin surface. Hold the barrel between the thumb and the index finger of the dominant hand and insert the needle completely to the hub. | ❏ | ❏ | ❏ |
| **10.** Holding the syringe steady, pull back on the syringe gently. If blood appears in the hub or the syringe, do not inject the medication; remove the needle and prepare a new injection. | ❏ | ❏ | ❏ |
| **11.** Inject the medication slowly by depressing the plunger. | ❏ | ❏ | ❏ |
| **12.** Place a gauze pad over the injection site and remove the needle.<br> **a.** Gently massage the injection site with the gauze pad.<br> **b.** Do not recap the used needle. Place in biohazard sharps container.<br> **c.** Apply an adhesive bandage if needed. | ❏ | ❏ | ❏ |
| **13.** **AFF** Explain how to respond to a patient who is visually impaired. | ❏ | ❏ | ❏ |

**PSY** PROCEDURE 9-5 **Administer an Intramuscular Injection**
(continued)

| | | | |
|---|---|---|---|
| | | | |
| | | | |
| | | | |
| | | | |
| | | | |
| **14.** Remove your gloves, and wash your hands. | ❏ | ❏ | ❏ |
| **15.** Notify the doctor of any reaction. (Be alert, anaphylaxis is possible.) | ❏ | ❏ | ❏ |
| **16.** **AFF** Log into the Electronic Medical Record (EMR) using your username and secure password OR obtain the paper medical record from a secure location and assure it is kept away from public access. Record the procedure noting the date, time, name of medication, dose administered, route of administration, and your name. | ❏ | ❏ | ❏ |
| **17.** When finished, log out of the EMR and/or replace the paper medical record in an appropriate and secure location. | ❏ | ❏ | ❏ |

**CALCULATION**

Total Possible Points: _____

Total Points Earned: _____ Multiplied by 100 = _____ Divided by Total Possible Points = _____ %

**PASS   FAIL   COMMENTS:**
❏        ❏

Student's signature _____ Date _____

Partner's signature _____ Date _____

Instructor's signature _____ Date _____

**PSY** PROCEDURE 9-6  **Administer an Intramuscular Injection Using the Z-Track Method**

Name: _____  Date: _____  Time: _____  Grade: _____

**EQUIPMENT/SUPPLIES:** Physician's order, medication for injection in ampule or vial, antiseptic wipes, gloves, appropriate-size needle and syringe, small gauze pad, biohazard sharps container, patient's medical record

**STANDARDS:** Given the needed equipment and a place to work, the student will perform this skill with _____ % accuracy in a total of _____ minutes. *(Your instructor will tell you what the percentage and time limits will be before you begin.)*

**KEY:**    4 = Satisfactory    0 = Unsatisfactory    NA = This step is not counted

| PROCEDURE STEPS | SELF | PARTNER | INSTRUCTOR |
|---|---|---|---|
| **1.** Follow steps 1 through 7 as described in Procedure 9-5. | ❏ | ❏ | ❏ |
| **2.** Pull the top layer of skin to the side and hold it with your non-dominant hand throughout the injection. | ❏ | ❏ | ❏ |
| **3.** While holding the syringe like a dart, use a quick, firm motion to insert the needle at a 90-degree angle to the skin surface. **a.** Hold the barrel between the thumb and index finger of the dominant hand. **b.** Insert the needle completely to the hub. | ❏ | ❏ | ❏ |
| **4.** Aspirate by withdrawing the plunger slightly. **a.** If no blood appears, push the plunger in slowly and steadily. **b.** Count to 10 before withdrawing the needle. | ❏ | ❏ | ❏ |
| **5.** Place a gauze pad over the injection site and remove the needle. **a.** Gently massage the injection site with the gauze pad. **b.** Do not recap the used needle. Place in the biohazard sharps container. **c.** Apply an adhesive bandage if needed. | ❏ | ❏ | ❏ |
| **6.** Remove your gloves, and wash your hands. | ❏ | ❏ | ❏ |
| **7.** Notify the doctor of any reaction. (Be alert, anaphylaxis is possible.) | ❏ | ❏ | ❏ |
| **8.** **AFF** Log into the Electronic Medical Record (EMR) using your username and secure password OR obtain the paper medical record from a secure location and assure it is kept away from public access. Record the procedure noting the date, time, name of medication, dose administered, route of administration, and your name. If instructions were given to the patient, document these also. | ❏ | ❏ | ❏ |
| **9.** When finished, log out of the EMR and/or replace the paper medical record in an appropriate and secure location. | ❏ | ❏ | ❏ |

**PSY** PROCEDURE 9-6 **Administer an Intramuscular Injection Using the Z-Track Method** (continued)

**CALCULATION**

Total Possible Points: _____

Total Points Earned: _____ Multiplied by 100 = _____ Divided by Total Possible Points = _____ %

**PASS    FAIL    COMMENTS:**
  ❏        ❏

Student's signature _____ Date _____

Partner's signature _____ Date _____

Instructor's signature _____ Date _____

## PROCEDURE 9-7   **Apply Transdermal Medications**

Name: _____   Date: _____   Time: _____   Grade: _____

**EQUIPMENT/SUPPLIES:** Physician's order, medication, gloves, patient's medical record

**STANDARDS:** Given the needed equipment and a place to work, the student will perform this skill with _____ % accuracy in a total of _____ minutes. *(Your instructor will tell you what the percentage and time limits will be before you begin.)*

**KEY:**          4 = Satisfactory          0 = Unsatisfactory          NA = This step is not counted

| PROCEDURE STEPS | SELF | PARTNER | INSTRUCTOR |
|---|---|---|---|
| **1.** Wash your hands. | ❏ | ❏ | ❏ |
| **2.** Review the physician's medication order and select the correct medication. <br> **a.** Compare the label with the physician's instructions. Note the expiration date. <br> **b.** Check the label three times: when taking it from the shelf, before taking it into the patient exam room, and before applying it to the patient's skin. | ❏ | ❏ | ❏ |
| **3.** Greet and identify the patient. Explain the procedure. | ❏ | ❏ | ❏ |
| **4.** Ask the patient about medication allergies that might not be noted on the medical record. | ❏ | ❏ | ❏ |
| **5.** Select the appropriate site and perform any necessary skin preparation. The sites are usually the upper arm, the chest or back surface, or behind the ear. <br> **a.** Ensure that the skin is clean, dry, and free from any irritation. <br> **b.** Do not shave areas with excessive hair; trim the hair closely with scissors. | ❏ | ❏ | ❏ |
| **6.** If there is a transdermal patch already in place, remove it carefully while wearing gloves. Discard the patch in the trash container. Inspect the site for irritation. | ❏ | ❏ | ❏ |
| **7.** Open the medication package by pulling the two sides apart. Do not touch the area of medication. | ❏ | ❏ | ❏ |
| **8.** Apply the medicated patch to the patient's skin, following the manufacturer's directions. <br> **a.** Press the adhesive edges down firmly all around, starting at the center and pressing outward. <br> **b.** If the edges do not stick, fasten with tape. | ❏ | ❏ | ❏ |
| **9.** **AFF** Explain how to respond to a patient who is uncomfortable exposing skin on areas such as the chest or arms due to cultural or religious beliefs. | ❏ | ❏ | ❏ |

**PSY** PROCEDURE 9-7 **Apply Transdermal Medications** (continued)

| | | | |
|---|---|---|---|
| | | | |

| | | | |
|---|---|---|---|
| **10.** Wash your hands. | ❏ | ❏ | ❏ |
| **11.** **AFF** Log into the Electronic Medical Record (EMR) using your username and secure password OR obtain the paper medical record from a secure location and assure it is kept away from public access. Record the procedure noting the date, time, name of medication, dose administered, route of administration, site of the new patch, and your name. | ❏ | ❏ | ❏ |
| **12.** When finished, log out of the EMR and/or replace the paper medical record in an appropriate and secure location. | ❏ | ❏ | ❏ |

**CALCULATION**

Total Possible Points: _____

Total Points Earned: _____ Multiplied by 100 = _____ Divided by Total Possible Points = _____ %

**PASS   FAIL   COMMENTS:**
  ❏        ❏

Student's signature _____ Date _____

Partner's signature _____ Date _____

Instructor's signature _____ Date _____

## FSY PROCEDURE 9-8 Complete an Incident Report Related to an Error in Patient Care

Name: _____ Date: _____ Time: _____ Grade: _____

**EQUIPMENT/SUPPLIES:** An incident form

**STANDARDS:** Given the needed equipment and a place to work, the student will perform this skill with _____ % accuracy in a total of _____ minutes. *(Your instructor will tell you what the percentage and time limits will be before you begin.)*

**KEY:** 4 = Satisfactory 0 = Unsatisfactory NA =This step is not counted

| PROCEDURE STEPS | SELF | PARTNER | INSTRUCTOR |
|---|---|---|---|
| **1.** Recognize the error in patient care (i.e., medication administration) and notify the physician immediately after assessing the patient and providing emergency procedures if appropriate. | ❏ | ❏ | ❏ |
| **2.** Once the patient is assessed and necessary interventions taken as per physician instructions, complete an incident report form. | ❏ | ❏ | ❏ |
| **3.** Sign and date the incident report form and file with the office or practice manager. | ❏ | ❏ | ❏ |
| **4.** ■AFF■ Advise the patient on any follow-up procedures as instructed by the physician. | ❏ | ❏ | ❏ |

**CALCULATION**

Total Possible Points: _____

Total Points Earned: _____ Multiplied by 100 = _____ Divided by Total Possible Points = _____ %

**PASS FAIL COMMENTS:**
❏ ❏

Student's signature _____ Date _____

Partner's signature _____ Date _____

Instructor's signature _____ Date _____

## Great Falls Medical Center Physician Offices
## Employee Incident/Injury Report Form

| | |
|---|---|
| Employee Name: | Title: |
| Location: | Date and Time of Injury/Illness: |
| Person or Employee the Injury/Illness Reported to: | Title of Person or Employee Injury or Illness Reported to: |

Describe the details of your accident, injury, or illness. Be as specific as possible:




Explain what you were doing at the time of your accident, injury, or illness:




For injuries, list the part or parts of your body that were injured. Be specific (i.e., right index finger, left ankle, etc...):


If there was a delay in reporting the injury or illness, explain the reason for this delay:


Names and Titles of Any Witnesses to your Injury or Illness:


| | |
|---|---|
| Employee Signature: | Date: |

# CHAPTER

# *10* Diagnostic Imaging

## Learning Outcomes

### COG Cognitive Domain

1. Spell and define the key terms
2. Explain the theory and function of x-rays and x-ray machines
3. State the principles of radiology
4. Describe routine and contrast media, fluoroscopy, computed tomography, sonography, magnetic resonance imaging, nuclear medicine, and mammographic examinations
5. Explain the role of the medical assistant in radiologic procedures
6. Describe body planes, directional terms, quadrants, and cavities
7. Identify critical information required for scheduling patient procedures

### PSY Psychomotor Domain

1. Assist with x-ray procedures (Procedure 10-1)

### AFF Affective Domain

1. Incorporate critical thinking skills when performing patient care
2. Show awareness of a patient's concerns related to the procedure being performed
3. Demonstrate respect for individual diversity including gender, race, religion, age, economic status, appearance
4. Explain to a patient the rationale for performance of a procedure
5. Demonstrate empathy, active listening, nonverbal communication

6. Protect the integrity of the medical record

### ABHES Competencies

1. Assist the physician with the regimen of diagnostic and treatment modalities as they relate to each body system
2. Comply with federal, state, and local health laws and regulations
3. Communicate on the recipient's level of comprehension
4. Serve as a liaison between the physician and others
5. Show empathy and impartiality when dealing with patients

Name: _____     Date: _____     Grade: _____

## COG MULTIPLE CHOICE

Circle the letter preceding the correct answer.

1. Which term below means lying face downward?
   a. Supine
   b. Prone
   c. Decubitus
   d. Recumbent
   e. Relaxed

2. Which of the following is a form of nuclear medicine?
   a. Radiopaque
   b. Barium
   c. Iodine
   d. Radionuclides
   e. Radiolucent

3. Noises heard during an x-ray exposure may come from:
   a. the x-ray tube.
   b. x-rays.
   c. the positioning aid.
   d. high voltage.
   e. the sheet of film.

4. Which of the following is an example of radiopaque tissue?
   a. Lungs
   b. Bone
   c. Muscle
   d. Fat
   e. Veins

5. A minimum of two x-rays should be taken at:
   a. 180 degrees of each other.
   b. 30 degrees of each other.
   c. 70 degrees of each other.
   d. 90 degrees of each other.
   e. 50 degrees of each other.

6. A type of radiography that creates cross-sectional images of the body is:
   a. fluoroscopy.
   b. echogram.
   c. computerized tomography.
   d. ultrasound.
   e. mammography.

7. Which of the following form of radiography does not use x-rays?
   a. MRI
   b. Nuclear medicine
   c. Fluoroscopy
   d. Teleradiology
   e. Tomography

8. Which procedure creates an image that depends on the chemical makeup of the body?
   a. Tomography
   b. Fluoroscopy
   c. MRI
   d. Mammography
   e. Nuclear medicine

9. Sonograms create images using:
   a. radioactive material.
   b. contrast media.
   c. magnetic resonance.
   d. chemotherapy.
   e. sound waves.

10. X-rays can be harmful to infants and young children because:
    a. their immune systems are not fully developed.
    b. their cells divide at a rapid pace.
    c. they have less muscle mass than adults.
    d. they have a smaller body mass.
    e. they have less body fat than adults.

11. Which of the following procedures may be done in a confined space?
    a. MRI
    b. Nuclear medicine
    c. Fluoroscopy
    d. Teleradiology
    e. Tomography

12. A physician who specializes in interpreting the images on the processed film is a(n):
    a. pulmonologist.
    b. internist.
    c. immunologist.
    d. ophthalmologist.
    e. radiologist.

*Scenario for questions 13 and 14:* A patient has come in for an x-ray. The physician wants you to get a clear image of the patient's liver.

13. What is another possible way to view the patient's liver without injections?
    a. Mammography
    b. Sonography
    c. Fluoroscopy
    d. Teleradiology
    e. Tomography

14. Which position would allow the best images of the liver?
    a. Supine
    b. Decubitus
    c. Posterior
    d. Left anterior oblique
    e. Right anterior oblique

15. Who owns the x-ray film after it has been developed?
    a. The patient
    b. The physician who ordered the x-rays
    c. The physician who will use the x-rays
    d. The lab that developed the film
    e. The site where the film was taken and developed.

16. You should wear a dosimeter to:
    a. lower the level of radiation.
    b. protect against radiation effects.
    c. monitor personal radiation exposure.
    d. enhance radiography images.
    e. collect data on different procedures.

17. Why do some tests require patients to be NPO before an administration of barium PO?
    a. Gastric juices may interfere with the readings.
    b. A full stomach may distort or alter an image.
    c. Patients are not allowed to relieve themselves.
    d. Undigested food might counteract contrast media.
    e. Instruments might become soiled during the procedure.

18. Images that partially block x-rays are called:
    a. radiographs.
    b. radiolucent.
    c. radiopaque.
    d. radionuclides.
    e. radiograms.

19. Why is radiology used as a form of cancer treatment?
    a. X-rays show the exact location of cancer.
    b. Radioactive cells produce more white blood cells.
    c. Radiation can destroy or weaken cancer cells.
    d. Radiation makes cancerous tumors benign.
    e. Chemotherapy is not as effective as radiation.

20. When explaining procedures to patients:
    a. let the physician go into detail.
    b. answer all the questions they ask.
    c. do not worry them with potential risk.
    d. soothe their fears without telling them anything.
    e. allow only the nurse to explain the procedure.

## OOG MATCHING

Grade: _____

Match each key term with its definition.

**Key Terms**

21. _____ cassette
22. _____ contrast medium
23. _____ film
24. _____ fluoroscopy
25. _____ magnetic resonance imaging
26. _____ nuclear medicine
27. _____ radiograph
28. _____ radiography
29. _____ radiologist
30. _____ radiology
31. _____ radiolucent
32. _____ radionuclide
33. _____ radiopaque
34. _____ teleradiology
35. _____ tomography
36. _____ ultrasound
37. _____ x-rays

**Definitions**

a. invisible electromagnetic radiation waves used in diagnosis and treatment of various disorders
b. a lightproof holder in which film is exposed
c. imaging technique that uses a strong magnetic field
d. a radioactive material with a short life that is used in small amounts in nuclear medicine studies
e. physician who interprets images to provide diagnostic information
f. imaging technique that uses sound waves to diagnose or monitor various body structures
g. not permeable to passage of x-rays
h. processed film that contains a visible image
i. a substance ingested or injected into the body to facilitate imaging of internal structures
j. the use of computed imaging and information systems to transmit diagnostic images to distant locations
k. a procedure in which the x-ray tube and film move in relation to each other during exposure, blurring out all structures except those in the focal plane

**Key Terms**

**Definitions**

**l.** a raw material on which x-rays are projected through the body; prior to processing, this does not contain a visible image

**m.** permitting the passage of x-rays

**n.** a special x-ray technique for examining a body part by immediate projection onto a fluorescent screen

**o.** the branch of medicine involving diagnostic and therapeutic applications of x-rays

**p.** a branch of medicine that uses radioactive isotopes to diagnose and treat disease

**q.** the art and science of producing diagnostic images with x-rays

## OOG MATCHING

Grade: _____

Match the different types of radiography techniques with their individual characteristics.

**Techniques**

**38.** _____ Fluoroscopy
**39.** _____ Tomography
**40.** _____ Mammography
**41.** _____ Ultrasound
**42.** _____ Magnetic resonance imaging
**43.** _____ Radiation therapy

**Characteristics**

**a.** the image depends on the chemical makeup of the body, commonly used in prenatal testing

**b.** can create three-dimensional images, so that organs can be viewed from all angles

**c.** the area of the body exposed must be defined exactly so that each treatment is identical

**d.** used as an aid to other types of treatment, such as reducing fractures and implanting devices such as pacemakers

**e.** a vital adjunct to biopsy

**f.** designed to concentrate on specific areas of the body

## OOG SHORT ANSWER

Grade: _____

**44.** List the four processes by which radiographic film is produced.

_____

_____

_____

_____

**45.** List five radiation safety procedures for patients.

_____

_____

_____

_____

**46.** Fill in the full names for the abbreviations below.

**a.** PET _____

**b.** SPECT _____

**c.** ALARA _____

**47.** Name two contrast mediums.

_____

_____

_____

_____

**48.** What are the three ways contrast media may be introduced into the body?

_____

_____

_____

_____

**49.** Name four types of interventional radiological procedures.

_____

_____

_____

_____

_____

**50.** List five side effects of radiation therapy.

_____

_____

_____

_____

_____

**51.** What is the difference between radiolucent and radiopaque tissues? How do these tissues appear differently on a radiograph? Give an example of each.

_____

_____

_____

_____

**52.** Why do x-ray examinations require a minimum of two exposures?

_____

_____

_____

_____

**53.** Why is it imperative to have an esophagogastroduodenoscopy done before other barium studies?

_____

_____

_____

**54.** Compare and contrast fluoroscopy with tomography. How do these procedures use movement?

_____

_____

_____

_____

**55.** You have a patient who will have a radiographic exam using contrast media next week. You find out this patient has an allergy to shellfish. What should you do?

_____

_____

_____

_____

## COG TRUE OR FALSE?

Grade: _____

Indicate whether the statements are true or false by placing the letter T (true) or F (false) on the line preceding the statement.

**56.** _____ A patient may hear noises during an x-ray procedure.

**57.** _____ A mammogram is a minimally invasive procedure.

**58.** _____ You need to be proficient in the operation of your facility's equipment.

**59.** _____ The best way to explain procedures to a patient is with lots of detail.

## COG AFF CASE STUDIES FOR CRITICAL THINKING

Grade: _____

**1.** Mrs. Kay has had several radiographic and contrast media studies over the past 5 years. She is now moving to another state and wants to know how to get copies of the films and reports to her new physician. What will you tell her about transferring these records?

_____

_____

_____

_____

**2.** You have a patient with a fear of enclosed spaces who is not able to have an open MRI at your outpatient radiographic center. How would you console this patient and explain x-ray procedures?

_____

_____

_____

**3.** You have a patient coming in for radiation therapy who has been experiencing side effects such as weight loss, loss of appetite, and hair loss. She has concerns about the radiation therapy that she has been receiving and feels that it may be too much for her body. What would you say to her to help her better understand the situation?

_____

_____

_____

_____

**4.** You have a patient who has had radiographs taken with a referring physician. This patient has already spoken to his referral physician about the finding in his x-rays and would now like to consult with his primary care physician. However, the referring physician has not yet sent a summary of findings. Your patient is very anxious. What should you say?

_____

_____

_____

_____

## PROCEDURE 10-1  Assist with x-Ray Procedures

**PSY**

Name: _____  Date: _____  Time: _____  Grade: _____

**EQUIPMENT/SUPPLIES:** Patient gown and drape

**STANDARDS:** Given the needed equipment and a place to work, the student will perform this skill with _____ % accuracy in a total of _____ minutes. *(Your instructor will tell you what the percentage and time limits will be before you begin.)*

**KEY:**   4 = Satisfactory   0 = Unsatisfactory   NA = This step is not counted

| PROCEDURE STEPS | SELF | PARTNER | INSTRUCTOR |
|---|---|---|---|
| **1.** Wash your hands. | ❏ | ❏ | ❏ |
| **2.** Greet the patient by name, introduce yourself, and escort him or her to the room where the x-ray equipment is maintained. | ❏ | ❏ | ❏ |
| **3.** Ask female patients about the possibility of pregnancy. If the patient is unsure or indicates pregnancy in any trimester, consult with the physician before proceeding with the x-ray procedure. | ❏ | ❏ | ❏ |
| **4.** **AFF** Explain how to respond to a patient who speaks English as a second language. | ❏ | ❏ | ❏ |
| _____ <br> _____ <br> _____ <br> _____ | | | |
| **5.** After explaining what clothing should be removed, if any, give the patient a gown and privacy. | ❏ | ❏ | ❏ |
| **6.** Notify the x-ray technician or physician that the patient is ready for the x-ray procedure. Stay behind the lead-lined wall during the x-ray procedure to avoid exposure to x-rays during the procedure. | ❏ | ❏ | ❏ |
| **7.** After the x-ray, ask the patient to remain in the room until the film has been developed and checked for accuracy and readability. | ❏ | ❏ | ❏ |
| **8.** Once you have determined that the exposed film is adequate for the physician to view for diagnosis, have the patient get dressed and escort him or her to the front desk. | ❏ | ❏ | ❏ |

| PSY   PROCEDURE  10-1    **Assist with x-Ray Procedures** (continued) | | | |
|---|---|---|---|
| 9. **AFF** Log into the Electronic Medical Record (EMR) using your username and secure password OR obtain the paper medical record from a secure location and assure it is kept away from public access. | ❑ | ❑ | ❑ |
| 10. When finished, log out of the EMR and/or replace the paper medical record in an appropriate and secure location. | ❑ | ❑ | ❑ |

**CALCULATION**

Total Possible Points: _____

Total Points Earned: _____ Multiplied by 100 = _____ Divided by Total Possible Points = _____ %

**PASS    FAIL    COMMENTS:**
  ❑          ❑

Student's signature _____ Date _____

Partner's signature _____ Date _____

Instructor's signature _____ Date _____

# CHAPTER

# *11* Medical Office Emergencies

---

## Learning Outcomes

### **COG** Cognitive Domain

1. Spell and define key terms
2. List principles and steps of professional/provider CPR
3. Describe basic principles of first aid as they pertain to the ambulatory health care setting.
4. Identify the five types of shock and the management of each
5. Describe how burns are classified and managed
6. Explain the management of allergic reactions
7. Describe the management of poisoning and the role of the poison control center
8. List the three types of hyperthermic emergencies and the treatment for each type
9. Discuss the treatment of hypothermia
10. Describe the role of the medical assistant in managing psychiatric emergencies

### **PSY** Psychomotor Domain

1. Administer oxygen (Procedure 11-1)
2. Perform cardiopulmonary resuscitation (Procedure 11-2)
3. Use an automatic external defibrillator (Procedure 11-3)
4. Manage a foreign body airway obstruction (Procedure 11-4)
5. Control bleeding (Procedure 11-5)
6. Respond to medical emergencies other than bleeding, cardiac/respiratory arrest, or foreign body airway obstruction (Procedure 11-6)
7. Document patient care accurately in the medical record

### **AFF** Affective Domain

1. Incorporate critical thinking skills in performing patient assessment
2. Incorporate critical thinking skills in performing patient care
3. Show awareness of patients' concerns related to the procedure being performed
4. Demonstrate empathy, active listening, nonverbal communication

5. Demonstrate respect for individual diversity including gender, race, religion, age, economic status, and appearance
6. Explain to a patient the rationale for performance of a procedure
7. Protect the integrity of the medical record
8. Demonstrate self-awareness in responding to an emergency situation

### ABHES Competencies

1. Document accurately
2. Recognize and respond to verbal and nonverbal communication
3. Adapt to individualized needs
4. Apply principles of aseptic techniques and infection control
5. Recognize emergencies and treatments and minor office surgical procedures
6. Use standard precautions
7. Perform first aid and CPR
8. Demonstrate professionalism by exhibiting a positive attitude and sense of responsibility

Name: _____    Date: _____    Grade: _____

## ⬡⬡⬡ MULTIPLE CHOICE

Circle the letter preceding the correct answer.

1. During a primary assessment, you should check:
   a. AVPU.
   b. pupils.
   c. responsiveness.
   d. vital signs.
   e. patient identification.

2. What signs and symptoms are consistent with heat stroke?
   a. Cyanotic skin
   b. Pale wet skin
   c. Ecchymosis
   d. Dry, flushed skin
   e. Waxy, gray skin

3. Superficial burns are categorized as:
   a. first degree.
   b. second degree.
   c. third degree.
   d. partial thickness.
   e. full thickness.

4. Which is an example of a closed wound?
   a. Abrasion
   b. Avulsion
   c. Contusion
   d. Laceration
   e. Ecchymosis

5. What is the BSA of the anterior portion of an adult's trunk?
   a. 1%
   b. 9%
   c. 13.5%
   d. 18%
   e. 36%

6. A patient with pneumonia is at risk for:
   a. hypothermia.
   b. hypovolemic shock.
   c. septic shock.
   d. seizures.
   e. hyperthermia.

7. The first step to take when discovering an unresponsive patient is to:
   a. begin CPR.
   b. check circulation.
   c. establish an airway.
   d. go find help.
   e. identify the patient.

8. During a physical examination of an emergency patient's abdomen, check for:
   a. cerebral fluid.
   b. distal pulses.
   c. paradoxical movement.
   d. tenderness, rigidity, and distension.
   e. lethargy and slow movements.

9. A potential complication from a splint could be:
   a. compartment syndrome.
   b. dislocation.
   c. hematoma.
   d. injury from sharp bone fragments.
   e. tissue ischemia and infarction.

10. Circulation after splinting can be tested using:
    a. blood pressure.
    b. brachial pulse.
    c. carotid pulse.
    d. distal pulse.
    e. femoral pulse.

*Scenario for questions 11 and 12:* A patient complains about tightness in the chest, a feeling of warmth, and itching. After a minute, the patient's breathing is labored.

11. You are most likely watching the early warning signs of:
    a. an allergic reaction.
    b. cardiogenic shock.
    c. a myocardial infarction.
    d. poisoning.
    e. ecchymosis.

12. What action is contraindicated should this patient go into shock?
    a. Cardiac monitoring
    b. Epinephrine (1:1,000)
    c. Establishing an IV line
    d. Intubation
    e. Providing high-flow oxygen

13. If a patient is having a seizure, you should:
    a. force something into the patient's mouth to protect the tongue.
    b. maintain spine immobilization.
    c. protect the patient from injury.
    d. restrain the patient.
    e. assist patient to supine position.

14. What is the difference between an emotional crisis and a psychiatric emergency?
    **a.** A psychiatric emergency results from substance abuse.
    **b.** A patient in a psychiatric emergency poses a physical threat to himself or others.
    **c.** An emotional crisis is a case of bipolar disorder.
    **d.** A psychiatric emergency involves a patient diagnosed with a psychiatric disorder.
    **e.** An emotional crisis does not include delusions.

15. A patient suffering hypothermia should be given:
    **a.** alcohol to promote circulation.
    **b.** hot chocolate to provide sugar.
    **c.** IV fluids for rehydration.
    **d.** warm coffee to raise his or her level of consciousness.
    **e.** dry heat to warm the surface.

16. What agency should be contacted first when a patient is exposed to a toxic substance?
    **a.** AMAA
    **b.** EMS
    **c.** MSDS
    **d.** Centers for Disease Control
    **e.** Poison Control Center

17. Which form of shock is an acute allergic reaction?
    **a.** Neurogenic shock
    **b.** Anaphylactic shock
    **c.** Cardiogenic shock
    **d.** Septic shock
    **e.** Hypovolemic shock

18. What does the "V" in AVPU stand for?
    **a.** Vocalization
    **b.** Vital signs
    **c.** Viscosity
    **d.** Voice recognition
    **e.** Verbal response

19. To manage open soft tissue injuries, you should:
    **a.** leave them open to the air.
    **b.** wrap loosely in bandages.
    **c.** immediately stitch closed.
    **d.** elevate the wound.
    **e.** apply direct pressure.

20. Which of the following items should be included in an emergency kit?
    **a.** Alcohol wipes
    **b.** Syringe
    **c.** Penicillin
    **d.** Oscilloscope
    **e.** Sample containers

## **COG MATCHING**

Grade: _____

Match each key term with its definition.

**Key Terms**

21. _____ allergen
22. _____ anaphylactic shock
23. _____ cardiogenic shock
24. _____ contusion
25. _____ ecchymosis
26. _____ full-thickness burn
27. _____ heat cramps
28. _____ heat stroke
29. _____ hematoma
30. _____ hyperthermia
31. _____ hypothermia
32. _____ hypovolemic shock
33. _____ infarction
34. _____ ischemia
35. _____ melena
36. _____ neurogenic shock
37. _____ partial-thickness burn
38. _____ seizure
39. _____ septic shock

**Definitions**

**a.** an abnormal discharge of electrical activity in the brain, resulting in erratic muscle movements, strange sensations, or a complete loss of consciousness
**b.** black, tarry stools caused by digested blood from the gastrointestinal tract
**c.** severe allergic reaction within minutes to hours after exposure to a foreign substance
**d.** an emergency where the body cannot compensate for elevated temperatures
**e.** a bruise or collection of blood under the skin or in damaged tissue
**f.** a burn limited to the epidermis
**g.** any device used to immobilize a sprain, strain, fracture, or dislocated limb
**h.** shock that results from dysfunction of the nervous system following a spinal cord injury
**i.** muscle cramping that follows a period of physical exertion and profuse sweating in a hot environment
**j.** a penetrating burn that has destroyed all skin layers
**k.** a characteristic black and blue mark from blood accumulation
**l.** below-normal body temperature
**m.** the general condition of excessive body heat
**n.** a blood clot that forms at an injury site
**o.** a burn that involves epidermis and varying levels of the dermis

**Key Terms**

40. _____ shock
41. _____ splint
42. _____ superficial burn

**Definitions**

p. a decrease in oxygen to tissue

q. a substance that causes manifestations of an allergy

r. shock that results from general infection in the bloodstream

s. shock caused by loss of blood or other body fluids

t. death of tissue due to lack of oxygen

u. condition resulting from the lack of oxygen to individual cells of the body

v. type of shock in which the left ventricle fails to pump enough blood for the body to function

## COG IDENTIFICATION

Grade: _____

43. As a medical assistant, you may be called on to assist during an emergency. Review the list of tasks below and determine which tasks you may be responsible for as a medical assistant. Place a check mark in the "Yes" column for those duties you might assist with as a medical assistant and place a check mark in the "No" column for those tasks that not be the responsibility of the medical assistant.

| Task | Yes | No |
|---|---|---|
| **a.** Obtain important patient information. | | |
| **b.** Perform CPR. | | |
| **c.** Set and splint bone fractures. | | |
| **d.** Remove foreign body airway obstructions. | | |
| **e.** Remain calm and react competently and professionally during a psychiatric crisis. | | |
| **f.** Coordinate multiple ongoing events while rendering patient care in a cardiac emergency. | | |
| **g.** Negotiate with or attempt to calm a violent patient during a psychiatric crisis. | | |
| **h.** Know what emergency system is used in the community. | | |
| **i.** Provide immediate care to the patient while the physician is notified. | | |
| **j.** Perform rapid sequence intubation (RSI) on a patient who is suffering respiratory failure. | | |
| **k.** Administer first aid. | | |
| **l.** Document all actions taken. | | |
| **m.** Complete routine scheduled tasks. | | |
| **n.** Assist EMS personnel as necessary. | | |
| **o.** Examine the patient for EMS personnel. | | |
| **p.** Direct care of the patient for EMS personnel. | | |
| **q.** Remove any obstacles that prevent speedy evacuation of the patient by stretcher. | | |
| **r.** Direct family members to the reception area or a private room. | | |

44. Identify the type of shock described in the following scenarios.

    **a.** A very ill patient has been complaining of increasing pain in the pelvis and legs. Blood is present in the urine. The patient's temperature was elevated but is dropping.

    _____

    **b.** An elderly patient falls on her back while attempting to get out of bed. Her heart rate becomes rapid and thready, and her blood pressure drops quickly.

    _____

    **c.** A patient presents with fluid in the lungs, difficulty breathing, and chest pain.

    _____

    **d.** A patient presents with labored breathing, grunting, wheezing, and swelling followed by fainting.

    _____

    **e.** A child is brought in for diarrhea. She has poor skin turgor and capillary refill. Her mental status appears to be deteriorating.

    _____

45. Put a check mark on the line next to the correct signs and symptoms of shock.

    **a.** _____ low blood pressure

    **b.** _____ high blood pressure

    **c.** _____ calm or lethargic

    **d.** _____ restlessness or signs of fear

    **e.** _____ thirst

    **f.** _____ polyuria

    **g.** _____ hunger

    **h.** _____ nausea

    **i.** _____ hot, sweaty skin

    **j.** _____ cool, clammy skin

    **k.** _____ pale skin with cyanosis (bluish color) at the lips and earlobes

    **l.** _____ flushed skin

    **m.** _____ rapid and weak pulse

    **n.** _____ bounding pulse

**46.** Classify the type, severity, and coverage of the burns in each of these scenarios.

**a.** A contractor installing medical equipment accidentally touches exposed wires. He has burns on his right arm, but no sensation of pain.

- Type:

_____

- Severity:

_____

- Coverage:

_____

**b.** A child spills bleach on one leg. The leg is blistering and causing severe pain.

- Type:

_____

- Severity:

_____

- Coverage:

_____

**c.** A man watches a welder installs handrails on your office's handicapped ramp. Now his face is red and painful, and his eyes have a painful itching sensation.

- Type:

_____

- Severity:

_____

- Coverage:

_____

**d.** A patient spills hot coffee while driving to your office, painfully blistering his genital area.

- Type:

_____

- Severity:

_____

- Coverage:

_____

**47.** Identify the hyperthermic and hypothermic emergencies from the list below and match them with the proper treatment. Place the number preceding the correct treatment on the line next to the heat or cold emergency.

**a.** _____ heat cramps

**1.** Remove wet clothing.
Cover the patient.
Give warm fluids by mouth if the patient is alert and oriented.

**b.** _____ frostbite

**2.** Move the patient to a cool area.
Remove clothing that may be keeping in the heat.
Place cool, wet clothes or a wet sheet on the scalp, neck, axilla, and groin.
Administer oxygen as directed by the physician and apply a cardiac monitor.
Notify the EMS for transportation to the hospital as directed by the physician.

**c.** _____ heat stroke

**3.** Immerse the affected tissue in lukewarm water (41°C, 105°F) until the area becomes pliable and the color and sensation return.
Do not apply dry heat.
Do not massage the area; massage may cause further tissue damage.
Avoid breaking any blisters that may form.
Notify the EMS for transportation to a hospital.

**d.** _____ hypothermia

**4.** Move the patient to a cool area.
Give fluids (commercial electrolyte solution) by mouth if uncomplicated.
Give IV fluids if patient presents with nausea.

**48.** What are your responsibilities for managing an allergic reaction? Circle the letter preceding all tasks that apply.

**a.** Leave the patient to bring the emergency kit or cart, oxygen, and to get a physician to evaluate the patient.

**b.** Assist the patient to a supine position.

**c.** Scrub the patient's skin to remove allergens and urticaria.

**d.** Assess the patient's respiratory and circulatory status by obtaining the blood pressure, pulse, and respiratory rates.

**e.** Observe skin color and warmth.

**f.** If the patient complains of being cold or is shivering, cover with a blanket.

**g.** Intubate the patient.

**h.** Upon the direction of the physician, start an intravenous line and administer oxygen.

**i.** Administer medications as ordered by the physician.

**j.** Document vital signs and any medications and treatments given, noting the time each set of vital signs is taken or medications are administered.

**k.** Communicate relevant information to the EMS personnel, including copies of the progress notes or medication record as needed.

**COG** **SHORT ANSWER** _____ Grade: _____

**49.** List nine interventions or steps to manage burns.

_____

_____

_____

_____

**50.** A sullen and moody patient suddenly becomes threatening. Name three things the medical assistant should do.

_____

_____

_____

_____

**51.** What six pieces of information should be included in your office's emergency plan?

_____

_____

_____

_____

**52.** What are the elements of the AVPU scale for assessing a patient's level of consciousness?

| A | |
|---|---|
| V | |
| P | |
| U | |

**53.** List the first three steps you should use to control bleeding from an open wound.

_____

_____

_____

_____

**54.** You enter an exam room and unexpectedly find someone sprawled on the floor. What four things do you check on your primary assessment?

_____

_____

_____

_____

**55.** At what point do you assess the general appearance of the patient?

_____

_____

_____

_____

**56.** A patient is found unconscious. You do not suspect trauma. In what order would you perform the physical examination?

_____

_____

_____

**57.** An examination of the eyes can be done according to the acronym "PEARL," meaning _Pupils Equal And Reactive to Light._ What does this examination reveal?

_____

_____

_____

**58.** A 55-year-old male begins complaining about nausea. He is clearly anxious or agitated. What could this be an early symptom of?

_____

_____

_____

## COG TRUE OR FALSE? _____ Grade: _____

Indicate whether the statements are true or false by placing the letter T (true) or F (false) on the line preceding the statement.

**59.** _____ During a primary assessment, you find a patient has inadequate respirations. You should proceed to the secondary assessment and physical examination to find out why.

**60.** _____ An impaled object should not be removed but requires careful immobilization of the patient and the injured area of the body.

**61.** _____ An allergic reaction will be evident immediately after exposure to an allergen.

**62.** _____ Closed wounds are not life threatening.

## COG AFF CASE STUDY FOR CRITICAL THINKING

Grade: _____

1. A male older adult falls in an exam room. He is conscious, but agitated and anxious. You are the first to discover him struggling on the floor. What is the only duty you will perform until others arrive, and why?

_____

_____

_____

_____

2. A patient in your office is in respiratory arrest. The physician is attending this patient. You have collected notes on the patient's vitals and SAMPLE history (signs and symptoms, allergies, medications, past pertinent history, last oral intake, and the events that led to the problem). A family member of the patient is present and is growing upset and intrusive. The EMTs arrive on the scene. What is your immediate responsibility? Explain.

_____

_____

_____

_____

3. A teenage patient is given an instant coldpack for an injury to the mouth. A few minutes later you discover the teenager misunderstood, and drank the contents of the cold pack. What information do you need to collect to prepare for a call to the poison control center?

_____

_____

_____

_____

4. Dante commutes to your office by public transportation. On a particularly cold day, Dante arrives late with cool, pale skin. He is lethargic and confused, with slow and shallow respirations and a slow and faint pulse. Describe what actions are appropriate.

_____

_____

_____

_____

5. You have just had a patient suffer anaphylactic shock and respiratory arrest due to an unsuspected penicillin allergy. EMS has transported the patient to a local hospital. The following week, the patient calls to ask what she can do to prevent this from happening in the future. What would you tell this patient? Are there any future precautions this patient should take? If so, what?

_____

_____

_____

_____

6. You have a 35-year-old patient who has religious reservations about some medical procedures. Normally, you and the physician carefully explain procedures to this patient so she has the opportunity to make informed consent decisions. Now she is lying unconscious in front of you with a medical emergency. How do you handle informed consent with an unconscious patient?

_____

_____

_____

_____

7. You have an elderly patient with a "do not resuscitate" order, because he does not want to receive CPR in the event of a heart attack. During treatment for another condition, he collapses in apparent anaphylactic shock. Do you provide emergency medical assistance?

_____

_____

_____

_____

## PSY PROCEDURE 11-1 Administer Oxygen

Name: _____ Date: _____ Time: _____ Grade: _____

**EQUIPMENT/SUPPLIES:** Oxygen tank with a regulator and flow meter, an oxygen delivery system (nasal cannula or mask)

**STANDARDS:** Given the needed equipment and a place to work, the student will perform this skill with _____ % accuracy in a total of _____ minutes. *(Your instructor will tell you what the percentage and time limits will be before you begin.)*

**KEY:**        4 = Satisfactory        0 = Unsatisfactory        NA = This step is not counted

| PROCEDURE STEPS | SELF | PARTNER | INSTRUCTOR |
|---|---|---|---|
| **1.** Wash your hands. | ❏ | ❏ | ❏ |
| **2.** Check the physician order for the amount of oxygen and the delivery method (nasal cannula, mask). | ❏ | ❏ | ❏ |
| **3.** Obtain the oxygen tank and nasal cannula or mask. | ❏ | ❏ | ❏ |
| **4.** Greet and identify the patient. | ❏ | ❏ | ❏ |
| **5. AFF** Explain how to respond to a patient who has dementia. | ❏ | ❏ | ❏ |
| **6.** Connect the distal end of the nasal cannula or mask tubing to the adapter on the oxygen tank regulator, which is attached to the oxygen tank. | ❏ | ❏ | ❏ |
| **7.** Place the oxygen delivery device into the patient's nares (nasal cannula) or over the patient's nose and mouth (mask). | ❏ | ❏ | ❏ |
| **8.** Turn the regulator dial to the liters per minute ordered by the physician. | ❏ | ❏ | ❏ |
| **9. AFF** Log into the Electronic Medical Record (EMR) using your username and secure password OR obtain the paper medical record from a secure location and assure it is kept away from public access. | ❏ | ❏ | ❏ |
| **10.** Record the procedure in the patient's medical record. | ❏ | ❏ | ❏ |
| **11.** When finished, log out of the EMR and/or replace the medical record in an appropriate and secure location to protect patient privacy. | ❏ | ❏ | ❏ |

**PSY** PROCEDURE 11-1 **Administer Oxygen** (continued)

**CALCULATION**

Total Possible Points: _____

Total Points Earned: _____ Multiplied by 100 = _____ Divided by Total Possible Points = _____ %

**PASS    FAIL    COMMENTS:**
❏           ❏

Student's signature _____ Date _____

Partner's signature _____ Date _____

Instructor's signature _____ Date _____

## PSY PROCEDURE 11-2 Perform Cardiopulmonary Resuscitation (Adult)

Name: _____ Date: _____ Time: _____ Grade: _____

**EQUIPMENT/SUPPLIES:** CPR mannequin, mouth-to-mouth barrier device, gloves

**STANDARDS:** Given the needed equipment and a place to work, the student will perform this skill with _____ % accuracy in a total of _____ minutes. *(Your instructor will tell you what the percentage and time limits will be before you begin.)*

**NOTE:** All health care professionals should receive training for proficiency in CPR in an approved program. This skill sheet is not intended to substitute for proficiency training with a mannequin and structured protocol.

**KEY:** 4 = Satisfactory  0 = Unsatisfactory  NA = This step is not counted

| PROCEDURE STEPS | SELF | PARTNER | INSTRUCTOR |
|---|---|---|---|
| 1. Determine unresponsiveness by shaking the patient and shouting "Are you okay?" | ❏ | ❏ | ❏ |
| 2. Instruct another staff member to get the physician, emergency cart/supplies, and AED. | ❏ | ❏ | ❏ |
| 3. Put on clean exam gloves. | ❏ | ❏ | ❏ |
| 4. If the patient does not respond, assess for cardiac function by feeling for a pulse using the carotid artery at the side of the patient's neck. | ❏ | ❏ | ❏ |
| 5. If no pulse is present, follow the protocol for chest compressions according to the standards for training provided by an approved basic life support provider. | ❏ | ❏ | ❏ |
| 6. After 30 compressions, check for airway patency and respiratory effort using the head-tilt, chin-lift maneuver with the patient in the supine position. | ❏ | ❏ | ❏ |
| 7. After opening the airway, begin rescue breathing by placing a mask over the patient's mouth and nose and giving two slow breaths, causing the chest to rise without overfilling the lungs. | ❏ | ❏ | ❏ |
| 8. Continue chest compressions and rescue breathing at a ratio of 30:1 until relieved by another health care provider or EMS arrives. | ❏ | ❏ | ❏ |
| 9. Utilize the recovery position if the patient regains consciousness or a pulse and adequate breathing. | ❏ | ❏ | ❏ |
| 10. Document the procedure and copy any records necessary for transport with EMS. | ❏ | ❏ | ❏ |

**PSY** PROCEDURE 11-2 **Perform Cardiopulmonary Resuscitation (Adult)** (continued)

**CALCULATION**

Total Possible Points: _____

Total Points Earned: _____ Multiplied by 100 = _____ Divided by Total Possible Points = _____ %

**PASS   FAIL   COMMENTS:**
❏         ❏

Student's signature _____ Date _____

Partner's signature _____ Date _____

Instructor's signature _____ Date _____

## PROCEDURE 11-3  Use an Automatic External Defibrillator (Adult)

**PSY**

Name: _____  Date: _____  Time: _____  Grade: _____

**EQUIPMENT/SUPPLIES:** Practice mannequin, training automatic external defibrillator with chest pads and connection cables, scissors, gauze, gloves

**STANDARDS:** Given the needed equipment and a place to work, the student will perform this skill with _____ % accuracy in a total of _____ minutes. *(Your instructor will tell you what the percentage and time limits will be before you begin.)*

**NOTE:** All health care professionals should receive training for proficiency in CPR and using an AED in an approved program. This skill sheet is not intended to substitute for proficiency training with a mannequin and structured protocol.

**KEY:**        4 = Satisfactory              0 = Unsatisfactory              NA =This step is not counted

| PROCEDURE STEPS | SELF | PARTNER | INSTRUCTOR |
|---|---|---|---|
| **1.** Determine unresponsiveness by shaking the patient and shouting "Are you okay?" | ❏ | ❏ | ❏ |
| **2.** Instruct another staff member to get the physician, emergency cart/supplies, and AED. | ❏ | ❏ | ❏ |
| **3.** While the other staff member continues CPR, remove the patient's shirt and prepare the chest for the AED electrodes: <br>**a.** If there are medication patches on the chest where the electrodes will be placed, remove them and wipe away any excess medication with a towel. <br>**b.** If there is excess hair on the chest that will prevent the AED electrodes from sticking, apply one set of electrodes and quickly remove, pulling any hair from the chest. <br>**c.** If the chest is wet, dry with a towel or other cloth before applying the electrodes. | ❏ | ❏ | ❏ |
| **4.** After removing the paper on the back of the AED electrodes, apply the electrodes to the chest area, one to the upper right chest area and the other on the lower left chest area. | ❏ | ❏ | ❏ |
| **5.** Explain what should be done in the event the patient has an implantable device in the area where the chest electrodes should be applied. | ❏ | ❏ | ❏ |
| **6.** With the electrodes securely on the chest, connect the wire from the electrodes to the AED unit and turn the AED on. | ❏ | ❏ | ❏ |
| **7.** Advise everyone to not touch the patient while the AED is analyzing the heart rhythm. | ❏ | ❏ | ❏ |
| **8.** If no shock is advised by the AED, resume CPR. | ❏ | ❏ | ❏ |
| **9.** If a shock is advised by the AED, make sure no one is touching the patient before pressing the appropriate button on the AED. | ❏ | ❏ | ❏ |
| **10.** After a shock is delivered by the AED, resume CPR until the AED advises you that the heart rhythm is being analyzed again. | ❏ | ❏ | ❏ |

**PSY** PROCEDURE 11-3 **Use an Automatic External Defibrillator (Adult)** (continued)

| | | | |
|---|---|---|---|
| **11.** Do not touch the patient while the heart rhythm is being reanalyzed at any point during the procedure. | ❑ | ❑ | ❑ |
| **12.** Continue to follow the instructions given by the AED and the physician until EMS has been notified and has arrived. | ❑ | ❑ | ❑ |
| **13.** Document the procedure and copy any records necessary for transport with EMS. | ❑ | ❑ | ❑ |

**CALCULATION**

Total Possible Points: _____

Total Points Earned: _____ Multiplied by 100 = _____ Divided by Total Possible Points = _____ %

**PASS    FAIL    COMMENTS:**
   ❑         ❑

Student's signature _____ Date _____

Partner's signature _____ Date _____

Instructor's signature _____ Date _____

## PSY PROCEDURE 11-4 Manage a Foreign Body Airway Obstruction (Adult)

**Name:** _____ **Date:** _____ **Time:** _____ **Grade:** _____

**EQUIPMENT/SUPPLIES:** Practice mannequin, mouth-to-mouth barrier device, gloves

**STANDARDS:** Given the needed equipment and a place to work, the student will perform this skill with _____ % accuracy in a total of _____ minutes. *(Your instructor will tell you what the percentage and time limits will be before you begin.)*

**NOTE:** All health care professionals should receive training for proficiency in managing a foreign body airway obstruction in an approved program. This skill sheet is not intended to substitute for proficiency training with a mannequin and structured protocol.

**KEY:** 4 = Satisfactory          0 = Unsatisfactory          NA = This step is not counted

| PROCEDURE STEPS | SELF | PARTNER | INSTRUCTOR |
|---|---|---|---|
| **1.** If the patient is conscious and appears to be choking, ask the patient, "Are you choking?" | ❏ | ❏ | ❏ |
| **2.** Do not perform abdominal thrusts if the patient can speak or cough because these are signs that the obstruction is not complete. | ❏ | ❏ | ❏ |
| **3.** If the patient cannot speak or cough but has indicated thate he or she is choking, move behind the patient, wrapping your arms around his or her abdomen. | ❏ | ❏ | ❏ |
| **4.** Place the fist of your dominant hand with the thumb against the patient's abdomen, between the navel and xiphoid process. | ❏ | ❏ | ❏ |
| **5.** Put your other hand against your dominant hand and give quick, upward thrusts, forceful enough to dislodge the obstruction in the airway. | ❏ | ❏ | ❏ |
| **6.** If the patient is obese or pregnant, place your hands against the middle of the sternum, above the xiphoid process and proceed with quick thrusts inward. | ❏ | ❏ | ❏ |
| **7.** Continue with the abdominal thrusts until the object is expelled and the patient can breathe or the patient becomes unconscious. | ❏ | ❏ | ❏ |
| **8.** If the patient becomes unconscious or is found unconscious, open the airway and give two rescue breaths. | ❏ | ❏ | ❏ |
| **9.** If rescue breaths are obstructed, reposition the head, and try again. | ❏ | ❏ | ❏ |
| **10.** If rescue breaths continue to be obstructed after repositioning, begin abdominal thrusts by placing your palm against the patient's abdomen with your fingers facing his or her head (you may need to straddle the patient's hips). The palm of the hand should be located between the navel and the xiphoid process. | ❏ | ❏ | ❏ |

**PSY** PROCEDURE 11-4 **Manage a Foreign Body Airway Obstruction (Adult)** (continued)

| | | | |
|---|---|---|---|
| **11.** Lace the fingers of the other hand into the fingers of the hand on the abdomen and give five abdominal thrusts. | ❏ | ❏ | ❏ |
| **12.** After five abdominal thrusts, open the patient's mouth using a tongue-jaw lift maneuver and do a finger- sweep of the mouth, removing any objects that may have been dislodged. | ❏ | ❏ | ❏ |
| **13.** If an item has been dislodged and can be removed easily, remove the object and attempt rescue breaths. Continue rescue breaths and chest compressions as necessary and appropriate. | ❏ | ❏ | ❏ |
| **14.** If the item has not been dislodged, attempt rescue breaths. If rescue breaths are successful, continue rescue breathing and chest compressions as necessary and appropriate. | ❏ | ❏ | ❏ |
| **15.** If the item has not been dislodged and rescue breaths are not successful, continue with abdominal thrusts. | ❏ | ❏ | ❏ |
| **16.** Repeat the pattern of abdominal thrusts, finger -sweep, and rescue breaths and follow the physician's orders until EMS is notified and arrives. | ❏ | ❏ | ❏ |
| **17.** Document the procedure and copy any records necessary for transport with EMS. | ❏ | ❏ | ❏ |

**CALCULATION**

Total Possible Points: _____

Total Points Earned: _____ Multiplied by 100 = _____ Divided by Total Possible Points = _____ %

**PASS   FAIL   COMMENTS:**
  ❏        ❏

Student's signature _____ Date _____

Partner's signature _____ Date _____

Instructor's signature _____ Date _____

## PSY PROCEDURE 11-5 **Control Bleeding**

Name: _____ Date: _____ Time: _____ Grade: _____

**EQUIPMENT/SUPPLIES:** Gloves, sterile gauze pads

**STANDARDS:** Given the needed equipment and a place to work, the student will perform this skill with ____ % accuracy in a total of ____ minutes. *(Your instructor will tell you what the percentage and time limits will be before you begin.)*

**KEY:**          4 = Satisfactory          0 = Unsatisfactory          NA = This step is not counted

| PROCEDURE STEPS | SELF | PARTNER | INSTRUCTOR |
|---|---|---|---|
| **1.** Identify the patient and assess the extent of the bleeding and type of accident. | ❑ | ❑ | ❑ |
| **2.** Take the patient to an examination room and notify the physician if appropriate. | ❑ | ❑ | ❑ |
| **3.** Give the patient some gauze pads and have him or her apply pressure to the area while you put on a pair of clean examination gloves and open additional sterile gauze pads. | ❑ | ❑ | ❑ |
| **4.** Observe the patient for signs of dizziness or lightheadedness. Have the patient lie down. | ❑ | ❑ | ❑ |
| **5.** Using several sterile gauze pads, apply direct pressure to the wound. | ❑ | ❑ | ❑ |
| **6.** Maintain pressure until the bleeding stops. | ❑ | ❑ | ❑ |
| **7.** If the bleeding continues or seeps through the gauze, apply additional gauze on top of the saturated gauze while continuing to apply direct pressure. | ❑ | ❑ | ❑ |
| **8.** If directed by the physician to do so, apply pressure to the artery delivering blood to this area while continuing to apply direct pressure to the wound to control bleeding. | ❑ | ❑ | ❑ |
| **9.** Once the bleeding is controlled, prepare to assist the physician with a minor office surgical procedure to close the wound. | ❑ | ❑ | ❑ |
| **10.** Continue to monitor the patient for signs of shock and be prepared to treat the patient appropriately. | ❑ | ❑ | ❑ |
| **11.** Document the treatment in the patient's medical record. | ❑ | ❑ | ❑ |

**CALCULATION**

Total Possible Points: _____

Total Points Earned: _____ Multiplied by 100 = _____ Divided by Total Possible Points = _____ %

**PASS    FAIL    COMMENTS:**
❑          ❑

Student's signature _____ Date _____

Partner's signature _____ Date _____

Instructor's signature _____ Date _____

## PSY PROCEDURE 11-6 Respond to Medical Emergencies Other than Bleeding, Cardiac/Respiratory Arrest, or Foreign Body Airway Obstruction

Name: _____ Date: _____ Time: _____ Grade: _____

**EQUIPMENT/SUPPLIES:** A medical emergency kit that contains a minimum of personal protective equipment including gloves, low-dose aspirin tablets, 2 × 2 and 4 × 4 sterile gauze pads, vinegar or acetic acid solution, blood pressure cuff and stethoscope, sterile water or saline for irrigation, ice bags, and towel or rolled gauze bandage material

**STANDARDS:** Given the needed equipment and a place to work, the student will perform this skill with _____ % accuracy in a total of _____ minutes. *(Your instructor will tell you what the percentage and time limits will be before you begin.)*

**KEY:**      4 = Satisfactory      0 = Unsatisfactory      NA = This step is not counted

| PROCEDURE STEPS | SELF | PARTNER | INSTRUCTOR |
|---|---|---|---|
| **1.** Identify the patient and assess the type of emergency involved. | ❏ | ❏ | ❏ |
| **2.** Escort the patient to an examination room. | ❏ | ❏ | ❏ |
| **3.** Have another staff member get the physician, medical emergency cart/supplies, and AED. | ❏ | ❏ | ❏ |
| **4.** Apply clean examination gloves and other PPE as appropriate. | ❏ | ❏ | ❏ |
| **5.** Assist the patient to the exam table and have him or her lie down. | ❏ | ❏ | ❏ |
| **6.** Treat the patient according to the physician's instructions and the most current guidelines for first aid procedures for the following:<br>**a.** Chest pain<br>**b.** Snakebite<br>**c.** Jellyfish sting<br>**d.** Dental injuries<br>　**(1) Chipped tooth**<br>　**(2) Cracked or broken tooth**<br>　**(3) Tooth removed**<br>　**(4) Broken jaw**<br>**e.** Fracture Injuries<br>**f.** Seizure<br>**g.** Shock<br>**h.** Syncope | ❏ | ❏ | ❏ |
| **7.** If the patient develops cardiac or respiratory arrest, follow the procedure for CPR according to the most recent standards and guidelines. | ❏ | ❏ | ❏ |
| **8.** Document the treatment in the patient's medical record. | ❏ | ❏ | ❏ |

**FSY** PROCEDURE 11-6 **Respond to Medical Emergencies Other than Bleeding, Cardiac/Respiratory Arrest, or Foreign Body Airway Obstruction** (continued)

**CALCULATION**

Total Possible Points: _____

Total Points Earned: _____ Multiplied by 100 = _____ Divided by Total Possible Points = _____ %

**PASS** **FAIL** **COMMENTS:**

❏ ❏

Student's signature _____ Date _____

Partner's signature _____ Date _____

Instructor's signature _____ Date _____

# *12* Disaster Preparedness and the Medical Assistant

## Learning Outcomes

### COG Cognitive Domain

1. Spell and define the key terms
2. Describe what is meant by a disaster and disaster preparedness
3. List several types of disasters
4. Identify critical elements of an emergency plan for response to a natural disaster or other emergency
5. Describe fundamental principles for evacuation of a health care setting
6. Identify emergency preparedness plans in your community
7. Discuss potential role(s) of the medical assistant in emergency preparedness

### PSY Psychomotor Domain

1. Respond to a simulated disaster (Procedure 12-1)

2. Maintain a list of community resources for emergency preparedness (Procedure 12-2)
3. Develop a personal safety plan (Procedure 12-3)

### AFF Affective Domain

1. Recognize the physical and emotional effects on persons involved in an emergency situation
2. Demonstrate self-awareness in responding to an emergency situation
3. Apply active listening skills
4. Use appropriate body language and other nonverbal skills in communicating with patients, family, and staff

### ABHES Competencies

1. Document accurately
2. Recognize and respond to verbal and nonverbal communication
3. Adapt to individualized needs
4. Apply principles of aseptic techniques and infection control
5. Recognize emergencies and treatments and minor office surgical procedures
6. Use standard precautions
7. Perform first aid and CPR
8. Demonstrate professionalism by exhibiting a positive attitude and sense of responsibility

Name: _____     Date: _____     Grade: _____

## COG MULTIPLE CHOICE

Circle the letter preceding the correct answer.

**1.** The 2001 discovery of anthrax in an envelope to be delivered to a U.S. Congressman is an example of a(n):
   **a.** bioterrorist attack.
   **b.** epidemic.
   **c.** pandemic.
   **d.** ergonomics.
   **e.** ADF.

**2.** An effective disaster plan for the medical office should include the input of which individuals?
   **a.** The physician or physicians
   **b.** The practice manager
   **c.** The medical assistants
   **d.** The receptionist
   **e.** All of the above

**3.** Which of these is not an example of a natural disaster?
   **a.** Flood
   **b.** Tornado
   **c.** Air quality advisory
   **d.** Hurricane
   **e.** Earthquake

**4.** An emergency action plan should include all of the following except:
   **a.** contact information for poison control.
   **b.** emergency procedures.
   **c.** the location of the emergency supplies.
   **d.** patient information sheets.
   **e.** contact information for local hospitals.

**5.** A well-written emergency plan is essential to being prepared for a disaster. What qualities are inherent in a well-written emergency plan?
   **a.** It is easy to read and include pictures.
   **b.** It is flexible and easily implemented.
   **c.** It is based on research and has references.
   **d.** It should include enough information to fill a 3-inch binder.
   **e.** It is written based on the reading level of the office personnel.

**6.** A location in or near the medical office should be identified to coordinate activities in a disaster, commonly known as a/n:
   **a.** central activities center.
   **b.** common planning center.
   **c.** central operation center.
   **d.** command center.
   **e.** operation command center.

**7.** An example of a manmade disaster includes all of the following except:
   **a.** drought.
   **b.** bioterriorism.
   **c.** a nuclear accident.
   **d.** contaminating a water source chemicals.
   **e.** none of the above.

**8.** A bioterrorism agent that is easily available, can be transferred to people easily, has the potential to cause injury and death to large amounts of people and other animals is included in which category?
   **a.** Category A
   **b.** Category B
   **c.** Category C
   **d.** Category D
   **e.** Category E

**9.** A disease that infects many people in a small geographical area is known as a/n:
   **a.** pandemic.
   **b.** Category C agent.
   **c.** infectious pathogen.
   **d.** bioterrorist.
   **e.** epidemic.

**10.** The role of the medical assistant in planning for emergencies and disasters includes assisting the physician with all of the following except:
   **a.** performing CPR if needed.
   **b.** transferring patients or victims.
   **c.** preparing and administering medications.
   **d.** diagnosing and treating illness and injuries caused by the emergency.
   **e.** collecting information and communicating clearly with everyone involved.

*Scenario for questions 11 through 15:* A tornado just came through the neighborhood where you are working in a family practice office. Although your office was not hit, several businesses around your office were damaged or destroyed. People are running into your office yelling for help for other victims who cannot get to the office or they are injured and bleeding themselves.

11. Your priority in assisting patients and victims in the office includes:
    a. asking nonpatients coming into the office to wait outside until the EMS arrives.
    b. remaining calm and implementing the emergency plan quickly and efficiently.
    c. asking the practice manager if you can leave to check on your family.
    d. standing outside to direct traffic and flag down emergency medical services.
    e. gathering equipment and supplies that may be needed for any injuries.

12. This is an example of which type of disaster?
    a. A pandemic
    b. A water emergency
    c. A bioterrorism disaster
    d. A manmade disaster
    e. A natural disaster

13. Your role in assisting in this disaster includes which of the following:
    a. Gathering medical information from patients and victims
    b. Assisting the physician with procedures and treatments
    c. Administering tetanus to everyone who is injured before they are seen by the physician.
    d. A and B.
    e. All of the above.

14. Because you are actively involved in assisting during this disaster, you are considered
    a. first-level victim.
    b. secondary-level victim.
    c. third-level victim.
    d. fourth-level victim.
    e. fifth-level victim.

15. One month after the disaster, you notice your coworker is unusually irritable and is unable to concentrate on simple tasks, making mistakes throughout the day. These behaviors are not typical of her personality and may be signs of:
    a. depression.
    b. posttraumatic stress disorder.
    c. a sleeping disorder.
    d. an anxiety disorder.
    e. a possible infectious disease contracted during the emergency.

## COG MATCHING

Grade: _____

Match each key term with its definition.

**Key Terms**

16. _____ bioterrorism
17. _____ disaster
18. _____ epidemic
19. _____ pandemic
20. _____ PTSD

**Definitions**

a. a disease that affects numerous people within a specific geographical area
b. a sudden and unplanned event that has the potential to cause damage to property or life; may be caused by an accident or by nature including weather events such as a hurricane.
c. a condition in some individuals who are affected by acute traumatic stress.
d. intentional release of a biologic agent with the intent to harm individuals.
e. a disease that affects numerous people in many areas of the world at the same time.

## ⬛OG IDENTIFICATION

_____ Grade: _____

**21.** You may be called upon to assist before, during, and after a disaster. Place a check mark in the "Yes" column for those duties you might assist with as a medical assistant and place a check mark in the "No" column for those tasks that not be the responsibility of the medical assistant with regard to disaster preparedness.

| Task | Yes | No |
|---|---|---|
| **a.** Obtain important patient information. | | |
| **b.** Perform first aid and CPR procedures. | | |
| **c.** Suture small lacerations. | | |
| **d.** Obtain vital signs. | | |
| **e.** Remain calm and react competently and professionally. | | |
| **f.** Coordinate multiple ongoing events. | | |
| **g.** Prescribe antibiotics to patients who may be infected | | |
| **h.** Know what emergency system is used in the community. | | |
| **i.** Provide immediate care to the patient while the physician is notified. | | |
| **j.** Advise victims with minor injuries to go home and take OTC medications for discomfort | | |
| **k.** Work as a law enforcement officer to manage victims exhibiting dangerous behaviors | | |
| **l.** Create medical records and document all actions taken. | | |
| **m.** Manage the temporary medical clinic | | |
| **n.** Assist EMS personnel as necessary. | | |

## ⬛OG SHORT ANSWER

_____ Grade: _____

**22.** What six pieces of information should be included in your office's emergency plan?

_____

_____

_____

_____

**23.** During a disaster, medical assistants must be able to coordinate multiple ongoing events while rendering patient care. What are the key components to managing a chaotic situation during a disaster?

_____

_____

_____

_____

**24.** Explain the purpose of a Central Operation Center.

_____

_____

_____

_____

**25.** How does the CDC determine that a biologic agent is a weapon?

_____

_____

_____

_____

## COG TRUE OR FALSE?

Grade: _____

Indicate whether the statements are true or false by placing the letter T (true) or F (false) on the line preceding the statement.

**26.** _____ A pandemic is a disease that affects many people within a very specific, localized geographic area.

**27.** _____ Having an alternative source of electricity is essential during a disaster.

**28.** _____ When evacuating an office during an emergency, you must first recognize the emergency as one that requires the removal from the area.

**29.** _____ Psychological first aid requires that you discuss all aspects of the disaster with coworkers and patients even if they do not wish to discuss the details.

**30.** _____ The primary defense mechanism used by individuals after a disaster is anxiety.

## COG IDENTIFICATION

Grade: _____

**31.** Place a checkmark in the appropriate box to indicate whether or not the statement should be considered to develop an evacuation plan for the medical office.

| Consideration for Evacuation Plan? | Yes | No |
| --- | --- | --- |
| **a.** Assign staff members to perform surgical procedures on victims who need immediate first aid. | | |
| **b.** Identify evacuation routes | | |
| **c.** Make sure everyone understands they are not to discuss patient/staff illness or injury during the evacuation. | | |
| **d.** Identify who is responsible for ordering the evacuation. | | |
| **e.** Do not allow anyone to reenter the facility after the disaster when the safety of everyone reentering the office has been established. | | |

| | | |
|---|---|---|
| **f.** Determine a location to move to and a backup site. | | |
| **g.** Define responsibilities of each staff member. | | |
| **h.** Do not waste time making sure patients and staff are accounted for during and after the evacuation. | | |
| **i.** Decide what supplies or equipment will need to be transported. | | |

## AFF CASE STUDY FOR CRITICAL THINKING

Grade: _____

1. You have been assigned to put together an emergency kit for the family practice office where you work. What items should you include in this kit?

   _____

   _____

   _____

   _____

2. There has just been an earthquake where you live and the medical office has stopped shaking, leaving patients and staff wondering what happened. There are items on the floor throughout the office that were shaken off the shelves and walls. What is your immediate responsibility? Explain.

   _____

   _____

   _____

   _____

3. An environmental safety plan was written for the office where you work and includes emergency procedures for all chemicals used in your office. When reviewing this plan, you notice that it does not include a plan to train employees on environmental safety guidelines. Is this important to include in the plan? Why or why not?

   _____

   _____

   _____

   _____

4. The practice manager at your office has scheduled a meeting to "test" the office emergency plan. He has asked the local fire department to assist in this training. How can you "test" an emergency plan and why would the local fire department be involved?

   _____

   _____

   _____

   _____

**5.** A tornado hit the community where you work 1 month ago, and there was significant property damage, injuries, and fatalities. A patient comes into the office today and complains that she is unable to sleep for more than 3 hours at a time as she "wakes up" frequently hearing tornado sirens and reliving the storm. What would you tell this patient? If so, what?

_____

_____

_____

_____

## PROCEDURE 12-1 Respond to a Simulated Disaster

**Name:** _____ **Date:** _____ **Time:** _____ **Grade:** _____

**EQUIPMENT/SUPPLIES:** Phone, disaster drill manual for a medical office, paper medical record forms and folders, pen, portable emergency kit.

**STANDARDS:** Given the needed equipment and a place to work, the student will perform this skill with _____ % accuracy in a total of _____ minutes. *(Your instructor will tell you what the percentage and time limits will be before you begin.)*

**KEY:** 4 = Satisfactory 0 = Unsatisfactory NA = This step is not counted

| PROCEDURE STEPS | SELF | PARTNER | INSTRUCTOR |
|---|---|---|---|
| **1.** Develop and/or review an emergency/ disaster procedure manual. | ❑ | ❑ | ❑ |
| **2.** Assume the role of an employee, patient, or visitor in a medical office. | ❑ | ❑ | ❑ |
| **3.** During a "normal" workday, a disaster occurs without warning. | ❑ | ❑ | ❑ |
| **4.** Follow the protocol and procedures for the disaster according to the emergency/disaster plan. | ❑ | ❑ | ❑ |
| **5.** After the mock disaster drill, discuss the event including the strengths and weaknesses of the emergency plan. | ❑ | ❑ | ❑ |
| **6.** **AFF** Complete a reflection paper about the mock disaster including your feelings, perceptions, and thoughts before, during, and after the mock disaster. | ❑ | ❑ | ❑ |

**CALCULATION**

Total Possible Points: _____

Total Points Earned: _____ Multiplied by 100 = _____ Divided by Total Possible Points = _____ %

**PASS   FAIL   COMMENTS:**
  ❑        ❑

Student's signature _____ Date _____

Partner's signature _____ Date _____

Instructor's signature _____ Date _____

**FSY** PROCEDURE 12-2 **Maintain a List of Community Resources for Emergency Preparedness**

Name: _____ Date: _____ Time: _____ Grade: _____

**EQUIPMENT/SUPPLIES:** Phone, computer with Internet access, paper and pen, binder

**STANDARDS:** Given the needed equipment and a place to work, the student will perform this skill with _____ % accuracy in a total of _____ minutes. *(Your instructor will tell you what the percentage and time limits will be before you begin.)*

**KEY:** 4 = Satisfactory  0 = Unsatisfactory  NA = This step is not counted

| PROCEDURE STEPS | SELF | PARTNER | INSTRUCTOR |
|---|---|---|---|
| 1. Determine the geographical area of your community including the city or town, county, and surrounding counties or towns as appropriate | ❏ | ❏ | ❏ |
| 2. Complete an Internet search of the possible resources that make up your community, beginning with the local resources. | ❏ | ❏ | ❏ |
| 3. Create a list of resources including the name of the agency, resources available, phone numbers, addresses, and web address if available. | ❏ | ❏ | ❏ |
| 4. Organize the resources you find in a binder or other notebook for easy reference | ❏ | ❏ | ❏ |

**CALCULATION**

Total Possible Points: _____

Total Points Earned: _____ Multiplied by 100 = _____ Divided by Total Possible Points = _____ %

**PASS   FAIL   COMMENTS:**
❏        ❏

Student's signature _____ Date _____

Partner's signature _____ Date _____

Instructor's signature _____ Date _____

## PROCEDURE 12-3 Develop a Personal Safety Plan

**Name:** _____ **Date:** _____ **Time:** _____ **Grade:** _____

**EQUIPMENT/SUPPLIES:** Phone, computer with Internet access, paper and pen, binder.

**STANDARDS:** Given the needed equipment and a place to work, the student will perform this skill with _____ % accuracy in a total of _____ minutes. *(Your instructor will tell you what the percentage and time limits will be before you begin.)*

**KEY:**        4 = Satisfactory        0 = Unsatisfactory        NA =This step is not counted

| PROCEDURE STEPS | SELF | PARTNER | INSTRUCTOR |
|---|---|---|---|
| **1.** Download an electronic version of a family or personal safety plan template from a reputable Web site. | ❑ | ❑ | ❑ |
| **2.** Gather information needed for inclusion in the safety plan. | ❑ | ❑ | ❑ |
| **3.** Speak with family members and decide how you will contact each other in the event of a disaster. Include the location where you will go and/or meet. | ❑ | ❑ | ❑ |
| **4.** Once the personal or family plan is developed, keep a copy in the emergency supply kit or another safe place. | ❑ | ❑ | ❑ |

**CALCULATION**

Total Possible Points: _____

Total Points Earned: _____ Multiplied by 100 = _____ Divided by Total Possible Points = _____ %

**PASS    FAIL    COMMENTS:**
❑          ❑

Student's signature _____ Date _____

Partner's signature _____ Date _____

Instructor's signature _____ Date _____

CHAPTER

# *13* Dermatology

## Learning Outcomes

### COG Cognitive Domain

1. Spell key terms
2. Define medical terms and abbreviations related to all body systems
3. Describe structural organization of the human body.
4. List major organs in each body system.
5. Identify the anatomical location of major organs in each body system.
6. Describe the normal function of each body system.
7. Identify common pathology related to each body system including signs, symptoms, and etiology.
8. Explain the difference between bandages and dressings and give the purpose of each
9. Identify the guidelines for applying bandages

### PSY Psychomotor Domain

1. Apply a warm or cold compress (Procedure 13-1)

2. Assist with therapeutic soaks (Procedure 13-2)
3. Apply a tubular gauze bandage (Procedure 13-3)

### AFF Affective Domain

1. Incorporate critical thinking skills when performing patient assessment
2. Incorporate critical thinking skills when performing patient care
3. Show awareness of a patient's concerns related to the procedure being performed
4. Demonstrate empathy, active listening, nonverbal communication
5. Demonstrate respect for individual diversity including gender, race, religion, age, economic status, appearance
6. Explain to a patient the rationale for performance of a procedure
7. Demonstrate sensitivity to patient rights
8. Protect the integrity of the medical record.

### ABHES Competencies

1. Assist the physician with the regimen of diagnostic and treatment modalities as they relate to each body system
2. Comply with federal, state, and local health laws and regulations
3. Communicate on the recipient's level of comprehension
4. Serve as a liaison between the physician and others
5. Show empathy and impartiality when dealing with patients

Name: _____     Date: _____     Grade: _____

## COG MULTIPLE CHOICE

Circle the letter preceding the correct answer.

1. Which of the following groups of people are most likely to develop impetigo?
   a. Older adults
   b. Women
   c. Young children
   d. Men
   e. Teenagers

2. What type of infection is herpes simplex?
   a. Bacterial
   b. Fungal
   c. Parasitic
   d. Viral
   e. Genetic

3. Public showers and swimming pools are common places to pick up fungal infections because:
   a. fungi thrive in moist conditions.
   b. areas that are highly populated increase the risk factor.
   c. sharing towels passes fungal infections from one person to another.
   d. fungi grow quickly on tile surfaces.
   e. antifungal medications do not work once they come into contact with water.

4. Which of these skin disorders may be caused by food allergies?
   a. Keloids
   b. Intertrigo
   c. Alopecia
   d. Eczema
   e. Seborrheic dermatitis

5. Which of the following statements is true about albinism?
   a. Respiratory problems are common among sufferers of albinism.
   b. Albinism is treated with benzoyl peroxide.
   c. Albinism usually occurs in exposed areas of the skin.
   d. People who suffer from albinism should have regular checkups.
   e. People who suffer from albinism should take particular care of their eyes in the sun.

6. Which statements are true about decubitus ulcers?
   a. They are frequently diagnosed in school-aged children.
   b. They are most common in aged, debilitated, and immobilized patients.
   c. They are highly contagious.
   d. They generally occur on the chin and forehead.
   e. They are effectively treated with antifungal creams.

7. When bandaging a patient, you should:
   a. fasten bandages only with safety pins.
   b. complete surgical asepsis before you begin.
   c. keep the area to be bandaged warm.
   d. leave fingers and toes exposed when possible.
   e. wrap the bandage as tightly as possible to prevent it from coming loose.

8. A person suffering from high stress levels is most likely to develop:
   a. urticaria.
   b. acne vulgaris.
   c. impetigo.
   d. leukoderma.
   e. herpes zoster.

9. How many people in the United States will typically develop malignant melanoma?
   a. 1 in 5
   b. 1 in 500
   c. 1 in 105
   d. 1 in 1,005
   e. 1 in 5,000

10. Which of the following conditions would be treated with topical antifungal cream?
    a. Folliculitis
    b. Vitiligo
    c. Tinea versicolor
    d. Urticaria
    e. Decubitus ulcers

11. What should patients do if they have an absence of melanin in their skin?
    a. Avoid coming into contact with other people.
    b. Protect their skin from the sun.
    c. Seek immediate medical assistance.
    d. Take supplementary vitamin pills.
    e. Stop sharing towels and bedding.

*Scenario for questions 12 and 13:* A male patient comes into the physician's office to have a wart removed from his finger. While you are preparing him for the procedure, he tells you that he regularly gets verrucae on his feet.

12. How would you advise the patient to avoid further viral infections?
    a. Wash all bedding and clothing at high temperatures.
    b. Avoid sharing combs and toiletries with anyone.
    c. Avoid coming into direct contact with skin lesions.
    d. Wear comfortable footwear and avoid walking long distances.
    e. Frequently wash hands with antibacterial soap.

13. The patient should look for over-the-counter wart medication that contains:
    a. podophyllum resin.
    b. acyclovir.
    c. selenium sulfide.
    d. permethrin.
    e. prednisone.

14. Before you apply a bandage to an open wound, you should:
    a. moisten the bandage.
    b. keep the bandage at room temperature.
    c. apply pressure to the wound.
    d. apply a sterile dressing to the wound.
    e. check to see how the patient would like the bandage fastened.

15. How can you tell that a patient is suffering from stage I decubitus ulcers?
    a. The skin is blistered, peeling, or cracked.
    b. Red skin does not return to normal when massaged.
    c. The skin is scaly, dry, and flaky.
    d. The skin is extremely itchy.
    e. The patient is unable to feel pressure on the area.

16. When a physician performs a shave biopsy, he:
    a. cuts the lesion off just above the skin line.
    b. removes a small section from the center of the lesion.
    c. removes the entire lesion for evaluation.
    d. cuts the lesion off just below the skin line.
    e. removes a small section from the edge of the lesion.

17. Which of these is thought to be a cause of skin cancer in areas not exposed to the sun?
    a. Chemicals in toiletries
    b. Pet allergies
    c. Frequent irritation
    d. Second-hand smoke
    e. Excessive scratching

18. Treatment of impetigo involves:
    a. washing the area two to three times a day followed by application of topical antibiotics.
    b. cleaning with alcohol sponges twice a day.
    c. washing towels, washcloths, and bed linens daily.
    d. oral antibiotics for severe cases.
    e. the physician removing the infected area.

19. Which of the following statements is true about nevi?
    a. Nevi are usually malignant.
    b. Nevi are usually found on the back or legs.
    c. It is common for nevi to bleed occasionally.
    d. Nevi are congenital pigmented skin blemishes.
    e. Nevi are extremely rare in young patients.

20. Which part of the body is affected by tinea capitis?
    a. Hands
    b. Feet
    c. Hair follicles
    d. Groin
    e. Scalp

## COG MATCHING

Grade: _____

Place the letter preceding the definition on the line next to the term.

**Key Terms**

21. _____ alopecia
22. _____ bulla
23. _____ carbuncle
24. _____ cellulitis
25. _____ dermatophytosis
26. _____ eczema
27. _____ erythema
28. _____ folliculitis
29. _____ furuncle
30. _____ herpes simplex
31. _____ herpes zoster
32. _____ impetigo
33. _____ macule
34. _____ neoplasm
35. _____ pediculosis
36. _____ pruritus
37. _____ psoriasis
38. _____ seborrhea
39. _____ urticaria
40. _____ verruca
41. _____ vesicle
42. _____ pustule

**Definitions**

a. a highly infectious skin infection causing erythema and progressing to honey-colored crusts
b. redness of the skin
c. an inflammation of hair follicles
d. a small, flat discoloration of the skin
e. an abnormal growth of new tissue; tumor
f. an infection of an interconnected group of hair follicles or several furuncles forming a mass
g. an inflammation or infection of the skin and deeper tissues that may result in tissue destruction if not treated properly
h. an infection caused by the herpes simplex virus
i. hives
j. an infection caused by reactivation of varicella zoster virus, which causes chicken pox
k. a wart
l. a large blister or vesicle
m. an infestation with parasitic lice
n. baldness
o. superficial dermatitis
p. itching
q. an overproduction of sebum by the sebaceous glands
r. an infection in a hair follicle or gland; characterized by pain, redness, and swelling with necrosis of tissue in the center
s. a skin lesion that appears as a small sac containing fluid; a blister
t. a fungal infection of the skin
u. a vesicle filled with pus
v. a chronic skin disorder that appears as red patches covered with thick, dry, silvery scales

## COG MATCHING

Grade: _____

Place the letter of the description on the line preceding the skin disorder.

**Disorders**

43. _____ vitiligo
44. _____ decubitus ulcer
45. _____ corn
46. _____ acne vulgaris
47. _____ carbuncle
48. _____ squamous cell carcinoma
49. _____ seborrheic dermatitis

**Descriptions**

a. a skin disease characterized by pimples, comedones, and cysts
b. a pigmentation disorder thought to be an autoimmune disorder in patients with an inherited predisposition
c. an infection in an interconnected group of hair follicles
d. a skin inflammation caused by an overproduction of sebum that affects the scalp, eyelids, face, back, umbilicus, and body folds
e. a hard, raised thickening of the stratum corneum on the toes
f. an ulcerative lesion caused by impaired blood supply and insufficient oxygen to an area
g. a type of skin cancer that is a slow-growing, malignant tumor

## OOG **MATCHING** _____ Grade: _____

Place the letter of the description on the line preceding the type of bandage.

**Bandages**

50. _____ roller bandages
51. _____ elastic bandages
52. _____ tubular gauze bandages

**Descriptions**

a. These bandages can be given to the patient to take home to wash and reuse. You should be careful when applying them so as not to compromise circulation.
b. These bandages are made of soft, woven materials and are available in various lengths and widths. They can be either sterile or clean.
c. These bandages are very stretchy and are used to enclose fingers, toes, arms, legs, head, and trunk.

## OOG **MATCHING** _____ Grade: _____

Although medical assistants do not prescribe treatments, match each of the following skin disorders with the most likely physician prescribed treatment. Place the letter of the possible treatment on the line next to the skin disorder.

**Disorders**

53. _____ decubitus ulcers
54. _____ basal cell carcinoma
55. _____ cellulitis
56. _____ folliculitis
57. _____ verruca
58. _____ urticaria

**Treatments**

a. saline soaks or compresses
b. antihistamines
c. antibiotic powder
d. surgical removal
e. keratolytic agents
f. antibiotics

## PSY **IDENTIFICATION** _____ Grade: _____

59. Which of the following skin disorders cannot be treated? Circle the correct answer.

   a. Impetigo

   b. Folliculitis

   c. Albinism

   d. Malignant melanoma

   e. Decubitus ulcers

60. How would a physician be able to confirm a suspected case of malignant melanoma? Circle the correct answer.

   a. Wood light analysis

   b. Inspection

   c. Urine test

**61.** As a medical assistant, you'll be responsible for helping the physician perform physical examinations of the skin. Review the list of tasks below and determine which tasks you may be responsible for as a medical assistant. Place a check mark in the "Yes" column for duties that you might assist with and a check mark in the "No" column for tasks that would be completed by someone else.

| Task | Yes | No |
|------|-----|-----|
| **a.** Assemble the equipment required by the physician. | | |
| **b.** Perform a skin biopsy. | | |
| **c.** Inject local anesthetic when needed. | | |
| **d.** Direct specimens to the appropriate laboratories. | | |
| **e.** Clean and disinfect the examination room. | | |
| **f.** Diagnose and treat common skin inflammations. | | |
| **g.** Reinforce the physician's instructions about caring for a skin condition at home. | | |

**62.** You are applying a bandage to a patient. Read the statements below and check the appropriate box to show whether the bandage has been applied correctly or incorrectly.

| | Applied Correctly | Applied Incorrectly |
|------|-------------------|---------------------|
| **a.** You have fastened the bandage with adhesive tape. | | |
| **b.** The area that you are about to bandage is clean and damp. | | |
| **c.** You have dressed two burned fingers separately and then bandaged them together. | | |
| **d.** The skin around the bandaged arm is pale and cool. | | |
| **e.** You have bandaged a wounded foot by covering the toes to make it neater. | | |
| **f.** You have bandaged an elbow with extra padding. | | |

**63.** Place a check mark in the appropriate box to show whether the person described is at a high risk or a low risk of developing impetigo.

| | High Risk | Low Risk |
|------|-----------|----------|
| **a.** A slightly overweight 34-year-old woman who showers twice a day | | |
| **b.** A 55-year-old man who works at a hospital laundry room and does not wash his hands | | |
| **c.** A 22-year-old woman with severe anorexia | | |

CHAPTER 13 Dermatology **197**

| **d.** An 18-year-old drug addict who lives in an abandoned warehouse | | |
|---|---|---|
| **e.** A 40-year-old mother of three who enjoys reading in the tub | | |

64. Read these descriptions of five of Dr. Marsh's patients then decide which of his patients is at the highest risk of developing malignant melanoma. Place a check mark on the line preceding the patient descriptions that are at the highest risk.

a. ＿＿＿＿＿＿ Mrs. Pearson, 42-year-old mother of two. Light brown hair, brown eyes, enjoys reading and watching movies.

b. ＿＿＿＿＿＿ Mr. Stevens, 50-year-old widower. Gray hair, brown eyes, enjoys walking and playing golf.

c. ＿＿＿＿＿＿ Jessica Phillips, 24-year-old college student. Red hair, blue eyes, enjoys playing volleyball and surfing.

d. ＿＿＿＿＿＿ Todd Andrews, 18-year-old student. Black hair, green eyes, enjoys running and swimming.

e. ＿＿＿＿＿＿ Mr. Archer, 39-year-old father of three. Blond hair, blue eyes, lives in Minnesota and enjoys skiing.

## COG **SHORT ANSWER** ＿＿＿＿＿＿＿＿＿＿＿＿＿＿ Grade: ＿＿＿＿＿＿

65. What are the symptoms of psoriasis?

＿＿＿＿＿＿＿＿＿＿＿＿＿＿＿＿＿＿＿＿＿＿＿＿＿＿＿＿＿＿＿＿＿＿＿＿＿＿

＿＿＿＿＿＿＿＿＿＿＿＿＿＿＿＿＿＿＿＿＿＿＿＿＿＿＿＿＿＿＿＿＿＿＿＿＿＿

＿＿＿＿＿＿＿＿＿＿＿＿＿＿＿＿＿＿＿＿＿＿＿＿＿＿＿＿＿＿＿＿＿＿＿＿＿＿

＿＿＿＿＿＿＿＿＿＿＿＿＿＿＿＿＿＿＿＿＿＿＿＿＿＿＿＿＿＿＿＿＿＿＿＿＿＿

66. A man brings his 85-year-old mother to the physician's office. He tells you that his mother lives in a local care home. When the physician examines the patient, you notice multiple decubitus ulcers on her body. Explain why this would be a particular cause of concern.

＿＿＿＿＿＿＿＿＿＿＿＿＿＿＿＿＿＿＿＿＿＿＿＿＿＿＿＿＿＿＿＿＿＿＿＿＿＿

＿＿＿＿＿＿＿＿＿＿＿＿＿＿＿＿＿＿＿＿＿＿＿＿＿＿＿＿＿＿＿＿＿＿＿＿＿＿

＿＿＿＿＿＿＿＿＿＿＿＿＿＿＿＿＿＿＿＿＿＿＿＿＿＿＿＿＿＿＿＿＿＿＿＿＿＿

＿＿＿＿＿＿＿＿＿＿＿＿＿＿＿＿＿＿＿＿＿＿＿＿＿＿＿＿＿＿＿＿＿＿＿＿＿＿

67. List the three types of skin biopsy performed by a physician.

＿＿＿＿＿＿＿＿＿＿＿＿＿＿＿＿＿＿＿＿＿＿＿＿＿＿＿＿＿＿＿＿＿＿＿＿＿＿

＿＿＿＿＿＿＿＿＿＿＿＿＿＿＿＿＿＿＿＿＿＿＿＿＿＿＿＿＿＿＿＿＿＿＿＿＿＿

＿＿＿＿＿＿＿＿＿＿＿＿＿＿＿＿＿＿＿＿＿＿＿＿＿＿＿＿＿＿＿＿＿＿＿＿＿＿

＿＿＿＿＿＿＿＿＿＿＿＿＿＿＿＿＿＿＿＿＿＿＿＿＿＿＿＿＿＿＿＿＿＿＿＿＿＿

**68.** List the three bacterial skin infections that develop in the hair follicles.

_____

_____

_____

_____

**69.** A patient has a band of lesions on his back made up of small red papules. What skin disorder does this person most likely have? Explain what causes the condition.

_____

_____

_____

_____

**70.** A father brings his 8-year-old son to the physician, who diagnoses the child with pediculosis. What advice could you give the father to ensure that no other members of the family become infected? List three things that the father could do to contain the problem.

_____

_____

_____

_____

**71.** What is the full version of the cancer prevention message "Slip! Slop! Slap! Wrap!"?

_____

_____

_____

_____

**72.** The physician suspects that a patient has ringworm. Explain what method the physician would most likely use to confirm the diagnosis?

_____

_____

_____

_____

## COG TRUE OR FALSE? 

Grade: _____

**73.** Indicate whether the statements are true or false by placing the letter T (true) or F (false) on the line preceding the statement.

**a.** _____ Before applying a bandage, you should perform surgical asepsis.

**b.** _____ Young women are more likely to develop keloids than young men.

**c.** _____ A wound culture is obtained by excising the wound.

**d.** _____ Erythema is best treated with antihistamines.

## COG AFF CASE STUDY FOR CRITICAL THINKING

Grade: _____

1. A patient has come into the physician's office for a skin biopsy on his thigh. After the physician has removed the tissue, she asks you to bandage the area. List three things you should do while you are bandaging the patient's thigh to ensure that it is both sterile and secure. Explain why they are important.

_____

_____

_____

_____

2. There are three patients waiting to be seen by a physician, and all of the appointments are slightly behind schedule. One of the patients is a young man who has clusters of wheals on his left arm. The second patient is a 7-year-old girl who has dry scaly crusts on her face and neck. The third patient is a 5-year-old boy with dried skin flakes and bald patches on his scalp. All three patients are itching, and the receptionist is concerned that they might be contagious. You have only one spare examination room. Which patient would you isolate in the examination room? Explain your answer.

_____

_____

_____

_____

3. Your patient is a 25-year-old female who has been to see the physician several times for severe sunburn. You know that her lifestyle can lead to long-term skin problems. Explain how you could educate her about staying safe in the sun. Include some of the early warning signs of skin cancer that she should keep an eye out for.

_____

_____

_____

_____

4. A mother brings her 8-year-old son to the physician's office, and the child is diagnosed with pediculosis. She insists that her child cannot possibly have lice because they live in a very clean home. The mother demands that the physician examines the child again. What do you say to the mother to calm her down? How do you reassure her?

_____

_____

_____

_____

**5.** A 14-year-old boy comes into the physician's office with severe acne vulgaris on his face and neck. He is embarrassed and depressed about his condition and is worried that it will never get better. He says that he has tried every over-the-counter medication and that this is his last hope. What would you say to this patient?

_____

_____

_____

_____

## PROCEDURE 13-1  Apply a Warm or Cold Compress

Name: _____  Date: _____  Time: _____  Grade: _____

**EQUIPMENT/SUPPLIES:** Warm compresses—appropriate solution (water with possible antiseptic if ordered), warmed to 110°F or recommended temperature; bath thermometer; absorbent material (cloths, gauze); waterproof barriers; hot water bottle (optional); clean or sterile basin; gloves. Cold compresses—appropriate solution; ice bag or cold pack; absorbent material (cloths, gauze); waterproof barriers; gloves

**STANDARDS:** Given the needed equipment and a place to work, the student will perform this skill with _____ % accuracy in a total of _____ minutes. *(Your instructor will tell you what the percentage and time limits will be before you begin.)*

**KEY:**  4 = Satisfactory  0 = Unsatisfactory  NA = This step is not counted

| PROCEDURE STEPS | SELF | PARTNER | INSTRUCTOR |
|---|---|---|---|
| 1. Wash your hands and put on gloves. | ❏ | ❏ | ❏ |
| 2. Check the physician's order and assemble the equipment and supplies. | ❏ | ❏ | ❏ |
| 3. Pour the appropriate solution into the basin. For hot compresses, check the temperature of the warmed solution. | ❏ | ❏ | ❏ |
| 4. Greet and identify the patient. Identify yourself including your title. Explain the procedure. | ❏ | ❏ | ❏ |
| 5. Ask patient to remove appropriate clothing. | ❏ | ❏ | ❏ |
| 6. Gown and drape accordingly. | ❏ | ❏ | ❏ |
| 7. **AFF** Explain how to respond to a patient who is hearing impaired. | ❏ | ❏ | ❏ |
|  |  |  |  |
|  |  |  |  |
| 8. Protect the examination table with a waterproof barrier. | ❏ | ❏ | ❏ |
| 9. Place absorbent material or gauze into the prepared solution. Wring out excess moisture. | ❏ | ❏ | ❏ |
| 10. Place the compress on the patient's skin and ask about comfort of temperature. | ❏ | ❏ | ❏ |
| 11. Observe the skin for changes in color. | ❏ | ❏ | ❏ |
| 12. Arrange the wet compress over the area. |  |  |  |

**PSY   PROCEDURE 13-1     Apply a Warm or Cold Compress** (continued)

| | | | |
|---|---|---|---|
| **13.** Insulate the compress with plastic or another waterproof barrier. | | | |
| **14.** Check the compress frequently for moisture and temperature.<br>  **a.** Hot water bottles or ice packs may be used to maintain the temperature.<br>  **b.** Rewet absorbent material as needed. | | | |
| **15.** After the prescribed amount of time, usually 20 to 30 minutes, remove the compress.<br>  **a.** Discard disposable materials.<br>  **b.** Disinfect reusable equipment. | | | |
| **16.** Remove your gloves and wash your hands. | | | |
| **17.** Log into the Electronic Medical Record (EMR) using your username and secure password OR obtain the paper medical record from a secure location and assure it is kept away from public access. Document the procedure including:<br>  **a.** Length of treatment, type of solution, temperature of solution<br>  **b.** Skin color after treatment, assessment of the area, and patient's reactions | | | |
| **18.** When finished, log out of the EMR and/or replace the paper medical record in an appropriate and secure location. | | | |

**CALCULATION**

Total Possible Points: _____

Total Points Earned: _____ Multiplied by 100 = _____ Divided by Total Possible Points = _____ %

**PASS   FAIL   COMMENTS:**
 ❑        ❑

Student's signature _____ Date _____

Partner's signature _____ Date _____

Instructor's signature _____ Date _____

**PSY** PROCEDURE 13-2 **Assist with Therapeutic Soaks**

Name: _____ Date: _____ Time: _____ Grade: _____

**EQUIPMENT/SUPPLIES:** Clean or sterile basin or container to comfortably contain the body part to be soaked; solution and/or medication; dry towels; bath thermometer; gloves

**STANDARDS:** Given the needed equipment and a place to work, the student will perform this skill with _____ % accuracy in a total of _____ minutes. *(Your instructor will tell you what the percentage and time limits will be before you begin.)*

**KEY:** 4 = Satisfactory 0 = Unsatisfactory NA =This step is not counted

| PROCEDURE STEPS | SELF | PARTNER | INSTRUCTOR |
|---|---|---|---|
| **1.** Wash your hands and apply your gloves. | ❏ | ❏ | ❏ |
| **2.** Assemble the equipment and supplies, including the appropriately sized basin or container. Pad surfaces of container for comfort. | ❏ | ❏ | ❏ |
| **3.** Fill the container with solution and check the temperature with a bath thermometer. The temperature should be below 110°F. | ❏ | ❏ | ❏ |
| **4.** Greet and identify the patient. Identify yourself including your credentials. Explain the procedure. | ❏ | ❏ | ❏ |
| **5. AFF** Explain how to respond to the patient who has dementia. | ❏ | ❏ | ❏ |
| _____ | | | |
| _____ | | | |
| _____ | | | |
| _____ | | | |
| **6.** Slowly lower the patient's extremity or body part into the container. | ❏ | ❏ | ❏ |
| **7.** Arrange the part comfortably and in easy alignment. | ❏ | ❏ | ❏ |
| **8.** Check for pressure areas and pad the edges as needed for comfort. | ❏ | ❏ | ❏ |
| **9.** Check the solution every 5 to 10 minutes for proper temperature. | ❏ | ❏ | ❏ |
| **10.** Soak for the prescribed amount of time, usually 15 to 20 minutes. | ❏ | ❏ | ❏ |
| **11.** Remove the body part from the solution and carefully dry the area with a towel. | ❏ | ❏ | ❏ |
| **12.** Properly care for the equipment; appropriately dispose of single-use supplies and wash your hands. | ❏ | ❏ | ❏ |

| FSY PROCEDURE 13-2 **Assist with Therapeutic Soaks** (continued) | | | |
|---|---|---|---|
| **13.** Log into the Electronic Medical Record (EMR) using your username and secure password OR obtain the paper medical record from a secure location and assure it is kept away from public access. Document the procedure including:<br>**a.** Length of treatment, type of solution, temperature of solution<br>**b.** Skin color after treatment, assessment of the area, and patient's reactions | ❏ | ❏ | ❏ |
| **14.** When finished, log out of the EMR and/or replace the paper medical record in an appropriate and secure location. | ❏ | ❏ | ❏ |

**CALCULATION**

Total Possible Points: _____

Total Points Earned: _____ Multiplied by 100 = _____ Divided by Total Possible Points = _____ %

**PASS    FAIL    COMMENTS:**
❏          ❏

Student's signature _____ Date _____

Partner's signature _____ Date _____

Instructor's signature _____ Date _____

**PSY** P R O C E D U R E  1 3 - 3   **Apply a Tubular Gauze Bandage**

Name: _____ Date: _____ Time: _____ Grade: _____

**EQUIPMENT/SUPPLIES:** Tubular gauze, applicator, tape, scissors

**STANDARDS:** Given the needed equipment and a place to work, the student will perform this skill with _____ % accuracy in a total of _____ minutes. *(Your instructor will tell you what the percentage and time limits will be before you begin.)*

**KEY:**         4 = Satisfactory         0 = Unsatisfactory         NA =This step is not counted

| PROCEDURE STEPS | SELF | PARTNER | INSTRUCTOR |
|---|---|---|---|
| **1.** Wash your hands and assemble the equipment. | ❏ | ❏ | ❏ |
| **2.** Greet and identify the patient. Identify yourself including your credentials. Explain the procedure. | ❏ | ❏ | ❏ |
| **3.** **AFF** Explain how to respond to a patient who is visually impaired. | ❏ | ❏ | ❏ |
| _____ | | | |
| _____ | | | |
| _____ | | | |
| _____ | | | |
| _____ | | | |
| **4.** Choose the appropriate-size tubular gauze applicator and gauze width. | ❏ | ❏ | ❏ |
| **5.** Select and cut or tear adhesive tape in lengths to secure the gauze ends. | ❏ | ❏ | ❏ |
| **6.** Place the gauze bandage on the applicator in the following manner: <br> **a.** Be sure that the applicator is upright (open end up) and placed on a flat surface. <br> **b.** Pull a sufficient length of gauze from the stock box, ready to cut. <br> **c.** Open the end of the length of gauze and slide it over the upper end of the applicator. <br> **d.** Push estimated amount of gauze needed for this procedure onto the applicator. <br> **e.** Cut the gauze when the required amount of gauze has been transferred to the applicator. | ❏ | ❏ | ❏ |
| **7.** Place applicator over the distal end of the affected part. Hold it in place as you move to Step 7. | ❏ | ❏ | ❏ |
| **8.** Slide applicator containing the gauze up to the proximal end of the affected part. | ❏ | ❏ | ❏ |

**PSY** PROCEDURE 13-3    **Apply a Tubular Gauze Bandage**
(continued)

| | | | |
|---|---|---|---|
| **9.** Pull the applicator 1 to 2 inches past the end of the affected part if the part is to be completely covered. | ❏ | ❏ | ❏ |
| **10.** Turn the applicator one full turn to anchor the bandage. | ❏ | ❏ | ❏ |
| **11.** Move the applicator toward the proximal part as before. | ❏ | ❏ | ❏ |
| **12.** Move the applicator forward about 1 inch beyond the original starting point. | ❏ | ❏ | ❏ |
| **13.** Repeat the procedure until the desired coverage is obtained. | ❏ | ❏ | ❏ |
| **14.** The final layer should end at the proximal part of the affected area. Remove the applicator. | ❏ | ❏ | ❏ |
| **15.** Secure the bandage in place with adhesive tape or cut the gauze into two tails and tie them at the base of the tear. | ❏ | ❏ | ❏ |
| **16.** Tie the two tails around the closest proximal joint. | ❏ | ❏ | ❏ |
| **17.** Use the adhesive tape sparingly to secure the end if not using a tie. | ❏ | ❏ | ❏ |
| **18.** Properly care for or dispose of equipment and supplies. | ❏ | ❏ | ❏ |
| **19.** Clean the work area. Wash your hands. | ❏ | ❏ | ❏ |
| **20.** Log into the Electronic Medical Record (EMR) using your username and secure password OR obtain the paper medical record from a secure location and assure it is kept away from public access. | ❏ | ❏ | ❏ |
| **21.** When finished, log out of the EMR and/or replace the paper medical record in an appropriate and secure location. | ❏ | ❏ | ❏ |

**CALCULATION**

Total Possible Points: _____

Total Points Earned: _____ Multiplied by 100 = _____ Divided by Total Possible Points = _____ %

**PASS    FAIL    COMMENTS:**
❏          ❏

Student's signature _____ Date _____

Partner's signature _____ Date _____

Instructor's signature _____ Date _____

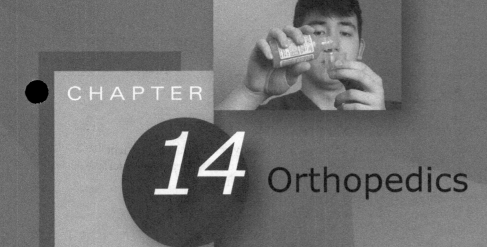

# CHAPTER 14 Orthopedics

## Learning Outcomes

**Cognitive Domain**

1. Spell key terms
2. Define medical terms and abbreviations related to all body systems
3. Describe structural organization of the human body
4. List major organs in each body system
5. Identify the anatomical location of major organs in each body system
6. Describe the normal function of each body system
7. Identify common pathology related to each body system including signs, symptoms, and etiology
8. Discuss the role of the medical assistant in caring for the patient with a musculoskeletal system disorder
9. Describe the various types of ambulatory aids

**Psychomotor Domain**

1. Apply an arm sling (Procedure 14-1)
2. Apply cold packs (Procedure 14-2)
3. Use a hot water bottle or commercial hot pack (Procedure 14-3)
4. Measure a patient for axillary crutches (Procedure 14-4)
5. Instruct a patient in various crutch gaits (Procedure 14-5)

**Affective Domain**

1. Incorporate critical thinking skills when performing patient assessment
2. Incorporate critical thinking skills when performing patient care.
3. Show awareness of a patient's concerns related to the procedure being performed
4. Demonstrate empathy, active listening, nonverbal communication
5. Demonstrate respect for individual diversity including gender, race, religion, age, economic status, appearance
6. Explain to a patient the rationale for performance of a procedure
7. Demonstrate sensitivity to patient rights
8. Protect the integrity of the medical record

**ABHES Competencies**

1. Assist the physician with the regimen of diagnostic and treatment modalities as they relate to each body system
2. Comply with federal, state, and local health laws and regulations
3. Communicate on the recipient's level of comprehension
4. Serve as a liaison between the physician and others
5. Show empathy and impartiality when dealing with patients
6. Document accurately

Name: _____    Date: _____    Grade: _____

## ⚙ MULTIPLE CHOICE

Circle the letter preceding the correct answer.

**1.** The rebound phenomenon happens:
   **a.** when the body secretes callus, which fills in fractures and mends damaged bone.
   **b.** when the body experiences bulging discs or biomechanical stress as a result of poor posture.
   **c.** when the body overcompensates for a muscle sprain by increasing use of unaffected muscles.
   **d.** when the body responds to extremes of temperature for long periods of time by exerting an opposite effect.
   **e.** when the body releases fat droplets from the yellow marrow of the long bones.

**2.** In which crutch gait do both legs leave the floor together?
   **a.** One-arm gait
   **b.** Two-point gait
   **c.** Three-point gait
   **d.** Four-point gait
   **e.** Swing-through gait

**3.** A fracture that occurs in flat bones (like those of the skull) and results in a fragment being driven below the surface of the bone is called a(n):
   **a.** depressed fracture.
   **b.** impacted fracture.
   **c.** pathological fracture.
   **d.** compression fracture.
   **e.** spiral fracture.

**4.** A possible cause of gout is:
   **a.** a liver disorder.
   **b.** a degenerative strain.
   **c.** a diet high in purines.
   **d.** the wear and tear on weight-bearing joints.
   **e.** the release of fat droplets from the marrow of long bones.

*Scenario for questions 5 and 6:* The physician has determined that a male patient will need to wear a short arm cast on his left arm as part of the treatment for his fracture. The physician asks you to help her apply the cast to the patient. You assemble the items needed to apply the cast. As the physician prepares the limb for casting, you soak the casting material and press it until it is no longer dripping. Then, the physician wraps the affected limb with the material. After the cast has dried, the physician asks you to apply an arm sling to the patient's left arm.

**5.** How should the physician wrap the patient's affected arm with the soaked casting material?
   **a.** From the axilla to mid palm
   **b.** From mid palm to the axilla
   **c.** From the elbow to mid palm
   **d.** From mid palm to the elbow
   **e.** From the axilla to the elbow

**6.** Which of these steps will you follow when applying the arm sling?
   **a.** Cover the left arm with soft knitted tubular material.
   **b.** Position the hand of the left arm at a 90-degree angle.
   **c.** Instruct the patient in various gaits using auxiliary crutches.
   **d.** Check the patient's circulation by pinching each of his fingers.
   **e.** Insert the elbow of the right arm into the pouch end of the sling.

**7.** Rheumatoid arthritis is a(n):
   **a.** joint failure.
   **b.** bone fracture.
   **c.** skeletal tumor.
   **d.** autoimmune disease.
   **e.** spine disorder.

**8.** Tendonitis that is caused by calcium deposits is called:
   **a.** fibromyalgia.
   **b.** iontophoresis.
   **c.** hardened tendons.
   **d.** calcific tendonitis.
   **e.** depository tendonitis.

*Scenario for questions 9 and 10:* A 20-year-old female patient is visiting your office because of pain in her knee. During the patient interview, the patient tells you that she experiences pain when walking down stairs and getting out of bed. You learn that she is very active and is a member of her university's track and field team.

**9.** What musculoskeletal disorder does this patient have?
   **a.** Plantar fasciitis
   **b.** Lateral humeral epicondylitis
   **c.** Dupuytren contracture
   **d.** Chondromalacia patellae
   **e.** Ankylosing spondylitis

10. What surgical procedure may need to be performed to repair or remove damaged cartilage if the patient's case is severe?
    a. Arthrogram
    b. Arthroplasty
    c. Arthroscopy
    d. Phonophoresis
    e. Electromyography

11. You should *not* apply cold to:
    a. open wounds.
    b. the pregnant uterus.
    c. acute inflammation.
    d. the very young and older adults.
    e. a contusion.

12. Proper cane length calls for the cane to be level with the user's greater trochanter and for the user's elbow to be bent at a:
    a. 30-degree angle.
    b. 50-degree angle.
    c. 60-degree angle.
    d. 80-degree angle.
    e. 90-degree angle.

13. A subluxation is a(n):
    a. dislocation of a facet joint.
    b. partial dislocation of a joint.
    c. complete dislocation of a joint.
    d. dislocation that damages the tendons.
    e. injury to a joint capsule.

14. How is immobilization during closed reduction achieved?
    a. Casting
    b. Surgery
    c. Exercise
    d. Splinting
    e. Ultrasound

15. You and the physician must wear goggles during a cast removal to protect against:
    a. flying particles.
    b. dangerous waves.
    c. unsanitary material.
    d. bloodborne pathogens.
    e. disease and infection.

16. If a fat embolus becomes lodged in a patient's pulmonary or coronary vessels, the patient may experience:
    a. limited mobility.
    b. pain and swelling.
    c. a warm sensation.
    d. an infarction and death.
    e. swelling and numbness.

17. The most common site of bursitis is the:
    a. foot.
    b. wrist.
    c. elbow.
    d. shoulder.
    e. ankle.

18. Your patient has just received a fiberglass leg cast. Which of the following is a sign that proper circulation is present?
    a. Red, hot toes
    b. Swollen toes
    c. Clammy toes
    d. Cold, blue toes
    e. Warm, pink toes

19. Osteoporosis is a condition in which the bones lack:
    a. bursae.
    b. calcium.
    c. vitamin D.
    d. malignancies.
    e. marrow.

20. Your patient is recovering from a strain in his Achilles tendon. He is unable to use one leg, but he has coordination and upper body strength. Which of the following ambulatory assist devices should this patient use to gain mobility?
    a. Cast
    b. Cane
    c. Sling
    d. Walker
    e. Crutches

## ◼◻◻ MATCHING

Grade: _____

Place the letter preceding the definition on the line next to the term.

**Key Terms**

21. _____ ankylosing spondylitis
22. _____ arthrogram
23. _____ arthroscopy
24. _____ arthroplasty
25. _____ bursae
26. _____ callus
27. _____ contracture
28. _____ contusion
29. _____ electromyography
30. _____ embolus
31. _____ goniometer
32. _____ iontophoresis
33. _____ kyphosis
34. _____ lordosis
35. _____ Paget disease
36. _____ phonophoresis
37. _____ prosthesis
38. _____ reduction
39. _____ scoliosis

**Definitions**

a. introduction of various chemical ions into the skin by means of electrical current

b. a deposit of new bone tissue that forms between the healing ends of broken bones

c. any artificial replacement for a missing body part, such as false teeth or an artificial limb

d. a mass of matter (thrombus, air, fat globule) freely floating in the circulatory system

e. small sacs filled with clear synovial fluid that surround some joints

f. a lateral curve of the spine, usually in the thoracic area, with a corresponding curve in the lumbar region, causing uneven shoulders and hips

g. an abnormal shortening of muscles around a joint caused by atrophy of the muscles and resulting in flexion and fixation

h. an abnormally deep ventral curve at the lumbar flexure of the spine; also known as swayback

i. ultrasound treatment used to force medications into tissues

j. surgical repair of a joint

k. an abnormally deep dorsal curvature of the thoracic spine; also known as humpback or hunchback

l. an examination of the inside of a joint through an arthroscope

m. x-ray of a joint

n. an instrument used to measure the angle of joints for range of motion

o. a collection of blood in tissues after an injury; a bruise

p. correcting a fracture by realigning the bones; may be closed (corrected by manipulation) or open (requires surgery)

q. a stiffening of the spine with inflammation

r. a recording of electrical nerve transmission in skeletal muscles

s. a degenerative bone disease usually in older persons with bone destruction and poor repair

## ◼◻◻ MATCHING

Grade: _____

Place the letter preceding the condition on the line preceding the ambulatory assist device.

**Devices**

40. _____ crutches
41. _____ cane
42. _____ walker

**Conditions**

a. Patient A is a 53-year-old female who has recently undergone hip replacement surgery. She is able to walk and needs only slight assistance until she has fully healed from her surgery.

b. Patient B is a 17-year-old male with a sprained ankle. His condition is temporary, but he needs assistance walking with one affected leg.

c. Patient C is a 79-year-old female with osteoarthritis. She has trouble maintaining her balance when walking.

## ∞ IDENTIFICATION

Grade: _____

**43.** Complete this chart to show the different types of fractures.

| Type of Fracture | Description |
|---|---|
| Avulsion | Tearing away of bone fragments caused by sharp twisting force applied to ligaments or tendons attached to bone |
| Comminuted | **a.** |
| Compound or open | Broken end of bone punctures and protrudes through skin |
| **b.** | Damage to bone caused by strong force on both ends of the bone, such as through a fall |
| Depressed | Fracture of flat bones (typically the skull) which causes bone fragment to be driven below the surface of the bone |
| Greenstick | **c.** |
| Impacted | One bone segment driven into another |
| **d.** | Break is slanted across the axis of the bone |
| Pathological | Related to a disease such as osteoporosis, Paget disease, bone cysts, tumors, or cancers |
| Simple or closed | **e.** |
| Spiral | Appears as an S-shaped fracture on radiographs and occurs with torsion or twisting injuries |
| **f.** | A fracture at right angles to axis of bone that is usually caused by excessive bending force or direct pressure on bone |

**44.** Complete this chart, which shows the variations of arthritis, the most commonly affected site, and the characteristics of the variation.

| Disease | Affected Site | Characteristics |
|---|---|---|
| Osteoarthritis | Weight-bearing joints | **a.** |
| **b.** | Synovial membrane lining of the joint | Usually begins in non–weight-bearing joints, but can spread to many other joints; results in inflammation, pain, stiffness, and crippling deformities |
| Ankylosing spondylitis (or Marie-Strümpell disease) | **c.** | Rheumatoid arthritis of the spine; results in extreme forward flexion of the spine and tightness in the hip flexors |
| **d.** | Joint, usually the great toe | An overproduction of uric acid leads to a deposit of uric acid crystals in the joint; results in a painful, hot, inflamed joint; can become chronic |

**45.** Review the list of tasks below and determine which tasks you may be responsible for as a medical assistant working in the clinical area. Place a check mark in the "Yes" column for those duties you may be responsible for doing and place a check mark in the "No" column for those tasks that you would not perform.

| Task | Yes | No |
|---|---|---|
| **a.** Instruct patients on how to use crutches, a cane, a walker, or a wheelchair. | | |
| **b.** Inform patients of the potential injury associated with heating pad use. | | |
| **c.** Perform arthroplasty to repair or remove cartilage damaged by chondromalacia patellae. | | |
| **d.** Assemble the supplies needed to cast a fractured bone. | | |
| **e.** Treat tendonitis with a transverse friction massage. | | |
| **f.** Help older adult patients avoid hip fractures by reviewing fall prevention techniques. | | |
| **g.** Observe and report signs of a musculoskeletal disorder, such as skin color, temperature, tone, and tenderness. | | |
| **h.** Give patients specific and detailed instructions for applying heat or cold at home. | | |
| **i.** Identify the type of fracture and decide the method of treatment. | | |

**46.** Use the word bank to fill in the blanks in this paragraph about bone tumors.
The cause of malignant skeletal tumors is unknown but may be linked to rapid development of _____ during youth. An early sign of bone tumors is bone pain, which is most intense at night. Some bone tumors have the potential to spread to the skin and muscles. Bone tumors are identified by _____ after a bone scan reveals the need for further diagnosis. Treatments include surgery, amputation, and _____.

**Word Bank:**
biopsy          bone tissue          chemotherapy
CT scan         osteosarcomas

## **COG** SHORT ANSWER

_____ Grade: _____

**47. Describe these three abnormal spine curvatures.**

**a.** Lordosis: _____

**b.** Kyphosis: _____

**c.** Scoliosis: _____

**48.** What is the difference between a sprain and a strain? How are they similar?

_____

_____

_____

_____

**49.** Name four common sites of dislocations.

_____

_____

_____

_____

**50.** Your patient is complaining of pain in his wrist. You learn that the pain began after he fell from a ladder and used his hand to break his fall. What would be signs that the patient has fractured his arm?

_____

_____

_____

_____

**51.** What is the difference between a spiral fracture and an avulsion fracture?

_____

_____

_____

_____

**52.** What test is performed that determines whether back pain results from a herniated intervertebral disc? How is the test done, and what is a positive indicator?

_____

_____

_____

_____

**53.** Both heat and cold treatments are used to relieve pain, but how do their uses differ?

_____

_____

_____

_____

**54.** List the five gaits utilized by patients who use crutches to assist them with walking.

_____

_____

_____

**55.** The physician has just applied a plaster cast to a patient. What instructions and information should you give to the patient regarding her plaster cast?

_____

_____

_____

## COG TRUE OR FALSE?

Grade: _____

Indicate whether the statements are true or false by placing the letter T (true) or F (false) on the line preceding the statement.

**56.** _____ Heat, such as heat from a heating pad or hot water bottle, should not be applied to the uterus of a pregnant woman.

**57.** _____ A greenstick fracture is a partial or incomplete fracture in which only one side of the bone is broken.

**58.** _____ The swing-through gait is the gait most commonly used to train patients to use crutches.

**59.** _____ Fibromyalgia is easy to diagnose because the symptoms are constant and centrally located in one joint socket.

## AFF CASE STUDY FOR CRITICAL THINKING

Grade: _____

**1.** Deirdre is a 52-year-old patient. She visits the office with a complaint of joint pain. After taking Deirdre's height and weight measurements, you notice that she is 1 and 1/2 inches shorter than she was just 2 years ago. After speaking with the patient, you learn that she does not exercise. The physician suspects Deirdre may have osteoporosis. What tests might the physician order to confirm his diagnosis? What preventative medicine information might be useful for Deirdre?

_____

_____

_____

_____

**2.** Maddy, a 9-year-old patient, needs to have her arm put into a cast after it is discovered that she has a greenstick fracture. The physician informs Maddy's mother that he will be using a fiberglass cast to immobilize Maddy's arm. Maddy's mother grows concerned after speaking with the physician. She has heard that fiberglass can be dangerous, and she wonders why the physician does not use a plaster like the cast she received when she was a child with a fractured arm. Explain to Maddy's mother the benefits of a fiberglass cast over a plaster cast, especially when the patient is a young, active child.

_____

_____

_____

_____

**3.** Your coworker Ben is moving some boxes from the reception area to a closet in the office. As you walk by, you observe him bending his back and lifting a box with extended arms. You know that this method of lifting could lead to serious back problems, so you decide to speak to Ben about avoiding back strain. What should you say to Ben? How would you respond if he laughs and tells you he is fine?

_____

_____

_____

_____

**4.** A 46-year-old patient has been advised by the physician to avoid using his strained knee. After you secure an ice pack to the patient's knee, you begin to instruct the patient in how to care for his knee at home. While you are speaking, the patient interrupts you saying that he has had this injury before and will "just throw a heating pad on there" like he has done in the past. How would you respond to the patient?

_____

_____

_____

_____

## PSY PROCEDURE 14-1 **Apply an Arm Sling**

Name: _____ Date: _____ Time: _____ Grade: _____

**EQUIPMENT/SUPPLIES:** A canvas arm sling with adjustable straps.

**STANDARDS:** Given the needed equipment and a place to work, the student will perform this skill with _____ % accuracy in a total of _____ minutes. *(Your instructor will tell you what the percentage and time limits will be before you begin.)*

**KEY:** 4 = Satisfactory     0 = Unsatisfactory     NA = This step is not counted

| PROCEDURE STEPS | SELF | PARTNER | INSTRUCTOR |
|---|---|---|---|
| **1.** Wash your hands. | ❏ | ❏ | ❏ |
| **2.** Assemble the equipment and supplies. | ❏ | ❏ | ❏ |
| **3.** Greet and identify the patient and explain the procedure. Identify yourself including your credentials. | ❏ | ❏ | ❏ |
| **4.** **AFF** Explain how to respond to a patient who does not speak English. | ❏ | ❏ | ❏ |
| _____ _____ _____ _____ | | | |
| **5.** Position the affected limb with the hand at slightly less than a 90-degree angle. | ❏ | ❏ | ❏ |
| **6.** Place the affected arm into the sling with the elbow snugly against the back of the sling, and the arm extended through the sling with the hand and/or fingers protruding out of the opposite end of the sling. | ❏ | ❏ | ❏ |
| **7.** Position the strap from the back of the sling around the patient's back, over the opposite shoulder. | ❏ | ❏ | ❏ |
| **8.** Secure the strap by inserting the end through the two metal rings on the top of the sling and further bringing the end of the strap back, looping it through the top metal ring only. | ❏ | ❏ | ❏ |
| **9.** Tighten the strap so that the patient's arm in the sling is slightly elevated. Make sure the strap coming around the patient's shoulder and neck is comfortable, padding if necessary to prevent friction and pressure areas. | ❏ | ❏ | ❏ |
| **10.** Check the patient's level of comfort and distal extremity circulation. | ❏ | ❏ | ❏ |

**FSY**   P R O C E D U R E   1 4 - 1      **Apply an Arm Sling** (continued)

| | | | |
|---|---|---|---|
| **11.** Wash your hands. | | | |
| **12.** **AFF** Log into the Electronic Medical Record (EMR) using your username and secure password OR obtain the paper medical record from a secure location and assure it is kept away from public access. Document the appliance in the patient's chart. | | | |
| **13.** When finished, log out of the EMR and/or replace the paper medical record in an appropriate and secure location. | | | |

**CALCULATION**

Total Possible Points: _____

Total Points Earned: _____ Multiplied by 100 = _____ Divided by Total Possible Points = _____ %

**PASS   FAIL   COMMENTS:**
❑        ❑

Student's signature _____ Date _____

Partner's signature _____ Date _____

Instructor's signature _____ Date _____

## PSY PROCEDURE 14-2 Apply Cold Packs

Name: _____ Date: _____ Time: _____ Grade: _____

**EQUIPMENT/SUPPLIES:** Ice bag and ice chips or small cubes, or disposable cold pack; small towel or cover for ice pack; gauze or tape.

**STANDARDS:** Given the needed equipment and a place to work, the student will perform this skill with _____ % accuracy in a total of _____ minutes. *(Your instructor will tell you what the percentage and time limits will be before you begin.)*

**KEY:** 4 = Satisfactory 0 = Unsatisfactory NA = This step is not counted

| PROCEDURE STEPS | SELF | PARTNER | INSTRUCTOR |
|---|---|---|---|
| **1.** Wash your hands. | ❏ | ❏ | ❏ |
| **2.** Assemble the equipment and supplies, checking the ice bag, if used, for leaks. If using a commercial cold pack, read the manufacturer's directions. | ❏ | ❏ | ❏ |
| **3.** Fill a nondisposable ice bag about two-thirds full.<br>**a.** Press it flat on a surface to express air from the bag.<br>**b.** Seal the container. | ❏ | ❏ | ❏ |
| **4.** If using a commercial chemical ice pack, activate it now. | ❏ | ❏ | ❏ |
| **5.** Cover the bag in a towel or other suitable cover. | ❏ | ❏ | ❏ |
| **6.** Greet and identify the patient. Identify yourself including your credentials. Explain the procedure. | ❏ | ❏ | ❏ |
| **7.** **AFF** Explain how to respond to a patient who has cultural or religious beliefs that prohibit disrobing. | ❏ | ❏ | ❏ |
| _____<br>_____<br>_____<br>_____ | | | |
| **8.** After assessing skin for color and warmth, place the covered ice pack on the area. | ❏ | ❏ | ❏ |
| **9.** Secure the ice pack with gauze or tape. | ❏ | ❏ | ❏ |
| **10.** Apply the treatment for the prescribed amount of time, but no longer than 30 minutes. | ❏ | ❏ | ❏ |
| **11.** During the treatment, assess the skin under the pack frequently for mottling, pallor, or redness. | ❏ | ❏ | ❏ |

## PSY PROCEDURE 14-2 **Apply Cold Packs** (continued)

| | | | |
|---|---|---|---|
| **12.** Properly care for or dispose of equipment and supplies. Wash your hands. | ❏ | ❏ | ❏ |
| **13. AFF** Log into the Electronic Medical Record (EMR) using your username and secure password OR obtain the paper medical record from a secure location and assure it is kept away from public access. | ❏ | ❏ | ❏ |
| **14.** Document the procedure, the site of the application, the results including the condition of the skin after the treatment, and the patient's reactions. | ❏ | ❏ | ❏ |
| **15.** When finished, log out of the EMR and/or replace the paper medical record in an appropriate and secure location. | ❏ | ❏ | ❏ |

**CALCULATION**

Total Possible Points: _____

Total Points Earned: _____ Multiplied by 100 = _____ Divided by Total Possible Points = _____ %

**PASS    FAIL    COMMENTS:**
❏          ❏

Student's signature _____ Date _____

Partner's signature _____ Date _____

Instructor's signature _____ Date _____

**PSY PROCEDURE 14-3   Use a Hot Water Bottle or Commercial Hot Pack**

Name: _____ Date: _____ Time: _____ Grade: _____

**EQUIPMENT/SUPPLIES:** A hot water bottle or commercial hot pack, towel or other suitable covering for the hot pack

**STANDARDS:** Given the needed equipment and a place to work, the student will perform this skill with _____ % accuracy in a total of _____ minutes. *(Your instructor will tell you what the percentage and time limits will be before you begin.)*

**KEY:**        4 = Satisfactory          0 = Unsatisfactory          NA = This step is not counted

| PROCEDURE STEPS | SELF | PARTNER | INSTRUCTOR |
|---|---|---|---|
| **1.** Wash your hands. | ❏ | ❏ | ❏ |
| **2.** Assemble equipment and supplies, checking the hot water bottle for leaks. | ❏ | ❏ | ❏ |
| **3.** Fill the hot water bottle about two-thirds full with warm (110°F) water.<br>**a.** Place the bottle on a flat surface and the opening up; "burp" it by pressing out the air.<br>**b.** If using a commercial hot pack, follow the manufacturer's directions for activating it. | ❏ | ❏ | ❏ |
| **4.** Wrap and secure the pack or bottle before placing it on the patient's skin. | ❏ | ❏ | ❏ |
| **5.** Greet and identify the patient. Identify yourself including your credentials. Explain the procedure. | ❏ | ❏ | ❏ |
| **6.** **AFF** Explain how to respond to a patient who is from a different generation (older) than you are. | ❏ | ❏ | ❏ |
| | | | |
| **7.** After assessing the color of the skin where the treatment is to be applied, place the covered hot pack on the area. | ❏ | ❏ | ❏ |
| **8.** Secure the hot pack with gauze or tape. | ❏ | ❏ | ❏ |
| **9.** Apply the treatment for the prescribed length of time, but no longer than 30 minutes. | ❏ | ❏ | ❏ |
| **10.** During treatment, assess the skin every 10 minutes for pallor (an indication of rebound), excessive redness (indicates temperature may be too high), and swelling (indicates possible tissue damage). | ❏ | ❏ | ❏ |

**FSY** PROCEDURE 14-3 **Use a Hot Water Bottle or Commercial Hot Pack** (continued)

| | | | |
|---|---|---|---|
| **11.** Properly care for or dispose of equipment and supplies. Wash your hands. | ❏ | ❏ | ❏ |
| **12.** **AFF** Log into the Electronic Medical Record (EMR) using your username and secure password OR obtain the paper medical record from a secure location and assure it is kept away from public access. | ❏ | ❏ | ❏ |
| **13.** Document the procedure, the site of the application, the results including the condition of the skin after the treatment, and the patient's reactions. | ❏ | ❏ | ❏ |
| **14.** When finished, log out of the EMR and/or replace the paper medical record in an appropriate and secure location. | ❏ | ❏ | ❏ |

**CALCULATION**

Total Possible Points: _____

Total Points Earned: _____ Multiplied by 100 = _____ Divided by Total Possible Points = _____ %

**PASS    FAIL    COMMENTS:**
❏          ❏

Student's signature _____ Date _____

Partner's signature _____ Date _____

Instructor's signature _____ Date _____

## PSY PROCEDURE 14-4   Measure a Patient for Axillary Crutches

Name: _____   Date: _____   Time: _____   Grade: _____

**EQUIPMENT/SUPPLIES:** Axillary crutches with tips, pads for the axilla, and hand rests, as needed

**STANDARDS:** Given the needed equipment and a place to work, the student will perform this skill with _____ % accuracy in a total of _____ minutes. *(Your instructor will tell you what the percentage and time limits will be before you begin.)*

**KEY:**          4 = Satisfactory          0 = Unsatisfactory          NA = This step is not counted

| PROCEDURE STEPS | SELF | PARTNER | INSTRUCTOR |
|---|---|---|---|
| **1.** Wash your hands. | ❏ | ❏ | ❏ |
| **2.** Assemble the equipment including the correct-size crutches. | ❏ | ❏ | ❏ |
| **3.** Greet and identify the patient. Identify yourself including your credentials. Explain the procedure. | ❏ | ❏ | ❏ |
| **4.** Ensure that the patient is wearing low-heeled shoes with safety soles. | ❏ | ❏ | ❏ |
| **5.** Have the patient stand erect. Support the patient as needed. | ❏ | ❏ | ❏ |
| **6.** **AFF** Explain how to respond to a patient who is hearing impaired. | ❏ | ❏ | ❏ |
| _____ _____ _____ _____ | | | |
| **7.** While standing erect, have the patient hold the crutches in the tripod position. | ❏ | ❏ | ❏ |
| **8.** Adjust the central support in the base. **a.** Tighten the bolts for safety when the proper height is reached. **b.** Adjust the handgrips. Tighten bolts for safety. **c.** If needed, pad axillary bars and handgrips. | ❏ | ❏ | ❏ |
| **9.** Wash your hands. | ❏ | ❏ | ❏ |
| **10.** **AFF** Log into the Electronic Medical Record (EMR) using your username and secure password OR obtain the paper medical record from a secure location and assure it is kept away from public access. | ❏ | ❏ | ❏ |

**PSY** P R O C E D U R E  1 4 - 4  **Measure a Patient for Axillary Crutches** (continued)

| | | | |
|---|---|---|---|
| **11.** Record the procedure, site of the application, results including the condition of the skin after the treatment, the patient's response, the date, time, and your name/credentials. | ❏ | ❏ | ❏ |
| **12.** When finished, log out of the EMR and/or replace the paper medical record in an appropriate and secure location. | ❏ | ❏ | ❏ |

**CALCULATION**

Total Possible Points: _____

Total Points Earned: _____ Multiplied by 100 = _____ Divided by Total Possible Points = _____ %

**PASS   FAIL   COMMENTS**:
❏        ❏

Student's signature _____ Date _____

Partner's signature _____ Date _____

Instructor's signature _____ Date _____

**PSY** P R O C E D U R E  1 4 - 5    **Instruct a Patient in Various Crutch Gaits**

Name: _____ Date: _____ Time: _____ Grade: _____

**EQUIPMENT/SUPPLIES:** Axillary crutches measured appropriately for a patient

**STANDARDS:** Given the needed equipment and a place to work, the student will perform this skill with _____ % accuracy in a total of _____ minutes. *(Your instructor will tell you what the percentage and time limits will be before you begin.)*

**KEY:** 　　　　　4 = Satisfactory 　　　　　0 = Unsatisfactory 　　　　　NA = This step is not counted

| PROCEDURE STEPS | SELF | PARTNER | INSTRUCTOR |
|---|---|---|---|
| **1.** Wash your hands. | ❏ | ❏ | ❏ |
| **2.** Have the patient stand up from a chair:<br>　**a.** The patient holds both crutches on the affected side.<br>　**b.** Then the patient slides to the edge of the chair.<br>　**c.** The patient pushes down on the chair arm on the unaffected side.<br>　**d.** Then the patient pushes to stand. | ❏ | ❏ | ❏ |
| **3.** With one crutch in each hand, rest on the crutches until balance is restored. | ❏ | ❏ | ❏ |
| **4.** Assist the patient to the tripod position. | ❏ | ❏ | ❏ |
| **5.** **AFF** Explain how to respond to a patient who is visually impaired. | ❏ | ❏ | ❏ |
| _____<br>_____<br>_____<br>_____ | | | |
| **6.** Depending upon the patient's weight-bearing ability, coordination, and general state of health, instruct the patient in one or more of the following gaits:<br>　**a.** Three-point gait<br>　**b.** Two-point gait<br>　**c.** Four-point gait<br>　**d.** Swing-through gait | ❏ | ❏ | ❏ |
| **7.** **AFF** Log into the Electronic Medical Record (EMR) using your username and secure password OR obtain the paper medical record from a secure location and assure it is kept away from public access. | ❏ | ❏ | ❏ |

| PSY PROCEDURE 14-5 **Instruct a Patient in Various Crutch Gaits** (continued) | | | |
|---|---|---|---|
| **8.** Record the patient education and instructions. | ❑ | ❑ | ❑ |
| **9.** When finished, log out of the EMR and/or replace the paper medical record in an appropriate and secure location. | ❑ | ❑ | ❑ |

**CALCULATION**

Total Possible Points: _____

Total Points Earned: _____ Multiplied by 100 = _____ Divided by Total Possible Points = _____ %

**PASS   FAIL   COMMENTS:**
  ❑       ❑

Student's signature _____ Date _____

Partner's signature _____ Date _____

Instructor's signature _____ Date _____

CHAPTER

# *15* Ophthalmology and Otolaryngology

## Learning Outcomes

### COG Cognitive Domain

1. Spell key terms
2. Define medical terms and abbreviations related to all body systems
3. Describe structural organization of the human body
4. List major organs in each body system
5. Identify the anatomical location of major organs in each body system
6. Describe the normal function of each body system
7. Identify common pathology related to each body system including signs, symptoms, and etiology
8. Describe patient education procedures associated with the eye, ear, nose, and throat

### PSY Psychomotor Domain

1. Measure distance visual acuity with a Snellen chart (Procedure 15-1)
2. Measure color perception with an Ishihara color plate book (Procedure 15-2)

3. Instill eye medication (Procedure 15-3)
4. Irrigate the eye (Procedure 15-4)
5. Irrigate the ear (Procedure 15-5)
6. Administer an audiometric hearing test (Procedure 15-6)
7. Instill ear medication (Procedure 15-7)
8. Instill nasal medication (Procedure 15-8)

### AFF Affective Domain

1. Incorporate critical thinking skills when performing patient assessment
2. Incorporate critical thinking skills when performing patient care
3. Show awareness of a patient's concerns related to the procedure being performed
4. Demonstrate empathy, active listening, nonverbal communication
5. Demonstrate respect for individual diversity including gender, race, religion, age, economic status, appearance

6. Explain to a patient the rationale for performance of a procedure
7. Demonstrate sensitivity to patient rights
8. Protect the integrity of the medical record

### ABHES Competencies

1. Assist the physician with the regimen of diagnostic and treatment modalities as they relate to each body system
2. Comply with federal, state, and local health laws and regulations
3. Communicate on the recipient's level of comprehension
4. Serve as a liaison between the physician and others
5. Show empathy and impartiality when dealing with patients
6. Document accurately

Name: _____    Date: _____    Grade: _____

## COG MULTIPLE CHOICE

Circle the letter preceding the correct answer.

**1.** The Ishihara method is used to test:
   **a.** hearing.
   **b.** color vision.
   **c.** cataract growth.
   **d.** corneal scarring.
   **e.** for multiple allergies.

**2.** A physician who specializes in disorders of the ears, nose, and throat is an:
   **a.** optician.
   **b.** ophthalmologist.
   **c.** optometrist.
   **d.** otolaryngologist.
   **e.** otitis externa.

**3.** A common cause of diminished hearing is:
   **a.** tinnitus.
   **b.** nasopharynx.
   **c.** cerumen.
   **d.** Ménière disease.
   **e.** strabismus.

**4.** Epistaxis is considered severe if bleeding continues how many minutes after treatment has begun?
   **a.** 5
   **b.** 10
   **c.** 15
   **d.** 20
   **e.** 30

**5.** Which of the following statements is true about preventive eye care?
   **a.** Patients should have regular checkups to maintain healthy eyes.
   **b.** Adults should wear UV-protected sunglasses, but children are not as susceptible.
   **c.** Goggles do not need to be worn if you are wearing your regular glasses.
   **d.** Patients should thoroughly wash hands before rubbing their eyes.
   **e.** Contact lenses cause scarring, so glasses are safer to use.

**6.** It's important to treat sinusitis immediately because:
   **a.** it can lead to severe cases of upper respiratory infections.
   **b.** new allergies might develop while the nasal membrane is infected.
   **c.** mucus may infect areas of throat, nose, and ears if left unchecked.
   **d.** vision may be affected from pressure of sinus cavities on the eyes.
   **e.** complications in the ear and brain may occur, causing damage.

**7.** One symptom of laryngitis is:
   **a.** earache.
   **b.** muscle soreness.
   **c.** coughing.
   **d.** inflamed tonsils.
   **e.** excessive mucus.

**8.** An infection of any of the lacrimal glands of the eyelids is:
   **a.** hordeolum.
   **b.** cataract.
   **c.** glaucoma.
   **d.** conjunctivitis.
   **e.** astigmatism.

**9.** Which of the following could the physician treat with a warm compress?
   **a.** Nosebleed
   **b.** Ear infection
   **c.** Tonsillitis
   **d.** Astigmatism
   **e.** Tinnitus

**10.** The common term for *otitis externa* is:
   **a.** pink eye.
   **b.** nosebleed.
   **c.** Ménière disease.
   **d.** swimmer's ear.
   **e.** presbycusis.

*Scenario for questions 11 and 12:* A patient comes in for an annual exam, and the physician diagnoses her with presbycusis and presbyopia. She complains of an intermittent, high whistling in her right ear and cloudy vision in both eyes.

11. Reading the symptoms and diagnosis above, the patient is most likely:
    a. an infant or a toddler.
    b. a young child to early teen.
    c. an older teen to early 30s.
    d. middle aged.
    e. a senior citizen.

12. One possible cause of the cloudy vision is:
    a. presbyopia.
    b. glaucoma.
    c. Ménière disease.
    d. cataracts.
    e. sinusitis.

13. What is a safe way to remove cerumen?
    a. Gently inserting a tissue into the ear canal
    b. Using a cotton swab and digging out as much as possible
    c. Drops of hydrogen peroxide dropped into the ear
    d. Using an otoscope to melt the earwax
    e. Blowing your nose

14. It's important not to use nasal preparations more than four times a day because they:
    a. severely damage your nasal cavity.
    b. may become addictive.
    c. dry out sinuses and cause congestion.
    d. cause irritation to the throat.
    e. can lead to allergies.

15. Color blindness is a result of:
    a. people failing the Ishihara test.
    b. patients being unable to differentiate between colors.
    c. a deficiency in the number of rods in the eye.
    d. a deficiency in the number of cones in the eye.
    e. the size and shape of the eye.

16. What important advice can you give children when dealing with contagious diseases like pink eye?
    a. Keep your hands washed and clean.
    b. Do not play with children who are sick.
    c. If you sneeze, immediately cover your face with your hand.
    d. Do not go to school if you are sick.
    e. Try to keep from touching anything others have already touched.

17. To test for pharyngitis or tonsillitis, the physician would most likely order:
    a. a blood sample.
    b. a urine sample.
    c. a reflex test.
    d. a throat culture.
    e. radiology.

18. Which form of strabismus is known as *convergent eyes*, in which the eyes are crossed?
    a. Esotropic
    b. Exotropic
    c. Hypotrophic
    d. Hypertrophic
    e. Nonconcomitant

19. The purpose of a hearing aid is to:
    a. fully restore the ability to hear.
    b. assist patients with permanent nerve damage.
    c. amplify sound waves.
    d. differentiate between tones.
    e. permanently correct hearing disabilities.

20. A common treatment for allergic rhinitis is:
    a. sleep.
    b. antihistamine medication.
    c. surgery.
    d. antibiotics.
    e. ear irrigation.

## MATCHING

Grade: _____

Place the letter preceding the definition on the line next to the term.

**Key Terms**

21. _____ astigmatism
22. _____ cerumen
23. _____ decibel
24. _____ fluorescein angiography
25. _____ hyperopia
26. _____ intraocular pressure
27. _____ myopia
28. _____ myringotomy
29. _____ ophthalmologist
30. _____ ophthalmoscope
31. _____ optician
32. _____ optometrist
33. _____ otolaryngologist
34. _____ otoscope
35. _____ presbycusis
36. _____ presbyopia
37. _____ refraction
38. _____ retinal degeneration
39. _____ tinnitus
40. _____ tonometry
41. _____ hordeolum
42. _____ strabismus

**Definitions**

a. physician who specializes in treatment of diseases and disorders of the ears, nose, and throat

b. an extraneous noise heard in one or both ears, described as whirring, ringing, whistling, roaring, etc.; may be continuous or intermittent

c. specialist who can measure for errors of refraction and prescribe lenses but who cannot treat diseases of the eye or perform surgery

d. an instrument used for visual examination of the ear canal and tympanic membrane

e. an incision into the tympanic membrane to relieve pressure

f. unit of intensity of sound

g. an unfocused refraction of light rays on the retina

h. a misalignment of eye movements usually caused by muscle incoordination

i. loss of hearing associated with aging

j. specialist who grinds lenses to correct errors of refraction according to prescriptions

k. yellowish or brownish waxlike secretion in the external ear canal; earwax

l. physician who specializes in treatment of disorders of the eyes

m. farsightedness

n. pathological changes in the cell structure of the retina that impair or destroy its function, resulting in blindness

o. infection of any of the lacrimal glands of the eyelids

p. intravenous injection of fluorescent dye; photographing blood vessels of the eye as dye moves through the vessels

q. measurement of intraocular pressure using a tonometer

r. lighted instrument used to examine the inner surfaces of the eye

s. bending of light rays that enter the pupil to reflect exactly on the fovea centralis, the area of greatest visual acuity

t. pressure within the eyeball

u. vision change (farsightedness) associated with aging

v. nearsightedness

## IDENTIFICATION

Grade: _____

43. Fill in the chart below with three types of vision testing charts, and when you should use each.

| Type of Vision Testing Chart | When You Would Use It |
| --- | --- |
| a. | |
| b. | |
| c. | |

44. Identify the seven causes of hearing loss.

a. _____

b. _____

c. _____

d. _____

e. _____

f. _____

g. _____

**OOG** **SHORT ANSWER**
_____ Grade: _____

45. List five preventive eye care tips that you may be asked to educate patients to follow.

a. _____

b. _____

c. _____

d. _____

e. _____

46. A patient complains of loss of vision and blurring, and cataracts are found in both eyes. How would surgery correct these symptoms?

_____

_____

_____

47. What is the difference between an optometrist and an optician?

_____

_____

_____

48. What is astigmatism?

_____

_____

_____

49. An examination of a patient's eye reveals an irregular corneal surface. What is the method used to diagnose a corneal ulcer?

_____

_____

_____

**50.** A patient comes in complaining of vertigo, nausea, and slight hearing loss. What might the patient be suffering from?

_____

_____

_____

_____

**51.** Why is otitis media so common in infants and young children?

_____

_____

_____

_____

**52.** What is the difference between audiometry and tympanometry?

_____

_____

_____

_____

**53.** List the initial therapy for common epistaxis.

_____

_____

_____

_____

**54.** Why is it so important to treat upper respiratory infections?

_____

_____

_____

_____

**55.** When is the physician likely to suggest that a patient receive a tonsillectomy?

_____

_____

_____

_____

**56.** What is a way to isolate the protein causing allergic reactions in a patient directly?

_____

_____

_____

**57.** Where do nasal polyps usually occur?

_____

_____

_____

_____

## COG TRUE OR FALSE?
Grade: _____

Indicate whether the statements are true or false by placing the letter T (true) or F (false) on the line preceding the statement.

**58.** _____ Diagnosis of vision loss of any type is done by testing the hearing using an audiometer.

**59.** _____ Swimmer's ear goes away on its own and does not need to be treated.

**60.** _____ Allergic rhinitis is another name for hay fever.

**61.** _____ A patient with tonsillitis should be told to rest his voice and speak as little as possible.

## COG AFF CASE STUDY FOR CRITICAL THINKING
Grade: _____

**1.** A patient calls in to the physician's office saying that pink eye is going around her son's school.
He has not been complaining of pain in either eye, but she has noticed that his eyes are red and that he has been sniffing and coughing lately. She wants to know if she should bring him in for a checkup. What should you tell her?

_____

_____

_____

_____

**2.** A patient is interested in getting LASIK surgery to correct her nearsightedness. She is 24 years old, and both of her parents have strong prescriptions for nearsightedness as well. She asks you what the surgery will be like, and if there is any chance that her eyes might revert back to their previous state. What is LASIK surgery and what are the advantages and disadvantages of this procedure? Are there any side effects?

_____

_____

_____

_____

3. A middle-aged patient comes in for a routine checkup and mentions a slight loss of hearing since the last exam. What tests would most likely be ordered by the physician to check his hearing? Are there any preventative education tips that you can give him about hearing loss?

_____

_____

_____

_____

4. A swimmer comes into the office complaining of recurrent swimmer's ear. She says she has used cotton swabs in the past to clear her ear canals, and asks if there is any particular medication she can apply to help keep her ear canals clean. How would you respond to this patient?

_____

_____

_____

_____

5. A young man comes in for a routine checkup and mentions that he will soon be learning to drive. However, the physician gives him the Ishihara test, and the teen fails to differentiate between colors. What information can you give him about color blindness, and what encouragement can you give him in regard to his upcoming driving test?

_____

_____

_____

_____

6. A young boy is brought in because he is complaining of headaches in school. The physician determines that the boy needs glasses and that the headaches are from eye strain. However, the boy states that he does not want glasses because he is afraid his classmates will make fun of him. What would you say to him?

_____

_____

_____

_____

## PSY PROCEDURE 15-1   Measure Distance Visual Acuity with a Snellen Chart

Name: _____   Date: _____   Time: _____   Grade: _____

**EQUIPMENT/SUPPLIES:** Snellen eye chart, paper cup or eye paddle

**STANDARDS:** Given the needed equipment and a place to work, the student will perform this skill with _____ % accuracy in a total of _____ minutes. *(Your instructor will tell you what the percentage and time limits will be before you begin.)*

**KEY:**          4 = Satisfactory          0 = Unsatisfactory          NA = This step is not counted

| PROCEDURE STEPS | SELF | PARTNER | INSTRUCTOR |
|---|---|---|---|
| **1.** Wash your hands. | ❏ | ❏ | ❏ |
| **2.** Prepare the examination area (well lit, distance marker 20 feet from the chart). | ❏ | ❏ | ❏ |
| **3.** Make sure the chart is at eye level. | ❏ | ❏ | ❏ |
| **4.** Greet and identify the patient. Identify yourself and your title. Explain the procedure. | ❏ | ❏ | ❏ |
| **5.** **AFF** Explain how to respond to a patient who is hearing impaired. | ❏ | ❏ | ❏ |
| _____ _____ _____ _____ _____ | | | |
| **6.** Position the patient in a standing or sitting position at the 20-foot marker. | ❏ | ❏ | ❏ |
| **7.** If he or she is not wearing glasses, ask the patient about contact lenses. Mark results accordingly. | ❏ | ❏ | ❏ |
| **8.** Have the patient cover the left eye with the eye paddle. | ❏ | ❏ | ❏ |
| **9.** Instruct the patient not to close the left eye, but to keep both eyes open during the test. | ❏ | ❏ | ❏ |
| **10.** Stand beside the chart and point to each row as the patient reads aloud. <br> **a.** Point to the lines, starting with the 20/200 line. <br> **b.** Record the smallest line that the patient can read with no errors. | ❏ | ❏ | ❏ |

**PSY** P R O C E D U R E   1 5 - 1    **Measure Distance Visual Acuity with a Snellen Chart** (continued)

| | | | |
|---|:---:|:---:|:---:|
| **11.** Repeat the procedure with the right eye covered and record. | ❏ | ❏ | ❏ |
| **12.** Wash your hands. | ❏ | ❏ | ❏ |
| **13.** **AFF** Log into the Electronic Medical Record (EMR) using your username and secure password OR obtain the paper medical record from a secure location and assure it is kept away from public access | ❏ | ❏ | ❏ |
| **14.** Record the procedure. | ❏ | ❏ | ❏ |
| **15.** When finished, log out of the EMR and/or replace the paper medical record in an appropriate and secure location. | ❏ | ❏ | ❏ |

**CALCULATION**

Total Possible Points: _____

Total Points Earned: _____ Multiplied by 100 = _____ Divided by Total Possible Points = _____ %

**PASS    FAIL    COMMENTS:**
  ❏          ❏

Student's signature _____ Date _____

Partner's signature _____ Date _____

Instructor's signature _____ Date _____

## PSY PROCEDURE 15-2 Measuring Color Perception

Name: _____ Date: _____ Time: _____ Grade: _____

**EQUIPMENT/SUPPLIES:** Ishihara color plates, gloves

**STANDARDS:** Given the needed equipment and a place to work, the student will perform this skill with _____ % accuracy in a total of _____ minutes. *(Your instructor will tell you what the percentage and time limits will be before you begin.)*

**KEY:** 4 = Satisfactory 0 = Unsatisfactory NA =This step is not counted

| PROCEDURE STEPS | SELF | PARTNER | INSTRUCTOR |
|---|---|---|---|
| **1.** Wash your hands, put on gloves, and obtain the Ishihara color plate book. | ❏ | ❏ | ❏ |
| **2.** Prepare the examination area (adequate lighting). | ❏ | ❏ | ❏ |
| **3.** Greet and identify the patient and yourself including your title. Explain the procedure. | ❏ | ❏ | ❏ |
| **4.** **AFF** Explain how to respond to a patient who is developmentally challenged. | ❏ | ❏ | ❏ |
| | | | |
| **5.** Hold the first bookplate about 30 inches from the patient. | ❏ | ❏ | ❏ |
| **6.** Ask if the patient can see the "number" within the series of dots. **a.** Record results of test by noting the number or figure the patient reports. **b.** If patient cannot distinguish a pattern, record plate number–x (e.g., 4–x). | ❏ | ❏ | ❏ |
| **7.** The patient should not take more than 3 seconds when reading the plates. **a.** The patient should not squint nor guess. These indicate that the patient is unsure. **b.** Record as plate number–x. | ❏ | ❏ | ❏ |
| **8.** Record the results for plates 1 through 10. **a.** Plate number 11 requires patient to trace a winding line between x's. **b.** Patients with a color deficit will not be able to trace the line. | ❏ | ❏ | ❏ |

**PSY** P R O C E D U R E   1 5 - 2   **Measuring Color Perception** (continued)

| | | | |
|---|---|---|---|
| **9.** Store the book in a closed, protected area to protect the integrity of the colors. | ❏ | ❏ | ❏ |
| **10.** Remove your gloves and wash your hands. | ❏ | ❏ | ❏ |
| **11.** **AFF** Log into the Electronic Medical Record (EMR) using your username and secure password OR obtain the paper medical record from a secure location and assure it is kept away from public access. | ❏ | ❏ | ❏ |
| **12.** Record the procedure in the medical record. | ❏ | ❏ | ❏ |
| **13.** When finished, log out of the EMR and/or replace the paper medical record in an appropriate and secure location. | ❏ | ❏ | ❏ |

**CALCULATION**

Total Possible Points: _____

Total Points Earned: _____ Multiplied by 100 = _____ Divided by Total Possible Points = _____ %

**PASS   FAIL   COMMENTS:**
  ❏         ❏

Student's signature _____ Date _____

Partner's signature _____ Date _____

Instructor's signature _____ Date _____

## PSY PROCEDURE 15-3 Instilling Eye Medication

Name: _____ Date: _____ Time: _____ Grade: _____

**EQUIPMENT/SUPPLIES:** Physician's order and patient record, ophthalmic medications, 2 × 2 gauze pad, tissues, gloves

**STANDARDS:** Given the needed equipment and a place to work, the student will perform this skill with _____ % accuracy in a total of _____ minutes. *(Your instructor will tell you what the percentage and time limits will be before you begin.)*

**KEY:**          4 = Satisfactory          0 = Unsatisfactory          NA = This step is not counted

| PROCEDURE STEPS | SELF | PARTNER | INSTRUCTOR |
|---|---|---|---|
| **1.** Wash your hands. | ❏ | ❏ | ❏ |
| **2.** Obtain the physician order, the correct medication, sterile gauze, and tissues. | ❏ | ❏ | ❏ |
| **3.** Greet and identify the patient. Identify yourself including your title. Explain the procedure. | ❏ | ❏ | ❏ |
| **4.** Ask the patient about any allergies not recorded in the chart. | ❏ | ❏ | ❏ |
| **5.** **AFF** Explain how to respond to a patient who does not speak English. | ❏ | ❏ | ❏ |
| _____ | | | |
| _____ | | | |
| _____ | | | |
| _____ | | | |
| **6.** Position the patient comfortably. Position the patient comfortably. | ❏ | ❏ | ❏ |
| **7.** Put on gloves. Ask the patient to look upward. | ❏ | ❏ | ❏ |
| **8.** Use gauze to gently pull lower lid down. Instill the medication: **a.** Ointment **b.** Drops | ❏ | ❏ | ❏ |
| **9.** Release the lower lid. Have the patient gently close the eyelid and roll the eye. | ❏ | ❏ | ❏ |
| **10.** Wipe off any excess medication with tissue. | ❏ | ❏ | ❏ |
| **11.** Instruct patient to apply light pressure on the puncta lacrimalia for several minutes. | ❏ | ❏ | ❏ |

**PSY** PROCEDURE 15-3 **Instilling Eye Medication** (continued)

| | | | |
|---|---|---|---|
| **12.** Properly care for or dispose of equipment and supplies. Clean the work area. | ❑ | ❑ | ❑ |
| **13.** Wash your hands. | ❑ | ❑ | ❑ |
| **14.** **AFF** Log into the Electronic Medical Record (EMR) using your username and secure password OR obtain the paper medical record from a secure location and assure it is kept away from public access. | ❑ | ❑ | ❑ |
| **15.** Record the procedure. | ❑ | ❑ | ❑ |
| **16.** When finished, log out of the EMR and/or replace the paper medical record in an appropriate and secure location. | ❑ | ❑ | ❑ |

**CALCULATION**

Total Possible Points: _____

Total Points Earned: _____ Multiplied by 100 = _____ Divided by Total Possible Points = _____ %

**PASS   FAIL   COMMENTS:**
❑        ❑

Student's signature _____ Date _____

Partner's signature _____ Date _____

Instructor's signature _____ Date _____

**PSY** PROCEDURE 15-4 **Irrigating the Eye**

Name: _____ Date: _____ Time: _____ Grade: _____

**EQUIPMENT/SUPPLIES:** Physician's order and patient record, small basin, irrigating solution and medication if ordered, protective barrier or towels, emesis basin, sterile bulb syringe or 15- to 20-mL syringe, tissues, gloves

**STANDARDS:** Given the needed equipment and a place to work, the student will perform this skill with _____ % accuracy in a total of _____ minutes. *(Your instructor will tell you what the percentage and time limits will be before you begin.)*

**KEY:**          4 = Satisfactory          0 = Unsatisfactory          NA = This step is not counted

| PROCEDURE STEPS | SELF | PARTNER | INSTRUCTOR |
|---|:---:|:---:|:---:|
| **1.** Wash your hands and put on your gloves. | ❏ | ❏ | ❏ |
| **2.** Assemble the equipment, supplies, and medication if ordered by the physician.<br>**a.** Check solution label three times.<br>**b.** Make sure that the label indicates for ophthalmic use. | ❏ | ❏ | ❏ |
| **3.** Greet and identify the patient. Identify yourself and your title. Explain the procedure. | ❏ | ❏ | ❏ |
| **4.** **AFF** Explain how to respond to a patient who is hard of hearing. | ❏ | ❏ | ❏ |
| _____<br>_____<br>_____<br>_____ | | | |
| **5.** Position the patient comfortably.<br>**a.** Sitting with head tilted with the affected eye lower.<br>**b.** Lying with the affected eye downward. | ❏ | ❏ | ❏ |
| **6.** Drape patient with the protective barrier or towel to avoid wetting the clothing. | ❏ | ❏ | ❏ |
| **7.** Place basin against upper cheek near eye with the towel under the basin.<br>**a.** Wipe the eye from the inner canthus outward with gauze to remove debris.<br>**b.** Separate the eyelids with your thumb and forefinger.<br>**c.** Lightly support your hand, holding the syringe, on the bridge of the patient's nose. | ❏ | ❏ | ❏ |

**PSY** P R O C E D U R E 1 5 - 4 **Irrigating the Eye** (continued)

| | | | |
|---|---|---|---|
| **8.** Holding syringe 1 inch above the eye, gently irrigate from inner to outer canthus.<br>**a.** Use gentle pressure and do not touch the eye.<br>**b.** The physician will order the period of time or amount of solution required. | ❏ | ❏ | ❏ |
| **9.** Use tissues to wipe any excess solution from the patient's face. | ❏ | ❏ | ❏ |
| **10.** Properly dispose of equipment or sanitize as recommended. | ❏ | ❏ | ❏ |
| **11.** Remove your gloves. Wash your hands. | ❏ | ❏ | ❏ |
| **12.** **AFF** Log into the Electronic Medical Record (EMR) using your username and secure password OR obtain the paper medical record from a secure location and assure it is kept away from public access. | ❏ | ❏ | ❏ |
| **13.** Record procedure, including amount, type, and strength of solution; which eye was irrigated; and any observations. | ❏ | ❏ | ❏ |
| **14.** When finished, log out of the EMR and/or replace the paper medical record in an appropriate and secure location. | ❏ | ❏ | ❏ |

**CALCULATION**

Total Possible Points: _____

Total Points Earned: _____ Multiplied by 100 = _____ Divided by Total Possible Points = _____ %

**PASS   FAIL   COMMENTS:**
❏        ❏

Student's signature _____ Date _____

Partner's signature _____ Date _____

Instructor's signature _____ Date _____

## PSY PROCEDURE 15-5 **Irrigating the Ear**

Name: _____ Date: _____ Time: _____ Grade: _____

**EQUIPMENT/SUPPLIES:** Physician's order and patient record, emesis basin or ear basin, waterproof barrier or towels, otoscope, irrigation solution, bowl for solution, gauze

**STANDARDS:** Given the needed equipment and a place to work, the student will perform this skill with _____ % accuracy in a total of _____ minutes. *(Your instructor will tell you what the percentage and time limits will be before you begin.)*

**KEY:**        4 = Satisfactory            0 = Unsatisfactory            NA = This step is not counted

| PROCEDURE STEPS | SELF | PARTNER | INSTRUCTOR |
|---|---|---|---|
| **1.** Wash your hands. | ❏ | ❏ | ❏ |
| **2.** Assemble the equipment and supplies. | ❏ | ❏ | ❏ |
| **3.** Greet and identify the patient. Identify yourself including your title. Explain the procedure. | ❏ | ❏ | ❏ |
| **4.** **AFF** Explain how to respond to a patient who has dementia. | ❏ | ❏ | ❏ |
| _____ _____ _____ _____ | | | |
| **5.** Position the patient comfortably in an erect position. | ❏ | ❏ | ❏ |
| **6.** View the affected ear with an otoscope to locate the foreign matter or cerumen.<br>   **a.** *Adults:* Gently pull up and back to straighten the auditory canal.<br>   **b.** *Children:* Gently pull slightly down and back to straighten the auditory canal. | ❏ | ❏ | ❏ |
| **7.** Drape the patient with a waterproof barrier or towel. | ❏ | ❏ | ❏ |
| **8.** Tilt the patient's head toward the affected side. | ❏ | ❏ | ❏ |
| **9.** Place the drainage basin under the affected ear. | ❏ | ❏ | ❏ |
| **10.** Fill the irrigating syringe or turn on the irrigating device | ❏ | ❏ | ❏ |
| **11.** Gently position the auricle as described above using your non-dominant hand. | ❏ | ❏ | ❏ |

## PROCEDURE 15-5 **Irrigating the Ear** (continued)

| | | | |
|---|---|---|---|
| **12.** With dominant hand, place the tip of the syringe into the auditory meatus. | ❏ | ❏ | ❏ |
| **13.** Direct the flow of the solution gently upward toward the roof of the canal. | ❏ | ❏ | ❏ |
| **14.** Irrigate for the prescribed period of time or until the desired results are obtained. | ❏ | ❏ | ❏ |
| **15.** Dry the patient's external ear with gauze. | ❏ | ❏ | ❏ |
| **16.** Inspect the ear with the otoscope to determine the results. | ❏ | ❏ | ❏ |
| **17.** Properly care for or dispose of equipment and supplies. Clean the work area. | ❏ | ❏ | ❏ |
| **18.** Wash your hands. | ❏ | ❏ | ❏ |
| **19.** **AFF** Log into the Electronic Medical Record (EMR) using your username and secure password OR obtain the paper medical record from a secure location and assure it is kept away from public access. | ❏ | ❏ | ❏ |
| **20.** Record the procedure in the patient's chart. | ❏ | ❏ | ❏ |
| **21.** When finished, log out of the EMR and/or replace the paper medical record in an appropriate and secure location. | ❏ | ❏ | ❏ |

**CALCULATION**

Total Possible Points: _____

Total Points Earned: _____ Multiplied by 100 = _____ Divided by Total Possible Points = _____ %

**PASS    FAIL    COMMENTS:**
  ❏          ❏

Student's signature _____ Date _____

Partner's signature _____ Date _____

Instructor's signature _____ Date _____

## PSY PROCEDURE 15-6   Perform an Audiometric Hearing Test

Name: _____   Date: _____   Time: _____   Grade: _____

**EQUIPMENT/SUPPLIES:** Audiometer, otoscope

**STANDARDS:** Given the needed equipment and a place to work, the student will perform this skill with _____ % accuracy in a total of _____ minutes. *(Your instructor will tell you what the percentage and time limits will be before you begin.)*

**KEY:**            4 = Satisfactory            0 = Unsatisfactory            NA = This step is not counted

| PROCEDURE STEPS | SELF | PARTNER | INSTRUCTOR |
|---|---|---|---|
| **1.** Wash your hands. | ❏ | ❏ | ❏ |
| **2.** Greet and identify the patient. Identify yourself and your title. Explain the procedure. | ❏ | ❏ | ❏ |
| **3.** **AFF** Explain how to respond to a patient who is visually impaired. | ❏ | ❏ | ❏ |
| _____ _____ _____ _____ _____ | | | |
| **4.** Take patient to a quiet area or room for testing. | ❏ | ❏ | ❏ |
| **5.** Visually inspect the ear canal and tympanic membrane before the examination. | ❏ | ❏ | ❏ |
| **6.** Choose the correct size tip for the end of the audiometer. | ❏ | ❏ | ❏ |
| **7.** Attach a speculum to fit the patient's external auditory meatus. | ❏ | ❏ | ❏ |
| **8.** With the speculum in the ear canal, retract the pinna:<br>**a.** *Adults:* Gently pull up and back to straighten the auditory canal.<br>**b.** *Children:* Gently pull slightly down and back to straighten the auditory canal. | ❏ | ❏ | ❏ |
| **9.** Follow audiometer instrument directions for use:<br>**a.** Screen right ear.<br>**b.** Screen left ear. | ❏ | ❏ | ❏ |
| **10.** If the patient fails to respond at any frequency, rescreening is required. | ❏ | ❏ | ❏ |
| **11.** If the patient fails rescreening, notify the physician. | ❏ | ❏ | ❏ |

**PSY** P R O C E D U R E   1 5 - 6     **Perform an Audiometric Hearing Test**
(continued)

| | | | |
|---|---|---|---|
| **12. AFF** Log into the Electronic Medical Record (EMR) using your username and secure password OR obtain the paper medical record from a secure location and assure it is kept away from public access. | ❏ | ❏ | ❏ |
| **13.** Record the results in the medical record | ❏ | ❏ | ❏ |
| **14.** When finished, log out of the EMR and/or replace the paper medical record in an appropriate and secure location. | ❏ | ❏ | ❏ |

**CALCULATION**

Total Possible Points: _____

Total Points Earned: _____ Multiplied by 100 = _____ Divided by Total Possible Points = _____ %

**PASS    FAIL    COMMENTS:**
❏           ❏

Student's signature _____ Date _____

Partner's signature _____ Date _____

Instructor's signature _____ Date _____

## PSY PROCEDURE 15-7 **Instilling Ear Medication**

Name: _____ Date: _____ Time: _____ Grade: _____

**EQUIPMENT/SUPPLIES:** Physician's order and patient record, otic medication with dropper, cotton balls

**STANDARDS:** Given the needed equipment and a place to work, the student will perform this skill with _____ % accuracy in a total of _____ minutes. *(Your instructor will tell you what the percentage and time limits will be before you begin.)*

**KEY:**        4 = Satisfactory        0 = Unsatisfactory        NA = This step is not counted

| PROCEDURE STEPS | SELF | PARTNER | INSTRUCTOR |
|---|---|---|---|
| **1.** Wash your hands. | ❏ | ❏ | ❏ |
| **2.** Assemble the equipment, supplies, and medication if ordered by the physician.<br>**a.** Check solution label three times.<br>**b.** Make sure that the label indicates for otic use. | ❏ | ❏ | ❏ |
| **3.** Greet and identify the patient. Identify yourself including your title. Explain the procedure. | ❏ | ❏ | ❏ |
| **4.** Ask patient about any allergies not documented. | ❏ | ❏ | ❏ |
| **5.** **AFF** Explain how to respond to a patient who does not speak English. | ❏ | ❏ | ❏ |
| _____ | | | |
| _____ | | | |
| _____ | | | |
| _____ | | | |
| **6.** Have the patient seated with the affected ear tilted upward. | ❏ | ❏ | ❏ |
| **7.** Draw up the ordered amount of medication.<br>**a.** Adults: Pull the auricle slightly up and back to straighten the S-shaped canal.<br>**b.** Children: Pull the auricle slightly down and back to straighten the S-shaped canal. | ❏ | ❏ | ❏ |
| **8.** Insert the tip of dropper without touching the patient's skin.<br>**a.** Let the medication flow along the side of the canal.<br>**b.** Have the patient sit or lie with affected ear upward for about 5 minutes. | ❏ | ❏ | ❏ |
| **9.** To keep medication in the canal, gently insert a moist cotton ball into the external auditory meatus. | ❏ | ❏ | ❏ |

**PSY** PROCEDURE 15-7 **Instilling Ear Medication** (continued)

| | | | |
|---|---|---|---|
| **10.** Properly care for or dispose of equipment and supplies. Clean the work area. | ❏ | ❏ | ❏ |
| **11.** Wash your hands. | ❏ | ❏ | ❏ |
| **12.** **AFF** Log into the Electronic Medical Record (EMR) using your username and secure password OR obtain the paper medical record from a secure location and assure it is kept away from public access. | ❏ | ❏ | ❏ |
| **13.** Record the procedure in the patient record. | ❏ | ❏ | ❏ |
| **14.** When finished, log out of the EMR and/or replace the paper medical record in an appropriate and secure location. | ❏ | ❏ | ❏ |

**CALCULATION**

Total Possible Points: _____

Total Points Earned: _____ Multiplied by 100 = _____ Divided by Total Possible Points = _____ %

**PASS   FAIL   COMMENTS**:
❏        ❏

Student's signature _____ Date _____

Partner's signature _____ Date _____

Instructor's signature _____ Date _____

## PSY PROCEDURE 15-8 Instilling Nasal Medication

Name: _____ Date: _____ Time: _____ Grade: _____

**EQUIPMENT/SUPPLIES:** Physician's order and patient record; nasal medication, drops, or spray; tissues; gloves

**STANDARDS:** Given the needed equipment and a place to work, the student will perform this skill with _____ % accuracy in a total of _____ minutes. *(Your instructor will tell you what the percentage and time limits will be before you begin.)*

**KEY:** 4 = Satisfactory 0 = Unsatisfactory NA = This step is not counted

| PROCEDURE STEPS | SELF | PARTNER | INSTRUCTOR |
|---|---|---|---|
| **1.** Wash your hands and put on gloves. | ❏ | ❏ | ❏ |
| **2.** Assemble the equipment and supplies. Check the medication label three times. | ❏ | ❏ | ❏ |
| **3.** Greet and identify the patient. Identify yourself including your title. Explain the procedure. | ❏ | ❏ | ❏ |
| **4.** Ask patient about any allergies not documented. | ❏ | ❏ | ❏ |
| **5.** **AFF** Explain how to respond to a patient who has dementia. | ❏ | ❏ | ❏ |
| _____ _____ _____ _____ | | | |
| **6.** Position the patient in a comfortable recumbent position. **a.** Extend patient's head beyond edge of examination table. **b.** Or place a pillow under the patient's shoulders. **c.** Support the patient's neck to avoid strain as the head is tilted back. | ❏ | ❏ | ❏ |
| **7.** Administering nasal medication: **a.** Nasal drops **(1)** Hold the dropper upright just above each nostril. **(2)** Drop the medication one drop at a time without touching the nares. **(3)** Keep the patient in a recumbent position for 5 minutes. **b.** Nasal spray **(1)** Place tip of the bottle at the naris opening without touching the patient. **(2)** Spray as the patient takes a deep breath. | ❏ | ❏ | ❏ |
| **8.** Wipe any excess medication from the patient's skin with tissues. | ❏ | ❏ | ❏ |

**PSY** P R O C E D U R E  1 5 - 8    **Instilling Nasal Medication** (continued)

| | | | |
|---|---|---|---|
| **9.** Properly care for or dispose of equipment and supplies. Clean the work area. | ❏ | ❏ | ❏ |
| **10.** Remove your gloves and wash your hands. | ❏ | ❏ | ❏ |
| **11.** **AFF** Log into the Electronic Medical Record (EMR) using your username and secure password OR obtain the paper medical record from a secure location and assure it is kept away from public access. | ❏ | ❏ | ❏ |
| **12.** Record the procedure in the patient's chart. | ❏ | ❏ | ❏ |
| **13.** When finished, log out of the EMR and/or replace the paper medical record in an appropriate and secure location. | ❏ | ❏ | ❏ |

**CALCULATION**

Total Possible Points: _____

Total Points Earned: _____ Multiplied by 100 = _____ Divided by Total Possible Points = _____ %

**PASS    FAIL    COMMENTS:**
  ❏          ❏

Student's signature _____ Date _____

Partner's signature _____ Date _____

Instructor's signature _____ Date _____

# CHAPTER 16 Pulmonary Medicine

## Learning Outcomes

### COG Cognitive Domain

1. Spell key terms
2. Define medical terms and abbreviations related to all body systems
3. Describe structural organization of the human body
4. List major organs in each body system
5. Identify the anatomical location of major organs in each body system
6. Describe the normal function of each body system
7. Identify common pathology related to each body system including signs, symptoms, and etiology
   a. Identify the primary defense mechanisms of the respiratory system
   b. Identify and explain diagnostic procedures of the respiratory system
   c. Describe the physician's examination of the respiratory system
8. Discuss the role of the medical assistant with regard to various diagnostic and therapeutic procedures

### PSY Psychomotor Domain

1. Instruct a patient in the use of the peak flow meter (Procedure 16-1)
2. Administer a nebulized breathing treatment (Procedure 16-2)
3. Collecting a Sputum Specimen (Procedure 16-3)
4. Perform a pulmonary function test (Procedure 16-4)

### AFF Affective Domain

1. Incorporate critical thinking skills when performing patient assessment
2. Incorporate critical thinking skills when performing patient care
3. Show awareness of a patient's concerns related to the procedure being performed
4. Demonstrate empathy, active listening, nonverbal communication
5. Demonstrate respect for individual diversity including gender, race, religion, age, economic status, appearance
6. Explain to a patient the rationale for performance of a procedure

7. Demonstrate sensitivity to patient rights
8. Protect the integrity of the medical record

### ABHES Competencies

1. Assist the physician with the regimen of diagnostic and treatment modalities as they relate to each body system
2. Comply with federal, state, and local health laws and regulations
3. Communicate on the recipient's level of comprehension
4. Serve as a liaison between the physician and others
5. Show empathy and impartiality when dealing with patients
6. Document accurately

Name: _____    Date: _____    Grade: _____

## ⬤OG MULTIPLE CHOICE

Circle the letter preceding the correct answer.

**1.** A pulmonary function test measures:
  **a.** arterial blood gases.
  **b.** oxygen saturation.
  **c.** sputum cells.
  **d.** tidal volume.
  **e.** fluid in the lungs.

**2.** A patient in need of an artificial airway will likely undergo:
  **a.** laryngectomy.
  **b.** tracheostomy.
  **c.** chemotherapy.
  **d.** bronchoscopy.
  **e.** pneumonectomy.

**3.** Which procedure necessitates a stethoscope?
  **a.** Percussion
  **b.** Palpation
  **c.** Inspection
  **d.** Radiation
  **e.** Auscultation

**4.** Which of the following would be a normal pulse oximetry reading for someone with no lung disease?
  **a.** 96%
  **b.** 94%
  **c.** 92%
  **d.** 90%
  **e.** 88%

**5.** One lower respiratory disorder is:
  **a.** laryngitis.
  **b.** bronchitis.
  **c.** sinusitis.
  **d.** pharyngitis.
  **e.** tonsillitis.

**6.** Which of the following is anesthetized by cigarette smoke?
  **a.** Alveoli
  **b.** Bronchioles
  **c.** Mucus
  **d.** Cilia
  **e.** Trachea

**7.** The most prominent symptom of bronchitis is:
  **a.** severe wheezing.
  **b.** repeated sneezing.
  **c.** productive cough.
  **d.** shortness of breath.
  **e.** coughing blood.

**8.** Viral pneumonia differs from bacterial pneumonia in that:
  **a.** it can be treated by antibiotics.
  **b.** it might result in hospitalization.
  **c.** it affects gas exchange in the lungs.
  **d.** it may lead to a fever and cough.
  **e.** it spreads throughout the lungs.

**9.** People with asthma have difficulty breathing because their:
  **a.** airways are narrow.
  **b.** cilia are inoperative.
  **c.** alveoli are collapsed.
  **d.** bronchioles are too wide.
  **e.** lungs are underdeveloped.

**10.** A productive cough refers to a cough that produces:
  **a.** blood.
  **b.** nasal mucus.
  **c.** sputum.
  **d.** oxygen.
  **e.** antibodies.

**11.** A type of medication that opens the bronchioles and controls bronchospasms is a(n):
  **a.** corticosteroid.
  **b.** bronchodilator.
  **c.** antibiotic.
  **d.** antihistamine.
  **e.** decongestant.

**12.** The public health department should be alerted about a diagnosis of:
  **a.** tuberculosis.
  **b.** pneumonia.
  **c.** bronchitis.
  **d.** asthma.
  **e.** COPD.

**13.** Which of the following is true of emphysema?
   **a.** It is not associated with bronchitis.
   **b.** It causes inflammation of the nasal passages.
   **c.** It can be cured with steroids.
   **d.** It is usually reversible.
   **e.** It usually takes many years to develop.

**14.** The purpose of a nebulizer is to:
   **a.** turn a vaporous medicine into a liquid.
   **b.** administer an asthma treatment.
   **c.** turn a liquid medicine into a vapor.
   **d.** cure COPD.
   **e.** pump oxygen.

**15.** Of the following diseases affecting the respiratory system, which, in most cases, is linked to cigarette smoking?
   **a.** Liver cancer
   **b.** Cystic fibrosis
   **c.** Laryngitis
   **d.** Lung cancer
   **e.** Allergic rhinitis

**16.** In the case of a patient receiving oxygen treatment, a cannula:
   **a.** stores the oxygen.
   **b.** separates oxygen from the air in a room.
   **c.** delivers oxygen to the airways.
   **d.** ensures proper flow of oxygen.
   **e.** prevents accidents caused by oxygen's flammability.

**17.** COPD patients may take medications that are also prescribed for patients with:
   **a.** Influenza
   **b.** Pneumonia
   **c.** Meningitis
   **d.** Lung cancer
   **e.** Asthma

**18.** One acute disease of the lower respiratory tract is:
   **a.** asthma.
   **b.** pneumonia.
   **c.** emphysema.
   **d.** sinusitis.
   **e.** COPD.

**19.** The best way to thin mucus in the airways is:
   **a.** oxygen therapy.
   **b.** steroid medication.
   **c.** to increase oral fluid intake.
   **d.** to consume a balanced diet.
   **e.** frequent exercise.

**20.** A physician may perform an arterial blood gas test to:
   **a.** determine how much gas is in a patient's lungs.
   **b.** determine whether a patient has a normal respiratory rate.
   **c.** determine when a patient will be ready for respiratory surgery.
   **d.** determine whether a patient will be receptive to oxygen therapy.
   **e.** determine whether the patient's lungs are adequately exchanging gases.

## COG MATCHING

_____ Grade: _____

Place the letter preceding the definition on the line next to the term.

**Key Terms**

**21.** _____ atelectasis
**22.** _____ chronic obstructive pulmonary disease (COPD)
**23.** _____ dyspnea
**24.** _____ forced expiratory volume (FEV)
**25.** _____ hemoptysis
**26.** _____ laryngectomy
**27.** _____ palliative
**28.** _____ status asthmaticus
**29.** _____ thoracentesis
**30.** _____ tidal volume
**31.** _____ tracheostomy

**Definitions**

**a.** coughing up blood from the respiratory tract
**b.** easing symptoms without curing
**c.** a permanent surgical stoma in the neck with an indwelling tube
**d.** a surgical puncture into the pleural cavity for aspiration of serous fluid or for injection of medication
**e.** a progressive, irreversible condition with diminished respiratory capacity
**f.** the volume of air forced out of the lungs
**g.** difficulty breathing
**h.** the amount of air inhaled and exhaled during normal respiration
**i.** an asthma attack that is not responsive to treatment
**j.** collapsed lung fields; incomplete expansion of the lungs, either partial or complete
**k.** the surgical removal of the larynx

## **COG** IDENTIFICATION

Grade: _____

**32.** Place a check mark on the line to indicate if each symptom is a possible symptom of laryngeal cancer.

**a.** _____ hoarseness lasting longer than 3 weeks

**b.** _____ pain in the throat when drinking hot liquids

**c.** _____ wheezing

**d.** _____ a feeling of a lump in the throat

**e.** _____ chest pain

**f.** _____ burning in the throat when drinking citrus juice

**g.** _____ dyspnea

**h.** _____ night sweats

**i.** _____ general malaise

**33.** Which of the following is/are an element/elements of the traditional examination of the chest? Circle the letter preceding all that apply.

**a.** Palpation

**b.** Auscultation

**c.** Sputum culture

**d.** Chest radiography

**e.** Inspection

**34.** Which of the following pulmonary diagnostic methods is considered invasive? Place a check mark on the line next to the appropriate diagnostic methods.

**a.** _____ Percussion

**b.** _____ Bronchoscopy

**c.** _____ Auscultation

**d.** _____ Sputum culture

**e.** _____ Posteroanterior x-ray

## **COG** SHORT ANSWER

Grade: _____

35. What is the most common cause of chronic obstructive pulmonary disease?

_____

_____

_____

_____

36. Why is the term *chronic obstructive pulmonary disease* used to characterize a patient suffering from emphysema and chronic bronchitis?

_____

_____

_____

_____

37. What are two of the most common causes of upper respiratory problems?

_____

_____

_____

_____

38. In the case of a pneumonia patient, what prevents effective gas exchange?

_____

_____

_____

_____

39. What is usually the etiology of chronic bronchitis?

_____

_____

_____

_____

40. What is a symptomatic difference between viral and bacterial pneumonia?

_____

_____

_____

_____

41. What is the role of the medical assistant in the collection and analysis of a sputum specimen?

_____

_____

_____

_____

42. What is the purpose of a peak flow meter?

_____

_____

_____

_____

43. Under what circumstance would a physician perform a laryngectomy?

_____

_____

_____

_____

44. Describe the difference between palliative care and a cure.

_____

_____

_____

_____

45. What measures ought to be taken in the case of an asthmatic patient who does not respond to medication?

_____

_____

_____

_____

46. If a patient is prescribed two bronchodilator inhalers, what is the most likely explanation? Why would two be prescribed?

_____

_____

_____

_____

**47.** Describe the typical prognosis of a lung cancer patient.

_____

_____

_____

_____

## COG TRUE OR FALSE?

Grade: _____

Indicate whether the statements are true or false by placing the letter T (true) or F (false) on the line preceding the statement.

**48.** _____ An asthma patient will, upon contracting the disease, suffer from it for her entire life.

**49.** _____ Emphysema entails chronic inflammation of the airways.

**50.** _____ A patient who tests positive for tuberculosis is contagious.

**51.** _____ Lung cancer, one of the most common causes of death in men and women, is believed to result usually from cigarette smoking.

## COG AFF CASE STUDY FOR CRITICAL THINKING

Grade: _____

**1.** Your patient comes to the office with shortness of breath. The physician asks you to perform an arterial blood gas and send it to the laboratory stat. How would you respond to the physician?

_____

_____

_____

**2.** A patient with a severe lung disease explains that she has been smoking for decades. You explain that she ought to quit, but she contends that it does not matter. She says she has already damaged her lungs enough that continuing to smoke will do no further harm. How do you respond to this patient?

_____

_____

_____

**3.** A patient receiving oxygen therapy calls to complain that his machine is not working. He does not know what to do. What suggestions do you have for the patient? What will you do to assist him?

_____

_____

**4.** Your patient has just been diagnosed with tuberculosis. Explain to him ways in which he should act to protect others while he undergoes treatment.

_____

_____

_____

**5.** A healthy patient worries that his exposure to secondhand smoke of his coworkers might cause his health to deteriorate. You are aware of research suggesting that this is so; however, much of the research is controversial. How would you advise the patient?

_____

_____

_____

**6.** A patient has just been diagnosed with lung cancer that the physician described as "not terribly aggressive and potentially curable." The patient asks you if this means that he will be okay. How do you respond?

_____

_____

_____

| **PSY** PROCEDURE 16-1 | **Instruct a Patient on Using the Peak Flow Meter** |
|---|---|

**Name:** _____ **Date:** _____ **Time:** _____ **Grade:** _____

**EQUIPMENT/SUPPLIES:** Peak flow meter, recording documentation form

**STANDARDS:** Given the needed equipment and a place to work, the student will perform this skill with _____ % accuracy in a total of _____ minutes. *(Your instructor will tell you what the percentage and time limits will be before you begin.)*

**KEY:** 4 = Satisfactory 0 = Unsatisfactory NA = This step is not counted

| PROCEDURE STEPS | SELF | PARTNER | INSTRUCTOR |
|---|---|---|---|
| **1.** Wash your hands. | ❑ | ❑ | ❑ |
| **2.** Assemble the peak flow meter, disposable mouthpiece, and patient documentation form. | ❑ | ❑ | ❑ |
| **3.** Greet and identify the patient. Identify yourself including your title and explain the procedure. | ❑ | ❑ | ❑ |
| **4.** Holding the peak flow meter upright, explain how to read and reset the gauge after each reading. | ❑ | ❑ | ❑ |
| **5.** **AFF** Explain how to respond to a patient who is visually impaired. | ❑ | ❑ | ❑ |
| _____<br><br>_____<br><br>_____<br><br>_____ | | | |
| **6.** Instruct the patient to place the peak flow meter mouthpiece into the mouth, forming a tight seal with the lips. After taking a deep breath, the patient should blow hard into the mouthpiece without blocking the back of the flow meter. | ❑ | ❑ | ❑ |
| **7.** Note the number on the flow meter denoting the level at which the sliding gauge stopped after the hard blowing into the mouthpiece. Reset the gauge to zero. | ❑ | ❑ | ❑ |
| **8.** Instruct the patient to perform this procedure a total of three times consecutively, in both the morning and at night, and to record the highest reading on the form. | ❑ | ❑ | ❑ |
| **9.** Explain to the patient the procedure for cleaning the mouthpiece of the flow meter by washing with soapy water and rinsing without immersing the flow meter in water. | ❑ | ❑ | ❑ |

**FSY** PROCEDURE 16-1 **Instruct a Patient on Using the Peak Flow Meter** (continued)

| | | | |
|---|---|---|---|
| 10. **AFF** Log into the Electronic Medical Record (EMR) using your username and secure password OR obtain the paper medical record from a secure location and assure it is kept away from public access. | ❏ | ❏ | ❏ |
| 11. Record the procedure including the name of the medication and the patient's response. | ❏ | ❏ | ❏ |
| 12. When finished, log out of the EMR and/or replace the paper medical record in an appropriate and secure location. | ❏ | ❏ | ❏ |

**CALCULATION**

Total Possible Points: _____

Total Points Earned: _____ Multiplied by 100 = _____ Divided by Total Possible Points = _____ %

**PASS    FAIL    COMMENTS:**
  ❏        ❏

Student's signature _____ Date _____

Partner's signature _____ Date _____

Instructor's signature _____ Date _____

| **PSY** PROCEDURE 16-2 | **Perform a Nebulized Breathing Treatment** |
|---|---|

Name: _____ Date: _____ Time: _____ Grade: _____

**EQUIPMENT/SUPPLIES:** Physician's order and patient's medical record, inhalation medication, nebulizer disposable setup, nebulizer machine

**STANDARDS:** Given the needed equipment and a place to work, the student will perform this skill with _____ % accuracy in a total of _____ minutes. *(Your instructor will tell you what the percentage and time limits will be before you begin.)*

**KEY:**            4 = Satisfactory            0 = Unsatisfactory            NA = This step is not counted

| PROCEDURE STEPS | SELF | PARTNER | INSTRUCTOR |
|---|---|---|---|
| **1.** Wash your hands. | ❑ | ❑ | ❑ |
| **2.** Assemble the equipment and medication, checking the medication label three times as indicated when administering any medications. | ❑ | ❑ | ❑ |
| **3.** Greet and identify the patient. Identify yourself including your title and explain the procedure. | ❑ | ❑ | ❑ |
| **4.** **AFF** Explain how you would respond to a patient who is deaf. | ❑ | ❑ | ❑ |
| _____ _____ _____ _____ | | | |
| **5.** Remove the nebulizer treatment cup from the setup and add the medication ordered by the physician. | ❑ | ❑ | ❑ |
| **6.** Place the top on the cup securely, attach the "T" piece to the top of the cup, and position the mouthpiece firmly on one end of the "T" piece. | ❑ | ❑ | ❑ |
| **7.** Attach one end of the tubing securely to the connector on the cup and the other end to the connector on the nebulizer machine. | ❑ | ❑ | ❑ |
| **8.** Ask the patient to place the mouthpiece into the mouth and make a seal with the lips, without biting the mouthpiece. Instruct the patient to breathe normally during the treatment, occasionally taking a deep breath. | ❑ | ❑ | ❑ |
| **9.** Turn the machine on using the on/off switch. The medication in the reservoir cup will become a fine mist that is inhaled by the patient breathing through the mouthpiece. | ❑ | ❑ | ❑ |

**PSY** P R O C E D U R E  1 6 - 2  **Perform a Nebulized Breathing Treatment** (continued)

| | | | |
|---|---|---|---|
| **10.** Before, during, and after the breathing treatment, take and record the patient's pulse. | ❏ | ❏ | ❏ |
| **11.** When the treatment is over and the medication is gone from the cup, turn the machine off and have the patient remove the mouthpiece. | ❏ | ❏ | ❏ |
| **12.** Disconnect the disposable treatment setup and dispose of all parts into a biohazard container. Properly put away the machine. | ❏ | ❏ | ❏ |
| **13.** Wash your hands. | ❏ | ❏ | ❏ |
| **14.** **AFF** Log into the Electronic Medical Record (EMR) using your username and secure password OR obtain the paper medical record from a secure location and assure it is kept away from public access. | ❏ | ❏ | ❏ |
| **15.** Record the procedure including the name of the medication and the patient's pulse before, during, and after the treatment. | ❏ | ❏ | ❏ |
| **16.** When finished, log out of the EMR and/or replace the paper medical record in an appropriate and secure location. | ❏ | ❏ | ❏ |

**CALCULATION**

Total Possible Points: _____

Total Points Earned: _____ Multiplied by 100 = _____ Divided by Total Possible Points = _____ %

**PASS   FAIL   COMMENTS:**
   ❏         ❏

Student's signature _____ Date _____

Partner's signature _____ Date _____

Instructor's signature _____ Date _____

## PSY  PROCEDURE 16-3   Collect a Sputum Specimen

**Name:** _____  **Date:** _____  **Time:** _____  **Grade:** _____

**EQUIPMENT/SUPPLIES:** Physician order, patient's medical record, sterile specimen container, gloves, biohazard transport bag, laboratory request

**STANDARDS:** Given the needed equipment and a place to work, the student will perform this skill with _____ % accuracy in a total of _____ minutes. *(Your instructor will tell you what the percentage and time limits will be before you begin.)*

**KEY:**          4 = Satisfactory          0 = Unsatisfactory          NA = This step is not counted

| PROCEDURE STEPS | SELF | PARTNER | INSTRUCTOR |
|---|---|---|---|
| **1.** Wash your hands. | ❏ | ❏ | ❏ |
| **2.** Assemble the equipment. | ❏ | ❏ | ❏ |
| **3.** Greet and identify the patient. Identify yourself including your title and explain the procedure. | ❏ | ❏ | ❏ |
| **4.** AFF Explain how to respond to a patient whose first language is not English. | ❏ | ❏ | ❏ |
| | | | |
| | | | |
| | | | |
| | | | |
| **5.** Provide the patient with a cup of water and instruct him or her to rinse the mouth with water. | ❏ | ❏ | ❏ |
| **6.** Ask the patient to cough deeply, using the abdominal muscles as well as the accessory muscles to bring secretions from the lungs and not just the upper airway. | ❏ | ❏ | ❏ |
| **7.** Instruct the patient to expectorate the specimen directly into the container without touching the inside of the container with the lips or tongue and without getting the specimen on the outside of the container. | ❏ | ❏ | ❏ |
| **8.** When the specimen is in the container, apply gloves and after taking the container from the patient, cap the container immediately and place into a biohazard bag for transport to the laboratory with a laboratory requisition. | ❏ | ❏ | ❏ |
| **9.** Once the specimen has been routed to the laboratory, remove your gloves and wash your hands. | ❏ | ❏ | ❏ |

**FSY** P R O C E D U R E  1 6 - 3    **Collect a Sputum Specimen** (continued)

| | | | |
|---|---|---|---|
| **10.** **AFF** Log into the Electronic Medical Record (EMR) using your username and secure password OR obtain the paper medical record from a secure location and assure it is kept away from public access. | ❑ | ❑ | ❑ |
| **11.** Record the procedure including the name of the medication and the patient's pulse before, during, and after the treatment. | ❑ | ❑ | ❑ |
| **12.** When finished, log out of the EMR and/or replace the paper medical record in an appropriate and secure location. | ❑ | ❑ | ❑ |

**CALCULATION**

Total Possible Points: _____

Total Points Earned: _____ Multiplied by 100 = _____ Divided by Total Possible Points = _____ %

**PASS    FAIL    COMMENTS:**
  ❑        ❑

Student's signature _____ Date _____

Partner's signature _____ Date _____

Instructor's signature _____ Date _____

## PSY   PROCEDURE 16-4   **Perform a Pulmonary Function Test**

Name: _____  Date: _____  Time: _____  Grade: _____

**EQUIPMENT/SUPPLIES:** Physician's order and patient's medical record, spirometer and appropriate cables, calibration syringe and log book, disposable mouthpiece, printer, nose clip

**STANDARDS:** Given the needed equipment and a place to work, the student will perform this skill with _____ % accuracy in a total of _____ minutes. *(Your instructor will tell you what the percentage and time limits will be before you begin.)*

**KEY:**          4 = Satisfactory          0 = Unsatisfactory          NA = This step is not counted

| PROCEDURE STEPS | SELF | PARTNER | INSTRUCTOR |
|---|---|---|---|
| **1.** Wash your hands. | ❑ | ❑ | ❑ |
| **2.** Assemble the equipment. | ❑ | ❑ | ❑ |
| **3.** Greet and identify the patient. Identify yourself including your title and explain the procedure. | ❑ | ❑ | ❑ |
| **4.** ■AFF■ Explain how to respond to a patient who has dementia. | ❑ | ❑ | ❑ |
| **5.** Turn the PFT machine on, and if the spirometer has not been calibrated according to the office policy, calibrate the machine using the calibration syringe according to the manufacturer's instructions, and record the calibration in the appropriate logbook. | ❑ | ❑ | ❑ |
| **6.** With the machine on and calibrated, attach the appropriate cable, tubing, and mouthpiece for the type of machine being used. | ❑ | ❑ | ❑ |
| **7.** Using the keyboard on the machine, input patient data into the machine including the patient's name or identification number, age, weight, height, sex, race, and smoking history. | ❑ | ❑ | ❑ |
| **8.** Ask the patient to remove any restrictive clothing, such as a necktie, and instruct the patient in applying the nose clip. | ❑ | ❑ | ❑ |
| **9.** Ask the patient to stand, breathe in deeply, and blow into the mouthpiece as hard as possible. He or she should continue to blow into the mouthpiece until the machine indicates that it is appropriate to stop blowing. A chair should be available in case the patient becomes dizzy or lightheaded. | ❑ | ❑ | ❑ |
| **10.** Continue the procedure until three adequate readings or maneuvers are performed. | ❑ | ❑ | ❑ |
| **11.** Properly care for the equipment and dispose of the mouthpiece into the biohazard container. | ❑ | ❑ | ❑ |
| **12.** Wash your hands. | ❑ | ❑ | ❑ |

**PSY** PROCEDURE 16-4 **Perform a Pulmonary Function Test**
(continued)

| | | | |
|---|---|---|---|
| **13.** **AFF** Log into the Electronic Medical Record (EMR) using your username and secure password OR obtain the paper medical record from a secure location and assure it is kept away from public access. | ❏ | ❏ | ❏ |
| **14.** Record the procedure including the patient's response. | ❏ | ❏ | ❏ |
| **15.** Print and/or scan the results and place into the medical record. | ❏ | ❏ | ❏ |
| **16.** When finished, log out of the EMR and/or replace the paper medical record in an appropriate and a secure location. | ❏ | ❏ | ❏ |

**CALCULATION**

Total Possible Points: _____

Total Points Earned: _____ Multiplied by 100 = _____ Divided by Total Possible Points = _____ %

**PASS    FAIL    COMMENTS:**
 ❏        ❏

Student's signature _____ Date _____

Partner's signature _____ Date _____

Instructor's signature _____ Date _____

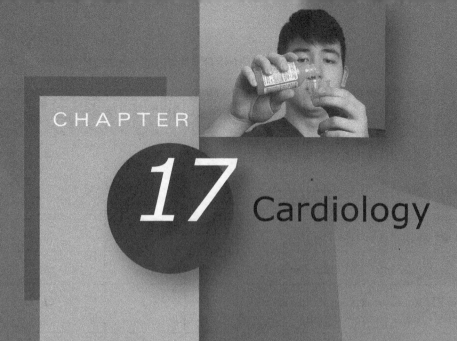

# CHAPTER 17 Cardiology

## Learning Outcomes

### COG Cognitive Domain

1. Spell key terms
2. Define medical terms and abbreviations related to all body systems
3. Describe structural organization of the human body
4. List major organs in each body system
5. Identify the anatomical location of major organs in each body system
6. Describe the normal function of each body system
7. Identify common pathology related to each body system including signs, symptoms, and etiology
   a. List and describe common cardiovascular disorders
   b. Identify and explain common cardiovascular procedures and tests
8. Describe the roles and responsibilities of the medical assistant during cardiovascular examinations and procedures
9. Discuss the information recorded on a basic 12-lead electrocardiogram
10. Explain the purpose of a Holter monitor

### PSY Psychomotor Domain

1. Perform electrocardiography (Procedure 17-1)
2. Apply a Holter monitor for a 24-hour test (Procedure 17-2)

### AFF Affective Domain

1. Incorporate critical thinking skills when performing patient assessment
2. Incorporate critical thinking skills when performing patient care
3. Show awareness of a patient's concerns related to the procedure being performed
4. Demonstrate empathy, active listening, nonverbal communication
5. Demonstrate respect for individual diversity including gender, race, religion, age, economic status, appearance
6. Explain to a patient the rationale for performance of a procedure
7. Demonstrate sensitivity to patient rights
8. Protect the integrity of the medical record

### ABHES Competencies

1. Assist the physician with the regimen of diagnostic and treatment modalities as they relate to each body system
2. Perform electrocardiograms
3. Comply with federal, state, and local health laws and regulations
4. Communicate on the recipient's level of comprehension
5. Serve as a liaison between the physician and others
6. Show empathy and impartiality when dealing with patients
7. Document accurately

Name: _____  Date: _____  Grade: _____

## COG MULTIPLE CHOICE

Circle the letter preceding the correct answer.

1. Chronic cases of myocarditis may lead to heart failure with:
   a. endocarditis.
   b. cardiomegaly.
   c. asthma.
   d. bronchitis.
   e. congestive heart failure.

2. To identify the causative agent, proper diagnosis of endocarditis requires a(n):
   a. chest radiograph.
   b. blood culture.
   c. electrocardiogram.
   d. x-ray.
   e. stool sample.

3. Arrhythmia may occur if the sinoatrial node initiates electrical impulses:
   a. too quietly or too loudly.
   b. too roughly or too smoothly.
   c. too fast or too slowly.
   d. always.
   e. 60 to 100 times a minute.

4. When a patient's heart conduction system cannot maintain normal sinus rhythm without assistance, an electrical source can be implanted to assist or replace the sinoatrial node. This device is called a(n):
   a. pacemaker.
   b. artifact.
   c. Holter monitor.
   d. aneurysm.
   e. lead.

5. Which condition may result from rheumatic heart disease?
   a. Valvular disease
   b. Cardiac arrhythmia
   c. Angina pectoris
   d. Mitral valve stenosis
   e. Endocarditis

6. One symptom of coronary artery disease is:
   a. bleeding around the heart.
   b. chronic head cold.
   c. swollen tongue.
   d. pressure or fullness in the chest.
   e. leg pain.

7. Patients who are considered hypertensive have a resting systolic blood pressure above _____ and a diastolic pressure above _____.
   a. 120 mm Hg; 70 mm Hg
   b. 130 mm Hg; 80 mm Hg
   c. 140 mm Hg; 90 mm Hg
   d. 150 mm Hg; 100 mm Hg
   e. 160 mm Hg; 110 mm Hg

8. Who is predisposed to varicose veins?
   a. People who use their brains more than their bodies
   b. People who run or jog excessively
   c. People who sit or stand for long periods of time without moving
   d. People who are obese over many years
   e. People who play a musical instrument

9. Another term for *thrombi* is:
   a. heart attack.
   b. blood clots.
   c. fever.
   d. racing heart.
   e. stroke.

10. Patients may refer to *anticoagulant medications* as:
    a. antipyretics.
    b. thrombolytics.
    c. sugar pills.
    d. thickening agents.
    e. blood thinners.

11. A common cause of cerebrovascular accident is:
    a. damage to the blood vessels in the heart.
    b. blockage of the cerebral artery by a thrombus.
    c. weakness or paralysis.
    d. pulmonary embolism.
    e. pleuritic chest pain.

12. Another term for *transient ischemic attack* is:
    a. peripheral vascular occlusion.
    b. mini-stroke.
    c. heart attack.
    d. brain damage.
    e. slurred speech.

13. Deficiencies in hemoglobin or in the numbers of red blood cells result in:
    a. tachycardia.
    b. thrombus.
    c. stroke.
    d. anemia.
    e. aneurysm.

14. During the physician's examination, what is used to evaluate the efficiency of the circulatory pathways and peripheral pulses?
    a. Palpation
    b. Blood pressure
    c. Weight
    d. Height
    e. Sign of fever

15. Electrocardiograms are not used to detect:
    a. ischemia.
    b. delays in impulse conduction.
    c. hypertrophy of the cardiac chambers.
    d. arrhythmias.
    e. heart murmurs.

16. How many leads does the standard ECG have?
    a. 2
    b. 10
    c. 12
    d. 18
    e. 20

17. A patient must keep a daily diary of activities when:
    a. wearing a Holter monitor.
    b. preparing for a cardiac examination.
    c. having an ECG.
    d. taking anticoagulants.
    e. completing a cardiac stress test.

18. Many patients with CHF have an enlarged:
    a. chest.
    b. throat.
    c. lung.
    d. heart.
    e. brain.

19. A person who can read and perform ECGs is called a(n):
    a. medical assistant.
    b. phlebotomist.
    c. ultrasonographer.
    d. sound technician.
    e. neurologist.

20. If atherosclerotic plaques are found during a catheterization, which procedure may be performed?
    a. Bypass graft
    b. Angioplasty
    c. Echocardiogram
    d. ECG
    e. Ultrasonograph

## **COG** MATCHING

_____ Grade: _____

Place the letter preceding the definition on the line next to the term.

**Key Terms**

21. _____ aneurysm
22. _____ angina pectoris
23. _____ artifact
24. _____ atherosclerosis
25. _____ bradycardia
26. _____ cardiomegaly
27. _____ cardiomyopathy
28. _____ cerebrovascular accident (CVA)
29. _____ congestive heart failure
30. _____ electrocardiography
31. _____ coronary artery bypass graft
32. _____ endocarditis
33. _____ leads
34. _____ myocardial infarction (MI)
35. _____ myocarditis
36. _____ palpitations

**Definitions**

a. a heart rate of less than 60 beats per minute
b. any disease affecting the myocardium
c. a surgical procedure that increases the blood flow to the heart by bypassing the occluded or blocked vessel with a graft
d. any activity recorded in an electrocardiogram caused by extraneous activity such as patient movement, loose lead, or electrical interference
e. a procedure that improves blood flow through a coronary artery by pressing the plaque against the wall of an artery with a balloon on a catheter, allowing for more blood flow
f. an inflammation of the inner lining of the heart
g. a death of cardiac muscle due to lack of blood flow to the muscle; also known as heart attack
h. a local dilation in a blood vessel wall
i. a heart rate of more than 100 beats per minute
j. an acute episode of cerebrovascular insufficiency, usually a result of narrowing of an artery by atherosclerotic plaques, emboli, or vasospasm; usually passes quickly, but should be considered a warning for predisposition to cerebrovascular accidents

**Key Terms**

37. _____ percutaneous transluminal coronary angioplasty (PTCA)
38. _____ pericarditis
39. _____ tachycardia
40. _____ transient ischemic attack (TIA)

**Definitions**

k. electrodes or electrical connections attached to the body to record electrical impulses in the body, especially the heart or brain
l. paroxysmal chest pain usually caused by a decrease in blood flow to the heart muscle due to coronary occlusion
m. ischemia of the brain due to an occlusion of the blood vessels supplying blood to the brain, resulting in varying degrees of debilitation
n. a buildup of fatty plaque on the interior lining of arteries
o. the feeling of an increased heart rate or pounding heart that may be felt during an emotional response or a cardiac disorder
p. a condition in which the heart cannot pump effectively
q. an inflammation of the sac that covers the heart
r. a procedure that produces a record of the electrical activity of the heart
s. an enlarged heart muscle
t. an inflammation of the myocardial layer of the heart

## MATCHING

Grade: _____

Place the letter preceding the description on the line preceding the cardiac condition.

**Conditions**

41. _____ congestive heart failure
42. _____ myocardial infarction
43. _____ ventricular tachycardia
44. _____ defibrillation
45. _____ arrhythmia

**Descriptions**

a. electrical signals originate from cells in the ventricles very rapidly.
b. a shock administered to restore normal cardiac electrical activity
c. symptoms may be similar to those felt during angina pectoris
d. occurs if the SA node initiates electrical impulses too fast or too slowly or the electrical signal originates from somewhere other than the SA node
e. failure of the left ventricle leads to pulmonary congestion

## MATCHING

Grade: _____

Place the letter preceding the description on the line preceding the cardiac procedure.

**Procedures**

46. _____ electrocardiogram
47. _____ chest radiography
48. _____ cardiac stress test
49. _____ echocardiography
50. _____ cardiac catheterization

**Descriptions**

a. provides valuable information about the anatomical location and gross structures of the heart, great vessels, and lungs
b. uses sound waves generated by a small device called a transducer
c. a graphic record of the electrical current as it progresses through the heart
d. common invasive procedure used to help diagnose or treat conditions affecting coronary arterial circulation
e. measures the response of the cardiac muscle to increased demands for oxygen

**COG IDENTIFICATION**

_____ Grade: _____

**51.** Cardiac inflammation, or carditis, is a disorder of the heart that is usually the result of infection. In the chart below are descriptions of the three types of carditis. Read the descriptions and fill in the missing boxes with the correct type of carditis.

| Disorder | Causes | Signs and Symptoms | Treatment |
|---|---|---|---|
| a. _____ | a pathogen, neoplasm, or autoimmune disorder, such as lupus erythematosus or rheumatoid arthritis | sharp pain in the same locations as myocardial infarction | relieving the symptoms and, if possible, correcting the underlying cause, including administering an antibiotic for bacterial infection |
| b. _____ | radiation, chemicals, and bacterial, viral, or parasitic infection | early signs: fever, fatigue, and mild chest pain chronic: cardiomegaly, arrhythmias, valvulitis | supportive care and medication as ordered by the physician to kill the responsible pathogen |
| c. _____ | infection or inflammation of the inner lining of the heart, the endocardium | reflux, or backflow, of the valves or blood | directed at eliminating the infecting organism |

Identify and circle the letter preceding the best answer.

**52.** Valvular disease is:

**a.** inflammatory lesions of the connective tissues, particularly in the heart joints, and subcutaneous tissues.

**b.** an acquired or congenital abnormality of any of the four cardiac valves.

**c.** a collection of fatty plaques made of calcium and cholesterol inside the walls of blood vessels.

**d.** a disordered blood flow within the valvular walls of the heart.

**53.** Atherosclerosis can sometimes result in:

**a.** rheumatic heart disease.

**b.** valvular disease.

**c.** coronary artery disease.

**d.** congestive heart failure.

**54.** Cerebrovascular accident (CVA) is sometimes called:

**a.** heart attack.

**b.** paralysis.

**c.** blood clot.

**d.** stroke.

55. Which of the following is a question you should ask the patient before a cardiovascular examination?

    a. Are you currently pregnant?

    b. How long have you had the pain/discomfort?

    c. How often do you exercise?

    d. What do you like to do in your free time?

56. A Holter monitor is used for:

    a. the diagnosis of intermittent cardiac arrhythmias and dysfunctions.

    b. obtaining a good-quality ECG without avoidable artifacts.

    c. obtaining basic information about the anatomical location and gross structures of the heart, great vessels, and lungs.

    d. measuring the response of the cardiac muscle to increased demands for oxygen.

57. Read the risk factors for developing thrombi below and indicate whether the risk factor is primary (P), or inherited, versus secondary (S), or acquired.

    a. _____ hemolytic anemia

    b. _____ long-term immobility

    c. _____ chronic pulmonary disease

    d. _____ thrombophlebitis

    e. _____ sickle cell disease

    f. _____ varicosities

    g. _____ defibrillation after cardiac arrest

58. Identify whether each description describes lead I, lead II, or lead III:

    a. _____ measures the difference in electrical potential between the right arm (RA) and the left leg (LL).

    b. _____ measures the difference in electrical potential between the right arm (RA) and the left arm (LA).

    c. _____ measures the difference in electrical potential between the left arm (LA) and the left leg (LL).

## COG SHORT ANSWER
_____ Grade: _____

59. List five symptoms of the various heart disorders.

_____

_____

_____

_____

**60.** List the four causes of congestive heart failure.

_____

_____

_____

_____

**61.** Explain how a pacemaker helps the heart maintain normal sinus rhythm.

_____

_____

_____

_____

**62.** List six potential causes of anemia.

_____

_____

_____

_____

**63.** Explain angiography, one of the procedures used to diagnose atherosclerosis.

_____

_____

_____

_____

**64.** Explain why a physician often requires several blood pressure readings before making the diagnosis of hypertension.

_____

_____

_____

_____

**65.** List the six elements that are taken into consideration during the ECG.

_____

_____

_____

_____

**66.** Explain the role of the medical assistant during an ECG.

_____

_____

_____

_____

## OOG TRUE OR FALSE?

Grade: _____

Indicate whether the statements are true or false by placing the letter T (true) or F (false) on the line preceding the statement.

67. _____ Congestive heart failure (CHF) is a condition in which the heart cannot pump effectively.

68. _____ Ventricular fibrillation is a medical emergency that occurs when the heart is contracting rather than quivering in an organized fashion.

69. _____ Diagnosis of atherosclerosis is often made by electrocardiography.

70. _____ Patients who have cerebrovascular accidents usually have varying degrees of weakness or paralysis of one side of the body.

## OOG AFF CASE STUDY FOR CRITICAL THINKING

Grade: _____

1. You are interviewing a patient prior to a physical examination of the cardiovascular system. This is his first time in a medical office after many years' absence, and he is considerably anxious. What do you say to him to calm him down? How would you explain the procedure?

_____

_____

_____

_____

2. A patient comes into the office complaining of chest pain, nausea, and vomiting. Will he likely be admitted to the hospital right away? Why or why not?

_____

_____

_____

_____

3. A patient is given an artificial pacemaker. She would like to know how the device works and what changes she can expect from it. What do you tell her?

_____

_____

_____

_____

4. Why is it important that a patient continue taking her prescribed antihypertensive medication, even if her blood pressure has reached a manageable level?

_____

_____

_____

_____

**5.** Many cardiac conditions are preventable with proper diet and exercise. It's important to stress prevention over cure, because in most instances, there is no quick "cure." How will you send this message to patients? What kinds of tools will you use?

_____

_____

_____

_____

## PROCEDURE 17-1 Perform a 12-Lead Electrocardiogram

**Name:** _____ **Date:** _____ **Time:** _____ **Grade:** _____

**EQUIPMENT/SUPPLIES:** Physician order, ECG machine with cable and lead wires, ECG paper, disposable electrodes that contain coupling gel, patient gown and drape, skin preparation materials including a razor and antiseptic wipes

**STANDARDS:** Given the needed equipment and a place to work, the student will perform this skill with _____ % accuracy in a total of _____ minutes. *(Your instructor will tell you what the percentage and time limits will be before you begin.)*

**KEY:**          4 = Satisfactory          0 = Unsatisfactory          NA =This step is not counted

| PROCEDURE STEPS | SELF | PARTNER | INSTRUCTOR |
|---|---|---|---|
| **1.** Wash your hands. | ❏ | ❏ | ❏ |
| **2.** Assemble the equipment. | ❏ | ❏ | ❏ |
| **3.** Greet and identify the patient. Identify yourself including your title and explain the procedure. | ❏ | ❏ | ❏ |
| **4.** Turn the ECG machine on and enter appropriate data into it. Include the patient's name and/or identification number, age, sex, height, weight, blood pressure, and medications. | ❏ | ❏ | ❏ |
| **5.** Instruct the patient to disrobe above the waist.<br>**a.** Provide a gown for privacy.<br>**b.** Female patients should also be instructed to remove any nylons or tights. | ❏ | ❏ | ❏ |
| **6.** Position patient comfortably in a supine position.<br>**a.** Provide pillows as needed for comfort.<br>**b.** Drape the patient for warmth and privacy. | ❏ | ❏ | ❏ |
| **7.** Prepare the skin as needed.<br>**a.** Wipe away skin oil and lotions with the antiseptic wipes.<br>**b.** Shave hair that will interfere with good contact between skin and electrodes. | ❏ | ❏ | ❏ |
| **8.** Apply the electrodes:<br>**a.** Arms and legs: snugly against the fleshy, muscular parts of upper arms and lower legs according to the manufacturer's directions.<br>**b.** Chest: $V_1$ through $V_6$. | ❏ | ❏ | ❏ |
| **9.** Connect the lead wires securely according to the color codes.<br>**a.** Untangle the wires before applying them to prevent electrical artifacts.<br>**b.** Each lead must lie unencumbered along the contours of the patient's body to decrease the incidence of artifacts.<br>**c.** Double check the placement. | ❏ | ❏ | ❏ |
| **10.** Determine the sensitivity and paper speed settings on the ECG machine. | ❏ | ❏ | ❏ |
| **11.** Depress the automatic button on the ECG machine to obtain the 12-lead ECG. | ❏ | ❏ | ❏ |
| **12.** When the tracing is printed, check the ECG for artifacts and standardization mark. | ❏ | ❏ | ❏ |

## PSY PROCEDURE 17-1 Perform a 12-Lead Electrocardiogram
(continued)

| | | | |
|---|---|---|---|
| **13.** If the tracing is adequate, turn off the machine.<br>  **a.** Remove the electrodes from the patient's skin.<br>  **b.** Assist the patient to a sitting position and help him or her with dressing if needed. | ❏ | ❏ | ❏ |
| **14.** **AFF** Explain how to respond to a patient who has dementia. | ❏ | ❏ | ❏ |
| _____<br>_____<br>_____<br>_____ | | | |
| **15.** For a single-channel machine, roll the ECG strip.<br>  **a.** Do not secure the roll with clips.<br>  **b.** This ECG will need to be mounted on an 8 × 11-inch paper or form. | ❏ | ❏ | ❏ |
| **16.** Discard disposable electrodes appropriately and put away the EKG machine. Wash your hands. | ❏ | ❏ | ❏ |
| **17.** **AFF** Log into the Electronic Medical Record (EMR) using your username and secure password OR obtain the paper medical record from a secure location and assure it is kept away from public access. | ❏ | ❏ | ❏ |
| **18.** Record the procedure. | ❏ | ❏ | ❏ |
| **19.** Place the printed results in the medical record or scan into the electronic medical record if appropriate. | ❏ | ❏ | ❏ |
| **20.** Let the physician know that the ECG has been completed and is ready for review. | ❏ | ❏ | ❏ |
| **21.** When finished, log out of the EMR and/or replace the paper medical record in an appropriate and secure location. | ❏ | ❏ | ❏ |

**CALCULATION**

Total Possible Points: _____

Total Points Earned: _____ Multiplied by 100 = _____ Divided by Total Possible Points = _____ %

**PASS**    **FAIL**    **COMMENTS:**
 ❏      ❏

Student's signature _____ Date _____

Partner's signature _____ Date _____

Instructor's signature _____ Date _____

**PSY** PROCEDURE 17-2 **Apply a Holter Monitor for a 24-Hour Test**

Name: _____ Date: _____ Time: _____ Grade: _____

**EQUIPMENT/SUPPLIES:** Physician's order, Holter monitor with appropriate lead wires, fresh batteries, carrying case with strap, disposable electrodes that contain coupling gel, adhesive tape, patient gown and drape, skin preparation materials including a razor and antiseptic wipes, patient diary

**STANDARDS:** Given the needed equipment and a place to work, the student will perform this skill with _____ % accuracy in a total of _____ minutes. *(Your instructor will tell you what the percentage and time limits will be before you begin.)*

**KEY:**        4 = Satisfactory            0 = Unsatisfactory            NA = This step is not counted

| PROCEDURE STEPS | SELF | PARTNER | INSTRUCTOR |
|---|---|---|---|
| **1.** Wash your hands. | ❑ | ❑ | ❑ |
| **2.** Assemble the equipment. | ❑ | ❑ | ❑ |
| **3.** Greet and identify the patient. Identify yourself including your title and explain the procedure. | ❑ | ❑ | ❑ |
| **4.** Explain the importance of carrying out all normal activities during the monitoring and the reason for the incident diary. Emphasize the need to use the diary at all times during the test. | ❑ | ❑ | ❑ |
| **5.** Ask the patient to remove all clothing from the waist up; gown and drape appropriately for privacy. | ❑ | ❑ | ❑ |
| **6.** Prepare the patient's skin for electrode attachment. **a.** Provide privacy and have the patient in a sitting position. **b.** Shave the skin if necessary and cleanse with antiseptic wipes. | ❑ | ❑ | ❑ |
| **7.** Apply the Holter electrodes at the specified sites: **a.** The right manubrium border. **b.** The left manubrium border. **c.** The right sternal border at the fifth rib level. **d.** The fifth rib at the anterior axillary line. **e.** The right lower rib cage over the cartilage as a ground lead. | ❑ | ❑ | ❑ |
| **8.** To do this, expose the adhesive backing of the electrodes and follow the manufacturer's instructions to attach each firmly. Check the security of the attachments. | ❑ | ❑ | ❑ |
| **9.** Position electrode connectors downward toward the patient's feet. | ❑ | ❑ | ❑ |
| **10.** Attach the lead wires and secure with adhesive tape. | ❑ | ❑ | ❑ |
| **11.** Connect the cable and run a baseline ECG by hooking the Holter monitor to the ECG machine with the cable hookup. | ❑ | ❑ | ❑ |
| **12.** Assist the patient to carefully redress with the cable extending through the garment opening. *Note:* Instruct the patient that clothing that buttons down the front is more convenient. | ❑ | ❑ | ❑ |

**PSY** PROCEDURE 17-2    **Apply a Holter Monitor for a 24-Hour Test**
(continued)

| | | | |
|---|---|---|---|
| **13.** Plug the cable into the recorder and mark the diary.<br>   **a.** If needed, explain the purpose of the diary to the patient again.<br>   **b.** Give instructions for a return appointment to evaluate the recording and the diary. | ❏ | ❏ | ❏ |
| **14.** Wash your hands. | ❏ | ❏ | ❏ |
| **15.** **AFF** Log into the Electronic Medical Record (EMR) using your username and secure password OR obtain the paper medical record from a secure location and assure it is kept away from public access. | ❏ | ❏ | ❏ |
| **16.** Record the procedure. | ❏ | ❏ | ❏ |
| **17.** When finished, log out of the EMR and/or replace the paper medical record in an appropriate and secure location. | ❏ | ❏ | ❏ |

**CALCULATION**

Total Possible Points: _____

Total Points Earned: _____ Multiplied by 100 = _____ Divided by Total Possible Points = _____ %

**PASS    FAIL    COMMENTS:**
   ❏        ❏

Student's signature _____ Date _____

Partner's signature _____ Date _____

Instructor's signature _____ Date _____

# CHAPTER

# *18* Gastroenterology

## Learning Outcomes

### COG Cognitive Domain

1. Spell key terms
2. Define medical terms and abbreviations related to all body systems
3. Describe structural organization of the human body
4. List major organs in each body system
5. Identify the anatomical location of major organs in each body system
6. Describe the normal function of each body system
7. Identify common pathology related to each body system including signs, symptoms, and etiology
   a. List and describe common disorders of the alimentary canal and accessory organs
   b. Identify and explain the purpose of common procedures and tests associated with the gastrointestinal system
8. Describe the roles and responsibilities of the medical assistant in diagnosing and treating

disorders of the gastrointestinal system

### PSY Psychomotor Domain

1. Assist with colon procedures (Procedure 18-1)
2. Test stool specimen for occult blood: Guaiac method (Procedure 18-2)

### AFF Affective Domain

1. Incorporate critical thinking skills when performing patient assessment
2. Incorporate critical thinking skills when performing patient care
3. Show awareness of a patient's concerns related to the procedure being performed
4. Demonstrate empathy, active listening, nonverbal communication
5. Demonstrate respect for individual diversity including gender, race, religion, age, economic status, appearance

6. Explain to a patient the rationale for performance of a procedure
7. Demonstrate sensitivity to patient rights
8. Protect the integrity of the medical record

### ABHES Competencies

1. Assist the physician with the regimen of diagnostic and treatment modalities as they relate to each body system
2. Prepare the patient for examinations and treatments
3. Recognize and understand various treatment protocols
4. Comply with federal, state, and local health laws and regulations
5. Communicate on the recipient's level of comprehension
6. Serve as a liaison between the physician and others
7. Show empathy and impartiality when dealing with patients
8. Document accurately

Name: _____   Date: _____   Grade: _____

## ◖◗ MULTIPLE CHOICE

Circle the letter preceding the correct answer.

1. Which of the following can trigger an outbreak of the herpes simplex virus?
   a. Food allergy
   b. Illness
   c. Lack of sleep
   d. Medication
   e. Poor diet

2. What commonly causes leukoplakia to develop?
   a. Hereditary genes
   b. Excessive alcohol intake
   c. Lack of exercise
   d. Tobacco irritation
   e. Obesity

3. Why should a patient complaining of heartburn be assessed immediately?
   a. The symptoms of gastroesophageal reflux disease may be similar to the chest pain of a patient with cardiac problems.
   b. A patient with heartburn is more likely to develop a serious heart condition.
   c. Heartburn is a symptom of a weak lower esophageal sphincter.
   d. It is important to assess any gastrointestinal disorder immediately because they are usually serious.
   e. Heartburn may be symptomatic of Barrett esophagus, which requires immediate surgery.

4. Abnormal contact between the upper teeth and lower teeth is:
   a. malocclusion.
   b. dental caries.
   c. stomatitis.
   d. candidiasis.
   e. gingivitis.

5. If a patient is suffering from peptic ulcers, the symptoms will be most severe when the patient:
   a. is hungry.
   b. has a bowel movement.
   c. lies on his back.
   d. chews his food.
   e. is digesting a meal.

6. Gastroenteritis could become life threatening if a patient:
   a. is pregnant.
   b. suffers from diabetes mellitus.
   c. needs a heart operation.
   d. consumes excess alcohol.
   e. does not receive treatment immediately.

7. The study of morbid obesity is called:
   a. orthodontistry.
   b. gerontology.
   c. bariatrics.
   d. gastroenterology.
   e. pediatrics.

8. What is the minimum body mass index that a patient must have to be considered for gastric bypass surgery?
   a. 25
   b. 30
   c. 35
   d. 40
   e. 45

9. Crohn disease becomes life threatening when:
   a. the bowel walls become inflamed and the lymph nodes enlarge.
   b. the fluid from the intestinal contents cannot be absorbed.
   c. edema of the bowel wall takes place.
   d. scarring narrows the colon and obstructs the bowel.
   e. patients have periods of constipation, anorexia, and fever.

10. How does irritable bowel syndrome differ from Crohn disease?
    a. It does not involve weight loss.
    b. It is easily treatable.
    c. It is thought to be genetic.
    d. It requires a colectomy.
    e. It causes scarring.

*Scenario for questions 11 and 12:* A patient is diagnosed with diverticulitis.

11. Which of the following treatments would the physician most likely recommend?
    a. Antibiotics
    b. Bed rest
    c. Antifungal agent
    d. Bland food
    e. Drinking less water

12. What advice might the physician have you give to the patient to help maintain good bowel habits in future?
    a. Never eat spicy foods.
    b. Get some form of daily exercise.
    c. Try to force a bowel movement at least once a day.
    d. Use laxatives when suffering from constipation.
    e. Cut out food products that contain wheat.

13. How can a patient decrease his or her risk of developing a hernia?
    a. Avoid lifting heavy objects.
    b. Switch from processed to organic foods.
    c. Maintain good bowel habits.
    d. Have regular medical checkups.
    e. Walk at least a mile every day.

14. What is the most effective treatment for appendicitis?
    a. Antibiotics
    b. Ileostomy
    c. Appendectomy
    d. Cryosurgery
    e. Radiation

15. Which of these factors increases the production of intestinal gas?
    a. Excess water
    b. Spicy or fatty foods
    c. Peristalsis
    d. Fast metabolism
    e. Lack of exercise

16. The most likely method of contracting hepatitis B is:
    a. contaminated food.
    b. poor hygiene.
    c. contaminated blood.
    d. stagnant water.
    e. weak immune system.

17. For which of the following procedures would the patient usually be put under anesthesia?
    a. Anoscopy
    b. Sigmoidoscopy
    c. Nuclear imaging
    d. Ultrasonography
    e. Endoscopic retrograde cholangiopancreatography

18. What is the caustic chemical secreted by the lining of the stomach that may cause erosion if too much of it is secreted?
    a. Pepsin
    b. Hydrochloric acid
    c. Insulin
    d. Oral mucosa
    e. Melena

19. How does lithotripsy break down gallstones to make them easy to pass?
    a. Lasers
    b. Sound waves
    c. Acidic liquid
    d. Heat
    e. Air pressure

20. Which piece of advice could best be given to a patient with a malabsorption syndrome by the physician?
    a. Drink more water.
    b. Eat less processed food.
    c. Take vitamin supplements.
    d. Cut out spicy foods.
    e. Exercise more often.

21. Which of these groups of people are at the highest risk of developing esophageal cancer?
    a. Teenagers
    b. Pregnant women
    c. Young children
    d. Elderly women
    e. Elderly men

22. A male patient comes to the physician's office complaining of an acute pain in his upper abdomen and back. He also suffers from indigestion and nausea, particularly when he tries to eat foods that have a high fat content. Which of the following gastrointestinal disorders does the patient probably have?
    a. Cholelithiasis
    b. Peptic ulcers
    c. Gastritis
    d. Leukoplakia
    e. Caries

## OOG **MATCHING**

Grade: _____

Place the letter preceding the definition on the line next to the term.

**Key Terms**

23. _____ anorexia
24. _____ ascites
25. _____ dysphagia
26. _____ guaiac
27. _____ hematemesis
28. _____ hepatomegaly
29. _____ hepatotoxin
30. _____ insufflator
31. _____ leukoplakia
32. _____ malocclusion
33. _____ melena
34. _____ metabolism
35. _____ obturator
36. _____ peristalsis
37. _____ sclerotherapy
38. _____ stomatitis
39. _____ turgor

**Definitions**

**a.** an enlarged liver
**b.** a substance used in a laboratory test for occult blood in the stool
**c.** a device for blowing air, gas, or powder into a body cavity
**d.** the sum of chemical processes that result in growth, energy production, elimination of waste, and body functions performed as digested nutrients are distributed
**e.** black, tarry stools caused by digested blood from the gastrointestinal tract
**f.** the contraction and relaxation of involuntary muscles of the alimentary canal, producing wavelike movements of products through the digestive system
**g.** difficulty speaking
**h.** loss of appetite
**i.** a substance that can damage the liver
**j.** an accumulation of serous fluid in the peritoneal cavity
**k.** the use of chemical agents to treat esophageal varices to produce fibrosis and hardening of the tissue
**l.** an inflammation of the mucous membranes of the mouth
**m.** an abnormal contact between the teeth in the upper and lower jaw
**n.** the normal tension in a cell or the skin
**o.** vomiting blood or bloody vomitus
**p.** the smooth, rounded, removable inner portion of a hollow tube, such as an anoscope, that allows for easier insertion
**q.** white, thickened patches on the oral mucosa or tongue that are often precancerous

## OOG **MATCHING**

Grade: _____

Place the letter preceding the description on the line next to the name of the gastrointestinal disorder.

**Disorders**

40. _____ esophageal varices
41. _____ cholecystitis
42. _____ peptic ulcers
43. _____ stomatitis
44. _____ gastroesophageal reflux disease (GERD)
45. _____ diverticulosis
46. _____ hiatal hernia

**Descriptions**

**a.** a chronic disorder characterized by discomfort in the chest due to the backflow of gastric contents into the esophagus
**b.** a condition that occurs when part of the stomach protrudes up through the diaphragm
**c.** varicose veins of the esophagus resulting from pressure within the esophageal veins
**d.** an acute or chronic inflammation of the gall bladder
**e.** erosions or sores in the GI tract left by sloughed tissue
**f.** a disorder that usually occurs in the sigmoid colon, attributed to a diet deficient in roughage
**g.** an inflammation of the oral mucosa, caused by a virus, bacteria, or fungus

## COG MATCHING

Grade: _____

Place the letter preceding the description on the line next to the examination method.

**Examination Methods**

47. _____ endoscopic studies
48. _____ nuclear imaging
49. _____ ultrasonography
50. _____ radiology studies
51. _____ sigmoidoscopy
52. _____ endoscopic retrograde cholangiopancreatography (ERCP)
53. _____ anoscopy

**Descriptions**

a. instilling barium into the GI tract orally or rectally to outline the organs and identify abnormalities
b. injecting radionuclides into the body and taking images using a nuclear scanning device to detect abnormalities
c. using high-frequency sound waves to diagnose disorders of internal structures
d. passing soft, flexible tubes into the stomach, small intestine, or colon for direct visualization of the organs
e. a method of injecting dye into the ducts of the gallbladder and pancreas; used to visualize the esophagus, stomach, proximal duodenum, and pancreas with a flexible endoscope
f. the insertion of a metal or plastic anoscope into the rectal canal to inspect the anus and rectum and swab for cultures
g. a visual examination of the sigmoid colon

## COG IDENTIFICATION

Grade: _____

54. A patient comes into the office with abdominal pain and indigestion. The physician diagnoses the patient with a hiatal hernia. Which of the following diet modifications and treatments would the physician most likely suggest to the patient? Circle the correct answers. There may be more than one.

a. Eat small, frequent meals.

b. Exercise vigorously three times a week.

c. Elevate the head of the bed when sleeping.

d. Do not eat for 2 hours before bedtime.

e. Drink less water.

f. Lose weight.

55. As a medical assistant, you may be called on to assist with colon procedures in the medical office. Place a check mark on the line next to the task(s) that the medical assistant would be responsible for performing in the medical office.

a. _____ Instruct the patient in the procedure of stool sample collection.

b. _____ Help to educate the patient about diet and the prevention of gastric disorders.

c. _____ Prescribe pain medication and antibiotics.

d. _____ Schedule radiographic and ultrasound procedures in an outpatient facility.

e. _____ Test the stool specimen when it is returned to the office.

f. _____ Compile detailed dietary regimens for obese patients.

g. _____ Assist the physician in performing colon examinations.

h. _____ Diagnose minor gastrointestinal disorders.

**56.** Which of the following factors increase a person's risk of developing pancreatic cancer? Circle all that apply.

   **a.** Being female

   **b.** Drinking alcohol

   **c.** Smoking

   **d.** Being of African American descent

   **e.** Being male

   **f.** Being of Caucasian descent

   **g.** Eating high-fat foods

   **h.** A history of working with industrial chemicals

**57.** Some gastrointestinal disorders require specialist knowledge and equipment outside of the physician's office. In the table below, place a check mark in the appropriate box to indicate whether a procedure could be carried out in the physician's office or would likely require an outpatient facility.

| Procedure | Physician's Office | Outpatient Facility |
|---|---|---|
| **a.** Ultrasonography | | |
| **b.** Anoscopy | | |
| **c.** Endoscopic retrograde cholangiopancreatography | | |
| **d.** Nuclear imaging | | |
| **e.** Sigmoidoscopy examination | | |

## COG SHORT ANSWER

_____ Grade: _____

**58.** Identify the part of the digestive system where the following gastrointestinal disorders occur.

   **a.** Appendicitis _____

   **b.** Hepatitis _____

   **c.** Cholelithiasis _____

   **d.** Crohn disease _____

   **e.** Peptic ulcers _____

   **f.** Ulcerative colitis _____

   **g.** Diverticulosis _____

**59.** List three symptoms that could indicate a patient is suffering from gastric cancer.

_____

_____

_____

_____

**60.** A 40-year-old woman comes to the physician's office complaining of severe stomach cramps and vomiting. To help the physician assess her condition and make a diagnosis, the medical assistant should obtain some personal information. List four things that the physician will ask the patient before continuing with the exam.

_____

_____

_____

_____

**61.** A 25-year-old woman comes to the physician's office complaining of fatigue and joint pain. She looks jaundiced, and when the physician asks her for her medical history, she says that she recently returned from a 3-month trip to Ghana. Which two tests will the physician most likely recommend?

_____

_____

_____

_____

**62.** As a medical assistant, part of your job may be to educate patients about the care of teeth and gums. List three things that you could tell a patient to do that might help to prevent dental caries.

_____

_____

_____

_____

**63.** Which is the more widely accepted instrument to use during an endoscopic study: a rigid sigmoidoscope or a flexible fiberoptic sigmoidoscope? Explain your answer.

_____

_____

_____

_____

## ⊙G TRUE OR FALSE?

_____ Grade: _____

Indicate whether the statements are true or false by placing the letter T (true) or F (false) on the line preceding the statement.

**64.** _____ Oral cancers are more common among people who smoke.

**65.** _____ Cancer of the esophagus is common and can easily be treated.

**66.** _____ A sign that a patient has a problem with malabsorption of fats includes stools that are loose.

**67.** _____ Irritable bowel syndrome usually results in chronic weight loss.

## ⊙G AFF CASE STUDY FOR CRITICAL THINKING

_____ Grade: _____

**1.** A 55-year-old woman comes to the physician's office and asks about gastric bypass surgery. She says that she has tried every diet available and is unable to lose weight. She suffers from shortness of breath and an inability to walk for long distances. You take the woman's vital signs and measure her height and weight. She appears to be in good health but is at least 60 pounds over the ideal weight for her height. The physician later confirms these facts. Is the patient likely to be a candidate for gastric bypass surgery? Explain your answer.

_____

_____

_____

_____

**2.** The physician tells a patient that he would like to schedule an endoscopic retrograde cholangiopancreatography in a local outpatient facility. After the physician leaves the room, you notice that the patient looks confused and worried. How would you explain the procedure to the patient to reassure him?

_____

_____

_____

_____

**3.** Mr. Thompson, a 50-year-old patient, is scheduled to have an endoscopic examination on Wednesday morning. You have given him all the necessary information to prepare for the examination, including taking a laxative the night before and eating only a light meal on Tuesday evening, with no breakfast Wednesday morning. Mr. Thompson calls you an hour before his appointment to tell you that he forgot to take the laxative the previous evening and has eaten breakfast. Explain what you would do.

_____

_____

_____

_____

**4.** A 15-year-old female patient comes into the physician's office with severe abdominal pains. She is extremely underweight for her height, and you suspect she might be anorexic. When the physician leaves the room, she confesses that she has been using laxatives every day to keep her weight down. Explain what you would do next.

_____

_____

_____

_____

**5.** A 50-year-old male patient has been diagnosed with pancreatic cancer. The patient is clearly devastated and tells you he has heard that people who develop pancreatic cancer have little chance of survival. What do you say to the patient?

_____

_____

_____

_____

## PSY PROCEDURE 18-1    **Assisting with Colon Procedures**

**Name:** _____    **Date:** _____    **Time:** _____    **Grade:** _____

**EQUIPMENT/SUPPLIES:** Appropriate instrument (flexible or rigid sigmoidoscope, anoscope, or proctoscope); water-soluble lubricant; patient gown and drape; cotton swabs; suction (if not part of the scope); biopsy forceps; specimen container with preservative; completed laboratory requisition form; personal wipes or tissues; equipment for assessing vital signs; examination gloves

**STANDARDS:** Given the needed equipment and a place to work, the student will perform this skill with _____ % accuracy in a total of _____ minutes. *(Your instructor will tell you what the percentage and time limits will be before you begin.)*

**KEY:**            4 = Satisfactory            0 = Unsatisfactory            NA = This step is not counted

| PROCEDURE STEPS | SELF | PARTNER | INSTRUCTOR |
|---|---|---|---|
| **1.** Wash your hands. | ❏ | ❏ | ❏ |
| **2.** Assemble the equipment and supplies.<br>**a.** Place the name of the patient on label on outside of specimen container.<br>**b.** Complete the laboratory requisition. | ❏ | ❏ | ❏ |
| **3.** Check the illumination of the light source if a flexible sigmoidoscope. Turn off the power after checking for working order. | ❏ | ❏ | ❏ |
| **4.** Greet and identify the patient and explain the procedure. Identify yourself including your title.<br>**a.** Inform patient that a sensation of pressure may be felt.<br>**b.** Tell the patient that the pressure is from the instrument.<br>**c.** Gas pressure may be felt when air is insufflated during the sigmoidoscopy. | ❏ | ❏ | ❏ |
| **5.** Instruct the patient to empty his or her urinary bladder. | ❏ | ❏ | ❏ |
| **6.** Assess the vital signs and record in the medical record. | ❏ | ❏ | ❏ |
| **7.** Have the patient undress from the waist down and gown and drape appropriately. | ❏ | ❏ | ❏ |
| **8.** Assist the patient onto the examination table.<br>**a.** If the instrument is an anoscope or a fiberoptic device, the Sims position or a side-lying position is most comfortable.<br>**b.** If a rigid instrument is used, position patient when doctor is ready: knee-chest position or on a proctological table.<br>**c.** Drape the patient. | ❏ | ❏ | ❏ |
| **9.** Assist the physician with lubricant, instruments, power, swabs, suction, etc. | ❏ | ❏ | ❏ |
| **10.** Monitor the patient's response and offer reassurance.<br>**a.** Instruct the patient to breathe slowly through pursed lips.<br>**b.** Encourage relaxing as much as possible. | ❏ | ❏ | ❏ |

**PSY** P R O C E D U R E 1 8 - 1 **Assisting with Colon Procedures** (continued)

| | | | |
|---|---|---|---|
| **11.** When the physician is finished:<br>   **a.** Assist the patient into a comfortable position and allow a rest period.<br>   **b.** Offer personal cleaning wipes or tissues.<br>   **c.** Take the patient's vital signs before allowing him or her to stand.<br>   **d.** Assist the patient from the table and with dressing as needed.<br>   **e.** Give the patient any instructions regarding postprocedure care. | ❏ | ❏ | ❏ |
| **12.** Clean the room and route the specimen to the laboratory with the requisition. | ❏ | ❏ | ❏ |
| **13.** Disinfect or dispose of the supplies and equipment as appropriate. | ❏ | ❏ | ❏ |
| **14.** Wash your hands. | ❏ | ❏ | ❏ |
| **15.** **AFF** Log into the Electronic Medical Record (EMR) using your username and secure password OR obtain the paper medical record from a secure location and assure it is kept away from public access. Document your part in preparing specimens obtained and patient instructions after the procedure. | ❏ | ❏ | ❏ |
| **16.** When finished, log out of the EMR and/or replace the paper medical record in an appropriate and secure location. | ❏ | ❏ | ❏ |

**CALCULATION**

Total Possible Points: _____

Total Points Earned: _____ Multiplied by 100 = _____ Divided by Total Possible Points = _____ %

**PASS  FAIL  COMMENTS:**
  ❏     ❏

Student's signature _____ Date _____

Partner's signature _____ Date _____

Instructor's signature _____ Date _____

**FSY** PROCEDURE 18-2 **Test Stool Specimen for Occult Blood: Guaiac Method**

Name: _____ Date: _____ Time: _____ Grade: _____

**EQUIPMENT/SUPPLIES:** Gloves, labeled specimen pack or packs (the patient may bring in up to three samples per the office policy), test developer or reagent drops, biohazardous waste container.

**STANDARDS:** Given the needed equipment and a place to work, the student will perform this skill with _____ % accuracy in a total of _____ minutes. *(Your instructor will tell you what the percentage and time limits will be before you begin.)*

**KEY:** 4 = Satisfactory 0 = Unsatisfactory NA = This step is not counted

| PROCEDURE STEPS | SELF | PARTNER | INSTRUCTOR |
|---|---|---|---|
| 1. Wash your hands. | ❑ | ❑ | ❑ |
| 2. Assemble the equipment and supplies and put on gloves. | ❑ | ❑ | ❑ |
| 3. Verify the stool sample collected by the patient appropriately labeled and that the physician has ordered a stool for occult blood. | ❑ | ❑ | ❑ |
| 4. Check the expiration date on the developer or reagent solution. | ❑ | ❑ | ❑ |
| 5. Open the test window on the back of each test pack. Apply one drop of the developer solution to each window according to the manufacturer's instructions. | ❑ | ❑ | ❑ |
| 6. Read the color change within the specified time period, usually 60 seconds. | ❑ | ❑ | ❑ |
| 7. Apply one drop of developer as directed on the control section or window of each test pack. Note whether the control results are positive or negative. | ❑ | ❑ | ❑ |
| 8. Explain the procedure to follow if the control is positive or negative. | ❑ | ❑ | ❑ |
| 9. Properly dispose of the test pack or packs and your gloves in a biohazardous waste container. | ❑ | ❑ | ❑ |
| 10. Wash your hands. | ❑ | ❑ | ❑ |
| 11. **AFF** Log into the Electronic Medical Record (EMR) using your username and secure password OR obtain the paper medical record from a secure location and assure it is kept away from public access. Document your part in preparing specimens obtained and patient instructions after the procedure. | ❑ | ❑ | ❑ |
| 12. When finished, log out of the EMR and/or replace the paper medical record in an appropriate and secure location. | ❑ | ❑ | ❑ |

**FSY** PROCEDURE 18-2 **Test Stool Specimen for Occult Blood:
Guaiac Method** (continued)

**CALCULATION**

Total Possible Points: _____

Total Points Earned: _____ Multiplied by 100 = _____ Divided by Total Possible Points = _____ %

**PASS    FAIL    COMMENTS:**
  ❑         ❑

Student's signature _____ Date _____

Partner's signature _____ Date _____

Instructor's signature _____ Date _____

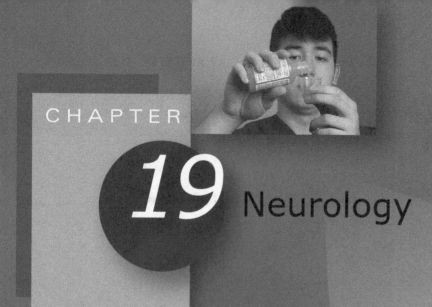

# CHAPTER 19 Neurology

## Learning Outcomes

### COG Cognitive Domain

1. Spell key terms
2. Define medical terms and abbreviations related to all body systems
3. Describe structural organization of the human body
4. List major organs in each body system
5. Identify the anatomical location of major organs in each body system
6. Describe the normal function of each body system
7. Identify common pathology related to each body system including signs, symptoms, and etiology
   a. List and describe common diseases of the nervous system
   b. Describe the physical and emotional effects of degenerative nervous system disorders
   c. List potential complications of a spinal cord injury
   d. Name and describe the common procedures for diagnosing nervous system disorders

### PSY Psychomotor Domain

1. Assist with a lumbar puncture (Procedure 19-1)

### AFF Affective Domain

1. Incorporate critical thinking skills when performing patient assessment
2. Incorporate critical thinking skills when performing patient care
3. Show awareness of a patient's concerns related to the procedure being performed
4. Demonstrate empathy, active listening, nonverbal communication
5. Demonstrate respect for individual diversity including gender, race, religion, age, economic status, appearance

6. Explain to a patient the rationale for performance of a procedure
7. Demonstrate sensitivity to patient rights
8. Protect the integrity of the medical record

### ABHES Competencies

1. Assist the physician with the regimen of diagnostic and treatment modalities as they relate to each body system
2. Comply with federal, state, and local health laws and regulations
3. Communicate on the recipient's level of comprehension
4. Serve as a liaison between the physician and others
5. Show empathy and impartiality when dealing with patients
6. Document accurately

Name: _____   Date: _____   Grade: _____

## COG MULTIPLE CHOICE

Circle the letter preceding the correct answer.

1. Initial symptoms of tetanus include:
   a. muscle spasms and stiff neck.
   b. paralysis and stiff neck.
   c. drooling and thick saliva.
   d. seizures and dysphagia.
   e. muscle spasms and clenched teeth.

2. What is another name for grand mal seizures?
   a. Absence seizures
   b. Tonic–clonic seizures
   c. Partial seizures
   d. Nervous seizures
   e. Flashing seizures

3. Febrile seizures occur in:
   a. teenagers.
   b. middle-aged men.
   c. young children.
   d. older adult women.
   e. people of all ages.

4. There may be no signs of external deformity with:
   a. meningocele.
   b. myelomeningocele.
   c. spina bifida occulta.
   d. amyotrophic lateral sclerosis.
   e. poliomyelitis.

5. To diagnose meningitis, the physician may order a(n):
   a. urine sample.
   b. x-ray.
   c. MRI.
   d. throat culture.
   e. complete blood count.

6. Hydrophobia often occurs after the onset of:
   a. rabies.
   b. tetanus.
   c. encephalitis.
   d. cerebral palsy.
   e. meningitis.

7. A herpes zoster breakout typically develops on:
   a. the legs and arms.
   b. the genitals and mouth.
   c. the stomach and chest.
   d. the face, back, and chest.
   e. the face and neck.

8. A disease closely related to poliomyelitis is:
   a. encephalitis.
   b. meningitis.
   c. Parkinson disease.
   d. PPMA syndrome.
   e. chicken pox.

9. Treatment for brain tumors may include:
   a. physical therapy and drug therapy.
   b. surgery and radiation therapy.
   c. surgery only.
   d. radiation therapy only.
   e. physical therapy and occupational therapy.

10. CSF removed and sent to the laboratory for a suspected diagnosis of meningitis may be tested for:
    a. red blood cell and white blood cell count.
    b. cholesterol and white blood cell count.
    c. red blood cells and viruses
    d. glucose and bacteria.
    e. glucose and fatty acids.

11. You should encourage slow, deep breathing for:
    a. electrical tests.
    b. a lumbar puncture.
    c. radiological tests.
    d. physical tests.
    e. the Romberg test.

12. Contrast medium helps distinguish between the soft tissues of the nervous system and:
    a. bones.
    b. tendons.
    c. tumors.
    d. muscles.
    e. arteries.

13. When assisting with a Queckenstedt test, you will be directed to:
    a. assist the patient into a side-curled position.
    b. support a forward-bending sitting position.
    c. maintain sterility of instruments.
    d. press against the patient's jugular vein.
    e. encourage the patient in slow, deep breathing.

14. AFP is generally performed:
    a. during the second trimester of pregnancy.
    b. during the first trimester of pregnancy.
    c. during the third trimester of pregnancy.
    d. before a woman gets pregnant.
    e. after the baby is born.

15. Which of the following is true of Lou Gehrig disease?
    a. It is officially known as multiple sclerosis.
    b. It is highly contagious.
    c. It is caused by a spinal cord injury.
    d. It is found most often in children.
    e. It is a terminal disease.

16. During the second phase of a grand mal seizure, the patient experiences:
    a. a tingling in extremities.
    b. a sensitivity to light.
    c. a complete loss of consciousness.
    d. an increased awareness of smell.
    e. a sense of drowsiness.

17. Which of the following is a cause of febrile seizures?
    a. Spinal cord damage
    b. Elevated body temperature
    c. Hypothermia
    d. Reye syndrome
    e. Neural tube defects

18. Paraplegia is:
    a. paralysis of all limbs.
    b. paralysis of the high thoracic vertebrae.
    c. paralysis on one side of the body, opposite the side of spinal cord involvement.
    d. paralysis of any part of the body above the point of spinal cord involvement.
    e. paralysis of any part of the body below the point of spinal cord involvement.

19. Which of the following is an infectious disorder of the nervous system?
    a. Tumors
    b. ALS
    c. Multiple sclerosis
    d. Encephalitis
    e. Febrile seizures

20. Parkinson disease is a:
    a. convulsive disorder.
    b. degenerative disorder.
    c. developmental disorder.
    d. neoplastic disorder.
    e. traumatic disorder.

## OOG MATCHING

Grade: _____

Place the letter preceding the definition on the line next to the term.

### Key Terms

21. _____ cephalalgia
22. _____ concussion
23. _____ contusion
24. _____ convulsion
25. _____ dysphagia
26. _____ dysphasia
27. _____ electroencephalogram (EEG)
28. _____ herpes zoster
29. _____ meningocele
30. _____ migraine
31. _____ myelogram
32. _____ myelomeningocele
33. _____ Queckenstedt test
34. _____ Romberg test
35. _____ seizure
36. _____ spina bifida occulta

### Definitions

a. tracing of the electrical activity of the brain
b. a headache
c. meninges protruding through the spinal column
d. the protrusion of the spinal cord through the spinal defect
e. an invasive radiological test in which dye is injected into the spinal fluid
f. a test to determine presence of obstruction in the CSF flow performed during a lumbar puncture
g. an injury to the brain due to trauma
h. difficulty speaking
i. sudden, involuntary muscle contraction of a voluntary muscle group
j. an infection caused by reactivation of varicella zoster virus, which causes chicken pox
k. a collection of blood tissues after an injury; a bruise
l. a type of severe headache, usually unilateral; may appear in clusters
m. a congenital defect in the spinal column caused by lack of union of the vertebrae
n. an abnormal discharge of electrical activity in the brain, resulting in involuntary contractions of voluntary muscles
o. a test for the inability to maintain body balance when eyes are closed and feet are together; indication of spinal cord disease
p. inability to swallow or difficulty in swallowing

## ⦿ MATCHING

_____ Grade: _____

Place the letter preceding the examination method on the line next to the cranial nerve.

**Cranial Nerves**

**37.** _____ Olfactory (I)
**38.** _____ Trochlear (IV)
**39.** _____ Facial (VII)
**40.** _____ Glossopharyngeal (IX)
**41.** _____ Vagus (X)

**Examination Methods**

**a.** Ask patient to raise eyebrows, smile, show teeth, puff out cheeks.
**b.** Test for downward, inward eye movement.
**c.** Test each nostril for smell reception, interpretation.
**d.** Ask patient to say "ah," yawn to observe upward movement of palate; elicit gag response, note ability to swallow.
**e.** Ask patient to swallow and speak; note hoarseness.

## ⦿ MATCHING

_____ Grade: _____

Place the letter preceding the response on the line next to the reflex. Responses may be used more than once.

**Reflexes**

**42.** _____ Brachioradialis
**43.** _____ Biceps
**44.** _____ Triceps
**45.** _____ Patellar
**46.** _____ Achilles
**47.** _____ Corneal

**Responses**

**a.** Closure of eyelid
**b.** Extension of elbow
**c.** Flexion of elbow
**d.** Plantar flexion of foot
**e.** Extension of leg

## ⦿ IDENTIFICATION

_____ Grade: _____

Indicate whether the following disorders are infectious (I), degenerative (DG), convulsive (C), developmental (DV), traumatic (T), neoplastic (N), or a type of headache (H) by placing the identifying letter(s) on the line preceding the disorder.

**48.** _____ Amyotrophic lateral sclerosis

**49.** _____ Focal or Jacksonian

**50.** _____ Hydrocephalus

**51.** _____ Meningitis

**52.** _____ Neural tube defects

**53.** _____ Poliomyelitis

**54.** _____ Brain astrocytoma

**55.** _____ Herpes zoster

**56.** _____ Cerebral palsy

**57.** _____ Tetanus

**58.** _____ Febrile seizures

**59.** _____ Multiple sclerosis

**60.** _____ Spinal cord injury

**61.** Identify whether the disorders listed below affect children, women, men, or older adults. Place a check mark on the line under the appropriate groups.

| Disorder | Children | Women | Men | Older Adults |
|---|---|---|---|---|
| **a.** Parkinson disease | | | | |
| **b.** Amyotrophic lateral sclerosis | | | | |
| **c.** Multiple sclerosis | | | | |
| **d.** Reye syndrome | | | | |
| **e.** Febrile seizures | | | | |

**62.** Indicate whether the following symptoms occur at the onset of a migraine or after the migraine begins. Place a check mark on the line under the word "onset" or "after."

| Symptoms | Onset | After Migraine Begins |
|---|---|---|
| **a.** experience of flashing lights | | |
| **b.** photophobia | | |
| **c.** nausea | | |
| **d.** experience of wavy lines | | |
| **e.** diplopia | | |

## COG SHORT ANSWER

_____ Grade: _____

**63.** Explain the difference between dysphagia and dysphasia.

_____

_____

_____

_____

**64.** Name three viral infections that lead to encephalitis.

_____

_____

_____

_____

**65.** What kind of outbreak might be caused by a varicella infection? What generally triggers this outbreak?

_____

_____

_____

_____

**66.** Which age group is most susceptible to traumatic brain injuries? Why? Which age group is most susceptible to spinal cord injuries? Why?

_____

_____

_____

_____

**67.** Name seven common diagnostic tests for the nervous system.

_____

_____

_____

_____

**68.** Explain the difference between the Romberg test and the Queckenstedt test and how or if you would assist the physician in each procedure.

_____

_____

_____

_____

**69.** List three responsibilities that you may have when working with patients with neurological disorders.

_____

_____

_____

_____

**70.** Below are some of the steps involved in assisting the physician with a lumbar puncture. Explain the reasons for performing each task listed.

**a.** Check that the consent form is signed and in the chart. Warn the patient not to move during the procedure. Tell the patient that the area will be numb but pressure may still be felt after the local anesthetic is administered.

_____

_____

_____

**b.** Throughout the procedure, observe the patient closely for signs such as dyspnea or cyanosis. Monitor the pulse at intervals and record the vital signs after the procedure. Note the patient's mental alertness and any leakage at the site, nausea, or vomiting. Assess lower limb mobility. Assist the physician as necessary.

_____

_____

_____

_____

**c.** If the Queckenstedt test is to be performed, you may be required to press against the patient's jugular veins in the neck (right, left, or both) while the physician monitors the pressure of CSF.

_____

_____

_____

_____

## COG TRUE OR FALSE?

Grade: _____

Indicate whether the statements are true or false by placing the letter T (true) or F (false) on the line preceding the statement.

**71.** _____ Ice and alcohol and sponge baths are preferable to cool compresses in returning a child's body temperature to normal.

**72.** _____ If a patient is bitten by an animal, a copy of the animal's rabies tag and certificate should be placed in the patient's chart.

**73.** _____ Multiple sclerosis is a contagious disease.

**74.** _____ A lumbar puncture is more commonly performed in outpatient clinics than in the medical office.

**75.** _____ Herpes zoster may develop in patients who had a previous varicella infection.

## COG AFF CASE STUDIES FOR CRITICAL THINKING

Grade: _____

**1.** A patient comes in for treatment because of a severe dog bite. The patient has already cleaned the wound himself and the physician attends to the wound immediately. Your patient then receives antibiotic and vaccine therapy. What is the next course of action and what may you be responsible for?

_____

_____

_____

_____

2. A patient in your clinic has been treated for epilepsy and is now seizure free. This patient has decided that she is going to stop her medication regimen. She has also expressed her excitement about being able to drive again soon. How might you advise this patient before she makes her decisions?

_____

_____

_____

_____

3. There is a patient who has recently started coming to your clinic for treatment for herpes zoster. She doesn't understand why she has shingles. She is a single mom who has been supporting her children and taking care of one child with severe Down syndrome. What would you explain as the likely cause for the herpes zoster outbreak? What kind of advice might you offer this patient toward improving her health?

_____

_____

_____

_____

4. A 40-year-old patient has been suffering from severe migraines for the last year. He is concerned about his condition because he is a truck driver. He is worried that it is just a matter time before a migraine sets in while he is driving. Taking rests while he is on the road is a near impossibility. He is usually very tired, and he drinks a lot of coffee to keep himself awake on his long rides. How might you advise and educate this patient?

_____

_____

_____

_____

5. A patient comes in to the office and complains of headaches, blurred vision, and memory loss. What would your immediate concern be? What type of tests may need to be performed to learn more about this patient's symptoms?

_____

_____

_____

_____

## PSY PROCEDURE 19-1  **Assist with a Lumbar Puncture**

Name: _____ Date: _____ Time: _____ Grade: _____

**EQUIPMENT/SUPPLIES:** Sterile gloves, examination gloves, 3- to 5-inch lumbar needle with a stylet (physician will specify gauge and length), sterile gauze sponges, specimen containers, local anesthetic and syringe, needle, adhesive bandages, fenestrated drape, sterile drape, antiseptic, skin preparation supplies (razor), biohazard sharps container, biohazard waste container

**STANDARDS:** Given the needed equipment and a place to work, the student will perform this skill with _____ % accuracy in a total of _____ minutes. *(Your instructor will tell you what the percentage and time limits will be before you begin.)*

**KEY:**         4 = Satisfactory              0 = Unsatisfactory              NA =This step is not counted

| PROCEDURE STEPS | SELF | PARTNER | INSTRUCTOR |
|---|---|---|---|
| **1.** Wash your hands. | ❏ | ❏ | ❏ |
| **2.** Assemble the equipment. | ❏ | ❏ | ❏ |
| **3.** Identify yourself including your title. | ❏ | ❏ | ❏ |
| **4.** Identify the patient, and explain the procedure. | ❏ | ❏ | ❏ |
| **5.** Check that the consent form is signed and available in the chart. | ❏ | ❏ | ❏ |
| **6.** Explain the importance of not moving during the procedure and explain that the area will be numbed but pressure may still be felt. | ❏ | ❏ | ❏ |
| **7.** Have the patient void. | ❏ | ❏ | ❏ |
| **8.** Direct the patient to disrobe and put on a gown with the opening in the back. | ❏ | ❏ | ❏ |
| **9.** Prepare the skin unless this is to be done as part of the sterile preparation. | ❏ | ❏ | ❏ |
| **10.** Assist as needed with administration of the anesthetic. | ❏ | ❏ | ❏ |
| **11.** Assist the patient into the appropriate position.<br>**a.** For the side-lying position:<br>(1) Stand in front of the patient and help by holding the patient's knees and top shoulder.<br>(2) Ask the patient to move, so the back is close to the edge of the table.<br>**b.** For the forward leaning, supported position:<br>(1) Stand in front of the patient and rest your hands on the patient's shoulders.<br>(2) Ask the patient to breathe slowly and deeply. | ❏ | ❏ | ❏ |
| **12.** Throughout the procedure, observe the patient closely for signs such as dyspnea or cyanosis.<br>**a.** Monitor the pulse at intervals and record the vital signs after the procedure.<br>**b.** Assess lower limb mobility. | ❏ | ❏ | ❏ |

**PSY** PROCEDURE 19-1 **Assist with a Lumbar Puncture** (continued)

| | | | |
|---|---|---|---|
| **13.** When the physician has the needle securely in place, if specimens are to be taken:<br>**a.** Put on gloves to receive the potentially hazardous body fluid.<br>**b.** Label the tubes in sequence as you receive them.<br>**c.** Label with the patient's identification and place them in bio-hazard bags. | ❏ | ❏ | ❏ |
| **14.** If the Queckenstedt test is to be performed, you may be required to press against the patient's jugular veins in the neck, either right, left, or both, while the physician monitors the CSF pressure. | ❏ | ❏ | ❏ |
| **15.** At the completion of the procedure:<br>**a.** Cover the site with an adhesive bandage and assist the patient to a flat position.<br>**b.** The physician will determine when the patient is ready to leave. | ❏ | ❏ | ❏ |
| **16.** Route the specimens as required. | ❏ | ❏ | ❏ |
| **17.** Clean the examination room and care for or dispose of the equipment as needed. | ❏ | ❏ | ❏ |
| **18.** Wash your hands. | ❏ | ❏ | ❏ |
| **19.** **AFF** Log into the Electronic Medical Record (EMR) using your username and secure password OR obtain the paper medical record from a secure location and assure it is kept away from public access. | ❏ | ❏ | ❏ |
| **20.** Document your part in preparing specimens obtained and patient instructions after the procedure. | ❏ | ❏ | ❏ |
| **21.** When finished, log out of the EMR and/or replace the paper medical record in an appropriate and secure location. | ❏ | ❏ | ❏ |

**CALCULATION**

Total Possible Points: _____

Total Points Earned: _____ Multiplied by 100 = _____ Divided by Total Possible Points = _____ %

**PASS   FAIL   COMMENTS:**
  ❏        ❏

Student's signature _____ Date _____

Partner's signature _____ Date _____

Instructor's signature _____ Date _____

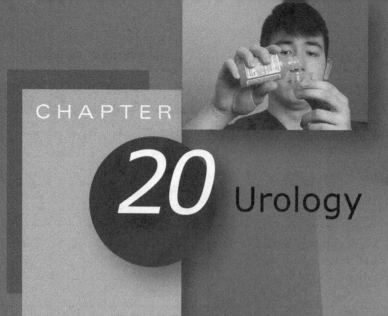

# CHAPTER

# *20* Urology

# Learning Outcomes

## **COG** Cognitive Domain

1. Spell key terms
2. Define medical terms and abbreviations related to all body systems
3. Describe structural organization of the human body
4. List major organs in each body system
5. Identify the anatomical location of major organs in each body system
6. Describe the normal function of each body system
7. Identify common pathology related to each body system including signs, symptoms, and etiology
   a. List and describe common diseases of the urinary system and the male reproductive system
   b. Describe and explain the purpose of various diagnostic procedures associated with the urinary system
   c. Name and describe the common procedures for diagnosing urinary system disorders

8. Discuss the role of the medical assistant in diagnosing and treating disorders of the urinary system and the male reproductive system

## **PSY** Psychomotor Domain

1. Perform a female urinary catheterization (Procedure 20-1)
2. Perform a male urinary catheterization (Procedure 20-2)
3. Instruct a male patient on the testicular self-examination (Procedure 20-3)

## **AFF** Affective Domain

1. Incorporate critical thinking skills when performing patient assessment
2. Incorporate critical thinking skills when performing patient care
3. Show awareness of a patient's concerns related to the procedure being performed
4. Demonstrate empathy, active listening, nonverbal communication
5. Demonstrate respect for individual diversity including gender, race,

religion, age, economic status, appearance
6. Explain to a patient the rationale for performance of a procedure
7. Demonstrate sensitivity to patient rights
8. Protect the integrity of the medical record

## **ABHES Competencies**

1. Assist the physician with the regimen of diagnostic and treatment modalities as they relate to each body system
2. Comply with federal, state, and local health laws and regulations
3. Communicate on the recipient's level of comprehension
4. Serve as a liaison between the physician and others
5. Show empathy and impartiality when dealing with patients
6. Document accurately

Name: _____    Date: _____    Grade: _____

## COG MULTIPLE CHOICE

Circle the letter preceding the correct answer.

1. Cystoscopy is:
   a. an inflammation of the urinary bladder.
   b. the direct visualization of the bladder and urethra.
   c. a procedure used to help patients pass calculi.
   d. the treatment used for men with an inguinal hernia.
   e. the use of a small camera inserted into the rectum.

2. Which of the following might contribute to psychogenic impotence?
   a. Disease in any other body system
   b. Injury to pelvic organs
   c. Medication
   d. Exhaustion
   e. Cardiovascular problems

3. Before scheduling a patient for an IVP or a retrograde pyelogram, you must check for a(n):
   a. protein allergy.
   b. lubricant allergy.
   c. iodine allergy.
   d. rubber allergy.
   e. latex allergy.

4. A procedure that cleanses the blood of waste products and excess fluid is:
   a. oliguria.
   b. lithotripsy.
   c. proteinuria.
   d. cystoscopy.
   e. dialysis.

5. Young girls are prone to urethritis because they:
   a. forget to practice good hand-washing technique.
   b. have a short urethra.
   c. don't take enough baths.
   d. urinate too frequently.
   e. wipe from front to back.

6. Which of the following instructions would be helpful for a patient trying to pass a stone?
   a. Eat a large amount of fiber.
   b. Get plenty of bed rest and relaxation.
   c. Drink lots of water.
   d. Go to the hospital when the stone passes.
   e. Do not consume anything until the stone has passed.

7. Orchiopexy is surgery to correct:
   a. undescended testes.
   b. enlarged prostate.
   c. inguinal hernia.
   d. impotence.
   e. hydrocele.

8. One common urinary disorder in females is:
   a. benign prostatic hyperplasia.
   b. nocturia.
   c. hydrocele.
   d. cryptorchidism.
   e. urinary tract infection.

*Scenario for questions 9 and 10:* An elderly patient comes in for a routine checkup, and the physician discovers his prostate gland is very enlarged.

9. What is a blood test you can run to look for prostate cancer?
   a. PSA test
   b. Proteinuria
   c. Snellen test
   d. Digital rectal exam
   e. Dialysis

10. A urinary condition that might indicate an enlarged prostate gland is:
    a. proteinuria.
    b. oliguria.
    c. nocturia.
    d. hematuria.
    e. pyuria.

11. Seventy-five percent of men with prostate cancer are over age:
    a. 15 years.
    b. 30 years.
    c. 34 years.
    d. 50 years.
    e. 75 years.

12. What kind of juice is recommended to patients to acidify urine?
    a. Tomato juice
    b. Orange juice
    c. Grape juice
    d. Cranberry juice
    e. Grapefruit juice

13. A patient should be given a catheter when:
    a. the patient suffers from nocturia.
    b. the patient has a urinary tract infection.
    c. the patient's urine has high PSA levels.
    d. the patient has calculi.
    e. the patient has dysuria.

14. Which of the following instruments is used to view the bladder and urethra?
    a. Catheter
    b. Cystoscope
    c. Dialysis machine
    d. Ultrasound
    e. Pyelogram

15. Which of the following patients is most likely to develop a urinary tract infection?
    a. A young boy who frequently urinates
    b. A teenaged girl who takes bubble baths
    c. An elderly woman who only wears loose-fitting dresses
    d. An adult woman who showers immediately after sexual intercourse
    e. A middle-aged man who does not wash his hands very often

16. Which of the following is the initial step in catheterization of a patient?
    a. Wash your hands.
    b. Open the catheterization kit.
    c. Put on sterile gloves.
    d. Use antiseptic swabs to clean area.
    e. Assist patient to assume position.

17. What is a symptom of hydronephrosis?
    a. Proteinuria
    b. Chills
    c. Swollen prostate
    d. Back pain
    e. High PSA levels

18. Which of the following is true for catheterizing both men and women?
    a. Tray may be placed on the patient's lap for easy access to tools.
    b. The patient's position is on his or her back, legs apart.
    c. Catheter is inserted 5 inches.
    d. Nondominant hand is contaminated.
    e. Coudé catheter may be used.

19. Which of the following is a cause of organic impotence?
    a. Exhaustion
    b. Anxiety
    c. Depression
    d. Stress
    e. Endocrine imbalance

20. Ultrasonography can be used to treat which of the following?
    a. Renal failure
    b. Hydronephrosis
    c. Calculi
    d. Urinary tract infection
    e. Inguinal hernia

## ᴄᴏɢ MATCHING

_____ Grade: _____

Place the letter preceding the definition on the line next to the term.

**Key Terms**

21. _____ anuria
22. _____ blood urea nitrogen
23. _____ catheterization
24. _____ cystoscopy
25. _____ dialysis
26. _____ dysuria
27. _____ enuresis
28. _____ hematuria
29. _____ impotence
30. _____ incontinence
31. _____ intravenous pyelogram (IVP)
32. _____ lithotripsy
33. _____ nephrostomy

**Definitions**

a. an inability to achieve or maintain an erection
b. painful or difficult urination
c. crushing a stone with sound waves
d. the removal of waste in blood not filtered by the kidneys by passing fluid through a semipermeable barrier that allows normal electrolytes to remain, either with a machine with circulatory access or by passing a balanced fluid through the peritoneal cavity
e. excessive urination at night
f. a blood test to determine the amount of nitrogen in blood or urea, a waste product normally excreted in urine
g. of psychological origin
h. a normal protein produced by the prostate that usually elevates in the presence of prostate cancer
i. the density of a liquid, such as urine, compared with water

**Key Terms**

34. _____ nocturia
35. _____ oliguria
36. _____ prostate-specific antigen
37. _____ proteinuria
38. _____ psychogenic
39. _____ pyuria
40. _____ retrograde pyelogram
41. _____ specific gravity
42. _____ ureterostomy
43. _____ urinalysis
44. _____ urinary frequency

**Definitions**

j. radiography using contrast medium to evaluate kidney function
k. direct visualization of the urinary bladder through a cystoscope inserted through the urethra
l. an examination of the physical, chemical, and microscopic properties of urine
m. failure of kidneys to produce urine
n. blood in the urine
o. the presence of large quantities of protein in the urine; usually a sign of renal dysfunction
p. scant urine production
q. the urge to urinate occurring more often than is required for normal bladder elimination
r. a surgical opening to the outside of the body from the ureter to facilitate drainage of urine from an obstructed kidney
s. pus in the urine
t. bed wetting
u. the placement of a catheter in the kidney pelvis to drain urine from an obstructed kidney
v. the inability to control elimination of urine, feces, or both
w. a procedure for introducing a flexible tube into the body
x. an x-ray of the urinary tract using contrast medium injected through the bladder and ureters; useful in diagnosing obstructions

## ⬤⬤⬤ SHORT ANSWER _____ Grade: _____

45. What is the difference between hemodialysis and peritoneal dialysis?

_____

_____

_____

_____

46. What are calculi?

_____

_____

_____

_____

47. List five microorganisms that may cause epididymitis.

a. _____

b. _____

c. _____

d. _____

e. _____

**48.** What are the symptoms of a possible tumor in the urinary system?

_____

_____

_____

_____

**49.** Are stones more likely to form when urine is alkaline or acidic?

_____

_____

_____

_____

**50.** Why is a woman more likely to have cystitis than a man?

_____

_____

_____

_____

**51.** Why are infections in the male urinary tract likely to spread to the reproductive system?

_____

_____

_____

_____

**52.** What are the three characteristics of the prostate that the physician is checking when performing a digital rectal examination?

_____

_____

_____

_____

**53.** An older adult male patient with prostatic hypertrophy must be given a catheter in order to obtain a urine sample. What is the best type of catheter to use, and why?

_____

_____

_____

_____

**54.** List three suggestions to help patients avoid urinary tract infections.

_____

_____

_____

_____

**55.** What is the difference between an intravenous pyelogram and a retrograde pyelogram? What might the medical assistant be responsible for with regards to the physician order for an intravenous pyelogram and retrograde pyelogram?

_____

_____

_____

_____

## COG TRUE OR FALSE? _____ Grade: _____

Indicate whether the statements are true or false by placing the letter T (true) or F (false) on the line preceding the statement.

**56.** _____ Orchiopexy refers to either one or both undescended testes.

**57.** _____ A nephrologist is a physician who specializes in the physical characteristics of the urinary system.

**58.** _____ No other form of birth control is needed after a man receives a vasectomy.

**59.** _____ Your office is obligated to notify a patient if a procedure or medication is still in clinical trials, but likely to be approved.

## COG AFF CASE STUDIES FOR CRITICAL THINKING _____ Grade: _____

**1.** A middle-aged patient in good shape comes in complaining of some pain in his groin. The physician suspects he might have an inguinal hernia. What is the procedure to diagnosis this, and how is it corrected?

_____

_____

_____

_____

**2.** An older adult patient has been diagnosed with renal failure and will need to undergo dialysis. However, he is not sure if hemodialysis or peritoneal dialysis would be better for his lifestyle. What information can you tell him about the two different processes, including the advantages and disadvantages of each?

_____

_____

_____

**3.** The physician asks you to give information to one of the patients about passing small calculi. What would you tell the patient about calculi, and what suggestions would you give to help the patient pass the stones?

_____

_____

_____

_____

**4.** A man in his early 20s has come in for his physical, and the physician has instructed you to teach him about testicular disease. You will also need to teach him how to perform a self-examination. However, the man is shy and embarrassed about the procedure. What can you say to him to help him overcome his discomfort?

_____

_____

_____

_____

**5.** An older adult woman has chronic renal failure, and the physician decides that she will need a catheter for peritoneal dialysis. The woman is upset that she needs this, because she believes that it will limit her movement and ability to participate in activities she likes. What can you tell her about catheters and how her lifestyle will change that might put her more at ease?

_____

_____

_____

_____

**PSY** P R O C E D U R E  2 0 - 1   **Perform a Female Urinary Catheterization**

Name: _____ Date: _____ Time: _____ Grade: _____

**EQUIPMENT/SUPPLIES:** Straight catheterization tray that includes a No. 14 or No. 16 French catheter, a sterile tray, sterile gloves, antiseptic, a specimen cup with a lid, lubricant, and a sterile drape; an examination light; an anatomically correct female torso model for performing the catheterization; a biohazard container

**STANDARDS:** Given the needed equipment and a place to work, the student will perform this skill with _____ % accuracy in a total of _____ minutes. *(Your instructor will tell you what the percentage and time limits will be before you begin.)*

**KEY:**          4 = Satisfactory                    0 = Unsatisfactory                    NA =This step is not counted

| PROCEDURE STEPS | SELF | PARTNER | INSTRUCTOR |
|---|---|---|---|
| **1.** Wash your hands. | ❑ | ❑ | ❑ |
| **2.** Greet the patient and identify yourself, including your title. | ❑ | ❑ | ❑ |
| **3.** Identify the patient and explain the procedure.<br>**a.** Have the patient disrobe from the waist down.<br>**b.** Provide adequate gowning and draping materials. | ❑ | ❑ | ❑ |
| **4.** Place the patient in the dorsal recumbent or lithotomy position.<br>**a.** Drape carefully to prevent unnecessary exposure.<br>**b.** Open the tray and place it between the patient's legs.<br>**c.** Adjust examination light to allow adequate visualization of the perineum. | ❑ | ❑ | ❑ |
| **5.** Remove the sterile glove package and put on the sterile gloves. | ❑ | ❑ | ❑ |
| **6.** Remove sterile drape and place it under the patient's buttocks. | ❑ | ❑ | ❑ |
| **7.** Open the antiseptic swabs and place them upright inside the catheter tray. | ❑ | ❑ | ❑ |
| **8.** Open the lubricant and squeeze a generous amount onto the tip of the catheter. | ❑ | ❑ | ❑ |
| **9.** Remove the sterile urine specimen cup and lid and place them to the side of the tray. | ❑ | ❑ | ❑ |
| **10.** Using your nondominant hand, carefully expose the urinary meatus. | ❑ | ❑ | ❑ |
| **11.** Using your sterile dominant hand, use antiseptic swabs to cleanse the urinary meatus by starting at the top and moving the swab down each side of the urinary meatus and down the middle, using a new swab for each side and the middle. Do not contaminate the glove on this hand. | ❑ | ❑ | ❑ |
| **12.** Pick up the catheter with the sterile, dominant hand and:<br>**a.** Carefully insert the lubricated tip into the urinary meatus approximately 3 inches.<br>**b.** Leave the other end of the catheter in the tray. | ❑ | ❑ | ❑ |

## PSY   PROCEDURE 20-1    **Perform a Female Urinary Catheterization**
(continued)

| | | | |
|---|:---:|:---:|:---:|
| **13.** Once the urine begins to flow into the catheter tray, hold the catheter in position with your nondominant hand. | ❏ | ❏ | ❏ |
| **14.** Use your dominant hand to direct the flow of urine into the specimen cup. | ❏ | ❏ | ❏ |
| **15.** Remove catheter when urine flow slows or stops or 1,000 mL has been obtained. | ❏ | ❏ | ❏ |
| **16.** Wipe the perineum carefully with the drape that was placed under the buttocks. | ❏ | ❏ | ❏ |
| **17.** Dispose of urine appropriately and discard supplies in a biohazard container.<br>　**a.** Label the specimen container and complete the necessary laboratory requisition.<br>　**b.** Process the specimen according to the guidelines of the laboratory. | ❏ | ❏ | ❏ |
| **18.** Remove your gloves and wash your hands. | ❏ | ❏ | ❏ |
| **19.** Instruct patient to dress and give any follow-up information. | ❏ | ❏ | ❏ |
| **20.** AFF Log into the Electronic Medical Record (EMR) using your username and secure password OR obtain the paper medical record from a secure location and assure it is kept away from public access. | ❏ | ❏ | ❏ |
| **21.** Document the procedure in the patient's medical record. | ❏ | ❏ | ❏ |
| **22.** When finished, log out of the EMR and/or replace the paper medical record in an appropriate and secure location. | ❏ | ❏ | ❏ |

**CALCULATION**

Total Possible Points: _____

Total Points Earned: _____ Multiplied by 100 = _____ Divided by Total Possible Points = _____ %

**PASS    FAIL    COMMENTS:**
　❏        ❏

Student's signature _____ Date _____

Partner's signature _____ Date _____

Instructor's signature _____ Date _____

**PSY** PROCEDURE 20-2 **Perform a Male Urinary Catheterization**

Name: _____ Date: _____ Time: _____ Grade: _____

**EQUIPMENT/SUPPLIES:** Straight catheterization tray that includes a No. 14 or No. 16 French catheter, a sterile tray, sterile gloves, antiseptic, a specimen cup with a lid, lubricant, and a sterile drape; an examination light; an anatomically correct male torso model for performing the catheterization; a biohazard container

**STANDARDS:** Given the needed equipment and a place to work, the student will perform this skill with _____ % accuracy in a total of _____ minutes. *(Your instructor will tell you what the percentage and time limits will be before you begin.)*

**KEY:** 4 = Satisfactory 0 = Unsatisfactory NA =This step is not counted

| PROCEDURE STEPS | SELF | PARTNER | INSTRUCTOR |
|---|---|---|---|
| **1.** Wash your hands. | ❑ | ❑ | ❑ |
| **2.** Greet the patient and identify yourself, including your title. | ❑ | ❑ | ❑ |
| **3.** Identify the patient.<br>**a.** Explain the procedure and have the patient disrobe from the waist down.<br>**b.** Provide adequate gowning and draping materials. | ❑ | ❑ | ❑ |
| **4.** Place the patient in the supine position.<br>**a.** Drape carefully to prevent unnecessary exposure.<br>**b.** Open the tray and place it to the side or on the patient's thighs.<br>**c.** Adjust examination light to allow adequate visualization of the perineum. | ❑ | ❑ | ❑ |
| **5.** Remove the sterile glove package and put on the sterile gloves. | ❑ | ❑ | ❑ |
| **6.** Carefully remove the sterile drape and place it under the glans penis. | ❑ | ❑ | ❑ |
| **7.** Open the antiseptic swabs and place them upright inside the catheter tray. | ❑ | ❑ | ❑ |
| **8.** Open lubricant and squeeze a generous amount onto the tip of the catheter. | ❑ | ❑ | ❑ |
| **9.** Remove sterile urine specimen cup and lid and place them to the side of the tray. | ❑ | ❑ | ❑ |
| **10.** Using your nondominant hand, pick up the penis to expose the urinary meatus. | ❑ | ❑ | ❑ |
| **11.** Using your sterile dominant hand, use antiseptic swabs to cleanse the urinary meatus by starting at the top and moving the swab around each side of the urinary meatus and down the middle, using a new swab for each side and the middle. Do not contaminate the glove on this hand. | ❑ | ❑ | ❑ |

## PROCEDURE 20-2 Perform a Male Urinary Catheterization
(continued)

| | | | |
|---|:---:|:---:|:---:|
| **12.** Using your sterile dominant hand, pick up the catheter.<br>**a.** Carefully insert the lubricated tip into the meatus approximately 4 to 6 inches.<br>**b.** The other end of the catheter should be left in the tray. | ❏ | ❏ | ❏ |
| **13.** Once the urine begins to flow into the catheter tray, hold the catheter in position. | ❏ | ❏ | ❏ |
| **14.** Use your dominant hand to direct the flow of urine into the specimen cup. | ❏ | ❏ | ❏ |
| **15.** Remove the catheter when urine flow slows or stops or 1,000 mL has been obtained. | ❏ | ❏ | ❏ |
| **16.** Wipe the glans penis carefully with the drape that was placed under the buttocks. | ❏ | ❏ | ❏ |
| **17.** Dispose of urine appropriately and discard supplies in a biohazard container. | ❏ | ❏ | ❏ |
| **18.** Label the specimen container and complete the necessary laboratory requisition. | ❏ | ❏ | ❏ |
| **19.** Process specimen according to the guidelines of the laboratory. | ❏ | ❏ | ❏ |
| **20.** Remove your gloves and wash your hands. | ❏ | ❏ | ❏ |
| **21.** Instruct patient to dress and give any follow-up information. | ❏ | ❏ | ❏ |
| **22.** **AFF** Log into the Electronic Medical Record (EMR) using your username and secure password OR obtain the paper medical record from a secure location and assure it is kept away from public access. | ❏ | ❏ | ❏ |
| **23.** Document the procedure in the patient's medical record. | ❏ | ❏ | ❏ |
| **24.** When finished, log out of the EMR and/or replace the paper medical record in an appropriate and secure location. | ❏ | ❏ | ❏ |

**CALCULATION**

Total Possible Points: _____

Total Points Earned: _____ Multiplied by 100 = _____ Divided by Total Possible Points = _____ %

**PASS    FAIL    COMMENTS:**
❏            ❏

Student's signature _____ Date _____

Partner's signature _____ Date _____

Instructor's signature _____ Date _____

**PSY** P R O C E D U R E  2 0 - 3 **Instruct a Male Patient on the Self-Testicular Examination**

Name: _____ Date: _____ Time: _____ Grade: _____

**EQUIPMENT/SUPPLIES:** A patient instruction sheet if available; a testicular examination model or pictures

**STANDARDS:** Given the needed equipment and a place to work, the student will perform this skill with _____ % accuracy in a total of _____ minutes. *(Your instructor will tell you what the percentage and time limits will be before you begin.)*

**KEY:** 4 = Satisfactory 0 = Unsatisfactory NA =This step is not counted

| PROCEDURE STEPS | SELF | PARTNER | INSTRUCTOR |
|---|---|---|---|
| **1.** Wash your hands. | ❑ | ❑ | ❑ |
| **2.** Greet the patient and identify yourself, including your title. | ❑ | ❑ | ❑ |
| **3.** Identify the patient and explain the procedure. | ❑ | ❑ | ❑ |
| **4.** Using the testicular model or pictures, explain the procedure. **a.** Tell the patient to examine each testicle by gently rolling between the fingers and the thumb with both hands. **b.** Check for lumps or thickenings. | ❑ | ❑ | ❑ |
| **5.** Explain that the epididymis is located on top of each testicle. **a.** Palpate to avoid incorrectly identifying it as an abnormal growth or lump. **b.** Instruct patient to report abnormal lumps or thickenings to the physician. | ❑ | ❑ | ❑ |
| **6.** Allow the patient to ask questions related to the testicular self-examination. | ❑ | ❑ | ❑ |
| **7. AFF** Log into the Electronic Medical Record (EMR) using your username and secure password OR obtain the paper medical record from a secure location and assure it is kept away from public access. | ❑ | ❑ | ❑ |
| **8.** Document the procedure in the patient's medical record. | ❑ | ❑ | ❑ |
| **9.** When finished, log out of the EMR and/or replace the paper medical record in an appropriate and secure location. | ❑ | ❑ | ❑ |

**CALCULATION**

Total Possible Points: _____

Total Points Earned: _____ Multiplied by 100 = _____ Divided by Total Possible Points = _____ %

**PASS FAIL COMMENTS:**
❑ ❑

Student's signature _____ Date _____

Partner's signature _____ Date _____

Instructor's signature _____ Date _____

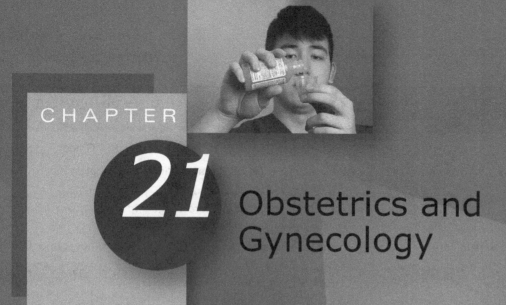

# CHAPTER

# *21* Obstetrics and Gynecology

## Learning Outcomes

### COG Cognitive Domain

1. Spell key terms
2. Define medical terms and abbreviations related to all body systems
3. Describe structural organization of the human body
4. List major organs in each body system
5. Identify the anatomical location of major organs in each body system
6. Describe the normal function of each body system
7. Identify common pathology related to each body system including signs, symptoms, and etiology
8. List and describe common gynecological and obstetric disorders
9. Identify your role in the care of gynecologic and obstetric patients
10. Describe the components of prenatal and postpartum patient care
11. Explain the diagnostic and therapeutic procedures associated with the female reproductive system
12. Identify the various methods of contraception
13. Describe menopause

### PSY Psychomotor Domain

1. Instruct the patient on the breast self-examination (Procedure 21-1)
2. Assist with the pelvic examination and Pap smear (Procedure 21-2)
3. Assist with colposcopy and cervical biopsy (Procedure 21-3)

### AFF Affective Domain

1. Incorporate critical thinking skills when performing patient assessment
2. Incorporate critical thinking skills when performing patient care
3. Show awareness of a patient's concerns related to the procedure being performed
4. Demonstrate empathy, active listening, nonverbal communication

5. Demonstrate respect for individual diversity including gender, race, religion, age, economic status, appearance
6. Explain to a patient the rationale for performance of a procedure
7. Demonstrate sensitivity to patient rights
8. Protect the integrity of the medical record

### ABHES Competencies

1. Assist the physician with the regimen of diagnostic and treatment modalities as they relate to each body system
2. Comply with federal, state, and local health laws and regulations
3. Communicate on the recipient's level of comprehension
4. Serve as a liaison between the physician and others
5. Show empathy and impartiality when dealing with patients
6. Document accurately

Name: _____     Date: _____     Grade: _____

## OOG MULTIPLE CHOICE

Circle the letter preceding the correct answer.

1. Within 24 hours before a gynecological examination, a patient should avoid:
   a. showering.
   b. using vaginal medication.
   c. taking a home pregnancy test.
   d. performing a breast self-examination.
   e. taking a medication containing aspirin.

2. A cesarean section is used to:
   a. diagnose gynecological cancers.
   b. screen the fetus for defects in the neural tube.
   c. analyze fluid from the amniotic sac for nervous system disorders.
   d. deliver an infant when vaginal delivery is not possible or advisable.
   e. stabilize an infant that was delivered before the 37th week of pregnancy.

3. Morning sickness that has escalated to a serious condition is known as:
   a. eclampsia.
   b. proteinuria.
   c. abruptio placentae.
   d. hyperemesis gravidarum.
   e. endometriosis.

4. A pessary may be used to treat:
   a. leiomyomas.
   b. ovarian cysts.
   c. endometriosis.
   d. uterine prolapse.
   e. ectopic pregnancy.

5. The most common sexually transmitted disease in the United States is:
   a. syphilis.
   b. gonorrhea.
   c. chlamydia.
   d. herpes genitalis.
   e. AIDS.

6. Which of the following methods of contraception works hormonally and is worn on the skin for 3 out of 4 weeks to prevent ovulation?
   a. Pill
   b. Ring
   c. Patch
   d. Condom
   e. Spermicide

7. Which of the following is a presumptive sign of pregnancy?
   a. Goodell sign
   b. Fetal heart tone
   c. Nausea and vomiting
   d. HCG in urine and blood
   e. Visualization of the fetus

8. A contraction stress test (CST) should be performed in the:
   a. hospital.
   b. patient's home.
   c. obstetrician's office.
   d. gynecologist's office.
   e. laboratory.

9. A hysterosalpingography is used to determine:
   a. the location and severity of cervical lesions.
   b. whether the patient will abort or miscarry a fetus.
   c. the presence of abnormal cells associated with cervical cancer.
   d. the position of the uterus and the patency of the fallopian tubes.
   e. the size of the pelvic anatomy for a vaginal delivery.

*Scenario for questions 10 and 11:* Your patient is a pregnant 32-year-old woman in her 22nd week of gestation. She is complaining of edema, headaches, blurred vision, and vomiting. After laboratory results confirm proteinuria, the physician concludes that the patient has preeclampsia.

10. Which of the following would the physician advise the patient to increase in her diet?
    a. Protein
    b. Sodium
    c. Calcium
    d. Folic acid
    e. Iron

11. What more severe condition could result if her present condition does not improve?
    a. Epilepsy
    b. Eclampsia
    c. Posteclampsia
    d. Premature labor
    e. Hyperemesis gravidarum

**12.** An undiagnosed ectopic pregnancy could lead to:
a. polymenorrhea.
b. salpingo-oophorectomy.
c. herniation of the ovaries.
d. displacement of the uterus.
e. rupture of the fallopian tube.

**13.** How should the lochia appear immediately and for up to 6 days after delivery?
a. White
b. Red
c. Green
d. Yellow
e. Clear

**14.** The onset of eclampsia is marked by:
a. seizures.
b. vomiting.
c. hypertension.
d. premature labor.
e. contractions.

**15.** A woman who is pregnant for the first time is:
a. nulligravida.
b. primigravida.
c. nullipara.
d. primipara.
e. multipara.

**16.** If animal research indicates no fetal risk concerning the use of a medication, but no human studies have been completed, the medication can be found in which category of drugs?
a. Category A
b. Category B
c. Category C
d. Category D
e. Category X

**17.** The onset of first menses is called:
a. menarche.
b. menses.
c. menorrhagia.
d. metrorrhagia.
e. polymenorrhea.

**18.** Surgery to occlude the vagina is called:
a. colporrhaphy.
b. laparoscopy.
c. ultrasound.
d. pessary.
e. colpocleisis.

**19.** The height of the fundus is determined each visit by:
a. ultrasound.
b. blood work.
c. urinalysis.
d. fetal heart monitor.
e. palpation.

**20.** Elevated AFP levels in a pregnant woman may indicate:
a. fetal nervous system deformities.
b. preeclampsia.
c. hyperemesis gravidarum.
d. placenta previa.
e. uterine contractions.

## **COG** MATCHING

Grade: _____

Place the letter preceding the definition on the line next to the term.

**Key Terms**

21. _____ abortion
22. _____ amenorrhea
23. _____ amniocentesis
24. _____ Braxton-Hicks
25. _____ Chadwick sign
26. _____ colpocleisis
27. _____ culdocentesis
28. _____ cystocele
29. _____ dysmenorrheal
30. _____ dyspareunia
31. _____ Goodell sign

**Definitions**

a. a woman who has never given birth to a viable fetus
b. softening of the cervix early in pregnancy
c. the presence of large amounts of protein in the urine; usually a sign of renal dysfunction
d. herniation of the rectum into the vaginal area
e. surgical puncture and aspiration of fluid from the vaginal cul-de-sac for diagnosis or therapy
f. when inserted into the vagina, device that supports the uterus
g. sign of early pregnancy in which the vaginal, cervical, and vulvar tissues develop a bluish violet color
h. herniation of the urinary bladder into the vagina

## Key Terms

32. _____ hirsutism
33. _____ human chorionic gonadotropin (HCG)
34. _____ hysterosalpingogram
35. _____ menorrhagia
36. _____ menarche
37. _____ metrorrhagia
38. _____ multipara
39. _____ nullipara
40. _____ pessary
41. _____ polymenorrhea
42. _____ primipara
43. _____ proteinuria
44. _____ puerperium
45. _____ rectocele
46. _____ salpingo-oophorectomy

## Definitions

i. period of time (about 6 weeks) from childbirth until reproductive structures return to normal
j. hormone secreted by the placenta and found in the urine and blood of a pregnant female
k. irregular uterine bleeding
l. puncture of the amniotic sac to remove fluid for testing
m. termination of pregnancy or products of conception prior to fetal viability and/or 20 weeks' gestation
n. condition of not menstruating
o. painful coitus or sexual intercourse
p. a woman who has given birth to one viable infant
q. abnormally frequent menstrual periods
r. surgery to occlude the vagina
s. a woman who has given birth to more than one fetus
t. surgical excision of both the fallopian tube and the ovary
u. sporadic uterine contractions during pregnancy
v. painful menstruation
w. abnormal or excessive hair growth in women
x. radiograph of the uterus and fallopian tubes after injection with a contrast medium
y. onset of first menstruation
z. excessive bleeding during menstruation

## **COG** MATCHING

Grade: _____

Place the letter preceding the description on the line next to the stage of lochia it describes.

## STDs

47. _____ AIDS
48. _____ Syphilis
49. _____ Chlamydia
50. _____ Condylomata acuminata
51. _____ Gonorrhea
52. _____ Herpes genitalis

## Microorganisms

a. Herpes simplex virus 2 (HSV2)
b. Human papilloma virus (HPV)
c. *Treponema pallidum*
d. *Chlamydia trachomatis*
e. Human immunodeficiency virus (HIV)
f. *Neisseria gonorrhoeae*

## **COG** MATCHING

Grade: _____

Match each of the following stages of lochia with the correct description.

## Lochia Stages

53. _____ Lochia rubra
54. _____ Lochia serosa
55. _____ Lochia alba

## Descriptions

a. Thin, brownish discharge lasting about 3 to 4 days after the previous stage
b. Blood-tinged discharge within 6 days of delivery
c. White discharge that has no evidence of blood that can last up to week 6

## PSY IDENTIFICATION

_____ Grade: _____

**56.** Identify which of the following tasks may be the responsibility of the medical assistant in the care of the gynecological and obstetric patient by placing a check mark on the line preceding the task.

**a.** _____ Give the patient instructions prior to her pelvic examination, such as refraining from douching, intercourse, and applying vaginal medication for 24 hours before her exam.

**b.** _____ Warm the speculum prior to the pelvic exam.

**c.** _____ Perform a breast examination.

**d.** _____ Instruct the patient to change into an examining gown.

**e.** _____ Inform patient of the effectiveness of different birth control methods.

**f.** _____ Confirm whether a patient is gravid.

**g.** _____ Decide whether a patient should go to the medical office, or go to the hospital after displaying signs and/or symptoms of labor.

**h.** _____ Determine if the patient's medical history includes any over-the-counter medications known to be harmful to a developing fetus.

**57.** Identify the obstetric disorder associated with the following signs and symptoms by writing the name of the disorder on the line following the signs and symptoms.

**a.** Nausea and vomiting (morning sickness) that has escalated to an unrelenting level, resulting in dehydration, electrolyte imbalance, and weight loss. _____
_____

**b.** The premature separation or detachment of the placenta from the uterus._____
_____

**c.** Hypertension that is directly related to pregnancy and can be classified as either preeclampsia or eclampsia. _____
_____

**d.** The loss of pregnancy before the fetus is viable; preceded by vaginal bleeding, uterine cramps, and lower back pain. _____
_____

**e.** A fertilized ovum that has implanted somewhere other than the uterine cavity, such as the fallopian tubes, the abdomen, the ovaries, and the cervical os, causing breast enlargement or tenderness, nausea, pelvic pain, syncope, abdominal symptoms, painful sexual intercourse, and irregular menstrual bleeding. _____
_____

**58.** During the first prenatal visit, you will be responsible for instructing the patient to contact the physician if she experiences certain alarming signs or symptoms. Below, eliminate the signs or symptoms that should not be included in the list by placing a check mark on the line next to the sign or symptom that should *not* be included.

**a.** _____ Vaginal bleeding or spotting

**b.** _____ Persistent vomiting

**c.** _____ Weight gain

**d.** _____ Increased appetite

**e.** _____ Fever or chills

**f.** _____ Dysuria

**g.** _____ Frequent urination

**h.** _____ Unusual food cravings

**i.** _____ Abdominal or uterine cramping

**j.** _____ Leaking amniotic fluid

**k.** _____ Alteration in fetal movement

**l.** _____ Depressed mood

**m.** _____ Dizziness or blurred vision

**59.** Review the list of contraceptive methods. Then place a check mark on the line under the column to identify the type of contraceptive that describes the method.

| Methods | Surgical | Hormonal | Barrier | Other |
|---|---|---|---|---|
| **a.** The pill | | | | |
| **b.** Vasectomy | | | | |
| **c.** Male condom | | | | |
| **d.** Spermicide | | | | |
| **e.** Injection | | | | |
| **f.** The patch | | | | |
| **g.** Emergency contraception | | | | |
| **h.** Female condom | | | | |
| **i.** The ring | | | | |
| **j.** Diaphragm/spermicide | | | | |
| **k.** Fertility awareness | | | | |
| **l.** IUD | | | | |

## **COG SHORT ANSWER**

_____ Grade: _____

**60.** Some ovarian cysts are functional, whereas others are problematic. Give an example of each.

_____

**61.** How is premenstrual dysphoric disorder (PMDD) diagnosed and treated?

_____

**62.** What is the difference between HIV and AIDS?

_____

**63.** A pregnant patient is listed as gr iv, pret 0, ab 2, p i. What does this listing describe?

_____

**64.** What is a cesarean section, and list the reasons that this procedure would be necessary?

_____

**65.** Which muscles are strengthened by Kegel exercises? How can these exercises benefit a patient?

_____

**66.** A patient has just learned she is pregnant. What will you tell her to expect during her first prenatal visit? How often will you schedule the patient's subsequent prenatal visits?

_____

**67.** After a patient's AFP (alpha-fetoprotein) levels were found to be abnormal, the physician has ordered an amniocentesis and a fetal ultrasonography. Describe the responsibilities of the medical assistant regarding these procedures performed in the medical office.

_____

**68.** What signs differentiate true labor from false labor?

_____

**69.** What should a patient nearing the age range of 45 to 50 years be told to expect during menopause?

_____

## COG COMPLETION

Grade: _____

**70.** Complete this chart, which shows common gynecological disorders, their signs and symptoms, and possible treatments.

| Disorder | Signs and Symptoms | Treatment |
|---|---|---|
| Dysfunctional uterine bleeding | a. | Hormone therapy, contraceptives, curettage, hysterectomy |
| Premenstrual syndrome | Severe physical, psychological, and behavioral signs and symptoms during the 7 to 10 days before menses | b. |
| Endometriosis | c. | Hormone and drug therapy, laparoscopic excision, hysterectomy, bilateral salpingo-oophorectomy |
| Uterine prolapse and displacement | Pelvic pressure, dyspareunia, urinary problems, constipation | d. |
| Leiomyomas | e. | Monitoring, myomectomy, hysterectomy |
| f. | Anovulation, irregular menses or amenorrhea, hirsutism | Hormone therapy, oral contraceptives |
| Infertility | Inability to conceive | g. |

**71.** Complete this chart, which shows common diagnostic and therapeutic procedures and their purposes.

| Procedure | Description | Purpose |
|---|---|---|
| Pelvic examination | a. | To identify or diagnose any abnormal conditions |
| Breast examination | Examination of the breast and surrounding tissue; performed with the hands | b. |
| Papanicolaou (Pap) test | c. | To detect signs of cervical cancer |
| Colposcopy | Visual examination of the vaginal and cervical surfaces using a stereoscopic microscope called a *colposcope* | d. |
| e. | Injection of a contrast medium into the uterus and fallopian tubes followed by a radiograph, using a hysterosalpingogram | To determine the configuration of the uterus and the patency of the fallopian tubes for patients with infertility |
| Dilation and curettage | f. | To remove uterine tissue for diagnostic testing, to remove endocrine tissue, to prevent or treat menorrhagia, or to remove retained products of conception after a spontaneous abortion or miscarriage |

# COG TRUE OR FALSE?

Grade: _____

Indicate whether the statements are true or false by placing the letter T (true) or F (false) on the line preceding the statement.

72. _____ A woman's first Pap test and pelvic examination should be performed about 3 years after her first sexual intercourse or by age 21 years, whichever comes first, as recommended by the American College of Obstetricians and Gynecologists (ACOG).

73. _____ A pelvic examination is performed for a pregnant patient during each prenatal visit to the obstetrician's office.

74. _____ The presence of Braxton-Hicks contractions is a conclusive sign of pregnancy and leads to a formal diagnosis of pregnancy.

75. _____ The date on which the patient last had sexual intercourse is used to calculate the expected date of delivery.

# COG AFF CASE STUDIES FOR CRITICAL THINKING

Grade: _____

**1.** A patient at your medical office tested positive for a sexually transmitted disease (STD). What will be your responsibilities in connection with this diagnosis?

_____

_____

_____

_____

**2.** While working at a gynecological/obstetrics office, you receive a frantic phone call from a pregnant patient who is experiencing vaginal bleeding, uterine cramps, and lower back pain. You put the patient on hold in order to consult the physician, but you learn that the physician has just been called to the hospital for a delivery. How would you handle this call?

_____

_____

_____

_____

**3.** Your 34-year-old patient is concerned about gynecological cancers because there are cases of breast cancer and cervical cancer in her family history. What can you recommend the patient do to ensure early detection of any gynecological problems? Describe these procedures to her in a way that will ease her anxieties.

_____

_____

_____

**4.** A 20-year-old female patient has made an appointment with the physician because she believes that she has PMDD, which she blames for her failing grades and damaged personal relationships. When you meet with the patient to assess her medical history, she asks you to write a note to her professors excusing her from any missed assignments. What should you do next?

_____

_____

_____

_____

**PSY**   PROCEDURE 21-1   **Instruct the Patient on the Breast Self-Examination**

Name: _____   Date: _____   Time: _____   Grade: _____

**EQUIPMENT/SUPPLIES:** Patient education instruction sheet, if available; breast examination model, if available

**STANDARDS:** Given the needed equipment and a place to work, the student will perform this skill with _____ % accuracy in a total of _____ minutes. *(Your instructor will tell you what the percentage and time limits will be before you begin.)*

**KEY:**         4 = Satisfactory         0 = Unsatisfactory         NA = This step is not counted

| PROCEDURE STEPS | SELF | PARTNER | INSTRUCTOR |
|---|---|---|---|
| **1.** Wash your hands. | ❏ | ❏ | ❏ |
| **2.** Greet the patient and identify yourself including your title. Identify the patient. | ❏ | ❏ | ❏ |
| **3.** Explain the purpose and frequency of examining the breasts. | ❏ | ❏ | ❏ |
| **4.** Describe three positions necessary for the patient to examine the breasts: in front of a mirror, in the shower, and while lying down. | ❏ | ❏ | ❏ |
| **5.** In front of a mirror: <br> **a.** Disrobe and inspect the breasts with her arms at sides and with arms raised above her head. <br> **b.** Look for any changes in contour, swelling, dimpling of the skin, or changes in the nipple. | ❏ | ❏ | ❏ |
| **6.** In the shower: <br> **a.** Feel each breast with hands over wet skin using the flat part of the first three fingers. <br> **b.** Check for any lumps, hard knots, or thickenings. <br> **c.** Use right hand to lightly press over all areas of left breast. <br> **d.** Use left hand to examine right breast. | ❏ | ❏ | ❏ |
| **7.** Lying down: <br> **a.** Place a pillow or folded towel under the right shoulder, and place the right hand behind head to examine the right breast. <br> **b.** With left hand, use flat part of the fingers to palpate the breast tissue. <br> **c.** Begin at the outermost top of the right breast. <br> **d.** Work in a small circular motion around the breast in a clockwise rotation. | ❏ | ❏ | ❏ |
| **8.** Encourage patient to palpate the breast carefully moving her fingers inward toward the nipple and palpating every part of the breast including the nipple. | ❏ | ❏ | ❏ |
| **9.** Repeat the procedure for the left breast. Place a pillow or folded towel under the left shoulder with the left hand behind the head. | ❏ | ❏ | ❏ |

**PSY** PROCEDURE 21-1 **Instruct the Patient on the Breast Self-Examination** (continued)

| | | | |
|---|---|---|---|
| **10.** Gently squeeze each nipple between the thumb and index finger.<br> **a.** Report any clear or bloody discharge to the physician.<br> **b.** Promptly report any abnormalities found in the breast self-examination to the physician. | ❑ | ❑ | ❑ |
| **11. AFF** Explain how to respond to a patient who is visually impaired. | ❑ | ❑ | ❑ |
| | | | |
| **12. AFF** Log into the Electronic Medical Record (EMR) using your username and secure password OR obtain the paper medical record from a secure location and assure it is kept away from public access. | ❑ | ❑ | ❑ |
| **13.** Document the patient education. | ❑ | ❑ | ❑ |
| **14.** When finished, log out of the EMR and/or replace the paper medical record in an appropriate and secure location. | ❑ | ❑ | ❑ |

**CALCULATION**

Total Possible Points: _____

Total Points Earned: _____ Multiplied by 100 = _____ Divided by Total Possible Points = _____ %

**PASS    FAIL    COMMENTS:**
  ❑        ❑

Student's signature _____ Date _____

Partner's signature _____ Date _____

Instructor's signature _____ Date _____

## PSY PROCEDURE 21-2 Assist with the Pelvic Examination and Pap Smear

Name: _____ Date: _____ Time: _____ Grade: _____

**EQUIPMENT/SUPPLIES:** Gown and drape; appropriate size vaginal speculum; cotton-tipped applicators; water-soluble lubricant; examination gloves; examination light; tissues; materials for Pap smear: cervical brush, liquid-based preservative (SurePath® or ThinPrep®), laboratory request form, identification labels, and other materials that may be required by laboratory; biohazard transport bag, and biohazard waste container.

**STANDARDS:** Given the needed equipment and a place to work, the student will perform this skill with _____ % accuracy in a total of _____ minutes. *(Your instructor will tell you what the percentage and time limits will be before you begin.)*

**KEY:** 4 = Satisfactory 0 = Unsatisfactory NA = This step is not counted

| PROCEDURE STEPS | SELF | PARTNER | INSTRUCTOR |
|---|---|---|---|
| **1.** Wash your hands. | ❏ | ❏ | ❏ |
| **2.** Assemble the equipment and supplies.<br>  **a.** Warm vaginal speculum by running under warm water.<br>  **b.** Do not use lubricant on the vaginal speculum before insertion. | ❏ | ❏ | ❏ |
| **3.** Label the outside of the liquid-based preservative container. | ❏ | ❏ | ❏ |
| **4.** Greet and identify yourself including your title. | ❏ | ❏ | ❏ |
| **5.** Identify the patient and explain the procedure. | ❏ | ❏ | ❏ |
| **6.** Ask the patient to empty her bladder and, if necessary, collect a urine specimen. | ❏ | ❏ | ❏ |
| **7.** Provide a gown and drape, and ask the patient to disrobe from the waist down. | ❏ | ❏ | ❏ |
| **8.** Position patient in the dorsal lithotomy position—buttocks at bottom edge of table. | ❏ | ❏ | ❏ |
| **9.** Adjust drape to cover patient's abdomen and knees but expose the genitalia. | ❏ | ❏ | ❏ |
| **10.** Adjust light over the genitalia for maximum visibility. | ❏ | ❏ | ❏ |
| **11.** Assist physician with the examination as needed. | ❏ | ❏ | ❏ |
| **12.** Put on examination gloves. Hold cytology liquid container for physician or insert brush as directed and mix with cytology liquid. | ❏ | ❏ | ❏ |
| **13.** Have a basin or other container ready to receive the now-contaminated speculum. | ❏ | ❏ | ❏ |
| **14.** Apply lubricant across the physician's two fingers. | ❏ | ❏ | ❏ |
| **15.** Encourage the patient to relax during the bimanual examination as needed. | ❏ | ❏ | ❏ |

**PSY** PROCEDURE 21-2 **Assist with the Pelvic Examination and Pap Smear** (continued)

| | | | |
|---|---|---|---|
| **16.** After the examination, assist the patient in sliding up to the top of the examination table and remove both feet at the same time from the stirrups. | ❑ | ❑ | ❑ |
| **17.** Offer the patient tissues to remove excess lubricant.<br>**a.** Assist her to a sitting position if necessary.<br>**b.** Watch for signs of vertigo.<br>**c.** Ask the patient to get dressed and assist as needed.<br>**d.** Provide for privacy as the patient dresses. | ❑ | ❑ | ❑ |
| **18.** Reinforce any physician instructions regarding follow-up appointments needed.<br>**a.** Advise patient on the procedure for obtaining results from the Pap smear. | ❑ | ❑ | ❑ |
| **19. AFF** Explain how to respond to a patient who has dementia. | ❑ | ❑ | ❑ |
| _____<br>_____<br>_____<br>_____<br>_____ | | | |
| **20.** Properly care for or dispose of equipment and clean the examination room. Prepare the specimen for transport to the laboratory. | ❑ | ❑ | ❑ |
| **21.** Remove your gloves and wash your hands. | ❑ | ❑ | ❑ |
| **22. AFF** Log into the Electronic Medical Record (EMR) using your username and secure password OR obtain the paper medical record from a secure location and assure it is kept away from public access. | ❑ | ❑ | ❑ |
| **23.** Document your responsibilities during the procedure. | ❑ | ❑ | ❑ |
| **24.** When finished, log out of the EMR and/or replace the paper medical record in an appropriate and secure location. | ❑ | ❑ | ❑ |

**CALCULATION**

Total Possible Points: _____

Total Points Earned: _____ Multiplied by 100 = _____ Divided by Total Possible Points = _____ %

**PASS   FAIL   COMMENTS**:
 ❑        ❑

Student's signature _____ Date _____

Partner's signature _____ Date _____

Instructor's signature _____ Date _____

## PSY  PROCEDURE 21-3  Assist with Colposcopy and Cervical Biopsy

Name: _____ Date: _____ Time: _____ Grade: _____

**EQUIPMENT/SUPPLIES:** Patient gown and drape, vaginal speculum, colposcope, specimen container with preservative (10% formalin), sterile gloves, appropriate size sterile cotton-tipped applicators, sterile normal saline solution, sterile 3% acetic acid, sterile povidone–iodine (Betadine), silver nitrate sticks or ferric subsulfate (Monsel solution), sterile biopsy forceps or punch biopsy instrument, sterile uterine curette, sterile uterine dressing forceps, sterile 4 × 4 gauze pad, sterile towel, sterile endocervical curette, sterile uterine tenaculum, sanitary napkin, examination gloves, examination light, tissues, biohazard container

**STANDARDS:** Given the needed equipment and a place to work, the student will perform this skill with _____ % accuracy in a total of _____ minutes. *(Your instructor will tell you what the percentage and time limits will be before you begin.)*

**KEY:** 4 = Satisfactory 0 = Unsatisfactory NA = This step is not counted

| PROCEDURE STEPS | SELF | PARTNER | INSTRUCTOR |
|---|---|---|---|
| **1.** Wash your hands. | ❏ | ❏ | ❏ |
| **2.** Verify that the patient has signed the consent form. | ❏ | ❏ | ❏ |
| **3.** Assemble the equipment and supplies. | ❏ | ❏ | ❏ |
| **4.** Check the light on the colposcope. | ❏ | ❏ | ❏ |
| **5.** Set up the sterile field without contaminating it. | ❏ | ❏ | ❏ |
| **6.** Pour sterile normal saline and acetic acid into their respective sterile containers. | ❏ | ❏ | ❏ |
| **7.** Cover the field with a sterile drape. | ❏ | ❏ | ❏ |
| **8.** Greet and identify yourself including your title. | ❏ | ❏ | ❏ |
| **9.** Identify the patient and explain the procedure. | ❏ | ❏ | ❏ |
| **10.** When the physician is ready to proceed with the procedure:<br>**a.** Assist the patient into the dorsal lithotomy position.<br>**b.** Put on sterile gloves after positioning the patient if necessary. | ❏ | ❏ | ❏ |
| **11.** Hand the physician:<br>**a.** The applicator immersed in normal saline.<br>**b.** Followed by the applicator immersed in acetic acid.<br>**c.** The applicator with the antiseptic solution (Betadine). | ❏ | ❏ | ❏ |
| **12.** If you did not apply sterile gloves to assist the physician:<br>**a.** Apply clean examination gloves.<br>**b.** Accept the biopsy specimen into a container of 10% formalin preservative. | ❏ | ❏ | ❏ |
| **13.** Provide the physician with Monsel solution or silver nitrate sticks. | ❏ | ❏ | ❏ |

**PSY** P R O C E D U R E  2 1 - 3   **Assist with Colposcopy and Cervical Biopsy** (continued)

| | | | |
|---|---|---|---|
| **14.** When the physician is finished with the procedure:<br>   **a.** Assist the patient from the stirrups and into a sitting position.<br>   **b.** Explain to the patient that a small amount of bleeding may occur.<br>   **c.** Have a sanitary napkin available for the patient.<br>   **d.** Ask the patient to get dressed and assist as needed.<br>   **e.** Provide for privacy as the patient dresses.<br>   **f.** Reinforce any physician instructions regarding follow-up appointments.<br>   **g.** Advise the patient on how to obtain the biopsy results. | ❏ | ❏ | ❏ |
| **15. AFF** Explain how to respond to a patient who does not speak English or speaks English as a second language. | ❏ | ❏ | ❏ |
| **16.** Label the specimen container with the patient's name and date.<br>   **a.** Prepare the laboratory request.<br>   **b.** Transport the specimen and form to the laboratory. | ❏ | ❏ | ❏ |
| **17.** Properly care for, or dispose of, equipment and clean the examination room. | ❏ | ❏ | ❏ |
| **18.** Wash your hands. | ❏ | ❏ | ❏ |
| **19. AFF** Log into the Electronic Medical Record (EMR) using your username and secure password OR obtain the paper medical record from a secure location and assure it is kept away from public access. | ❏ | ❏ | ❏ |
| **20.** Document your responsibilities during the procedure. | ❏ | ❏ | ❏ |
| **21.** When finished, log out of the EMR and/or replace the paper medical record in an appropriate and secure location. | ❏ | ❏ | ❏ |

**CALCULATION**

Total Possible Points: _____

Total Points Earned: _____ Multiplied by 100 = _____ Divided by Total Possible Points = _____ %

**PASS   FAIL   COMMENTS:**
  ❏     ❏

Student's signature _____ Date _____

Partner's signature _____ Date _____

Instructor's signature _____ Date _____

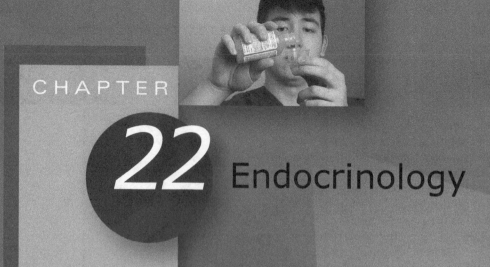

# CHAPTER 22 Endocrinology

## Learning Outcomes

Name: _____     Date: _____     Grade: _____

## COG MULTIPLE CHOICE

Circle the letter preceding the correct answer:

1. A patient with hypothyroidism must take hormone replacements:
   a. for as many years as he has had the disease.
   b. until the conclusion of puberty.
   c. for his entire life.
   d. until middle age.
   e. for 10 years.

2. Diabetics may need supplemental insulin to:
   a. test blood glucose levels.
   b. reverse vascular changes.
   c. reduce the presence of ketones.
   d. restore pancreatic function.
   e. control blood glucose levels.

3. One symptom of ketoacidosis is:
   a. shallow respirations.
   b. low blood glucose levels.
   c. overhydration.
   d. abdominal pain.
   e. pale, moist skin.

4. Diabetes mellitus affects metabolism of which type of molecule?
   a. Neurotransmitters
   b. Carbohydrates
   c. Hormones
   d. Vitamins
   e. Lipids

5. One symptom of type 1 diabetes mellitus is:
   a. polyuria.
   b. exophthalmia.
   c. anorexia.
   d. weight gain.
   e. a goiter.

6. Hyperpigmentation of the skin might be an indication of:
   a. Cushing syndrome.
   b. Hashimoto thyroiditis.
   c. Graves disease.
   d. Addison disease.
   e. diabetes insipidus.

7. To control gestational diabetes, a blood glucose specimen should be taken from a pregnant woman between:
   a. 28 and 32 weeks of gestation.
   b. 24 and 28 weeks of gestation.
   c. 20 and 24 weeks of gestation.
   d. 16 and 20 weeks of gestation.
   e. 12 and 16 weeks of gestation.

8. Cushing syndrome sufferers may experience accelerated:
   a. Addison disease.
   b. endocarditis.
   c. osteoporosis.
   d. arthritis.
   e. dementia.

9. Acromegaly results primarily in:
   a. an increase in bone width.
   b. muscular atrophy.
   c. an increase in bone length.
   d. muscular hypertrophy.
   e. an increase in bone density.

10. Growth can be stimulated for children with dwarfism by:
    a. repairs in the pituitary gland.
    b. administration of growth hormone.
    c. psychotherapy.
    d. increased physical activity.
    e. a high-protein diet.

11. Diabetes insipidus results from a deficiency of:
    a. adrenocorticotropic hormone.
    b. anterior pituitary hormones.
    c. human growth hormone.
    d. antidiuretic hormone.
    e. thyroid hormones.

12. Insulin shock is a result of:
    a. Cushing syndrome.
    b. Addison disease.
    c. Graves disease.
    d. hyperglycemia.
    e. hypoglycemia.

13. Diabetes mellitus patients need to care for their feet because:
    a. they regularly develop ingrown toenails.
    b. their peripheral circulation may be poor.
    c. they suffer severe joint pain.
    d. they have weak calves.
    e. foot pain occurs.

14. Exophthalmia is a protrusion of the:
    a. thyroid gland.
    b. pancreas.
    c. gall bladder.
    d. eyes.
    e. liver.

15. Patients taking corticosteroids may be at risk for:
    a. Cushing disease.
    b. Addison disease.
    c. type 2 diabetes mellitus.
    d. Graves disease.
    e. Hashimoto thyroiditis.

16. The A1C test determines how well blood glucose has been controlled during the previous:
    a. 2 to 3 hours.
    b. 2 to 3 days.
    c. 2 to 3 weeks.
    d. 2 to 3 months.
    e. 2 to 3 years.

17. Gigantism is a disorder of the:
    a. adrenal glands.
    b. pancreas.
    c. liver.
    d. thyroid.
    e. pituitary gland.

18. A thyroid scan relies on a radioactive isotope of what element?
    a. Iodine
    b. Barium
    c. Indium
    d. Bismuth
    e. Iridium

19. Addison disease is a disorder of the:
    a. pituitary gland.
    b. pancreas.
    c. thyroid.
    d. adrenal gland.
    e. salivary glands.

20. Both Graves disease and goiters are examples of:
    a. hypothyroidism.
    b. hypoglycemia.
    c. hyperthyroidism.
    d. hyperglycemia.
    e. hypertension.

## COG MATCHING

_____ Grade: _____

Place the letter preceding the definition on the line next to the term.

**Key Terms**

21. _____ acromegaly
22. _____ Addison disease
23. _____ Cushing syndrome
24. _____ diabetes insipidus
25. _____ dwarfism
26. _____ endocrinologist
27. _____ exophthalmia
28. _____ gigantism
29. _____ glycosuria
30. _____ goiter
31. _____ Graves disease
32. _____ Hashimoto thyroiditis
33. _____ hormones
34. _____ hyperglycemia
35. _____ hyperplasia
36. _____ hypoglycemia
37. _____ insulin-dependent diabetes mellitus

**Definitions**

a. an enlargement of the thyroid gland
b. a substance that is produced by an endocrine gland and travels through the blood to a distant organ or gland where it acts to modify the structure or function of that gland or organ
c. an adrenal gland disorder that results in an increased production of ACTH from the pituitary glands
d. excess quantities of thyroid hormone in tissues
e. excessive proliferation of normal cells in the normal tissue arrangement of an organism
f. the end products of fat metabolism
g. itching
h. pronounced hyperthyroidism with signs of enlarged thyroid and exophthalmos
i. a type of diabetes in which patients do not require insulin to control blood sugar
j. a deficiency in insulin production that leads to an inability to metabolize carbohydrates

**Key Terms**

38. _____ ketoacidosis
39. _____ ketones
40. _____ non–insulin-dependent diabetes mellitus
41. _____ polydipsia
42. _____ polyphagia
43. _____ polyuria
44. _____ pruritus
45. _____ radioimmunoassay
46. _____ thyrotoxicosis

**Definitions**

k. partial or complete failure of the adrenal cortex functions, causing general physical deterioration
l. the presence of glucose in the urine
m. a disease of the immune system in which the tissue of the thyroid gland is replaced with fibrous tissue
n. excessive thirst
o. abnormal underdevelopment of the body with extreme shortness but normal proportion; achondroplastic dwarfism is an inherited growth disorder characterized by shortened limbs and a large head but almost normal trunk proportions
p. acidosis accompanied by an accumulation of ketones in the body
q. excessive size and stature caused most frequently by hypersecretion of the human growth hormone
r. deficiency of sugar in the blood
s. an unusual protrusion of the eyeballs as a result of a thyroid disorder
t. a disorder of metabolism characterized by polyuria and polydipsia; caused by a deficiency in ADH or an inability of the kidneys to respond to ADH
u. excessive excretion and elimination of urine
v. hyperfunction of the anterior pituitary gland near the end of puberty that results in increased bone width.
w. the introduction of radioactive substances in the body to determine the concentration of a substance in the serum, usually the concentration of antigens, antibodies, or proteins
x. a doctor who diagnoses and treats disorders of the endocrine system and its hormone-secreting glands
y. abnormal hunger
z. an increase in blood sugar, as in diabetes mellitus

## COG IDENTIFICATION

_____ Grade: _____

47. Read the following list of symptoms. Are these symptoms representative of hyperglycemia or hypoglycemia? Place the prefix "hyper" on the line preceding the symptoms for hyperglycemia and "hypo" for hypoglycemia.

a. _____ Pale complexion

b. _____ Deep respirations

c. _____ Moist skin

d. _____ Shallow respirations

e. _____ Abdominal pain

f. _____ Rapid, bounding pulse

g. _____ Fruity breath

h. _____ Subnormal blood glucose levels

**COG SHORT ANSWER**

_____ Grade: _____

**48.** When does ketoacidosis occur?

_____

_____

_____

_____

**49.** A patient is stunned to learn that she has been diagnosed with type 2 diabetes mellitus. She is 43 years old and in excellent health. As a personal trainer and nutritionist, she has always taken good care of her body. What potential cause of type 2 diabetes mellitus might she be overlooking?

_____

_____

_____

_____

**50.** A patient complains that, lately, his appetite has been ferocious, but he is actually losing weight. He does not understand why this is happening. What do you tell him?

_____

_____

_____

_____

**51.** Why is it difficult for many sufferers of endocrine disorders to comply with physicians' orders?

_____

_____

_____

_____

**52.** A patient who has been diagnosed with type 2 diabetes mellitus explains that a friend told him the disease is sometimes called _non–insulin-dependent diabetes mellitus_. He asks if this means that he will not need to take insulin. Is he correct? Why, or why not?

_____

_____

_____

_____

**53.** Who might be at risk for gestational diabetes mellitus?

_____

_____

_____

_____

**54.** What is the cause of hypoglycemia?

_____

_____

_____

_____

**55.** How is Addison disease treated?

_____

_____

_____

_____

**56.** A patient is diagnosed with dwarfism, and the patient's mother is extremely distressed, wondering if certain body parts will grow normally while others will not. She also wonders if her daughter could ever grow normally. What could you tell the mother?

_____

_____

_____

_____

**57.** What do the fasting glucose test and glucose tolerance test for diabetes mellitus have in common?

_____

_____

_____

_____

**58.** What is the purpose of the A1C blood test?

_____

_____

_____

_____

**59.** Cushing syndrome and Addison disease are both disorders of which gland?

_____

_____

_____

_____

**60.** Why is it important that patients with diseases of the endocrine system wear a medical alert bracelet or necklace?

_____

_____

_____

_____

## COG TRUE OR FALSE?

Grade: _____

Indicate whether the statements are true or false by placing the letter T (true) or F (false) on the line preceding the statement.

**61.** _____ Endocrine glands are unlike other glands in the body because they are ductless.

**62.** _____ Hashimoto thyroiditis is a disease of the endocrine system.

**63.** _____ Type 1 diabetes mellitus occurs only in children and young adults.

**64.** _____ Addison disease has no effect on the pituitary gland.

## COG AFF CASE STUDIES FOR CRITICAL THINKING

Grade: _____

**1.** A patient is worried that a thyroid function test requires the use of radioactive material. Explain, to the best of your ability, how the test works and why there is no need to be concerned about radiation. If necessary, do additional research on thyroid function tests to prepare your answer.

_____

_____

_____

_____

**2.** After an examination, a pregnant patient asks why the physician performed a test on her blood glucose level. She says she does not have diabetes. Explain why the physician chose to do the test.

_____

_____

_____

_____

**3.** Young children are sometimes afflicted with diabetes mellitus. This can be difficult for both the child and the family. What is your perspective of the medical assistant's role in this situation?

_____

_____

_____

_____

**4.** A patient with hyperthyroidism says she would prefer not to be treated because she has few negative symptoms, and the increased metabolic rate helps keep her thin. How would you respond to this?

_____

_____

_____

_____

## PSY PROCEDURE 22-1  Manage a Patient with a Diabetic Emergency

Name: _____ Date: _____ Time: _____ Grade: _____

**EQUIPMENT/SUPPLIES:** Gloves, blood glucose monitor and strips, fruit juice or oral glucose tablets

**STANDARDS:** Given the needed equipment and a place to work, the student will perform this skill with _____ % accuracy in a total of _____ minutes. *(Your instructor will tell you what the percentage and time limits will be before you begin.)*

**KEY:**          4 = Satisfactory          0 = Unsatisfactory          NA = This step is not counted

| PROCEDURE STEPS | SELF | PARTNER | INSTRUCTOR |
|---|---|---|---|
| **1.** Wash your hands. | ❑ | ❑ | ❑ |
| **2.** Recognize the signs and symptoms of hyperglycemia and hypoglycemia. | ❑ | ❑ | ❑ |
| **3.** Greet the patient and identify yourself including your title. Identify the patient. | ❑ | ❑ | ❑ |
| **4.** Escort the patient into the examination room while making the observation that there is a problem. | ❑ | ❑ | ❑ |
| **5.** Determine if the patient has been previously diagnosed with diabetes mellitus and acknowledge that the patient is a diabetic. | ❑ | ❑ | ❑ |
| **6.** Ask the patient if he or she has eaten today or taken any medication. | ❑ | ❑ | ❑ |
| **7.** Notify the physician about the patient and perform a capillary stick for a blood glucose as directed. | ❑ | ❑ | ❑ |
| **8.** Notify the physician with the results of the blood glucose and treat the patient as ordered by the physician.<br>**a.** Administer insulin subcutaneously to a patient with hyperglycemia.<br>**b.** Administer a quick-acting sugar, such as an oral glucose tablet or fruit juice, for a patient with hypoglycemia. | ❑ | ❑ | ❑ |
| **9.** AFF Explain how to respond to a patient who is developmentally challenged. | ❑ | ❑ | ❑ |

_____

_____

_____

_____

**FSY** P R O C E D U R E  2 2 - 1    **Manage a Patient with a Diabetic Emergency** (continued)

| | | | |
|---|---|---|---|
| **10.** Be prepared to notify EMS as directed by the physician if the symptoms do not improve or worsen. | ❏ | ❏ | ❏ |
| **11.** **AFF** Log into the Electronic Medical Record (EMR) using your username and secure password OR obtain the paper medical record from a secure location and assure it is kept away from public access. | ❏ | ❏ | ❏ |
| **12.** Document any observations and treatments given. | ❏ | ❏ | ❏ |
| **13.** Document any observations and treatments given. | ❏ | ❏ | ❏ |

**CALCULATION**

Total Possible Points: _____

Total Points Earned: _____ Multiplied by 100 = _____ Divided by Total Possible Points = _____ %

**PASS    FAIL    COMMENTS:**
❏           ❏

Student's signature _____ Date _____

Partner's signature _____ Date _____

Instructor's signature _____ Date _____

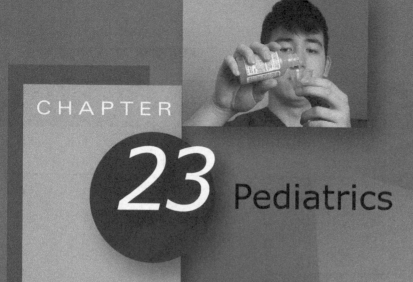

# CHAPTER

# 23 Pediatrics

---

## Learning Outcomes

### COG Cognitive Domain

1. Spell key terms
2. Define medical terms and abbreviations related to all body systems
3. Compare structure and function of the human body across the life span
4. Analyze health care results as reported in graphs and tables
5. Identify common pathology related to each body system including signs, symptoms, and etiology
6. List safety precautions for the pediatric office
7. Explain the difference between a well-child and a sick-child visit
8. List types and schedule of immunizations
9. Describe the types of feelings a child might have during an office visit
10. List and explain how to record the anthropometric measurements obtained in a pediatric visit
11. Identify two injection sites to use on an infant and two used on a child
12. Describe the role of the parent during the office visit
13. List the names, symptoms, and treatments for common pediatric illnesses

### PSY Psychomotor Domain

1. Obtain an infant's length and weight (Procedure 23-1)
2. Obtain the head and chest circumference (Procedure 23-2)
3. Apply a urinary collection device (Procedure 23-3)

### AFF Affective Domain

1. Incorporate critical thinking skills when performing patient assessment
2. Incorporate critical thinking skills when performing patient care
3. Show awareness of a patient's concerns related to the procedure being performed
4. Demonstrate empathy, active listening, nonverbal communication

5. Demonstrate respect for individual diversity including gender, race, religion, age, economic status, appearance
6. Explain to a patient the rationale for performance of a procedure
7. Demonstrate sensitivity to patient rights
8. Protect the integrity of the medical record

### ABHES Competencies

1. Assist the physician with the regimen of diagnostic and treatment modalities as they relate to each body system
2. Comply with federal, state, and local health laws and regulations
3. Communicate on the recipient's level of comprehension
4. Serve as a liaison between the physician and others
5. Show empathy and impartiality when dealing with patients
6. Document accurately

Name: _____     Date: _____     Grade: _____

## OOG MULTIPLE CHOICE

Circle the letter preceding the correct answer.

1. The top priority in a pediatric office is:
   a. organization.
   b. safety.
   c. efficiency.
   d. location.
   e. size.

2. In a pediatrician's waiting room, it's most important that the toys are:
   a. trendy.
   b. interesting to all age groups.
   c. large enough to share.
   d. washable.
   e. educational.

3. Which method of taking a temperature is most readily accepted by children of all ages?
   a. Tympanic
   b. Oral
   c. Rectal
   d. Axillary
   e. Touch

4. One symptom of meningitis is:
   a. dysuria.
   b. disorientation.
   c. coughing.
   d. stiff neck.
   e. chills.

5. Which of the following has been associated with Reye syndrome?
   a. Pyloric stenosis
   b. Aspirin
   c. Cerebral palsy
   d. Phenylalanine hydroxylase
   e. Otitis media

6. Which of the following is something that is routinely done at a child's wellness exam?
   a. Blood test
   b. Urine test
   c. Immunization
   d. Radiography
   e. Measurements

7. To minimize a child's anxiety during a visit, you should:
   a. avoid talking to the child.
   b. speak directly to the parent.
   c. be gentle but firm.
   d. ask the child to be quiet.
   e. spend as little time in the room as possible.

8. Which of the following statements is true?
   a. The reflexes present in a newborn disappear by age 3 months.
   b. A pediatrician is responsible for a child's physical and mental health.
   c. Disinfectants should be kept in patient rooms for easy access.
   d. Vaccination Information Statements may be provided upon request.
   e. The DDST measures all physical and mental aspects of a child.

9. One warning sign of child abuse is a child who:
   a. comes in with scraped knees.
   b. shrinks away as you approach.
   c. has a poor growth pattern.
   d. has a bloody nose.
   e. screams when you administer a shot.

10. What might make the examination more fun for a 4- or 5-year-old child?
    a. Allowing the child to crawl on the floor
    b. Answering all the questions he or she asks
    c. Showing the child medical pictures
    d. Letting the child listen to his or her heartbeat
    e. Asking the parent to assist with the exam

*Scenario for questions 11 and 12:* A child comes in for a well-child visit and begins to panic when she hears she will need to get a vaccination.

11. What should you do?
    a. Let another assistant give her the shot.
    b. Ask the parent or caregiver to calm her down.
    c. Show her the needle ahead of time.
    d. Tell her gently that it won't hurt at all.
    e. Hide the needle until you give her the shot.

12. After you administer the medication, the girl becomes sullen and withdrawn. What is the best way to address this behavior?
    a. Leave and allow her mother to comfort her.
    b. Praise and comfort her before you leave.
    c. Ask her if the shot was really that bad.
    d. Promise it won't hurt so much next time.
    e. Laugh and say it was just a little shot.

13. Which of the following disorders has symptoms that may become obvious only with the passage of time?
    a. Meningitis
    b. Croup
    c. Epiglottitis
    d. Cerebral palsy
    e. Pyloric stenosis

14. Children are more likely to develop ear infections than adults because they have:
    a. an immature nervous system.
    b. short and straight Eustachian tubes.
    c. decreased resistance to diseases.
    d. more exposure to bacteria.
    e. poor hand-washing skills.

15. Which infant reflex is a result of the cheek being stroked?
    a. Rooting
    b. Moro
    c. Stepping
    d. Fencing
    e. Babinski

16. Children have lower blood pressure than adults because:
    a. they cannot sit still for long periods of time.
    b. they require a smaller cuff for measurements.
    c. their hearts do not pump as quickly as adults' hearts.
    d. their vessels are softer and less resistant.
    e. you must use a standard sphygmomanometer.

17. At what age does a child's respiratory rate slow to that of an adult's?
    a. 0 to 1 year
    b. 1 to 5 years
    c. 5 to 10 years
    d. 10 to 15 years
    e. 15 to 20 years

18. Which of the following can help a physician test an infant for pyloric stenosis?
    a. Blood tests
    b. Urine tests
    c. Parental history
    d. Percentile comparisons
    e. Weight

19. Which of the following disorders cannot be cured at this time?
    a. Meningitis
    b. Impetigo
    c. Tetanus
    d. Syphilis
    e. Cerebral palsy

20. A sharp barking cough is a symptom of:
    a. meningitis.
    b. croup.
    c. tetanus.
    d. encephalitis.
    e. impetigo.

## COG MATCHING

_____ Grade: _____

Place the letter preceding the definition on the line next to the term.

**Key Terms**
21. _____ aspiration
22. _____ autonomous
23. _____ congenital anomaly
24. _____ immunization
25. _____ neonatologist
26. _____ pediatrician

**Definitions**
a. to control or confine movement
b. a physician who specializes in the care and treatment of newborns
c. a viral infection manifested by the characteristic rash of successive crops of vesicles that scab before resolution; also called chicken pox
d. a physician who specializes in the care of infants, children, and adolescents
e. a visit to the medical office for the administration of immunizations and evaluation of growth and development

**Key Terms**

27. _____ pediatrics
28. _____ psychosocial
29. _____ restrain
30. _____ sick-child visit
31. _____ varicella zoster
32. _____ well-child visit

**Definitions**

f. drawing in or out by suction, as in breathing objects into the respiratory tract or suctioning substances from a site

g. an abnormality, either structural or functional, present at birth

h. a pediatric visit for the treatment of illness or injury

i. a specialty of medicine that deals with the care of infants, children, and adolescents

j. existing or functioning independently

k. relating to mental and emotional aspects of social encounters

l. the act or process of rendering an individual immune to specific disease

## COG MATCHING

Grade: _____

Place the letter preceding the pulse rate range on the line preceding the appropriate age.

**Ages**

33. _____ newborn
34. _____ 3 months to 2 years
35. _____ 2 years to 10 years
36. _____ 10 years and older

**Pulse Rate Ranges**

a. 80 to 150/minute
b. 60 to 100/minute
c. 100 to 180/minute
d. 65 to 130/minute

## PSY IDENTIFICATION

Grade: _____

37. Review the most current pediatric immunization schedule on the CDC (Center for Disease Control and Prevention website) to answer the following questions:

a. How many doses of the rotavirus vaccine are given? When?

_____

b. How many immunizations do children receive at 4 months? Which ones?

_____

c. When do children start receiving a yearly influenza vaccination?

_____

d. How many doses of the hepatitis B vaccine are administered?

_____

38. What are five different ways to check a child's temperature?

a. _____

b. _____

c. _____

d. _____

e. _____

**39.** What are the seven "rights" of drug administration?

a. _____

b. _____

c. _____

d. _____

e. _____

f. _____

g. _____

**40.** Identify six symptoms of meningitis:

_____

**COG** **SHORT ANSWER** _____ Grade: _____

**41.** What does the Federal Child Abuse Prevention and Treatment Act mandate?

_____

_____

_____

_____

**42.** What is the VIS? Why do you give the parent or caregiver of a child a copy?

_____

_____

_____

_____

**43.** Why do sick-child visits occur frequently during early childhood?

_____

_____

_____

_____

**44.** What is the difference between a well-child and a sick-child visit?

_____

_____

_____

_____

**45.** List five feelings a child might have during an office visit.

_____

_____

_____

_____

**46.** What role does a parent or caregiver play in the child's exam?

_____

_____

_____

_____

**47.** How is a child's medication dosage calculated?

_____

_____

_____

_____

**48.** Why is epiglottitis considered more serious than croup?

_____

_____

_____

_____

**49.** If a child has been reported as being easily distracted, forgetful, extremely talkative, impulsive, and showing a dislike for school activities, does the child have ADHD?

_____

_____

_____

**50.** A worried mother calls in because her newborn baby is vomiting. She wants to know if she should bring her baby into the office for examination. What do you tell her?

_____

_____

_____

## OG COMPLETION

_____ Grade: _____

**51.** Complete the chart below with information about childhood reflexes. Briefly describe each response and note the age it generally disappears.

| Reflex | Response | Age When It Generally Disappears |
|---|---|---|
| **a.** Sucking, or rooting | | |
| **b.** Moro, or startle | | |
| **c.** Grasp | | |
| **d.** Tonic neck, or fencing | | |
| **e.** Placing, or stepping | | |
| **f.** Babinski | | |

## OG TRUE OR FALSE?

_____ Grade: _____

Indicate whether the statements are true or false by placing the letter T (true) or F (false) on the line preceding the statement.

**52.** _____ Infant scales should always be placed on the floor next to the adult scale.

**53.** _____ It is a violation of HIPAA to have two separate waiting rooms for sick children and well children.

**54.** _____ There should be no toys in the waiting room because they may help spread germs.

**55.** _____ Children outgrow child-sized furniture too quickly, so it is not a worthwhile investment.

**56.** _____ Many childhood diseases are highly contagious and can be controlled by stringent hand-washing measures.

**57.** _____ Immunization schedules change every 5 years.

**58.** _____ A child's heartbeat is much slower than an adult's heart rate.

**59.** _____ Asthma is a respiratory problem that usually develops after puberty.

**60.** _____ Minors do not need to be informed of what you're going to do.

**COG** **AFF** **CASE STUDIES FOR CRITICAL THINKING** _____ Grade: _____

1. A mother calls in, saying her 15-month-old daughter has been fussy and tugging at her ear. There is no fever, but the girl has been tired and had a cold a few days before. What do you tell her to do?

_____

_____

_____

_____

2. A young boy, accompanied by his mother, greets you in the examination room and starts asking all kinds of questions about things you do. He enjoys helping you test his reflexes and reading the vision chart, but he firmly refuses to cooperate when you try to give him a shot. What can you or his mother do to get him settled down enough to give him the shot?

_____

_____

_____

_____

3. A 16-year-old boy has been diagnosed as obese, and his parents have come in to find out what they can do to help their son achieve a healthy weight. The physician wants the boy to exercise at a local gym and to return in 6 months to check his progress. What education can you provide that will help the boy and his parents start a healthier lifestyle?

_____

_____

_____

_____

4. A young child has come in with a broken arm. During the examination, you notice the child also has several scrapes and bruises on his legs and feet as well. His mother says he got them from playing outdoors. Do you report this as child abuse to the physician? If not, what do you do?

_____

_____

_____

_____

5. Spanking children for misbehaving is sometimes considered child abuse. However, the parents who spank their children say that they were spanked when they were young, and they believe it is the best way to safely punish bad behavior. They also say that children who are not spanked become spoiled and difficult to control. What do you think? Is it your duty to report spanking as child abuse?

_____

_____

_____

_____

## PSY  PROCEDURE 23-1   Obtain an Infant's Length and Weight

Name: _____  Date: _____  Time: _____  Grade: _____

**EQUIPMENT/SUPPLIES:** Examining table with clean paper, tape measure, infant scale, protective paper for the scale, appropriate growth chart

**STANDARDS:** Given the needed equipment and a place to work, the student will perform this skill with _____ % accuracy in a total of _____ minutes. *(Your instructor will tell you what the percentage and time limits will be before you begin.)*

**KEY:**          4 = Satisfactory                    0 = Unsatisfactory                    NA = This step is not counted

| PROCEDURE STEPS | SELF | PARTNER | INSTRUCTOR |
|---|---|---|---|
| **1.** Wash your hands. | ❑ | ❑ | ❑ |
| **2.** Greet the patient and caregiver and identify yourself including your title. | ❑ | ❑ | ❑ |
| **3.** Explain the procedure to the parent or caregiver. | ❑ | ❑ | ❑ |
| **4.** Ask parent to remove the infant's clothing except for the diaper. | ❑ | ❑ | ❑ |
| **5.** Place the child on a firm examination table covered with clean table paper. | ❑ | ❑ | ❑ |
| **6.** Fully extend the child's body by holding the head in the midline. | ❑ | ❑ | ❑ |
| **7.** Grasp the knees and press flat onto the table gently but firmly. | ❑ | ❑ | ❑ |
| **8.** Make a mark on table paper with pen at the top of the head and heel of the feet. | ❑ | ❑ | ❑ |
| **9.** Measure between marks in either inches or centimeters. | ❑ | ❑ | ❑ |
| **10.** Record the child's length on the growth chart and in the patient's chart. | ❑ | ❑ | ❑ |
| **11.** Either carry the infant or have the parent carry the infant to the scale. | ❑ | ❑ | ❑ |
| **12.** Place a protective paper on the scale and balance the scale. | ❑ | ❑ | ❑ |
| **13.** Remove the diaper just before laying the infant on the scale. | ❑ | ❑ | ❑ |
| **14.** Place the child gently on the scale. Keep one of your hands over or near the child on the scale at all times. | ❑ | ❑ | ❑ |
| **15.** Balance the scale quickly but carefully. | ❑ | ❑ | ❑ |
| **16.** Pick the infant up and instruct the parent to replace the diaper if removed. | ❑ | ❑ | ❑ |
| **17.** Wash your hands. | ❑ | ❑ | ❑ |

**FSY** PROCEDURE 23-1 **Obtain an Infant's Length and Weight**
(continued)

| | | | |
|---|---|---|---|
| **18.** **AFF** Log into the Electronic Medical Record (EMR) using your username and secure password OR obtain the paper medical record from a secure location and assure it is kept away from public access. | ❑ | ❑ | ❑ |
| **19.** Record the infant's weight on the growth chart and in the patient medical record. | ❑ | ❑ | ❑ |
| **20.** When finished, log out of the EMR and/or replace the paper medical record in an appropriate and secure location. | ❑ | ❑ | ❑ |

**CALCULATION**

Total Possible Points: _____

Total Points Earned: _____ Multiplied by 100 = _____ Divided by Total Possible Points = _____ %

**PASS   FAIL   COMMENTS:**
  ❑        ❑

Student's signature _____ Date _____

Partner's signature _____ Date _____

Instructor's signature _____ Date _____

## PROCEDURE 23-2 Obtain the Head and Chest Circumference

Name: _____ Date: _____ Time: _____ Grade: _____

**EQUIPMENT/SUPPLIES:** Paper or cloth measuring tape, growth chart

**STANDARDS:** Given the needed equipment and a place to work, the student will perform this skill with _____ % accuracy in a total of _____ minutes. *(Your instructor will tell you what the percentage and time limits will be before you begin.)*

**KEY:** 4 = Satisfactory 0 = Unsatisfactory NA = This step is not counted

| PROCEDURE STEPS | SELF | PARTNER | INSTRUCTOR |
|---|---|---|---|
| 1. Wash your hands. | ❑ | ❑ | ❑ |
| 2. Place the infant in the supine position on the examination table, or ask the parent to hold the infant. | ❑ | ❑ | ❑ |
| 3. Measure around the head above the eyebrow and posteriorly at the largest part of the occiput. | ❑ | ❑ | ❑ |
| 4. Record the child's head circumference on the growth chart. | ❑ | ❑ | ❑ |
| 5. With the infant's clothing removed from the chest, measure around the chest at the nipple line, keeping the measuring tape at the same level anteriorly and posteriorly. | ❑ | ❑ | ❑ |
| 6. Wash your hands. | ❑ | ❑ | ❑ |
| 7. **AFF** Log into the Electronic Medical Record (EMR) using your username and secure password OR obtain the paper medical record from a secure location and assure it is kept away from public access. | ❑ | ❑ | ❑ |
| 8. Record the child's chest circumference on the growth chart. | ❑ | ❑ | ❑ |
| 9. When finished, log out of the EMR and/or replace the paper medical record in an appropriate and secure location. | ❑ | ❑ | ❑ |

**CALCULATION**

Total Possible Points: _____

Total Points Earned: _____ Multiplied by 100 = _____ Divided by Total Possible Points = _____ %

**PASS   FAIL   COMMENTS:**
  ❑        ❑

Student's signature _____ Date _____

Partner's signature _____ Date _____

Instructor's signature _____ Date _____

# CHAPTER

# 24 Geriatrics

## Learning Objectives

### COG Cognitive Domain

1. Spell key terms
2. Define medical terms and abbreviations related to all body systems
3. Compare structure and function of the human body across the life span
4. Identify common pathology related to each body system including signs, symptoms, and etiology
5. Explain how aging affects thought processes
6. Describe methods to increase compliance with health maintenance programs among older adults
7. Discuss communication problems that may occur with the older adult and list steps to maintain open communication

8. Recognize and describe the coping mechanisms used by the older adult to deal with multiple losses
9. Name the risk factors and signs of elder abuse
10. Explain the types of long-term care facilities available
11. Describe the effects of aging on the way the body processes medication
12. Discuss the responsibility of medical assistants with regard to teaching older adult patients
13. List and describe physical changes and diseases common to the aging process

### AFF Affective Domain

1. Incorporate critical thinking skills when performing patient assessment
2. Incorporate critical thinking skills when performing patient care

3. Demonstrate empathy, active listening, nonverbal communication
4. Demonstrate respect for individual diversity including gender, race, religion, age, economic status, appearance

### ABHES Competencies

1. Assist the physician with the regimen of diagnostic and treatment modalities as they relate to each body system
2. Comply with federal, state, and local health laws and regulations
3. Communicate on the recipient's level of comprehension
4. Serve as a liaison between the physician and others
5. Show empathy and impartiality when dealing with patients
6. Document accurately

Name: _____  Date: _____  Grade: _____

## ⬤⬤G MULTIPLE CHOICE

Circle the letter preceding the correct answer.

1. Which of the following statements is true about older adult patients who require long-term medication?
   a. If older adult patients take their medication every day, they are unlikely to forget a dosage.
   b. Compliance over a long period of time can become problematic in older adult patients.
   c. With a chronic illness, an older adult patient can neglect to take his or her medication for a few weeks with no side effects.
   d. Patients who take their medications for a long period of time will eventually notice a significant improvement.
   e. Older adult patients will eventually become immune to long-term medication.

2. Which of these conditions can sometimes be improved by taking the herbal supplement gingko?
   a. Arthritis
   b. Parkinson disease
   c. Loss of appetite
   d. Poor concentration
   e. Alzheimer disease

3. The purpose of an advance directive is to:
   a. divide a person's possessions in the event of death.
   b. inform the physician of any allergies that an individual has to specific medications.
   c. outline a person's wishes about end-of-life care.
   d. transfer a patient's medical records between physicians' offices.
   e. order a physician not to resuscitate a patient under any circumstances.

4. Which of these is a task performed by a home health aide?
   a. Light housecleaning
   b. Refilling prescriptions
   c. Reorganizing bulky furniture
   d. Writing daily task lists and reminders
   e. Keeping the older adult occupied

5. Which of these is a good place to find information about respite care for older adult relatives?
   a. Local newspaper
   b. Television advertisement
   c. Community senior citizen program
   d. Local business directory
   e. Library bulletin board

6. What is an example of passive neglect of an older adult patient?
   a. Withholding medication from the patient
   b. Locking the patient in a room
   c. Overmedicating the patient to make him or her easier to care for
   d. Isolating the patient from friends and family
   e. Forgetting to give the patient regular baths

7. Which of the following statements is true about the aging process?
   a. Longevity is based entirely on environmental factors.
   b. People who have dangerous occupations will not live as long as people who do not.
   c. Longevity is hereditary, so it does not make a difference how you live your life.
   d. Longevity is largely hereditary, but environmental factors play a significant role.
   e. An obese, physically inactive smoker will have a shorter lifespan than a healthy nonsmoker.

8. What is the best way to deal with a patient who is hearing impaired?
   a. Raise your voice until the patient can hear you.
   b. Give written instructions whenever possible.
   c. Talk to the patient with your back to the light.
   d. Talk directly into the patient's ear.
   e. Find a coworker who is able to communicate using sign language.

*Scenario for questions 9 to 11:* A 55-year-old patient comes into the physician's office and tells you that he thinks he is suffering from Parkinson disease.

9. The physician would diagnose the patient by:
   a. taking a blood test.
   b. performing dexterity tasks.
   c. excluding other causes.
   d. performing an MRI scan.
   e. testing his reflexes.

10. How would you explain deep brain stimulation to the patient?
    a. It increases the levels of dopamine in the brain.
    b. It lowers a person's acetylcholine levels.
    c. It blocks the impulses that cause tremors.
    d. It controls a person's stress and anxiety levels.
    e. It acts as a muscle relaxant and prevents rigidity.

11. What would you tell the patient about Levodopa?
    a. It has no serious side effects.
    b. It remains effective for the entire length of the disease.
    c. It can cause headaches and migraines.
    d. It should not be taken with alcohol.
    e. It may aggravate stomach ulcers.

12. When older adult patients are beginning a new exercise regime, it is a good idea for them to:
    a. rest when they get tired.
    b. start with a brisk 30-minute jog.
    c. keep to the same weekly routine.
    d. exercise alone so they are not distracted.
    e. work through any initial pain or discomfort.

13. Which of the following statements is true about the nutritional requirements of older adult patients?
    a. Older adult patients need less food and water than younger patients because older adults are not as active.
    b. It is easier for older adult patients to maintain good nutrition because they have more time to prepare meals.
    c. Vitamin and mineral requirements are lower in older adult patients than in younger patients.
    d. Older adult patients should eat smaller, more frequent meals to aid digestion.
    e. Older adult patients can replace meals with liquid dietary supplements without damaging their health.

14. A caregiver can help increase safety in the home of an older adult patient by:
    a. installing handrails in the bathtub and near the commode.
    b. placing childproof locks on the kitchen cupboards.
    c. encouraging the patient to exercise regularly.
    d. covering highly polished floors with scatter rugs.
    e. keeping the patient's medicine in a locked bathroom cabinet.

15. What action should you take if you suspect older adult abuse?
    a. Try to separate the caregiver from the patient for the examination.
    b. Tell the caregiver you will be reporting him or her to the authorities.
    c. Question the patient about suspicious injuries until she tells you the truth.
    d. Call the police while the patient is in the examination room.
    e. Wait to inform the physician of your suspicions until you are sure they are correct.

16. What does the acronym HOH mean in a patient's chart?
    a. Has ordinary hearing
    b. Head of household
    c. Has own home
    d. Hard on health
    e. Hard of hearing

17. Another name for the herbal supplement gingko is:
    a. folic acid.
    b. kew tree.
    c. aloe vera.
    d. green tea.
    e. milk thistle.

18. What is the best advice to give a patient who is having difficulty swallowing medication?
    a. Grind the medication into powder.
    b. Ask the pharmacist for smaller pills.
    c. Put the medication on the back of the tongue, and drink water with a straw.
    d. Lie down and swallow the medication with a lot of water.
    e. Dissolve the medication in a hot drink.

19. A physician who specializes in disorders that affect the aging population is called a(n):
    a. gastroenterologist.
    b. gerontologist.
    c. oncologist.
    d. otorhinolaryngologist.
    e. rheumatologist.

20. An eye condition that causes increased intraocular pressure and intolerance to light is:
    a. cataracts.
    b. kyphosis.
    c. bradykinesia.
    d. osteoporosis.
    e. glaucoma.

## OG MATCHING

Grade: _____

Place the letter preceding the definition on the line next to the term.

**Key Terms**

21. _____ activities of daily living (ADL)
22. _____ biotransform
23. _____ bradykinesia
24. _____ cataracts
25. _____ cerebrovascular accident (CVA)
26. _____ compliance
27. _____ degenerative joint disease (DJD)
28. _____ dementia
29. _____ dysphagia
30. _____ gerontologist
31. _____ glaucoma
32. _____ Kegel exercises
33. _____ keratosis (senile)
34. _____ kyphosis (dowager's hump)
35. _____ lentigines
36. _____ osteoporosis
37. _____ potentiation
38. _____ presbycusis
39. _____ presbyopia
40. _____ senility
41. _____ syncope
42. _____ transient ischemic attack (TIA)
43. _____ vertigo

**Definitions**

a. a specialist who studies aging
b. general mental deterioration associated with old age
c. to convert the molecules of a substance from one form to another, as in medications within the body
d. a sensation of whirling of oneself or the environment, dizziness
e. abnormally slow voluntary movements
f. a sudden fall in blood pressure or cerebral hypoxia resulting in loss of consciousness
g. progressive organic mental deterioration with loss of intellectual function
h. a skin condition characterized by overgrowth and thickening
i. difficulty speaking
j. an abnormal porosity of the bone, most often found in the older adult, predisposing the affected bony tissue to fracture
k. an acute episode of cerebrovascular insufficiency, usually a result of narrowing of an artery by atherosclerotic plaques, emboli, or vasospasm; usually passes quickly but should be considered a warning for predisposition to cerebrovascular accidents
l. a progressive loss of transparency of the lens of the eye, resulting in opacity and loss of sight
m. describes the actions of two drugs taken together in which the combined effects are greater than the sum of the independent effects
n. a vision change (farsightedness) associated with aging
o. isometric exercises in which the muscles of the pelvic floor are voluntarily contracted and relaxed while urinating
p. brown skin macules occurring after prolonged exposure to the sun; freckles
q. a loss of hearing associated with aging
r. an abnormally deep dorsal curvature of the thoracic spine; also known as humpback or hunchback
s. activities usually performed in the course of the day, i.e., bathing, dressing, feeding oneself
t. also known as *osteoarthritis*; arthritis characterized by degeneration of the bony structure of the joints, usually noninflammatory
u. willingness of a patient to follow a prescribed course of treatment
v. ischemia of the brain due to an occlusion of the blood vessels supplying the brain, resulting in varying degrees of debilitation
w. an abnormal increase in the fluid of the eye, usually as a result of obstructed outflow, resulting in degeneration of the intraocular components and blindness

## ⬢og MATCHING

Place the letter preceding the description of the facility on the line preceding the type of facility.

**Facilities**

44. _____ Group homes or assisted living facilities
45. _____ Long-term care facilities
46. _____ Skilled-nursing facilities

**Descriptions**

a. Facilities for those who need help with most areas of personal care and moderate medical supervision
b. Facilities for those who are gravely or terminally ill and need constant supervision
c. Facilities for those who can tend to their own activities of daily living but need companionship and light supervision for safety

## ⬢og IDENTIFICATION

47. Some older adult patients suffer from memory loss, which may make it difficult for them to remember to take their medications. As a medical assistant, it is important to give these patients tools to help them remember and maintain their medication regimens. Identify and list five ways you can help older adult patients remember their medication regimens.

_____

_____

_____

_____

48. Which of the following are common reasons for older adult patients not taking their medications correctly? Place a check mark on the line next to all that apply.

a. _____ Financial difficulties

b. _____ To attract attention

c. _____ Forgetfulness

d. _____ Tiring of the constraints of taking long-term medication

e. _____ Deliberate defiance

49. Mrs. Kim is 89 years old and suffers from memory lapses. It is apparent that she is both frustrated and lonely. Identify and list three ways that you can maintain good communication with her and help her express her feelings.

_____

_____

_____

**50.** Mrs. Driscoll is 84 years old with poor eyesight who suffers from forgetfulness. She needs to take two different types of medication three times a day. Identify and list four ways that you could help ensure that Mrs. Driscoll adheres to her medication regimen.

_____

_____

_____

_____

**51.** Patients who react negatively to moving to a long-term care facility can show signs of grief. Identify and list five symptoms that could indicate that a patient is suffering from a sense of loss.

_____

_____

_____

_____

**52.** Sometimes an older adult patient will turn to alcohol as a way of coping. The effects of drinking alcohol can often be mistaken for other ailments. Identify and list three conditions that exhibit symptoms similar to the influence of alcohol.

_____

_____

_____

_____

**53.** Suicide is a risk for older adult patients, especially those who have recently lost a spouse to death or divorce. Which of the following warning signs indicate that an older adult patient is contemplating suicide? Place a check mark on the line next to all that apply.

**a.** _____ Giving away favored objects

**b.** _____ Increased interest in family affairs

**c.** _____ Secretive behavior

**d.** _____ Increased anger, hostility, or isolation

**e.** _____ Increased forgetfulness

**f.** _____ Increased alcohol or drug use

**g.** _____ Loss of interest in matters of health

**54.** Which of the following indicate that a patient is suffering from older adult abuse? Place a check mark on the line preceding all that apply.

a. _____ Disturbed sleep patterns

b. _____ Signs of restraint on the wrists or ankles

c. _____ Large, deep pressure ulcers

d. _____ Incontinence

e. _____ Poor hygiene or poor nutrition

f. _____ Untreated injury or condition

g. _____ Dehydration not caused by disease

**55.** Which of the following are symptoms of Parkinson disease? Circle the letter preceding all that apply.

**a.** Muscle rigidity

**b.** Increased anger

**c.** Involuntary tremors

**d.** Difficulty walking

**e.** Loss of memory

**f.** Dysphagia and drooling

**g.** Expressionless face and infrequent blinking

**56.** Identify and list three reasons why an older adult patient can have difficulty maintaining good nutrition.

a. _____

b. _____

c. _____

## COG SHORT ANSWER                                                  Grade: _____

**57.** You ask Mr. Walton if he is taking his blood pressure medication and he tells you that he is taking it every day. Later, the physician tells you that Mr. Walton has been taking three pills a day instead of just one. How could this situation be avoided with other older adult patients?

_____

_____

_____

_____

**58.** Mrs. Dawson is a widow who lives in a long-term care facility. Her family is worried that she has recently become withdrawn and uncommunicative. Before her husband died, Mrs. Dawson led an active life and took a large role in running the household. What could you say to Mrs. Dawson's family to help her cope with the loss of her spouse and her independence?

_____

_____

_____

_____

**59.** Mr. Gonzalez is an 85-year-old patient who lives alone. He is still fairly active and is able to carry out most activities of daily living by himself. However, members of his family have expressed some concerns that he is lonely and that they are not able to visit him as often as they would like. What options could you discuss with the family?

_____

_____

_____

_____

## COG COMPLETION

_____ Grade: _____

**60.** Older adult patients whose health and economic situation are unstable may experience feelings of grief and loss. These feelings can be about both specific and nonspecific aspects of their lives. Fill in the chart below, listing five specific and nonspecific losses older adult patients may find difficult to cope with.

| | Specific Losses | Nonspecific Losses |
|---|---|---|
| a. | | |
| b. | | |
| c. | | |
| d. | | |
| e. | | |

**61.** The passage below describes how medications affect the body of an older adult. However, some of the important terms are missing. Read the passage and fill in the correct words from the list below.

The _____ system no longer moves medications along as efficiently because _____ has slowed. The _____ system does not absorb dissolved medication from the _____ or the _____ and deliver it to the target tissue as quickly. The _____ does not _____ medication as quickly, causing medications to remain in the body longer than desirable and possibly add to the cumulative effect. Finally, the _____ receive less blood, so less medication is filtered and removed from the body. These decreases in body system function can result in possible _____ of medications in the older adult.

circulatory system    gastrointestinal system    intestines    biotransform    kidneys
toxic effects                                       liver         peristalsis     injection site

**62.** Complete the following table by indicating whether the following suggestions are appropriate for a patient with Parkinson disease or for a patient with Alzheimer disease. Place a checkmark in the appropriate box.

| Suggestion | Patient with Parkinson Disease | Patient with Alzheimer Disease |
|---|---|---|
| **a.** Speak calmly and without condescension. | | |
| **b.** Do not argue with the patient. | | |
| **c.** Tell the patient to take small bites and chew each mouthful carefully before swallowing. | | |
| **d.** Encourage the patient to use no-spill cups, plates with high sides, and special utensils. | | |
| **e.** Free the home from rugs and loose cords that may cause tripping. | | |
| **f.** Speak in short, simple, direct sentences and explain one action at a time. | | |
| **g.** Listen to the patient and stimulate his intelligence. | | |
| **h.** Remind the patient who you are and what you must do. | | |

## COG TRUE OR FALSE?

Grade: _____

Indicate whether the statements are true or false by placing the letter T (true) or F (false) on the line preceding the statement.

**63.** _____ Newspaper word puzzles are just a temporary distraction to help entertain older adults.

**64.** _____ Attempts to commit suicide by older adults are usually just a cry for help.

**65.** _____ If a patient has an advance directive on file somewhere other than the medical office, it should be noted in her medical record.

**66.** _____ Most older adult abuse is committed by workers in long-term care facilities.

## OOG AFF CASE STUDIES FOR CRITICAL THINKING

Grade: _____

1. Read the following case studies and think about what you know about the causes of older adult abuse. Circle the letter preceding the case study that describes the patient who falls in the highest risk category for abuse.

   a. Mr. Simpson is an 89-year-old widower who lives alone. He is still fairly active and is able to carry out most daily activities by himself. He has a daughter and a son, who take turns visiting him every week and doing his shopping and laundry for him. Mr. Simpson takes medication for high blood pressure and angina.

   b. Mrs. Lewis is an 83-year-old patient who lives in a long-term care facility. She suffers from mild senile dementia, which her family sometimes finds frustrating, but is learning to cope with. Mrs. Lewis has a home health aide and private nurse to help her carry out activities of daily living. She sleeps for most of the day.

   c. Mrs. Beddowes is a 90-year-old widow who lives with her son. She suffers from senile dementia, incontinence, and insomnia. Her family members cannot afford to place her in a long-term care facility, so they share the responsibility of taking care of her. However, most of the responsibility falls onto her son, who helps Mrs. Beddowes carry out most activities of daily living.

   d. Mr. Williams is an 81-year-old patient who lives in an assisted living facility. He was recently widowed and is having difficulty coming to terms with his wife's death. Mr. Williams used to be extremely active but has recently become withdrawn and has started drinking heavily. He has two daughters who visit him regularly.

2. Your patient is a 90-year-old man with various age-associated health problems. He has been recently diagnosed with dementia, but during his recent visits to the physician's office, you have smelled alcohol on his breath. How would you handle this situation? What would you do?

   _____

   _____

   _____

   _____

3. Your patient is an 82-year-old woman who suffers from mild hearing loss. She recently lost her husband and has been making frequent appointments at the physician's office for minor complaints. You suspect that the patient is lonely and is visiting the office for company and human interaction. Explain what you would do.

   _____

   _____

   _____

   _____

**4.** Your patient is an 80-year-old woman who has recently lost a noticeable amount of weight. She tells you that she has not been very hungry lately and has not felt like eating very much. The physician has asked you to write a list of nutritional guidelines for her to follow and explain why they are important. What would you put in the guidelines?

_____

_____

_____

_____

**5.** Your patient is a 91-year-old man with Alzheimer disease. After his appointment with the physician, you overhear his family trying to get him into the car. The patient has forgotten where he is and refuses to leave the physician's office. His daughter loses her temper and shouts at her father loudly until he complies. What would you do? Explain your actions.

_____

_____

_____

_____

**6.** You overhear a coworker asking a 77-year-old patient about her medical history. When the patient tells your coworker that she is taking gingko to improve her memory, your coworker tells her that she needs to know only about actual medications. What would you say to your coworker?

_____

_____

_____

_____

# PART

# 2

# The Clinical Laboratory

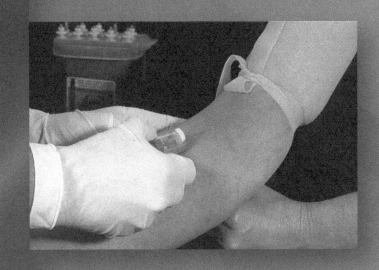

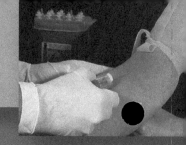

# UNIT THREE   FUNDAMENTALS OF LABORATORY PROCEDURES

## CHAPTER

# 25

# Introduction to the Physician Office Laboratory

## Learning Outcomes

### 🧠 Cognitive Domain

1. Spell key terms
2. Define medical terms and abbreviations related to all body systems
3. List the various types of clinical laboratories including the physician office laboratory
4. Explain the types of departments found in most large laboratories
5. Describe common laboratory tests ordered to diagnose disease and illness
6. Explain the significance of CLIA and how to maintain compliance in the physician office laboratory

7. Identify disease processes that are indications for CLIA-waived tests
8. Identify equipment found in the physician office laboratory and routine maintenance
9. List and describe the parts of a microscope
10. Discuss the role of the medical assistant in clinical laboratory testing
11. Define critical values
12. Analyze charts, graphs, and/or tables in the interpretation of health care results

### 🖐 Psychomotor Domain

1. Care of the microscope (Procedure 25-1)
2. Screen test results (Procedure 25-2)
3. Maintain laboratory test results using flow sheets (Procedures 25-3 and 25-4)

### ABHES Competencies

1. Incorporate critical thinking skills when performing patient assessment
2. Distinguish between normal and abnormal test results

Name: _____ Date: _____ Grade: _____

## ⬤ᴼᴳ MULTIPLE CHOICE

1. Laboratory test results are evaluated to determine the relative health of body systems or organs by comparison with:
   a. panels.
   b. constituents.
   c. reference intervals.
   d. calibration ranges.
   e. quality control ranges.

2. A large facility in which thousands of tests of various types are performed each day is a:
   a. hospital laboratory.
   b. POL.
   c. waived-testing laboratory.
   d. clinical chemistry laboratory.
   e. referral laboratory.

3. A Pap test specimen would be sent to which department for analysis?
   a. Histology
   b. Cytology
   c. Immunohematology
   d. Microbiology
   e. Clinical chemistry

4. Hematology includes the study of:
   a. etiology, diagnosis, and treatment of blood diseases.
   b. analysis of body fluids.
   c. the study of hormones.
   d. the study of the immune system and antibodies.
   e. the study of drugs.

5. Mycology is the study of:
   a. protozoa and worms.
   b. viruses.
   c. bacteria.
   d. tuberculosis.
   e. fungi and yeasts.

6. The test panel defined by the American Medical Association (AMA) for national standardization of nomenclature and testing used to test cholesterol, triglycerides, HDL, and LDL is the:
   a. comprehensive metabolic panel.
   b. basic metabolic panel.
   c. electrolyte panel.
   d. hepatic panel.
   e. lipid panel.

7. A laboratory must have a written quality assurance policy that:
   a. is communicated to all staff.
   b. is stored neared the site of use.
   c. includes all HazCom requirements.
   d. includes all MSDSs supplied by the manufacturers.
   e. is updated once a week.

8. The best source of normal values for the POL is:
   a. the *Physicians' Desk Reference.*
   b. the manufacturer's packaging insert.
   c. the ICD-9 CM.
   d. the Laboratory Procedure Manual.
   e. the CLIA certificate.

9. The presence of a panic value in test results indicates:
   a. an outbreak of a contagious virus.
   b. imminent death of the patient.
   c. general good health.
   d. a potentially life-threatening situation.
   e. negligence on the part of the laboratory.

10. Who provides quality control instructions for a given test?
    a. FDA
    b. CLSI
    c. Laboratory director
    d. Manufacturer
    e. OSHA

11. Urine dipsticks and pregnancy tests are examples of:
    a. waived tests.
    b. moderately complex tests.
    c. provider-performed microscopy.
    d. high complexity tests.
    e. referral tests.

12. What CLIA-waived test may be ordered on a patient presenting with a sore throat?
    a. Hematocrit
    b. Urine dipstick
    c. Glucose meter measurement
    d. Rapid strep test
    e. CBC

13. You bring your lunch to work and need to refrigerate it. You would:
    a. store it in the laboratory refrigerator. It is nearest to you while you work.
    b. store it in the refrigerator in the break room. That refrigerator does not have a biohazard label.
    c. store it in the refrigerator with drugs and vaccines.
    d. store it in a drawer in the laboratory.
    e. store it in an empty drawer in the procedure room.

## COG MATCHING

Grade: _____

Match the following key terms to their definitions.

**Key Terms**

14. _____ aliquots
15. _____ analytes
16. _____ antibodies
17. _____ antigen
18. _____ anticoagulant
19. _____ autoimmunity
20. _____ centrifugation
21. _____ centers for Medicare and Medicaid Services (CMS)
22. _____ coagulation
23. _____ cytogenetics
24. _____ cytology
25. _____ hematology
26. _____ histology
27. _____ immunodeficiency
28. _____ immunohematology
29. _____ immunology
30. _____ microbiology

**Definitions**

a. substance or constituent for which a laboratory conducts testing
b. anything that prevents or delays blood clotting
c. testing based on the reactions of antibodies in the presence of antigens
d. proteins formed in the body in response to foreign substances
e. substance that, when introduced into the body, cause the development of immune responses
f. disorder of the immune system in which parts of the immune system fail to provide an adequate response
g. disorders of the immune system in which the immune system attacks its own host's body
h. study of the microscopic structure of tissue; samples of tissue are prepared, stained, and evaluated under a microscope to determine whether disease is present
i. involves a wide variety of procedures used in donor selection, component preparation and use, and techniques used to detect antigen/antibody reactions that may adversely affect a patient receiving a transfusion
j. study of the microscopic structure of cells; individual cells in body fluids and other specimens are evaluated microscopically for the presence of disease such as cancer.
k. genetic structure of the cells obtained from tissue, blood, or body fluids, such as amniotic fluid, is examined or tested for chromosome deficiencies related to genetic disease.
l. the process of separating blood or other body fluid cells from liquid components
m. portions of the original specimen
n. require the use of test panels created by the AMA
o. the study of blood and blood forming tissues
p. the study of the blood's ability to clot
q. the study of pathogen identification and antibiotic susceptibility determination.

## OOG MATCHING

Grade: _____

Match the following key terms to their definitions.

**Key Terms**

31. _____ aerosol
32. _____ calibration
33. _____ confirmatory test
34. _____ control
35. _____ critical values
36. _____ external control
37. _____ internal control
38. _____ qualitative test
39. _____ quantitative test
40. _____ reconstitution
41. _____ shifts
42. _____ therapeutic range
43. _____ trends

**Definitions**

a. an additional more specific test performed to rule out or confirm a preliminary test result to provide a final result.
b. a device or solution used to monitor the test for accuracy and precision.
c. life-threatening test results
d. a method provided by the manufacturer to standardize a test or laboratory instrument.
e. control built into the testing device.
f. control that acts just like a patient specimen
g. particles suspended in gas or air.
h. the test result range the physician wants for the patient.
i. test has positive or negative results.
j. tests are measured and reported in a number value.
k. when QC results make an obvious change
l. when results increase or decrease over time
m. adding water to bring a material back to its liquid state

## OOG MATCHING

Grade: _____

Match the following key terms to their definitions.

**Key Terms**

44. _____ oncology
45. _____ panels
46. _____ pathogen
47. _____ physician office laboratory (POL)
48. _____ plasma
49. _____ product insert
50. _____ quality assurance (QA)
51. _____ quality control (QC)
52. _____ reference intervals
53. _____ referral laboratory
54. _____ serum
55. _____ specimens
56. _____ surgical pathology
57. _____ toxicology
58. _____ unitized test device
59. _____ urinalysis
60. _____ whole blood

**Definitions**

a. acceptable ranges for a healthy population
b. designed to ensure thorough patient care
c. procedures to monitor and evaluate testing procedures, supplies, and equipment to ensure accuracy in laboratory performance
d. standard groups of laboratory tests organized to effectively evaluate disease processes or organ systems
e. contains instructions and critical details for performing a test
f. top layer of a whole blood specimen if the specimen was anticoagulated and not allowed to clot
g. the study and medical treatment of cancer
h. a limited testing laboratory in a medical office
i. a large facility in which thousands of tests of various types are performed each day
j. blood containing all its cellular and liquid components
k. disease-causing microorganism
l. the liquid portion of the blood after the blood has been allowed to clot.
m. examination of the physical, chemical, and microscopic properties of urine
n. the pathologist in this department gives a diagnosis of the presence or absence of disease in tissue that is surgically removed from a patient.
o. used for a single test and discarded after testing
p. small portions of anything used to evaluate the nature of the whole
q. branch of chemistry that studies the amounts and identification of chemicals foreign to the body

## **COG** IDENTIFICATION

_____ Grade: _____

Each of the medical assistants below needs a laboratory test completed for a patient. Review the task that must be performed and then decide which laboratory department should handle each task.

**61.** Ericka needs to send in blood for a complete blood count. _____

**62.** Kwon needs results of the chemical properties of a patient's urine. _____

**63.** Darren has to send a patient to the lab for glucose testing. _____

**64.** Don has a mole removed and sent to the lab for analysis. _____

**65.** Rochelle collects a clean-catch urine for culture. _____

## **COG** SHORT ANSWER

_____ Grade: _____

**66.** Why does the laboratory need the patient's birth date and gender?

_____

_____

_____

_____

**67.** How does the laboratory use the date and time of collection?

_____

_____

_____

_____

**68.** List six good laboratory practices for POLs performing POC testing.

_____

_____

_____

_____

**69.** Identify the source of instrument maintenance and calibration instructions.

_____

_____

_____

_____

**70.** In the context of laboratory medical testing, what is the purpose of a control?

_____

_____

_____

**71.** Explain the difference between qualitative and quantitative tests.

_____

_____

_____

_____

**72.** How do you identify whether patient values are inside or outside the reference interval?

_____

_____

_____

_____

**73.** In reviewing patient results, how do you determine patient values requiring follow-up?

_____

_____

_____

_____

## COG PSY AFF CASE STUDIES FOR CRITICAL THINKING Grade: _____

**1.** The physician in the family practice office where you work asks you to perform a streptococcus test on a throat specimen. You know that the test is performed using a waived-testing kit; however, when you open the box, the package insert is missing. This insert is necessary to use as a guide to perform the test and contains the instructions. How do you obtain directions for performing the test?

**2.** A test is showing systematically low results; that is, in each case, the result is proportionately lower than expected. The results are precise but inaccurate. What must you do to ensure proper results?

_____

_____

_____

_____

**3.** You are performing a glucose test on your patient using a glucose meter. The patient's glucose result is below the level the meter can detect. The glucose meter can detect values as low as 40 mg/dL. What kind of value is this and what steps should you take with the test results?

_____

_____

_____

_____

## PROCEDURE 25-1    Care of the Microscope

**Name:** _____ **Date:** _____ **Time:** _____ **Grade:** _____

**EQUIPMENT/SUPPLIES:** Lens paper, lens cleaner, gauze, mild soap solution, microscope, hand disinfectant, surface disinfectant

**STANDARDS:** Given the needed equipment and a place to work, the student will perform this skill with _____ % accuracy in a total of _____ minutes. *(Your instructor will tell you what the percentage and time limits will be before you begin practicing.)*

**KEY:**          4 = Satisfactory          0 = Unsatisfactory          NA =This step is not counted

| PROCEDURE STEPS | SELF | PARTNER | INSTRUCTOR |
|---|---|---|---|
| **1.** Wash your hands. | ❑ | ❑ | ❑ |
| **2.** Assemble the equipment. | ❑ | ❑ | ❑ |
| **3.** If you need to move the microscope, carry it in both hands, one holding the base and the other holding the arm. | ❑ | ❑ | ❑ |
| **4.** Clean the optical areas.<br>  **a.** Place a drop or two of lens cleaner on a piece of lens paper.<br>  **b.** Wipe each eyepiece thoroughly with the lens paper. Do not touch the optical areas with your fingers. Wipe each eyepiece with lens paper and lens cleaner.<br>  **c.** Wipe each objective lens, starting with the lowest power and continuing to the highest power (usually an oil immersion lens). If the lens paper appears to have dirt or oil on it, use a clean section of the lens paper or a new piece of lens paper with cleaner. Wipe each objective lens with lens paper and lens cleaner. Clean the oil objective last so you do not carry its oil to the other objective lenses.<br>  **d.** Using a new piece of dry lens paper, wipe each eyepiece and objective lens so that no cleaner remains.<br>  **e.** With a new piece of lens paper moistened with lens cleaner, clean the condenser and illuminator optics. Clean and dry the condenser and illuminator optics. | ❑ | ❑ | ❑ |
| **5.** Clean the areas other than the optics.<br>  **a.** Moisten gauze with mild soap solution or use an alcohol wipe and wipe all areas other than the optics, including the stage, base, and adjustment knobs.<br>  **b.** Moisten another gauze with water and rinse the washed areas. | ❑ | ❑ | ❑ |
| **6.** To store the cleaned microscope, ensure that the light source is turned off. Rotate the nosepiece so that the low-power objective is pointed down toward the stage. Cover the microscope with the plastic dust cover that came with it or a small trash bag. | ❑ | ❑ | ❑ |
| **7.** Document microscope cleaning on the microscope maintenance log sheet (sample instrument log sheet). | ❑ | ❑ | ❑ |

**PSY** PROCEDURE 25-1 **Care of the Microscope** (continued)

_____

_____

_____

_____

**CALCULATION**

Total Possible Points: _____

Total Points Earned: _____ Multiplied by 100 = _____ Divided by Total Possible Points = _____ %

**PASS   FAIL   COMMENTS:**
  ❏         ❏

Student's signature _____ Date _____

Partner's signature _____ Date _____

Instructor's signature _____ Date _____

## PROCEDURE 25-2   Screen and Follow Up Test Results

**Name:** _____ **Date:** _____ **Time:** _____ **Grade:** _____

**EQUIPMENT/SUPPLIES:** Patient laboratory results, critical values list for office, patient medical record

**STANDARDS:** Given the needed equipment and a place to work, the student will perform this skill with _____ % accuracy in a total of _____ minutes. *(Your instructor will tell you what the percentage and time limits will be before you begin practicing.)*

**KEY:**         4 = Satisfactory         0 = Unsatisfactory         NA =This step is not counted

| PROCEDURE STEPS | SELF | PARTNER | INSTRUCTOR |
|---|---|---|---|
| **1.** Review laboratory reports received from reference laboratory. | ❏ | ❏ | ❏ |
| **2.** Note which reports may be placed directly on the patient's chart and which require immediate notification due to critical results. | ❏ | ❏ | ❏ |
| **3.** Notify the physician of the result. Take any immediate instructions from the physician. | ❏ | ❏ | ❏ |
| **4.** Follow instructions and document notification and follow-up. | ❏ | ❏ | ❏ |
| **5.** Chart remaining reports appropriately. | ❏ | ❏ | ❏ |

**CALCULATION**

Total Possible Points: _____

Total Points Earned: _____ Multiplied by 100 = _____ Divided by Total Possible Points = _____ %

**PASS    FAIL    COMMENTS:**
 ❏          ❏

Student's signature _____ Date _____

Partner's signature _____ Date _____

Instructor's signature _____ Date _____

## PSY PROCEDURE 25-3 Use a Laboratory Flow Sheet

Name: _____ Date: _____ Time: _____ Grade: _____

**EQUIPMENT/SUPPLIES:** Flow sheet for documenting a patient's anticoagulation therapy and test results; scenarios for patient Jacob Wisliki.

**STANDARDS:** Patient Jacob Wisliki is on Coumadin (warfarin) therapy following a stroke. Dr. Wilson requests that you maintain a flow sheet on this patient and orders weekly INR (coagulation) testing.

The student will perform this skill with _____% accuracy in a total of _____ minutes. *(Your instructor will tell you what the percentage and time limits will be before you begin practicing.)*

**PATIENT SCENARIOS:**

- Today is November 1, 2016. Mr. Wisliki's INR is 1.8, which is below Dr. Wilson's target range. Dr. Wilson increases Mr. Wisliki's dose to 2.5 mg qd and requests that Mr. Wisliki return in a week for another INR.

- Mr. Wisliki returns and his INR is 2.1, which is in Dr. Wilson's therapeutic range. Dr. Wilson would like to see the value higher so he increases Mr. Wisliki's Coumadin dose to 3.5 mg qd and have another INR performed in 1 week.

- The following week, Mr. Wisliki returns and his INR result is 3.5, which is higher than Dr. Wilson's therapeutic range. Dr. Wilson decreases Mr. Wisliki's dose to 3.0 mg qd and requests Mr. Wisliki to return in 1 week.

- Mr. Wisliki returns on schedule the following week and his INR is 3.1. Dr. Wilson is concerned that Mr. Wisliki's INR did not respond as usual to the decrease in the dose. Mr. Wisliki is instructed to avoid eating green leafy vegetables while on anticoagulant therapy and his dose is not changed. He is instructed to return in a week as ordered by Dr. Wilson.

- Mr. Wisliki is back for his weekly INR check, and today, it is 2.5. Dr. Wilson is pleased with this INR result and does not change the dose. You instruct Mr. Wisliki to return in a week as Dr. Wilson ordered.

- Mr. Wisliki is back for his INR, which is 2.5. Because his INR is stable, Dr. Wilson does not change his dose.

**KEY:**     4 = Satisfactory          0 = Unsatisfactory          NA = This step is not counted

| PROCEDURE STEPS | SELF | PARTNER | INSTRUCTOR |
|---|---|---|---|
| 1. Obtain the anticoagulant flow sheet and the scenarios and data for Jacob Wisliki. | ❏ | ❏ | ❏ |
| 2. Record the INR results, medication dosage change (new dose), and your name (first initial, last name) on the first line (date 11/01/2016) of the flow sheet. | ❏ | ❏ | ❏ |
| 3. Record the date, INR results, medication dosage change, and your name for the 2nd week of the scenario. | ❏ | ❏ | ❏ |
| 4. Record the date, INR results, medication dosage change, and your name for each of the following weeks (weeks # 2, 3, 4, 5, and 6). | ❏ | ❏ | ❏ |
| 5. Each weekly entry is complete, legible, and accurate. | ❏ | ❏ | ❏ |
| 6. Explain that the flow sheet is maintained in the patient medical record. | ❏ | ❏ | ❏ |

**PSY** PROCEDURE 25-3 **Use a Laboratory Flow Sheet** (continued)

**CALCULATION**

Total Possible Points: _____

Total Points Earned: _____ Multiplied by 100 = _____ Divided by Total Possible Points = _____ %

**PASS** **FAIL** **COMMENTS:**
❏ ❏

Student's signature _____ Date _____

Partner's signature _____ Date _____

Instructor's signature _____ Date _____

## PROCEDURE 25-4 Anticoagulant Flow Sheet

Name: _____ Date: _____ Time: _____ Grade: _____

**PATIENT'S NAME:** Jacob Wisliki

**DATE OF BIRTH:** 03/20/1940

**TARGET INTERNATIONAL NORMALIZED RATIO (INR):** √ 2.0–3.0 ☐ 2.5–3.5 Other: _____

| Date | Current Dose | INR | Medication | New Dose | Signature |
|------|-------------|-----|-----------|----------|-----------|
| 11/01/2016 | 2 mg qd | | | | |
| | | | | | |
| | | | | | |
| | | | | | |
| | | | | | |
| | | | | | |
| | | | | | |

# CHAPTER

# 26 Phlebotomy

## Learning Outcomes

### COG Cognitive Domain

1. Spell and define the key terms
2. Define medical terms and abbreviations related to all body systems
3. Identify equipment and supplies used to obtain a routine venous specimen and a routine capillary skin puncture
4. Describe proper use of specimen collection equipment
5. List the major anticoagulants, their color codes, and the suggested order in which they are filled during a venipuncture
6. Describe the location and selection of the blood collection sites using capillaries and veins
7. Differentiate between the feel of a vein, tendon, and artery
8. Describe care for a puncture site after blood has been drawn
9. Explain quality assessment issues in specimen collection procedures

### PSY Psychomotor Domain

1. Obtain a blood specimen by evacuated tube or winged infusion set (Procedure 26-1)
   a. Perform venipuncture
   b. Instruct and prepare a patient for a procedure or treatment
   c. Coach patients appropriately considering cultural diversity,

developmental life stage, communication barriers
   d. Document patient care accurately in the medical record.
2. Obtain a blood specimen by capillary puncture (Procedure 26-2)
   a. Perform capillary puncture
   b. Instruct and prepare a patient for a procedure or treatment
   c. Coach patients appropriately considering cultural diversity, developmental life stage, communication barriers
   d. Document patient care accurately in the medical record.

### AFF Affective Domain

1. Incorporate critical thinking skills when performing patient assessment.
2. Incorporate critical thinking skills when performing patient care.
3. Show awareness of a patient's concerns related to the procedure being performed.
4. Demonstrate empathy, active listening, nonverbal communication
5. Demonstrate respect for individual diversity including gender, race, religion, age, economic status, appearance.
6. Explain to a patient the rationale for performance of a procedure

7. Demonstrate sensitivity to patient rights
8. Protect the integrity of the medical record.

### ABHES Competencies

1. Define and use entire basic structure of medical words and be able to accurately identify in the correct context, that is, root, prefix, suffix, combinations, spelling, and definitions
2. Build and dissect medical terms from roots/suffixes to understand the word element combinations that create medical terminology
3. Document accurately
4. Comply with federal, state, and local health laws and regulations
5. Identify and respond appropriately when working/caring for patients with special needs
6. Maintain inventory equipment and supplies
7. Communicate on the recipient's level of comprehension
8. Use pertinent medical terminology
9. Recognize and respond to verbal and nonverbal communication
10. Use standard precautions
11. Dispose of biohazardous materials
12. Collect, label, and process specimens
13. Perform venipuncture
14. Perform capillary puncture

Name: _____     Date: _____     Grade: _____

## OOG MULTIPLE CHOICE

Circle the letter preceding the correct answer.

1. When obtaining a blood specimen from a winged infusion set you need all of the following except:
   a. evacuated tubes.
   b. tourniquet.
   c. gauze pads.
   d. syringe.
   e. permanent marker.

2. A source of error in venipuncture is:
   a. puncturing the wrong area of an infant's heel.
   b. inserting needle bevel side down.
   c. prolonged tourniquet application.
   d. pulling back on syringe plunger too forcefully.
   e. all of the above

3. When your patient is feeling faint during venipuncture, you should do all of the following except:
   a. remove the tourniquet and withdraw the needle.
   b. divert attention from the procedure.
   c. have patient breathe deeply.
   d. loosen a tight collar or tie.
   e. apply a cold compress or washcloth.

4. To avoid hemoconcentration, the phlebotomist should:
   a. ensure the tourniquet is not too tight.
   b. have patient make a fist.
   c. use occluded veins.
   d. draw blood from the heel.
   e. use a needle with a small diameter.

5. If you accidentally puncture an artery, you should:
   a. hold pressure over the site for a full 5 minutes.
   b. use a cold compress to reduce pain.
   c. perform a capillary puncture.
   d. use a multisample needle instead.
   e. use a flatter angle when inserting the needle.

6. What is the difference between NPO and fasting?
   a. Fasting is no food, and NPO is no water.
   b. Fasting and NPO are basically the same.
   c. Fasting allows the patient to drink water, whereas NPO does not.
   d. NPO requires that the patient drink water, whereas fasting does not.
   e. Fasting is for surgery, and NPO is for getting true test results.

7. Aseptic techniques to prevent infection of the venipuncture site include:
   a. using sterile gloves.
   b. wearing a lab coat.
   c. using a gel separator.
   d. not opening bandages ahead of time.
   e. not speaking while you draw blood.

8. When collecting a blood sample from the fingers, you should use:
   a. the thumb.
   b. the second finger.
   c. the fifth finger.
   d. all fingers.
   e. the third and fourth fingers.

9. You should not draw blood using a small gauge needle because:
   a. there is a greater likelihood of it breaking off in the vein.
   b. blood cells will rupture, causing hemolysis of the specimen.
   c. the luer adaptor will not fit venipuncture cuffs.
   d. the small needles are awkward to hold and manipulate.
   e. the small needles do not allow you to collect enough blood.

10. Which of the following may trigger hematoma formation?
    a. Pressure is applied after venipuncture.
    b. The needle is removed after the tourniquet is removed.
    c. The needle penetrates all the way through the vein.
    d. The needle is fully inserted into the vein.
    e. The patient has not properly followed preparation instructions.

11. The most commonly used antiseptic for routine blood collection is:
    a. 70% isopropyl alcohol.
    b. povidone iodine.
    c. 0.5% chlorhexidine gluconate.
    d. benzalkonium chloride.
    e. sodium chloride.

12. Which tubes must be first in the order of the draw?
    a. Blood culture tubes
    b. Coagulation tubes
    c. Heparin tubes
    d. Serum separator tubes (SSTs)
    e. Plain tubes

13. Which of the following is true of ethylenediaminetetraacetic acid (EDTA) tubes?
    a. They cause the least interference in tests.
    b. They should be filled after hematology tubes.
    c. They are the same as PSTs.
    d. They minimize the chance of microbial contamination.
    e. They elevate sodium and potassium levels.

14. What safety features are available for the holder used with the evacuated tube system?
    a. Shields that cover the needle, or devices that retract the needle into the holder
    b. A self-locking cover for recapping the needle
    c. A gripper to clamp the holder to the Vacutainer tube, preventing slippage
    d. Orange color as a reminder to discard in biohazard container
    e. A beveled point on only one end

15. What example explains the best advantage of using the evacuated tube system?
    a. Multiple tubes may be filled from a single venipuncture.
    b. The tubes are color coded according to the tests to be done.
    c. The vacuum draws the blood into the tubes.
    d. It is a universal system, used in all phlebotomy laboratories around the country.
    e. It is the least painful way to draw blood from a patient.

## COG MATCHING

_____ Grade: _____

Match each key term with the correct definition.

**Key Terms**

16. _____ antecubital space
17. _____ anticoagulant
18. _____ blood cultures
19. _____ breathing the syringe
20. _____ butterfly
21. _____ cultured
22. _____ evacuated tube
23. _____ fasting
24. _____ gel separator
25. _____ hemochromatosis
26. _____ hematocrit
27. _____ hematoma
28. _____ hemoconcentration
29. _____ hemolysis
30. _____ luer adapter

**Definitions**

a. blood collection tube additive used because it prevents clotting

b. forms a physical barrier between the cellular portion of a specimen and the serum or plasma portion after the specimen has been centrifuged

c. specimens drawn to culture the blood for pathogens

d. winged infusion set

e. grown in the laboratory

f. pull back the plunger to about halfway up the barrel, and then push it back

g. the inside of the elbow

h. the patient must eat nothing after midnight until the blood specimen is drawn, including chewing gum, breath mints, and coffee; the patient can have water

i. formation caused by blood leaking into the tissues during or after venipuncture

j. packed red blood cell volume

k. a condition that causes an elevated hematocrit

l. disorder that increases the amount of iron in the blood to dangerous levels

m. tubes that fill with a predetermined volume of blood because of the vacuum inside the tube (the vacuum is premeasured by the manufacturer to draw the precise amount of blood into the tube; the tube fills until the vacuum is exhausted)

n. rupturing of red blood cells, causing release of intracellular contents into the plasma

o. needle holder

## ᴄᴏɢ MATCHING

Match each key term with the correct definition.

**Key Terms**

31. _____ lymphedema
32. _____ multisample needle
33. _____ order of draw
34. _____ palpate
35. _____ peak level
36. _____ polycythemia vera
37. _____ prophylaxis
38. _____ thrombosed
39. _____ trough level
40. _____ venipuncture

**Definitions**

a. protective treatment for the prevention of disease once exposure has occurred
b. the process of puncturing a vein with a needle for the purpose of obtaining a blood sample for analysis; also known as a phlebotomy procedure.
c. system that facilitates collecting multiple tubes with a single venipuncture
d. tube filling sequence for both collection of evacuated tubes and filling evacuated tubes from a syringe
e. disease of having too many red blood cells; abnormally high hematocrit
f. veins that have been injured, lack resilience, and roll easily
g. lymphatic obstruction
h. the highest serum level of a drug in a patient based on a dosing schedule, which is usually measured about 60 minutes after the end of the infusion
i. drug level drawn immediately prior to a dose
j. using the tip of the index finger to evaluate veins by feeling to determine their suitability

## ᴄᴏɢ SHORT ANSWER

41. List four techniques you can use to avoid hemoconcentration in a blood specimen.

a. _____

b. _____

c. _____

d. _____

42. Name three issues that can be avoided by using the correct order of draw.

_____

_____

_____

_____

43. Describe six sites to avoid when performing a venipuncture.

_____

_____

_____

_____

**44.** What should you do if a hematoma begins to form during venipuncture?

_____

_____

_____

_____

**45.** Name eight sources of error in venipuncture procedure.

_____

_____

_____

_____

## COG MATCHING

_____ Grade: _____

Match each tube with its description.

**Tubes**

**46.** _____ Heparin tubes
**47.** _____ Tubes for coagulation testing
**48.** _____ EDTA tubes
**49.** _____ Tubes for blood cultures
**50.** _____ PST tubes
**51.** _____ Serum separator gel tubes
**52.** _____ Plain (nonadditive) tubes

**Descriptions**

**a.** Drawn first to minimize chance of microbial contamination
**b.** Prevents contamination by additives in other tubes
**c.** Must be the first additive tube in the order because all other additive tubes affect coagulation tests
**d.** Come after coagulation tests because silica particles activate clotting and affect coagulation tests; carryover of silica into subsequent tubes can be overridden by the anticoagulant in them
**e.** Affects coagulation tests and interferes in collection of serum specimens; causes the least interference in tests other than coagulation tests
**f.** Causes more carryover problems than any other additive; elevates sodium and potassium levels; chelates and decreases calcium and iron levels; elevates prothrombin time and partial thromboplastin time results
**g.** Causes the least interference in tests other than coagulation tests and contains a gel separator to separate plasma from the blood cells in the specimen

## COG TRUE OR FALSE?

_____ Grade: _____

Indicate whether the statements are true or false by placing the letter T (true) or F (false) on the line preceding the statement.

**53.** _____ Winged sets cause increased numbers of needlesticks to phlebotomists.

**54.** _____ For finger puncture sites, it is best to have the hand below the heart.

**55.** _____ Never believe patients when they say they faint during venipuncture.

**56.** _____ Warmers decrease blood flow before the skin is punctured.

**57.** _____ Excessive massaging of the puncture site is a source of error in skin puncture.

**COG SHORT ANSWER**

_____ Grade: _____

**58.** List the use of each item of equipment listed that may be used during a routine venipuncture and/or a routine capillary skin puncture.

**a.** Evacuated collection tubes:

_____

_____

_____

_____

**b.** Multisample needles:

_____

_____

_____

_____

**c.** Winged infusion sets:

_____

_____

_____

_____

**d.** Holders/adapters:

_____

_____

_____

_____

**e.** Tourniquets:

_____

_____

_____

_____

**f.** Puncture devices:

_____

_____

_____

_____

**g.** Microhematocrit tubes:

_____

_____

_____

_____

**h.** Microcollection containers:

_____

_____

_____

_____

**59.** Supply the color code for each type of blood collection tube.

**a.** Blood cultures _____

**b.** Coagulation tests _____

**c.** Serum separator tubes _____

**d.** Ethylenediaminetetraacetic acid _____

**e.** Plain (nonadditive) tubes _____

**f.** Plasma tubes and plasma separator tubes _____

## COG IDENTIFICATION

_____ Grade: _____

**60.** Fill in artery (A), tendon (T), or vein (V) by the feeling when palpating a vein.

**a.** _____ cordlike

**b.** _____ lacks resilience

**c.** _____ most elastic

**d.** _____ palpable

**e.** _____ pulsatile

**f.** _____ resilient

**g.** _____ trackable

**COG PLACE IN ORDER**                                                                 Grade: _____

**61.** Numbering from 1 to 25, place the steps for performing a venipuncture in the correct order.

_____ Greet and identify the patient. Explain the procedure. Ask for and answer any questions.

_____ Tap the tubes that contain additives to ensure that the additive is dislodged from the stopper and wall of the tube. Insert the tube into the adaptor until the needle slightly enters the stopper. Do not push the top of the tube stopper beyond the indentation mark. If the tube retracts slightly, leave it in the retracted position.

_____ Check the physician order and fill out a laboratory requisition form if necessary.

_____ If a fasting specimen is required, ask the patient the last time he or she ate or drank anything other than water.

_____ Select a vein by palpating. Use your gloved index finger to trace the path of the vein and judge its depth.

_____ Wash your hands.

_____ Apply the tourniquet around the patient's arm 3 to 4 inches above the elbow.

_____ Cleanse the venipuncture site with an alcohol pad, starting in the center of puncture site and working outward in a circular motion. Allow the site to dry or dry the site with sterile gauze. Do not touch the area after cleansing.

_____ With the bevel up, line up the needle with the vein approximately one quarter to half an inch below the site where the vein is to be entered. At a 15- to 30-degree angle, rapidly and smoothly insert the needle through the skin. Place two fingers on the flanges of the adapter, and with the thumb, push the tube onto the needle inside the adapter. Allow the tube to fill to capacity. Release the tourniquet and allow the patient to release the fist. When blood flow ceases, remove the tube from the adapter by gripping the tube with your nondominant hand and placing your thumb against the flange during removal. Twist and gently pull out the tube. Steady the needle in the vein. Avoid pulling up or pressing down on the needle while it is in the vein. Insert any other necessary tubes into adapter and allow each to fill to capacity.

_____ Assemble the equipment. Check the expiration date on the tubes.

_____ Record the procedure.

_____ Put on nonsterile latex or vinyl gloves. Use other personal protective equipment as defined by facility policy.

_____ Place a sterile gauze pad over the puncture site at the time of needle withdrawal. Do not apply any pressure to the site until the needle is completely removed. After the needle is removed, immediately activate the safety device and apply pressure or have the patient apply direct pressure for 3 to 5 minutes. Do not bend the arm at the elbow.

_____ Instruct the patient to sit with a well-supported arm.

_____ Label the tubes with patient information as defined in facility protocol.

_____ Release the tourniquet after palpating the vein if it has been left on for more than 1 minute. Have patient release his or her fist.

_____ Test, transfer, or store the blood specimen according to the medical office policy.

_____ Remove the needle cover. Hold the needle assembly in your dominant hand, thumb on top of the adaptor and fingers under it. Grasp the patient's arm with the other hand, using your thumb to draw the skin taut over the site. This anchors the vein about 1 to 2 inches below the puncture site and helps keep it in place during needle insertion.

_____ If the vacuum tubes contain an anticoagulant, they must be mixed immediately by gently inverting the tube 8 to 10 times. Do not shake the tube.

_____ If blood being drawn for culture will be used in diagnosing a septic condition, make sure the specimen is sterile. To do this, apply alcohol to the area for 2 full minutes. Then apply a 2% iodine solution in ever widening circles. Never move the wipes back over areas that have been cleaned; use a new wipe for each sweep across the area.

_____ Thank the patient. Instruct the patient to leave the bandage in place at least 15 minutes and not to carry a heavy object (such as a purse) or lift heavy objects with that arm for 1 hour.

_____ Properly care for or dispose of all equipment and supplies. Clean the work area. Remove personal protective equipment and wash your hands.

_____ Reapply the tourniquet if it was removed after palpation. Ask patient to make a fist.

_____ Check the puncture site for bleeding. Apply a dressing, a clean 2 × 2 gauze pad folded in quarters, and hold in place by an adhesive bandage or 3-inch strip of tape.

_____ With the tourniquet released, remove the tube from the adapter before removing the needle from the arm.

62. Numbering from 1 to 16, place the steps for performing a capillary puncture in the correct order.

_____ Thank the patient. Instruct the patient to leave the bandage in place at least 15 minutes.

_____ Greet and identify the patient. Explain the procedure. Ask for and answer any questions.

_____ Check the physician order and fill out a laboratory requisition form if necessary.

_____ Select the puncture site. Use the appropriate puncture device for the site selected.

_____ Obtain the first drop of blood. Wipe away the first drop of blood with dry gauze. Apply pressure toward the site but do not milk the site.

_____ Wash your hands.

_____ Grasp the finger firmly between your nondominant index finger and thumb, or grasp the infant's heel firmly with your index finger wrapped around the foot and your thumb wrapped around the ankle. Cleanse the selected area with 70% isopropyl alcohol and allow to air dry.

_____ Record the procedure.

_____ Assemble the equipment.

_____ Hold the patient's finger or heel firmly and make a swift, firm puncture. Perform the puncture perpendicular to the whorls of the fingerprint or footprint. Dispose of the used puncture device in a sharps container.

_____ Test, transfer, or store the specimen according to the medical office policy.

_____ Put on gloves.

_____ Collect the specimen in the chosen container or slide. Touch only the tip of the collection device to the drop of blood. Blood flow is encouraged if the puncture site is held downward and gentle pressure is applied near the site. Cap microcollection tubes with the caps provided and mix the additives by gently tilting or inverting the tubes 8 to 10 times.

_____ Make sure the site chosen is warm and not cyanotic or edematous. Gently massage the finger from the base to the tip or massage the infant's heel.

_____ Properly care for or dispose of equipment and supplies. Clean the work area. Remove gloves and wash your hands.

_____ When collection is complete, apply clean gauze to the site with pressure. Hold pressure or have the patient hold pressure until bleeding stops. Label the containers with the proper information. Do not apply a dressing to a skin puncture of an infant under age 2 years. Never release a patient until the bleeding has stopped.

## ⓒⓞⓖ TRUE OR FALSE?

Grade: _____

Indicate whether the statements are true or false by placing the letter T (true) or F (false) on the line preceding the statement.

**63.** _____ After the needle is removed, activate the safety device as soon as possible.

**64.** _____ The phlebotomy equipment should be easily accessible by everyone in the medical office.

**65.** _____ A safety device locks the armrest in place in front of the patient to prevent falling from the chair if fainting occurs.

**66.** _____ Needle holders do not include a safety device, so needle safety devices are required.

**67.** _____ The Needlestick Safety and Prevention Act requires each phlebotomist to be responsible for his or her own safety.

**68.** _____ Quick activation of the safety device relieves the phlebotomist of concern for caution.

**69.** _____ Holder safety features may include a shield that covers the needle or a device that retracts the needle into the holder after it is withdrawn from the vein.

**70.** _____ Regardless of safety features, immediately dispose of used needles, lancets, and other sharp objects in a puncture-resistant, leak-proof disposable container called a sharps container.

## ⓒⓞⓖ FILL IN THE BLANK

Grade: _____

**71.** Postural changes (_____, _____, _____) are known to vary laboratory results of some analytes. The differences in these lab values have been attributed to shifts in _____ _____. Fluids tend to stay in the vascular compartment (bloodstream) when the patient is _____ or _____. This tends to _____ the blood. There is a _____ of fluids to the interstitial spaces upon standing or ambulation. The lab tests that are the most affected by this phenomenon are proteins (_____, _____, _____) and protein-bound substances, such as _____, _____, _____, and _____.

**72.** The maximum time limit for leaving the tourniquet in place is _____ minutes. Extending the time limit can alter test results by causing _____ and _____. The _____ of fluid in hemoconcentrated blood results in a(n) _____ of cellular components in that blood. This _____ elevation results in _____ laboratory measurement of _____, _____, and some _____. _____ tourniquet placement may significantly increase total protein, aspartate aminotransferase (AST), total lipids, cholesterol, iron, and hematocrit.

**73.** The most common complication of venipuncture is _____ formation caused by blood leaking into the tissues during or after venipuncture.

**74.** Situations that may trigger hematoma formation include:

**a.** The vein is _____ or too _____ for the needle.

**b.** The needle _____ all the way through the _____.

**c.** The needle is only _____ _____ into the vein.

**d.** Excessive or _____ _____ is used to find the vein.

**e.** The needle is removed while the _____ _____ _____ _____.

**f.** _____ is not adequately applied after venipuncture.

**75.** _____ veins (lack resilience) feel like rope or cord and _____ easily.

**76.** Accidental puncture of an _____ is recognized by the blood's bright red color and the _____ of the specimen into the tube.

**77.** Permanent _____ damage may result from _____ site selection, movement of the _____ during needle insertion, inserting the needle too _____ or _____, or excessive blind _____.

**78.** Make sure the needle fully _____ the _____ most wall of the vein. (Partial _____ allow blood to leak into the soft tissue surrounding the vein by way of the needle _____.)

**79.** If an insufficient amount or no blood is collected:

**a.** Change the _____ of the _____. Move it forward (it may not be in the _____). Or, move it backward (it may have _____ _____ _____).

**b.** Adjust the angle (the _____ may be against the vein _____).

**c.** Loosen the tourniquet; it may be _____ blood _____.

**d.** Try _____ tube. There may be no _____ in the _____ _____ _____.

**e.** _____ the vein. Veins sometimes _____ _____ from the _____ of the needle and puncture site.

**f.** The vein may have _____; _____ the tourniquet to increase _____ filling. If this is not successful, remove the _____, take care of the _____ site, and _____.

**g.** The _____ may have pulled _____ _____ _____ _____ when switching tubes. _____ equipment firmly and place _____ against the patient's arm, using the _____ for leverage when withdrawing and inserting _____.

## AFF PSY CASE STUDIES FOR CRITICAL THINKING
_____ Grade: _____

**1.** You have a patient who says that he always becomes nervous at the sight of his own blood but has never fainted before. You ask the patient to lie down during the procedure. Your patient is fine with the needle insertion, but as soon as he sees the sight of his own blood, he passes out. What should you do?

_____

_____

_____

_____

2. You are reviewing test results received from the referral laboratory. You notice that the HIV results on your neighbor, Alice Sihotang, are positive. Your friend Kaylene Oyakawa meets you for lunch. She tells you that all of your neighbors are worried about Alice because she looks so ill and has been losing weight. Kaylene says that she knows Alice is a patient at your medical office and asks you what is wrong with Alice. What do you say?

_____

_____

_____

_____

3. After drawing blood with a winged set, you inadvertently stick yourself with the needle. How would you handle this situation?

_____

_____

_____

_____

4. Your last patient of the day, a young child accompanied by her mother, accidentally knocks over your collection tubes that were within her reach as you were disposing of sharps. How would you handle this situation?

_____

_____

_____

_____

5. The medical office has closed and you are completing preparation of specimens for the reference laboratory pick-up. You find you have two requisitions without labeled specimens to accompany them. You have two unlabeled blood tubes. There is no way to identify the two specimens. What do you do?

_____

_____

_____

_____

## PSY PROCEDURE 26-1    Obtain a Blood Specimen by Evacuated Tube or Winged Infusion Set

Name: _____ Date: _____ Time: _____ Grade: _____

**EQUIPMENT/SUPPLIES:** Multisample needle and adaptor or winged infusion set, evacuated tubes, tourniquet, sterile gauze pads, bandages, sharps container, 70% alcohol pad, permanent marker or pen, appropriate personal protective equipment (e.g., gloves, impervious gown, face shield)

**STANDARDS:** Given the needed equipment and a place to work, the student will perform this skill with _____ % accuracy in a total of _____ minutes. *(Your instructor will tell you what the percentage and time limits will be before you begin practicing.)*

**KEY:**          4 = Satisfactory          0 = Unsatisfactory          NA =This step is not counted

| PROCEDURE STEPS | SELF | PARTNER | INSTRUCTOR |
|---|---|---|---|
| 1. Check the physician order and complete the requisition slip if appropriate. | ❏ | ❏ | ❏ |
| 2. Wash your hands and assemble the equipment. | ❏ | ❏ | ❏ |
| 3. Check the expiration date on the tubes. Discard expired supplies according to office policy and procedure. | ❏ | ❏ | ❏ |
| 4. **AFF** Greet and identify the patient and yourself including your title. Explain the procedure. | ❏ | ❏ | ❏ |
| 5. **AFF** Demonstrate recognition of the patient's level of understanding communications. Apply active listening skills. Modify communication to the patient's level of understanding, or obtain assistance with language differences. | ❏ | ❏ | ❏ |
| 6. Ask the patient about any dietary restrictions and the use of medications that increase bleeding time. If a fasting or NPO specimen is required, ask the patient for the last time he or she ate or drank anything. | ❏ | ❏ | ❏ |
| 7. Put on nonsterile latex or vinyl gloves. Use other personal protective equipment as defined by office policy. | ❏ | ❏ | ❏ |
| 8. *For evacuated tube collection*: Break the seal of the needle cover and thread the sleeved needle into the adaptor, using the needle cover as a wrench.   *For winged infusion set collection*: Extend the tubing. Thread the sleeved needle into the adaptor.   *For both methods*: Tap the tubes that contain additives to ensure that the additive is dislodged from the stopper and wall of the tube. Insert the tube into the adaptor until the needle slightly enters the stopper. Do not push the top of the tube stopper beyond the indentation mark. If the tube retracts slightly, leave it in the retracted position. | ❏ | ❏ | ❏ |
| 9. Instruct the patient to sit with a well-supported arm. | ❏ | ❏ | ❏ |

**PROCEDURE 26-1** **Obtain a Blood Specimen by Evacuated Tube or Winged Infusion Set** (continued)

| | | | |
|---|---|---|---|
| 10. After reviewing veins in both arms, choose one arm and apply the tourniquet 3 –to 4 inches above the elbow.<br>  **a.** Apply the tourniquet snuggly, but not too tightly.<br>  **b.** Secure the tourniquet by using the half-bow knot.<br>  **c.** Make sure the tails of the tourniquet extend upward to avoid contaminating the venipuncture site.<br>  **d.** Ask the patient to make a fist and hold it, but not to pump the fist. | ❏ | ❏ | ❏ |
| 11. Select a vein by palpating. Use your gloved index finger to trace the path of the vein and judge its depth. | ❏ | ❏ | ❏ |
| 12. Release tourniquet after palpating the vein if it has been left on for more than one minute. Have patient release fist. | ❏ | ❏ | ❏ |
| 13. Cleanse the venipuncture site with an alcohol pad, starting in the center of puncture site and working outward in a circular motion. Allow the site to dry or dry the site with sterile gauze. Do not touch the area after cleansing. | ❏ | ❏ | ❏ |
| 14. If blood is being drawn for a blood culture, make sure the area is cleansed using a 2% iodine solution for 2 full minutes. | ❏ | ❏ | ❏ |
| 15. Reapply the tourniquet if it was removed after palpation. Ask patient to make a fist. | ❏ | ❏ | ❏ |
| 16. Remove the needle cover. Hold the needle assembly in your dominant hand, thumb on top of the adaptor and fingers under it. Grasp the patient's arm with the other hand, using your thumb to draw the skin taut over the site. This anchors the vein about 1 –to 2 inches below the puncture site and helps keep it in place during needle insertion. | ❏ | ❏ | ❏ |
| 17. With the bevel up, line up the needle with the vein approximately one quarter to half an inch below the site where the vein is to be entered. At a 15- to 30-degree angle, rapidly and smoothly insert the needle through the skin. Use a lesser angle for winged infusion set collections. Place two fingers on the flanges of the adapter and with the thumb push the tube onto the needle inside the adapter. Allow the tube to fill to capacity. Release the tourniquet and allow the patient to release the fist. When blood flow ceases, remove the tube from the adapter by gripping the tube with your non-dominant hand and placing your thumb against the flange during removal. Twist and gently pull out the tube. Steady the needle in the vein. Avoid pulling up or pressing down on the needle while it is in the vein. Insert any other necessary tubes into adapter and allow each to fill to capacity. | ❏ | ❏ | ❏ |

**PSY** PROCEDURE 26-1   **Obtain a Blood Specimen by Evacuated Tube or Winged Infusion Set** (continued)

| | | | |
|---|---|---|---|
| **18.** With the tourniquet released, remove the tube from the adapter before removing the needle from the arm. | ❏ | ❏ | ❏ |
| **19.** Place a sterile gauze pad over the puncture site at the time of needle withdrawal. Do not apply any pressure to the site until the needle is completely removed.<br>**a.** After the needle is removed, immediately activate the safety device and apply pressure or have the patient apply direct pressure for 3 to 5 minutes. Do not bend the arm at the elbow. | ❏ | ❏ | ❏ |
| **20.** After the needle is removed, immediately activate the safety device and apply pressure, or have the patient apply direct pressure for 3 to 5 minutes. Do not bend the arm at the elbow. | ❏ | ❏ | ❏ |
| **21.** If the vacuum tubes contain an anticoagulant, they must be mixed immediately by gently inverting the tube 8 to 10 times. Do not shake the tube. | ❏ | ❏ | ❏ |
| **22.** Label the tubes with patient information as defined by the office or laboratory protocol. | ❏ | ❏ | ❏ |
| **23.** Check the puncture site for bleeding. Apply a dressing, a clean 2 × 2 gauze pad folded in quarters, and hold in place by an adhesive bandage or 3-inch strip of tape. | ❏ | ❏ | ❏ |
| **24.** **AFF** Thank the patient. Instruct the patient to leave the bandage in place at least 15 minutes and not to carry a heavy object (such as a purse) or lift heavy objects with that arm for 1 hour. | ❏ | ❏ | ❏ |
| **25.** Properly care for or dispose of all equipment and supplies. Clean the work area. Remove personal protective equipment and wash your hands. | ❏ | ❏ | ❏ |
| **26.** Test, transfer, or store the blood specimen according to the medical office policy. | ❏ | ❏ | ❏ |
| **27.** Log into the Electronic Medical Record (EMR) using your username and secure password OR obtain the paper medical record from a secure location and assure it is kept away from public access. Record the procedure noting the date, time, site of the venipuncture, test results for CLIA-waived POC procedures or the name of the lab where the specimen was sent, and your name. | ❏ | ❏ | ❏ |
| **28.** When finished, log out of the EMR and/or replace the paper medical record in an appropriate and secure location. | ❏ | ❏ | ❏ |

## PROCEDURE 26-1 Obtain a Blood Specimen by Evacuated Tube or Winged Infusion Set (continued)

| | | | |
|---|---|---|---|
| **29.** **AFF** Explain how to respond to a patient who is deaf, hearing impaired, visually impaired, developmentally challenged, or speaks English as a second language (ESL) or who has dementia, cultural or religious concerns, or generational differences. | ❏ | ❏ | ❏ |

_____

_____

_____

_____

_____

**CALCULATION**

Total Possible Points: _____

Total Points Earned: _____ Multiplied by 100 = _____ Divided by Total Possible Points = _____ %

**PASS** **FAIL** **COMMENTS:**
❏ ❏

Student's signature _____ Date _____

Partner's signature _____ Date _____

Instructor's signature _____ Date _____

## PSY PROCEDURE 26-2 Obtain a Blood Specimen by Capillary Puncture

Name: _____ Date: _____ Time: _____ Grade: _____

**EQUIPMENT/SUPPLIES:** Skin puncture device, 70% alcohol pads, 2 × 2 gauze pads, microcollection tubes or containers, heel warming device if needed, small band aids, pen or permanent marker and personal protective equipment (e.g., gloves, impervious gown, face shield)

**STANDARDS:** Given the needed equipment and a place to work the student will perform this skill with _____ % accuracy in a total of _____ minutes. *(Your instructor will tell you what the percentage and time limits will be before you begin.)*

**KEY:** 4 = Satisfactory  0 = Unsatisfactory  NA =This step is not counted

| PROCEDURE STEPS | SELF | PARTNER | INSTRUCTOR |
|---|---|---|---|
| **1.** Check the physician order and complete the requisition slip if appropriate. | ❏ | ❏ | ❏ |
| **2.** Wash your hands. | ❏ | ❏ | ❏ |
| **3.** Assemble the equipment. | ❏ | ❏ | ❏ |
| **4.** **AFF** Greet and identify the patient and yourself including your title. Explain the procedure. | ❏ | ❏ | ❏ |
| **5.** **AFF** Evaluate your patient for his or her ability to understand your instructions. When indicated, whether the problem is deafness, hearing impairment, visual impairment, a developmental challenge, English as a second language (ESL), dementia, cultural or religious concerns, or generational differences, you are responsible for helping the patient understand the procedure before beginning the phlebotomy. This may include help from the person who brought the patient to the office or from a translator. | ❏ | ❏ | ❏ |
| **6.** Put on gloves. | ❏ | ❏ | ❏ |
| **7.** Ask the patient or caregiver of an infant or small child about any dietary restrictions and the use of medications that increase bleeding time as appropriate. If a fasting or NPO specimen is required, ask the patient for the last time he or she ate or drank anything. | ❏ | ❏ | ❏ |
| **8.** Select the puncture site (the lateral portion of the tip of the middle or ring finger of the non-dominant hand or lateral curved surface of the heel of an infant). The puncture should be made in the fleshy central portion of the second or third finger, slightly to the side of center, and perpendicular to the grooves of the fingerprint. Perform heel puncture only on the plantar surface of the heel, medial to an imaginary line extending from the middle of the great toe to the heel, and lateral to an imaginary line drawn from between the fourth and fifth toes to the heel. Use the appropriate puncture device for the site selected. | ❏ | ❏ | ❏ |

**PSY** PROCEDURE 26-2 **Obtain a Blood Specimen by Capillary Puncture** (continued)

| | | | |
|---|---|---|---|
| 9. Make sure the site chosen is warm and not cyanotic or edematous. Gently massage the finger from the base to the tip or massage the infant's heel. | ❑ | ❑ | ❑ |
| 10. Grasp the finger firmly between your nondominant index finger and thumb, or grasp the infant's heel firmly with your index finger wrapped around the foot and your thumb wrapped around the ankle. Cleanse the selected area with 70% isopropyl alcohol and allow to air dry. | ❑ | ❑ | ❑ |
| 11. Hold the patient's finger or heel firmly and make a swift, firm puncture. Perform the puncture perpendicular to the whorls of the fingerprint or footprint. Dispose of the used puncture device in a sharps container. | ❑ | ❑ | ❑ |
| 12. Obtain the first drop of blood.<br>**a.** Wipe away the first drop of blood with dry gauze.<br>**b.** Apply pressure toward the site but do not milk the site. | ❑ | ❑ | ❑ |
| 13. Collect the specimen in the chosen container or slide. Touch only the tip of the collection device to the drop of blood. Blood flow is encouraged if the puncture site is held downward, and gentle pressure is applied near the site. Cap micro-collection tubes with the caps provided and mix the additives by gently tilting or inverting the tubes 8 to 10 times. | ❑ | ❑ | ❑ |
| 14. When collection is complete, apply clean gauze to the site with pressure. Hold pressure or have the patient or caregiver hold pressure until bleeding stops. Label the containers with the proper information. Do not apply a dressing to a skin puncture of an infant under age 2 years. Never release a patient until the bleeding has stopped. | ❑ | ❑ | ❑ |
| 15. **AFF** Thank the patient. Instruct the patient to leave the bandage in place at least 15 minutes if appropriate. | ❑ | ❑ | ❑ |
| 16. Properly care for or dispose of equipment and supplies. Clean the work area. Remove gloves and wash your hands. | ❑ | ❑ | ❑ |
| 17. Test, transfer, or store the specimen according to the medical office policy. | ❑ | ❑ | ❑ |
| 18. Log into the Electronic Medical Record (EMR) using your username and secure password OR obtain the paper medical record from a secure location and assure it is kept away from public access. Record the procedure noting the date, time, site of the capillary puncture, test results for CLIA-waived POC procedures or the name of the lab where the specimen was sent, and your name. | ❑ | ❑ | ❑ |
| 19. When finished, log out of the EMR and/or replace the paper medical record in an appropriate and secure location. | ❑ | ❑ | ❑ |

**PSY**   PROCEDURE 26-2   **Obtain a Blood Specimen by Capillary Puncture** (continued)

_____

_____

_____

_____

**CALCULATION**

Total Possible Points: _____

Total Points Earned: _____ Multiplied by 100 = _____ Divided by Total Possible Points = _____ %

**PASS   FAIL   COMMENTS:**
❑        ❑

Student's signature _____ Date _____

Partner's signature _____ Date _____

Instructor's signature _____ Date _____

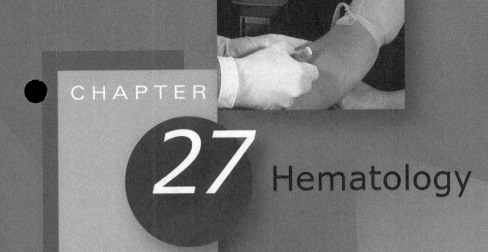

# CHAPTER

# *27* Hematology

## COG Cognitive Domain

1. Spell key terms
2. Define medical terms and abbreviations related to all body systems
3. List the parameters measured in the complete blood count and their normal ranges
4. State the conditions associated with selected abnormal complete blood count findings
5. Explain the functions of the three types of blood cells
6. Discuss the purpose of testing for the erythrocyte sedimentation rate
7. List the leukocytes seen normally in the blood and the functions of each.
8. Analyze charts, graphs, and/or tables in the interpretation of health care results

## PSY Psychomotor Domain

1. Perform hemoglobin determination (Procedure 27-1)
   a. Perform CLIA-waived hematology testing
   b. Instruct and prepare a patient for a procedure or treatment

   c. Coach patients appropriately considering cultural diversity, developmental life stage, communication barriers
   d. Document patient care accurately in the medical record
2. Perform microhematocrit determination (Procedure 27-2)
   a. Perform CLIA-waived hematology testing
   b. Instruct and prepare a patient for a procedure or treatment
   c. Coach patients appropriately considering cultural diversity, developmental life stage, communication barriers
   d. Document patient care accurately in the medical record

## AFF Affective Domain

1. Incorporate critical thinking skills when performing patient assessment.
2. Incorporate critical thinking skills when performing patient care.
3. Show awareness of a patient's concerns related to the procedure being performed.

4. Demonstrate empathy, active listening, nonverbal communication
5. Demonstrate respect for individual diversity including gender, race, religion, age, economic status, appearance.
6. Explain to a patient the rationale for performance of a procedure
7. Demonstrate sensitivity to patient rights
8. Protect the integrity of the medical record.

## ABHES Competencies

1. Apply principles of aseptic techniques and infection control
2. Collect and process specimens
3. Perform selected CLIA-waived tests that assist with diagnosis and treatment
4. Dispose of biohazardous waste
5. Practice standard precautions
6. Perform hematology testing
7. Document appropriately
8. Use methods of quality control
9. Adhere to OSHA compliance rules and regulations

Name: _____   Date: _____   Grade: _____

## **COG** MULTIPLE CHOICE

Circle the letter preceding the correct answer.

**1.** Leukocytosis is most likely caused by:
   **a.** chemical toxicity.
   **b.** inflammation.
   **c.** nutritional deficiencies.
   **d.** infection.
   **e.** anticoagulant therapy.

**2.** What indicates a vitamin $B_{12}$ deficiency?
   **a.** The presence of bands
   **b.** Macrocytosis or a mean corpuscular volume (MCV) of higher than 100 fL
   **c.** High numbers of lymphocytes
   **d.** Erythrocytes that lack a nucleus
   **e.** Microcytosis or a mean cell volume (MCV) less than 80 fL

**3.** Which white blood cells produce antibodies?
   **a.** Neutrophils
   **b.** Eosinophils
   **c.** Monocytes
   **d.** Lymphocytes
   **e.** Basophils

**4.** Where in the body are red blood cells produced?
   **a.** Bone marrow
   **b.** Fatty tissue
   **c.** Liver
   **d.** Kidney
   **e.** Heart

**5.** A parasitic infection is indicated by increased numbers of which leukocytes?
   **a.** Neutrophils
   **b.** Lymphocytes
   **c.** Eosinophils
   **d.** Monocytes
   **e.** Basophils

**6.** Which condition could be caused by chemotherapy?
   **a.** Anemia
   **b.** Folate deficiency
   **c.** Leukocytosis
   **d.** Monocytosis
   **e.** Thrombocytopenia

**7.** One symptom of vitamin K deficiency is:
   **a.** left shift.
   **b.** macrocytosis.
   **c.** prolonged ESR.
   **d.** prolonged PT.
   **e.** thrombocytosis.

**8.** ESR tests should be read:
   **a.** after 1 minute.
   **b.** at 15 minutes.
   **c.** at 30 minutes.
   **d.** at 60 minutes.
   **e.** at any time; the exact time is not important.

**9.** Microcytosis indicates:
   **a.** iron deficiency.
   **b.** the presence of gamma globins.
   **c.** liver disorders.
   **d.** $B_{12}$ deficiency.
   **e.** sickle cell anemia.

**10.** Patients with iron deficiencies should be encouraged to eat:
   **a.** dairy.
   **b.** fish.
   **c.** fruit.
   **d.** tofu.
   **e.** liver.

**11.** Erythropoiesis is driven by chemical signals from:
   **a.** the brain.
   **b.** the kidneys.
   **c.** the liver.
   **d.** the marrow.
   **e.** the spleen.

**12.** What is the most direct measurement of the blood's ability to deliver oxygen available in the CBC?
   **a.** RBC count
   **b.** Hemoglobin (Hgb) determination
   **c.** Hematocrit (Hct) determination
   **d.** Mean cell volume (MCV)
   **e.** Mean corpuscular hemoglobin (MCH)

**13.** A patient has a platelet count of 75,000/mm³. What visible symptom might appear on the patient?
  **a.** Circular rash
  **b.** Edema
  **c.** Bruising
  **d.** Sloughing of skin
  **e.** Hair loss

**14.** Which is a normal platelet count?
  **a.** 4,300 to 10,800 /μL
  **b.** 150,000 to 400,000/μL
  **c.** 4.2 to 5.4 million/μL
  **d.** 4.6 to 6.2 million/μL
  **e.** 27 to 31 million/μL

**15.** Which is the normal RBC count for women?
  **a.** 4,300 to 10,800/mm³
  **b.** 200,000 to 400,000/mm³
  **c.** 3.9 to 5.2 million/mm³
  **d.** 4.4 to 5.8 million/mm³
  **e.** 27 to 31 million/mm³

## ᴄᴏɢ MATCHING

Grade: _____

Match each key terms with the correct definition.

**Key Terms**

**16.** _____ band
**17.** _____ basophil
**18.** _____ complete blood count
**19.** _____ eosinophil
**20.** _____ erythrocytes
**21.** _____ erythrocyte indices
**22.** _____ erythrocyte sedimentation rate
**23.** _____ erythropoietin
**24.** _____ hematocrit
**25.** _____ hemoglobin
**26.** _____ leukocytes
**27.** _____ monocyte
**28.** _____ morphology
**29.** _____ neutrophil
**30.** _____ differential

**Definitions**

**a.** red blood cells or RBCs
**b.** white blood cells or WBCs
**c.** the functioning unit of the red blood cell
**d.** influences RBC production when it is released from the kidneys
**e.** cell type that makes up only a small portion of the number of white blood cells but are important parts of the body's immune response
**f.** cells active at the end of allergic responses and of parasite elimination
**g.** third most abundant leukocyte that engulfs foreign material
**h.** cell that defends against foreign invaders by engulfing them
**i.** a younger, less mature version of the neutrophils
**j.** contains WBC count and differential, RBC count, hemoglobin (Hgb) determination, hematocrit (Hct) determination, mean cell volume (MCV), mean corpuscular hemoglobin (MCH), mean corpuscular hemoglobin concentration (MCHC), and platelet count
**k.** WBCs are counted, tallied according to type, and reported as percentages
**l.** how cells appear under the microscope
**m.** percentage of RBCs in whole blood
**n.** measurements indicating the size of the RBC and how much hemoglobin the RBC holds
**o.** the rate in millimeters per hour at which RBCs settle out in a tube

## COG FILL IN THE BLANK

Grade: _____

List the parameters measured in the complete blood count and their normal ranges

| Test | Reference Interval |
|---|---|
| 31. | |
| 32. | |
| 33. | |
| 34. | |
| 35. | |
| 36. | |
| 37. | |
| 38. | |

## COG MATCHING

Grade: _____

Match each condition with the correct abnormal finding.

**Conditions**

39. _____ Increased bleeding

40. _____ Infection

41. _____ Anemia

42. _____ Low iron level

43. _____ Dehydration

44. _____ Liver disorders

45. _____ Microcytic anemia

**Abnormal Findings**

a. hemoglobin of 10 g/dL

b. thrombocytopenia

c. hematocrit of 55%

d. leukocytosis

e. macrocytosis

f. red cell count of 3.9 million/mL

g. MCH of 22 picograms/red cell

## COG IDENTIFICATION

Grade: _____

Indicate whether following cell function is that of a red blood cell (RBC), a white blood cell (WBC), or a platelet (PLA).

46. _____ body's primary defense against bacteria found inside cells

47. _____ contribute to inflammatory reactions

48. _____ critical elements of clot formation

49. _____ defend against foreign invaders by engulfing them

50. _____ important parts of the body's immune response

51. _____ may indicate any of a variety of acute conditions that necessitate immediate attention

52. _____ plug can arrest bleeding

53. _____ process the antigens and through a series of cell transitions, produce the antibodies that can now fight that antigen in the body

54. _____ release carbon dioxide that was picked up from the tissues and then bind oxygen

55. _____ signal of a viral infection

## COG FILL IN THE BLANK

Grade: _____

56. Fill in the blanks in this description of the purpose of testing for the erythrocyte sedimentation rate.

The reference interval for men under 50 years of age is _____, and for women under 50 years, it is _____. Elevations in ESR values are _____ _____ for any disorder but indicate either _____ or any other condition that causes increased or altered _____ in the blood (e.g., rheumatoid arthritis). The more _____ the RBCs fall in the column, the greater the degree of inflammation. The ESR can be elevated with infection and _____.

## COG FILL IN THE BLANK

Grade: _____

List the leukocytes seen normally in the blood and their functions.

| White Blood Cell Type | Function |
|---|---|
| 57. | |
| 58. | |
| 59. | |
| 60. | |
| 61. | |

## ⚙️ ANALYSIS

Grade: _____

**62.** Analyze a graph in the interpretation of health care results.

You have centrifuged your capillary collection tubes to calculate the patient's hematocrit.

**a.** Which tube is placed correctly on the measurement grid? (Place the letter identifying the correct tube in the space provided.) _____

**b.** How did you verify the correct placement of the tube on the grid?

_____

_____

_____

_____

**c.** Because this graph is difficult to interpret, estimate the approximate hematocrit for this patient. _____

## ⚙️ IDENTIFICATION

Grade: _____

Indicate whether each laboratory result is normal (N) or abnormal (A).

**63.** _____ Platelet count = 110,000/μL

**64.** _____ Hemoglobin in a male = 16 g/dL

**65.** _____ Hematocrit in a male = 49%

**66.** _____ MCV = 75 fL

**67.** _____ MCH = 29 picograms

**68.** _____ MCHC = 35 g/dL

**69.** _____ RBC in a female = 3.71 million/mm$^3$

**70.** _____ ESR = 5 mm/hour

## 🔶 CASE STUDY FOR CRITICAL THINKING

Grade: _____

**1.** Men over age 35 years and alcoholics frequently have difficulty absorbing vitamin B. What symptoms would you expect to see in an older male who drinks, and how could these be best addressed?

_____

_____

_____

_____

**2.** A trauma patient arrives in the hospital with extensive bleeding and internal injuries. The next day you are asked to run lab tests on this patient's bloodwork. How do you expect her results to differ from those of a healthy patient?

_____

_____

_____

_____

**3.** Your patient presents with a persistent headache and nasal congestion. His WBC count is normal, but the eosinophil count is high. What is the probable cause of the patient's complaint?

_____

_____

_____

_____

**4.** You are performing an erythrocyte sedimentation rate. After 60 minutes, you look at the tube to report the test results. You cannot determine the separation between the cells and the plasma. The separation is not straight, and there are bubbles in the tube. What are the probable causes of your problem?

_____

_____

_____

_____

**5.** You are preparing to collect a fingerstick specimen from your patient for a PT and INR test. The puncture wound continues to bleed heavily after the specimen is completed. How do you stop the bleeding and reassure the patient?

_____

_____

_____

_____

**6.** Explain the rationale used when explaining a procedure to the patient within parameters set by the physician.

_____

_____

_____

_____

**7.** Your patient arrives for a fingerstick hematocrit test. She tells you she is worried because she continues to have anemia and treatment does not seem to be helping. How do you show awareness of the patient's feelings within the scope of practice of a medical assistant?

_____

_____

_____

_____

## PSY PROCEDURE 27-1 Performing a Hemoglobin Determination

Name: _____ Date: _____ Time: _____ Grade: _____

**EQUIPMENT/SUPPLIES:** Hemoglobin meter, applicator sticks, whole blood, hand disinfectant, surface disinfectant, gloves, biohazard container, medical record

**STANDARDS:** Given the needed equipment and a place to work, the student will perform this skill with _____ % accuracy in a total of _____ minutes. *(Your instructor will tell you what the percentage and time limits will be before you begin practicing.)*

**KEY:** 4 = Satisfactory 0 = Unsatisfactory NA = This step is not counted

| PROCEDURE STEPS | SELF | PARTNER | INSTRUCTOR |
|---|---|---|---|
| **1.** Check the physician order and wash your hands. Put on personal protective equipment. | ❏ | ❏ | ❏ |
| **2.** Assemble the necessary equipment and supplies. Check the expiration dates on supplies that require this and ensure the equipment is in good working order. Perform any calibration or quality control procedures as required per the manufacturer and office policy and procedure. | ❏ | ❏ | ❏ |
| **3.** Take the equipment and supplies to the patient examination room or take the patient to the phlebotomy station if available. | ❏ | ❏ | ❏ |
| **4.** Greet and identify the patient and yourself including your title. Explain the procedure and put on gloves. | ❏ | ❏ | ❏ |
| **5.** Explain how you would respond to an elderly patient. | ❏ | ❏ | ❏ |
| **6.** Obtain a blood specimen from the patient by capillary puncture. | ❏ | ❏ | ❏ |
| **7.** Place well-mixed whole blood into the hemoglobinometer chamber or place the blood specimen on the reagent strip as described by the manufacturer. | ❏ | ❏ | ❏ |
| **8.** Slide the chamber into the hemoglobinometer or process the specimen using the CLIA-waived machine as required by the manufacturer. Slide the chamber into the hemoglobin meter. | ❏ | ❏ | ❏ |
| **9.** Record the hemoglobin level from the digital readout. | ❏ | ❏ | ❏ |
| **10.** Dispose of the contaminated supplies into a biohazard waste receptacle according to office policy and procedure. Clean the work area with surface disinfectant. Remove gloves and wash your hands. *Note:* This procedure may vary with the instrument. | ❏ | ❏ | ❏ |

| **PSY** PROCEDURE 27-1 | **Performing a Hemoglobin Determination** (continued) | | | |
|---|---|---|---|---|

| | | | |
|---|---|---|---|
| **11.** Log into the Electronic Medical Record (EMR) using your username and secure password OR obtain the paper medical record from a secure location and assure it is kept away from public access. Record the procedure, noting the date, time, site of the venipuncture, test results for CLIA-waived POC procedures or the name of the lab where the specimen was sent, and your name. | ❏ | ❏ | ❏ |
| **12.** When finished, log out of the EMR and/or replace the paper medical record in an appropriate and secure location. | ❏ | ❏ | ❏ |

_____

_____

_____

_____

_____

**CALCULATION**

Total Possible Points: _____

Total Points Earned: _____ Multiplied by 100 = _____ Divided by Total Possible Points = _____ %

**PASS    FAIL    COMMENTS:**
  ❏        ❏

Chart Documentation _____ Date _____

Student's signature _____ Date _____

Partner's signature _____ Date _____

Instructor's signature _____ Date _____

## FSY PROCEDURE 27-2 Performing a Microhematocrit Determination

Name: _____ Date: _____ Time: _____ Grade: _____

**EQUIPMENT/SUPPLIES:** Microcollection tubes, sealing clay, microhematocrit centrifuge, microhematocrit reading device, hand disinfectant, surface disinfectant, gloves, biohazard container, sharps container, medical record

**STANDARDS:** Given the needed equipment and a place to work, the student will perform this skill with _____ % accuracy in a total of _____ minutes. *(Your instructor will tell you what the percentage and time limits will be before you begin practicing.)*

**KEY:** 4 = Satisfactory     0 = Unsatisfactory          NA = This step is not counted

| PROCEDURE STEPS | SELF | PARTNER | INSTRUCTOR |
|---|---|---|---|
| **1.** Check the physician order and wash your hands. | ❑ | ❑ | ❑ |
| **2.** Assemble the equipment and supplies. Check the expiration dates on supplies that require this and ensure the equipment is in good working order. Perform any calibration or quality control procedures as required per the manufacturer and office policy and procedure. | ❑ | ❑ | ❑ |
| **3.** Take the equipment and supplies to the patient examination room or take the patient to the phlebotomy station if available. | ❑ | ❑ | ❑ |
| **4.** Greet and identify the patient and yourself including your title. Explain the procedure and put on gloves. | ❑ | ❑ | ❑ |
| **5.** Explain how you would respond to a patient who does not speak English as their first language. | ❑ | ❑ | ❑ |
| **6.** Obtain a blood specimen from the patient by capillary puncture. Draw blood into the capillary tube by holding the capillary microhemaocrit microhematocrit tube horizontally and touching one end of the tube to the blood coming from the capillary puncture. Allow the tube to fill to ¾ or the indicated mark on the capillary tube. | ❑ | ❑ | ❑ |
| **7.** With the microhematocrit tube in a horizontal position, place your forefinger over the opposite end of the tube, lift it up, and push the tube into the clay sealant with the blood side in the clay. | ❑ | ❑ | ❑ |
| **8.** Draw a second specimen in the same manner using a second microhematocrit tube. | ❑ | ❑ | ❑ |
| **9.** Place the tubes, clay-sealed end out, in the radial grooves of the microhematocrit centrifuge opposite each other. Put the lid on the grooved area and tighten by turning the knob clockwise. Close the centrifuge lid. Spin for 5 minutes or as directed by the centrifuge manufacturer. | ❑ | ❑ | ❑ |
| **10.** Remove the tubes from the centrifuge and read the results; instructions are printed on the device. Results should be within 5% of each other. Take the average and report as a percentage. | ❑ | ❑ | ❑ |

**FSY** P R O C E D U R E  2 7 - 2  **Performing a Microhematocrit Determination** (continued)

| | | | |
|---|---|---|---|
| **11.** Dispose of the contaminated supplies into a biohazard waste receptacle according to office policy and procedure. Clean the work area with surface disinfectant. Dispose of equipment and supplies appropriately. Remove gloves and wash your hands. *Note:* Some microhematocrit centrifuges have the scale printed in the machine at the radial grooves. | ❏ | ❏ | ❏ |
| **12.** Log into the Electronic Medical Record (EMR) using your username and secure password OR obtain the paper medical record from a secure location and assure it is kept away from public access. Record the procedure, noting the date, time, site of the venipuncture, test results for CLIA-waived POC procedures or the name of the lab where the specimen was sent, and your name. | ❏ | ❏ | ❏ |
| **13.** When finished, log out of the EMR and/or replace the paper medical record in an appropriate and secure location. | ❏ | ❏ | ❏ |

_____

_____

_____

_____

_____

**CALCULATION**

Total Possible Points: _____

Total Points Earned: _____ Multiplied by 100 = _____ Divided by Total Possible Points = _____ %

**PASS**  **FAIL**  **COMMENTS:**
  ❏      ❏

Chart Documentation _____ Date _____

Student's signature _____ Date _____

Partner's signature _____ Date _____

Instructor's signature _____ Date _____

# CHAPTER

## 28 Clinical Chemistry

# Learning Outcomes

## COG Cognitive Domain

1. Spell key terms
2. Define medical terms and abbreviations related to all body systems
3. List the common electrolytes and explain the relationship of electrolytes to acid–base balance
4. Describe the nonprotein nitrogenous compounds and name conditions with abnormal values
5. Identify CLIA-waived tests associated with common diseases
6. Analyze health care results as reported in graphs and tables
7. List and describe the substances commonly tested in liver function assessment
8. Describe glucose use and regulation and the purpose of the various glucose tests
9. Describe the function of cholesterol and other lipids and their correlation to heart disease

## PSY Psychomotor Domain

1. Perform blood glucose testing (Procedure 28-1)
2. Perform blood cholesterol testing (Procedure 28-2)

## AFF Affective Domain

1. Distinguish between normal and abnormal test results
2. Incorporate critical thinking skills when performing patient assessment
3. Incorporate critical thinking skills when performing patient care
4. Show awareness of a patient's concerns related to the procedure being performed.
5. Demonstrate empathy, active listening, nonverbal communication
6. Demonstrate respect for individual diversity including gender, race, religion, age, economic status, appearance

7. Explain to a patient the rationale for performance of a procedure
8. Demonstrate sensitivity to patient rights
9. Protect the integrity of the medical record

## ABHES Competencies

1. Perform CLIA-waived tests that assist with diagnosis and treatment
2. Perform chemistry testing
3. Perform routine maintenance of clinical equipment safely
4. Screen and follow up patient test results
5. Use standard precautions

Name: _____     Date: _____     Grade: _____

## OOG AFF MULTIPLE CHOICE

Circle the letter preceding the correct answer.

1. Sodium is used to maintain:
   a. blood urea nitrogen.
   b. TSH stimulation.
   c. waste materials.
   d. fluid balance.
   e. blood oxygen.

2. An enzyme is a(n):
   a. cell that speeds up the production of proteins.
   b. protein that quickens chemical reactions.
   c. chemical reaction that ionizes electrolytes.
   d. ion that has an electrical charge.
   e. specialized cell that deals with blood levels.

3. Which of the following is formed in the liver?
   a. Urea
   b. TSH
   c. Creatinine
   d. Lipase
   e. Amylase

4. A patient's blood work shows her amylase level is found to be high. What other substance would indicate pancreatitis?
   a. Hemoglobin
   b. Triglycerides
   c. Potassium
   d. Lipase
   e. Lipoproteins

5. The function of LDLs is to:
   a. transport enzymes to the heart and lungs.
   b. assist in the production of lipoproteins.
   c. store energy in adipose tissue.
   d. move cholesterol from the liver to arteries.
   e. carry cholesterol from the cells to the liver.

6. Chloride, bicarbonate, and electrolytes are all a part of:
   a. maintaining thyroid function.
   b. bile formation.
   c. red blood cell maturation.
   d. glucose storage.
   e. acid-base balance.

7. Women are screened for gestational diabetes:
   a. before they conceive.
   b. during the first month of pregnancy.
   c. during the second trimester.
   d. during the third trimester.
   e. after the baby is born.

8. When blood sugar levels go below 45 mg/dL, a person may experience:
   a. trembling.
   b. vomiting.
   c. diarrhea.
   d. chills.
   e. a high temperature.

9. If you are testing for a substance only found in serum, what should you do with a blood specimen?
   a. Use reagent strips to check for serum presence.
   b. Create a slide and analyze it under a microscope.
   c. Put the clotted specimen in the centrifuge to separate.
   d. Allow the specimen a few days to sit and separate.
   e. Run tests without doing anything to the specimen.

10. What is the body's normal blood pH range?
    a. 7.35 to 7.45
    b. 6.9 to 7.35
    c. 7.0 to 7.5
    d. 6.0 to 6.5
    e. 7.45 to 8.25

11. Hemoglobin A1C is tested to measure the patient's:
    a. fasting glucose.
    b. level of anemia.
    c. glucose that is attached to hemoglobin molecules.
    d. hemoglobin attached to glucose molecules.
    e. glucose tolerance.

12. Why is fasting required to accurately measure lipid levels?
    a. To evaluate how the body handles fat intake
    b. To establish fasting glucose levels
    c. To measure how much water is in body fat
    d. To limit the action of digestion on increasing lipid levels
    e. To lower HDL levels

## COG MATCHING

_____ Grade: _____

Match each key term with the correct definition.

**Key Terms**

13. _____ acidosis
14. _____ alkalosis
15. _____ amylase
16. _____ azotemia
17. _____ bicarbonate
18. _____ buffer systems
19. _____ creatinine
20. _____ electrolyte
21. _____ enzyme
22. _____ ions
23. _____ lipase
24. _____ lipoproteins
25. _____ urea

**Definitions**

a. electrically charged atoms
b. any substance-containing ions
c. an electrolyte with a negative charge formed when carbon dioxide dissolves in the blood
d. keeps the pH changes balanced
e. blood pH is below 7.4 caused by too much acid or too little base
f. blood pH is above 7.4 caused by too much base or too little acid
g. waste product from the body's metabolism of protein
h. abnormally high levels of nitrogen-containing compounds
i. a protein produced by living cells that speeds up chemical reactions
j. helps in the digestion of fats
k. breaks down starch into sugar
l. substances composed of lipids and proteins
m. a waste product from making the energy muscles use to function

## COG IDENTIFICATION

_____ Grade: _____

Identify the electrolyte by the stated relationship to acid–base balance.

| Relationship | Electrolyte |
|---|---|
| 26. It causes the most problems when its level is not stable | |
| 27. When the level is extremely low, it becomes difficult for the patient to breathe | |
| 28. Can be made unstable if the patient is suffering diabetic ketoacidosis and metabolic acidosis | |
| 29. Most important electrolyte used in acid–base balance | |
| 30. Low levels are seen in patients experiencing a long-term severe illness | |
| 31. Low levels result from inadequate absorption from the diet, GI losses, electrolyte shifts, and endocrine disorders | |
| 32. A waste product of oxygen metabolism | |

## COG IDENTIFY

Grade: _____

The following table lists nonprotein nitrogenous compound descriptions and associated abnormal conditions. Identify the nonprotein nitrogenous compound that is described.

| Compound | Description | Abnormal Condition |
|---|---|---|
| 33. | Waste product from the body's metabolism of protein | Dehydration, renal disease, inadequate dialysis, azotemia |
| 34. | Waste product from making the energy muscles use to function | Kidney damage, kidney disease |
| 35. | Waste product from breaking down protein | Gout, kidney stones |

## COG FILL IN THE BLANK

Grade: _____

36. _____ is elevated in MI.

37. Most of the CK is located in _____ muscle.

38. CK has three parts: _____, _____, and _____.

39. The _____ _____ is present in both cardiac and skeletal muscle.

40. The _____ _____ is much more specific for cardiac muscle.

41. The CKMB fraction increases within _____ following MI.

42. Troponins will begin to rise following MI within _____.

43. _____ levels are the best indicator of MI.

44. Rise in myoglobin can help to determine the _____ of an infarction.

45. Since inflammation is part of MI, _____ _____ is tested to predict the diagnosis of MI.

## COG SHORT ANSWER

Grade: _____

46. What is pancreatitis, and what two enzymes are elevated in this condition?

_____

_____

_____

_____

47. The pancreas makes two endocrine hormones that are important in diabetes. What are they and what do they do?

_____

_____

_____

_____

48. What are the two hormones that regulate the process of storing glucose as glycogen?

   a. _____

   b. _____

49. What glucose test is used for screening?

   _____

   _____

   _____

   _____

50. What glucose test is used to monitor insulin therapy?

   _____

   _____

   _____

   _____

51. How does hemoglobin A1C gives the physician a picture of the patient's glucose levels over the past 3 months?

   _____

   _____

   _____

   _____

52. What are the four fats measured in a lipid panel?

   _____

   _____

   _____

   _____

# AFF CASE STUDIES

Grade: _____

1. Your patient is a 5-year-old girl. The physician has ordered a fingerstick glucose. The mother of the child accompanied her to the office and gave the child a piece of candy because she thought her sugar might be low. You collect the specimen and run the test. The glucose is 60 mg/dL. You realize that you forgot to help the child wash her hands before the test. How could the result be affected if traces of the candy were on the child's finger? What do you do? What will make it difficult to do the right thing? How do you manage the parent and the child?

   _____

   _____

   _____

   _____

2. Your patient, Sarah Ingle, had an electrolyte panel ordered by Dr. Willis. The results are back from the reference lab, and your job includes screening test results. What are the reference intervals (normal ranges) you expect to see for these tests: sodium, potassium, chloride, and $CO_2$? You find that the potassium level is 6.0 mmol/L. What action do you take, and how do you document your action?

_____

_____

_____

_____

3. Melissa Woermann had a glucose tolerance test, and her results are noted on the graph is below. Her fasting glucose was 90 mg/dL. Estimate Ms. Woermann's 1/2-, 1-, 2-, and 3-hour glucose levels. What are the criteria proposed by the National Diabetes Data Group and the World Health Organization and endorsed by the ADA for a diagnosis of diabetes? Does it appear from the graph that Ms. Woermann could be diagnosed with diabetes?

_____

_____

_____

_____

## PSY PROCEDURE 28-1   **Perform Blood Glucose Testing**

Name: _____ Date: _____ Time: _____ Grade: _____

**EQUIPMENT/SUPPLIES:** Glucose meter, glucose reagent strips, control solutions, capillary puncture device, personal protective equipment, gauze, paper towel, adhesive bandage, lancet, alcohol pad, hand sanitizer, surface sanitizer, contaminated waste container.

**NOTE:** These are generic instructions for using a glucose meter. Refer to the manufacturer's instructions shipped with the meter for instructions specific to the instrument in use.

**STANDARDS:** Given the needed equipment and a place to work, the student will perform this skill with _____ % accuracy in a total of _____ minutes. *(Your instructor will tell you what the percentage and time limits will be before you begin practicing.)*

**KEY:**          4 = Satisfactory          0 = Unsatisfactory          NA = This step is not counted

| PROCEDURE STEPS | SELF | PARTNER | INSTRUCTOR |
|---|---|---|---|
| **1.** Check the physician order and wash your hands | ❑ | ❑ | ❑ |
| **2.** Assemble the equipment and supplies. | ❑ | ❑ | ❑ |
| **3.** Review the instrument manual for your glucose meter. | ❑ | ❑ | ❑ |
| **4.** Turn on the instrument and verify that it is calibrated. | ❑ | ❑ | ❑ |
| **5.** Perform the test on the quality control (QC) material. Record results. Determine whether QC is within control limits. If yes, proceed with patient testing. If no, take corrective action and recheck controls. Document corrective action. Proceed with patient testing when acceptable QC results are obtained. | ❑ | ❑ | ❑ |
| **6.** Remove one reagent strip, lay it on the paper towel, and recap the container. | ❑ | ❑ | ❑ |
| **7.** **AFF** Greet and identify the patient. Identify yourself including your title. Explain the procedure. Ask for and answer any questions. | ❑ | ❑ | ❑ |
| **8.** Have the patient wash hands in warm water. Put on gloves. | ❑ | ❑ | ❑ |
| **9.** Cleanse the selected puncture site (finger) with alcohol. | ❑ | ❑ | ❑ |
| **10.** Perform a capillary puncture and wipe away the first drop of blood. | ❑ | ❑ | ❑ |
| **11.** Turn the patient's hand palm down and gently squeeze the finger to form a large drop of blood. | ❑ | ❑ | ❑ |
| **12.** Bring the reagent strip up to the finger and touch the pad to the blood. **a.** Do not touch the finger. **b.** Completely cover the pad or fill the testing chamber with blood. | ❑ | ❑ | ❑ |

**PSY** PROCEDURE 28-1 **Perform Blood Glucose Testing** (continued)

| | | | |
|---|---|---|---|
| **13.** Insert the reagent strip into the analyzer.<br>  **a.** Meanwhile, apply pressure to the puncture wound with gauze.<br>  **b.** The meter will continue to incubate the strip and measure the reaction. | ❏ | ❏ | ❏ |
| **14.** The instrument reads the reaction strip and displays the result on the screen in mg/dL. | ❏ | ❏ | ❏ |
| **15.** Apply a small adhesive bandage to the patient's fingertip. | ❏ | ❏ | ❏ |
| **16.** Properly care for or dispose of equipment and supplies. | ❏ | ❏ | ❏ |
| **17.** Clean the work area. Remove personal protective equipment and wash your hands. | ❏ | ❏ | ❏ |
| **18.** Log into the Electronic Medical Record (EMR) using your username and secure password OR obtain the paper medical record from a secure location and assure it is kept away from public access. Record the procedure noting the date, time, test results for CLIA-waived POC procedure, and your name. | ❏ | ❏ | ❏ |
| **19.** When finished, log out of the EMR and/or replace the paper medical record in an appropriate and secure location. | ❏ | ❏ | ❏ |

_____

_____

_____

_____

**CALCULATION**

Total Possible Points: _____

Total Points Earned: _____ Multiplied by 100 = _____ Divided by Total Possible Points = _____ %

**PASS    FAIL    COMMENTS:**
  ❏          ❏

Student's signature _____ Date _____

Partner's signature _____ Date _____

Instructor's signature _____ Date _____

## PSY PROCEDURE 28-2    **Perform Blood Cholesterol Testing**

Name: _____  Date: _____  Time: _____  Grade: _____

**EQUIPMENT/SUPPLIES:** Cholesterol meter and supplies or test kit, control solutions, capillary puncture equipment or blood specimen as indicated by manufacturer, personal protective equipment, hand sanitizer, surface sanitizer, contaminated waste container

**NOTE:** These are generic instructions for using a cholesterol meter or test kit. Refer to the manufacturer's instructions shipped with the testing tool for instructions specific for the instrument in use.

**STANDARDS:** Given the needed equipment and a place to work, the student will perform this skill with _____ % accuracy in a total of _____ minutes. *(Your instructor will tell you what the percentage and time limits will be before you begin practicing.)*

**KEY:**         4 = Satisfactory              0 = Unsatisfactory              NA = This step is not counted

| PROCEDURE STEPS | SELF | PARTNER | INSTRUCTOR |
|---|---|---|---|
| **1.** Check the physician order and wash your hands. Wash your hands. | ❏ | ❏ | ❏ |
| **2.** Assemble the equipment and supplies. | ❏ | ❏ | ❏ |
| **3.** Review the instrument manual for your cholesterol meter or kit. Put on gloves. | ❏ | ❏ | ❏ |
| **4.** Perform the test on the quality control material. Record results. Determine whether QC is within control limits. If yes, proceed with patient testing. If no, take corrective action and recheck controls. Document corrective action. Proceed with patient testing when acceptable QC results are obtained. | ❏ | ❏ | ❏ |
| **5.** Follow manufacturer's instructions in using a patient specimen obtained by capillary puncture or from evacuation a tube. | ❏ | ❏ | ❏ |
| **6.** Follow manufacturer's instructions for applying the sample to the testing device and inserting the device into the analyzer. Record results. | ❏ | ❏ | ❏ |
| **7.** Properly care for or dispose of equipment and supplies. | ❏ | ❏ | ❏ |
| **8.** Clean the work area. Remove personal protective equipment and wash your hands. | ❏ | ❏ | ❏ |
| **9.** AFF Log into the Electronic Medical Record (EMR) using your username and secure password OR obtain the paper medical record from a secure location and assure it is kept away from public access. Record the procedure noting the date, time, test results for CLIA-waived POC procedure, and your name. | ❏ | ❏ | ❏ |
| **10.** When finished, log out of the EMR and/or replace the paper medical record in an appropriate and secure location. | ❏ | ❏ | ❏ |

**PSY** PROCEDURE 28-2 **Perform Blood Cholesterol Testing**
(continued)

_____

_____

_____

_____

**CALCULATION**

Total Possible Points: _____

Total Points Earned: _____ Multiplied by 100 = _____ Divided by Total Possible Points = _____ %

**PASS**  **FAIL**  **COMMENTS:**
 ❏       ❏

Student's signature _____ Date _____

Partner's signature _____ Date _____

Instructor's signature _____ Date _____

CHAPTER

# 29 Microbiology and Immunology

## Learning Outcomes

### COG Cognitive Domain

1. Spell the key terms
2. Define medical terms and abbreviations related to all body systems
3. Identify CLIA-waived tests associated with common diseases
4. Analyze health care results as reported in graphs and tables
5. List major types of infectious agents
6. Discuss quality control issues related to handling microbiological specimens

### PSY Psychomotor Domain

1. Collect throat specimens (Procedure 29-1)
2. Collect nasopharyngeal specimens (Procedure 29-2)
3. Collect wound specimens (Procedure 29-3)
4. Collect stool specimen for ova and parasites (Procedure 29-4)

5. Inoculate a culture (Procedure 29-5)
6. Perform mononucleosis testing (Procedure 29-6)
7. Perform HCG pregnancy testing (Procedure 29-7)
8. Perform rapid group A strep testing (Procedure 29-8)

### AFF Affective Domain

1. Incorporate critical thinking skills when performing patient assessment.
2. Incorporate critical thinking skills when performing patient care.
3. Show awareness of a patient's concerns related to the procedure being performed.
4. Demonstrate empathy, active listening, nonverbal communication
5. Demonstrate respect for individual diversity including gender, race, religion, age, economic status, appearance.

6. Explain to a patient the rationale for performance of a procedure
7. Demonstrate sensitivity to patient rights
8. Protect the integrity of the medical record.

### ABHES Competencies

1. Document patient care
2. Perform quality control measures
3. Screen test results
4. Perform immunology testing
5. Practice standard precautions
6. Perform handwashing
7. Obtain specimens for microbiology testing
8. Perform CLIA-waived microbiology testing
9. Perform pregnancy test
10. Perform strep A test
11. Instruct patients in the collection of fecal specimens

Name: _____ Date: _____ Grade: _____

## ⬤⬤⬤ MULTIPLE CHOICE

Circle the letter preceding the correct answer.

1. A pregnancy test detects the presence of:
   a. RhoGAM.
   b. protein.
   c. genetic defects.
   d. HCG.
   e. immune-D serum.

2. Where will the medical assistant find instructions for the correct method for collecting and transporting microbiology specimens?
   a. The test requisition
   b. The patient's chart
   c. A textbook
   d. The laboratory's procedure manual
   e. The physician

3. The result of a laboratory test is only as good as:
   a. the physician.
   b. the medical assistant.
   c. the laboratory equipment.
   d. the specimen.
   e. the patient.

4. Sensitivity tests monitor the microorganism's sensitivity to:
   a. RhoGAM.
   b. antibiotics.
   c. light.
   d. color.
   e. other microorganisms.

5. Bacilli can be recognized by their:
   a. globular shape.
   b. long, spiral shape.
   c. rigid, spiral shape.
   d. comma-like shape.
   e. rod-like shape.

6. Why is it important to transport or process microbiology specimens as soon as possible?
   a. So the organism does not die
   b. To get the results to the physician as soon as possible
   c. To start the patient on antibiotics
   d. So normal flora bacteria do not overgrow the specimen
   e. So the infection will not be contagious

7. Antigens are:
   a. proteins the body creates as a defensive measure against foreign substances.
   b. foreign substances that cause the body to initiate a defense response.
   c. reagents used to detect the presence of antibodies in a culture dish.
   d. media used to create an environment suitable for organism growth.
   e. dyes used to stain cells that are prepared for microscope slides.

8. How long is a culture incubated to verify there is no bacterial growth from the specimen?
   a. 8 hours
   b. 12 hours
   c. 24 hours
   d. 48 hours
   e. 72 hours

9. Which of these conditions is caused by a virus?
   a. Impetigo
   b. Tuberculosis
   c. Strep throat
   d. Ringworm
   e. Rabies

10. What organism results in Lyme disease?
    a. *Clostridium botulinum*
    b. *Clostridium tetani*
    c. *Chlamydia trachomatis*
    d. *Borrelia burgdorferi*
    e. Bacteroides species

## COG MATCHING

Grade: _____

Match each key term with the correct definition.

**Key Terms**

11. _____ aerobes
12. _____ agar
13. _____ anaerobes
14. _____ bacilli (singular, bacillus)
15. _____ broth
16. _____ cocci
17. _____ culture
18. _____ differential stain
19. _____ diplococci
20. _____ Gram negative
21. _____ Gram positive
22. _____ Gram stain
23. _____ immunity
24. _____ isolate
25. _____ media
26. _____ mordant
27. _____ mycology
28. _____ normal flora
29. _____ nosocomial infection
30. _____ resistant
31. _____ sensitive
32. _____ sensitivity testing
33. _____ smear
34. _____ specificity
35. _____ spirochetes

**Definitions**

a. bacteria that require oxygen to survive
b. bacteria that require a lack of oxygen to survive
c. an environment that provides the bacteria a place to grow
d. liquid media in glass tubes or bottles
e. the most widely used solid media
f. stain used to identify differences in cells
g. bacteria that will lose the purple color in a Gram stain and stain red with safranin
h. bacteria that are spherical in shape
i. spherical cocci in pairs
j. bacteria that are rod shaped and are usually aerobic
k. bacteria that normally live on the body and do not cause disease
l. infections acquired in a medical setting
m. a mixture of substances that nourish pathogens to support the growth of microorganisms for identification
n. materials that have been dried on a glass slide
o. primary stain used in the microbiology lab
p. bacteria that keep the purple color even when exposed to the ethyl alcohol step of the Gram stain
q. Gram's iodine is one, used to fix the dye on the smear to make it more intense
r. long, spiral, flexible organisms
s. testing to determine if an antibiotic will be effective in stopping growth of an organism (also identifies antibiotics that will not stop the growth of an organism)
t. organisms that are inhibited by an antimicrobial agent
u. organisms that grow even in the presence of an antimicrobial agent
v. separate from any other microorganisms present
w. the study of fungi
x. the response to foreign bodies
y. an antibody combines with only one antigen

## COG MATCHING

Grade: _____

Match each category of organisms to its description.

**Key Terms**

36. _____ rickettsia
37. _____ chlamydia
38. _____ mycoplasma
39. _____ viruses
40. _____ eukaryotic microorganisms
41. _____ fungi
42. _____ protozoa and helminths
43. _____ nematodes
44. _____ arthropods
45. _____ prokaryotic cells

**Definitions**

a. cause blindness, pneumonia, and lymphogranuloma venereum
b. cause atypical pneumonia and genitourinary infections
c. cells with no nuclei including bacteria
d. lice, fleas, and ticks
e. not susceptible to antibiotics and are extremely difficult to treat
f. pathogens include the groups fungi, algae, protozoans, and parasites
g. small organisms like bacteria with the potential to produce disease in susceptible hosts
h. parasites
i. round worm parasites
j. organisms carried on arthropods

## COG FILL IN THE BLANK

Grade: _____

**46.** If the specimen is not fully and correctly labeled, the laboratory may be required to _____ of the specimen.

**47.** Use the appropriate _____ media, if indicated.

**48.** Transport specimens at the _____ temperature.

**49.** Correct steps are important for keeping the pathogen _____ until it reaches the laboratory.

**50.** Handle all specimens as if _____. Follow standard precautions.

## COG AFF IDENTIFICATION

Grade: _____

**51.** List six autoimmune diseases.

_____

_____

_____

_____

_____

**52.** How is an antigen–antibody reaction identified?

_____

_____

_____

_____

**53.** Using immunoassay test kits, how is a positive antigen indicated?

_____

_____

_____

_____

**54.** How does the medical assistant assure the accuracy of testing with an immunoassay test kit?

_____

_____

_____

_____

**55.** How are normal and abnormal test results identified using immunoassay test kits?

_____

_____

_____

_____

**COG** **AFF** **CASE STUDIES**

_____ Grade: _____

**1.** Your patient is concerned that others may learn of the results to her laboratory test. How do you reassure her this will not happen?

_____

_____

_____

_____

**2.** Your patient is a little girl being evaluated for sexual abuse by her father. How do you display sensitivity to the mother regarding her distress about collecting the specimens? How do you explain the rationale for performing the procedure? How do you demonstrate your awareness of the patient's concerns regarding perceptions related to the procedure being performed? How do you demonstrate empathy in communicating with the patient and her mother? How will you use active listening skills in this scenario? How will you demonstrate awareness of the territorial boundaries of the child and her mother? How will you demonstrate your sensitivity to the situation?

_____

_____

_____

_____

**3.** Your patient is a 7-year-old boy. The doctor has ordered a throat culture, and the boy is obviously apprehensive. How do you use body language and other nonverbal skills to reassure the boy and also collect a good specimen?

_____

_____

_____

_____

## PSY PROCEDURE 29-1 Collect a Throat Specimen

Name: _____ Date: _____ Time: _____ Grade: _____

**EQUIPMENT/SUPPLIES:** Tongue blade, light source, sterile specimen container and swab, personal protective equipment, hand sanitizer, surface sanitizer and biohazard transport bag (if to be sent to the laboratory for analysis)

**STANDARDS:** Given the needed equipment and a place to work, the student will perform this skill with _____ % accuracy in a total of _____ minutes. *(Your instructor will tell you what the percentage and time limits will be before you begin practicing.)*

**KEY:**         4 = Satisfactory             0 = Unsatisfactory             NA =This step is not counted

| PROCEDURE STEPS | SELF | PARTNER | INSTRUCTOR |
|---|---|---|---|
| **1.** Check the physician order. Wash your hands. | ❑ | ❑ | ❑ |
| **2.** Assemble the equipment and supplies. | ❑ | ❑ | ❑ |
| **3.** Apply gloves. | ❑ | ❑ | ❑ |
| **4.** **AFF** Greet and identify the patient. Identify yourself including your title. Explain the rationale of the performance of the collection to the patient. | ❑ | ❑ | ❑ |
| **5.** **AFF** If the patient is hearing impaired, you need to speak clearly and distinctly in front of the patient's face. | ❑ | ❑ | ❑ |
| **6.** **AFF** Use active listening to observe patients' body language and detect a lack of understanding of instructions. Obtain assistance when you realize that you are not able to communicate with the patient. | ❑ | ❑ | ❑ |
| **7.** **AFF** Allow time for the adult or patient or caregiver if the patient is a child to ask questions. | ❑ | ❑ | ❑ |
| **8.** **AFF** Display empathy for the patient and family. | ❑ | ❑ | ❑ |
| **9.** Have the patient sit with a light source directed the throat. | ❑ | ❑ | ❑ |
| **10.** Carefully remove the sterile swab from the container. If performing both the rapid strep and culture or confirming negative results with a culture, swab with two swabs held together. | ❑ | ❑ | ❑ |
| **11.** Have the patient say "Ah" as you press down on the midpoint of the tongue with the tongue depressor. If the tongue depressor is placed too far forward, it will not be effective; if it is placed too far back, the patient will gag unnecessarily. | ❑ | ❑ | ❑ |
| **12.** Swab the mucous membranes, especially the tonsillar area, the crypts, and the posterior pharynx in a "figure 8" motion. Turn the swab to expose all of its surfaces to the membranes. Avoid touching teeth, sides of mouth, and uvula. | ❑ | ❑ | ❑ |

## PROCEDURE 29-1 Collect a Throat Specimen (continued)

| | | | |
|---|---|---|---|
| **13.** Maintain the tongue depressor position while withdrawing the swab from the patient's mouth. | ❏ | ❏ | ❏ |
| **14.** Follow the instructions on the specimen container for transferring the swab or processing the specimen in the office using a commercial kit. Label the specimen with the patient's name, the date and time of collection, and the origin of the material. | ❏ | ❏ | ❏ |
| **15.** Properly dispose of the equipment and supplies in a biohazard waste container. Remove PPE and wash your hands. | ❏ | ❏ | ❏ |
| **16.** Route the specimen or store it appropriately until routing can be completed. | ❏ | ❏ | ❏ |
| **17.** **AFF** Log into the Electronic Medical Record (EMR) using your username and secure password OR obtain the paper medical record from a secure location and assure it is kept away from public access. Record the procedure noting the date, time, specimen collected, and specimen processing procedure (i.e., sent to lab, tested using CLIA-waived test, etc.). Include your name and title according to office policy and procedure. | ❏ | ❏ | ❏ |

_____

_____

_____

_____

**CALCULATION**

Total Possible Points: _____

Total Points Earned: _____ Multiplied by 100 = _____ Divided by Total Possible Points = _____ %

**PASS   FAIL   COMMENTS:**
❏        ❏

Student's signature _____ Date _____

Partner's signature _____ Date _____

Instructor's signature _____ Date _____

**PSY** PROCEDURE 29-2 **Collect a Nasopharyngeal Specimen**

**Name:** _____ **Date:** _____ **Time:** _____ **Grade:** _____

**EQUIPMENT/SUPPLIES:** Penlight, tongue blade, sterile flexible wire swab, transport media, personal protective equipment, hand sanitizer, surface sanitizer and biohazard transport bag (if to be sent to the laboratory for analysis)

**STANDARDS:** Given the needed equipment and a place to work, the student will perform this skill with _____ % accuracy in a total of _____ minutes. *(Your instructor will tell you what the percentage and time limits will be before you begin practicing.)*

**KEY:** 4 = Satisfactory      0 = Unsatisfactory      NA = This step is not counted

| PROCEDURE STEPS | SELF | PARTNER | INSTRUCTOR |
|---|---|---|---|
| **1.** Check the physician order. Wash your hands. | ❑ | ❑ | ❑ |
| **2.** Assemble the equipment and supplies. | ❑ | ❑ | ❑ |
| **3.** Put on gloves. | ❑ | ❑ | ❑ |
| **4.** **AFF** Greet and identify the patient. Greet and identify the patient. Identify yourself including your title. Explain the rationale of the performance of the collection to the patient. | ❑ | ❑ | ❑ |
| **5.** **AFF** If your patient is developmentally challenged, have the individual who transported the patient to the office assist you with communicating with the patient. The developmentally challenged patient may struggle if you have to proceed with something he or she does not understand. Have another medical assistant available to help you should extra support be necessary to support the patient. | ❑ | ❑ | ❑ |
| **6.** **AFF** Leave time for the adult patient or caregiver of a child to ask questions. | ❑ | ❑ | ❑ |
| **7.** Position the patient with his head tilted back. | ❑ | ❑ | ❑ |
| **8.** Using a penlight, inspect the nasopharyngeal area. | ❑ | ❑ | ❑ |
| **9.** Gently pass the swab through the nostril and into the nasopharynx, keeping the swab near the septum and floor of the nose. Rotate the swab quickly and then remove it and place it in the transport media. | ❑ | ❑ | ❑ |
| **10.** Label the specimen with the patient's name, the date and time of collection, and the origin of repeated. | ❑ | ❑ | ❑ |
| **11.** Properly dispose of the equipment and supplies in a biohazard waste container. Remove gloves and wash your hands. | ❑ | ❑ | ❑ |

**PSY** PROCEDURE 29-2 **Collect a Nasopharyngeal Specimen**
(continued)

| | | | |
|---|---|---|---|
| **12.** Route the specimen or store it appropriately until routing can be completed. | ❑ | ❑ | ❑ |
| **13.** **AFF** Log into the Electronic Medical Record (EMR) using your username and secure password OR obtain the paper medical record from a secure location and assure it is kept away from public access. Record the procedure noting the date, time, specimen collected, and specimen processing procedure (i.e., sent to lab, tested using CLIA-waived test, etc.). Include your name and title according to office policy and procedure. | ❑ | ❑ | ❑ |

_____

_____

_____

_____

**CALCULATION**

Total Possible Points: _____

Total Points Earned: _____ Multiplied by 100 = _____ Divided by Total Possible Points = _____ %

**PASS   FAIL   COMMENTS:**
  ❑       ❑

Student's signature _____ Date _____

Partner's signature _____ Date _____

Instructor's signature _____ Date _____

## PSY PROCEDURE 29-3 Collect a Wound Specimen

Name: _____ Date: _____ Time: _____ Grade: _____

**EQUIPMENT/SUPPLIES:** Sterile swab, transport media, personal protective equipment, hand sanitizer, surface sanitizer, and biohazard transport bag (if to be sent to the laboratory for analysis)

**STANDARDS:** Given the needed equipment and a place to work, the student will perform this skill with _____ % accuracy in a total of _____ minutes. *(Your instructor will tell you what the percentage and time limits will be before you begin practicing.)*

**KEY:** 4 = Satisfactory 0 = Unsatisfactory NA =This step is not counted

| PROCEDURE STEPS | SELF | PARTNER | INSTRUCTOR |
|---|---|---|---|
| **1.** Check the physician order. Wash your hands. | ❏ | ❏ | ❏ |
| **2.** Assemble the equipment and supplies. | ❏ | ❏ | ❏ |
| **3.** Put on gloves. | ❏ | ❏ | ❏ |
| **4.** **AFF** Greet and identify the patient. Identify yourself including your title. Explain the procedure. | ❏ | ❏ | ❏ |
| **5.** **AFF** If your patient is struggling with dementia, be prepared to gently repeat yourself as necessary until you have collected your specimen. You may have to physically adjust your patient as necessary to collect the specimen. Be gentle but remember to speak to the patient as an adult. | ❏ | ❏ | ❏ |
| **6.** If dressing is present, remove it and dispose of it in biohazard container. Assess the wound by observing color, odor, and amount of exudate. Remove contaminated gloves and put on clean gloves. | ❏ | ❏ | ❏ |
| **7.** Use the sterile swab to sample the exudate. Saturate swab with exudate, avoiding the skin edge around the wound. | ❏ | ❏ | ❏ |
| **8.** Place swab back into container and crush the ampule of transport medium. | ❏ | ❏ | ❏ |
| **9.** Label the specimen with the patient's name, the date and time of collection, and the origin of specimen. | ❏ | ❏ | ❏ |
| **10.** Route the specimen or store it appropriately until routing can be completed. | ❏ | ❏ | ❏ |
| **11.** Clean the wound and apply a sterile dressing using sterile technique. | ❏ | ❏ | ❏ |
| **12.** Properly dispose of the equipment and supplies in a biohazard waste container. Remove gloves and wash your hands. | ❏ | ❏ | ❏ |

**PSY** P R O C E D U R E   2 9 - 3    **Collect a Wound Specimen** (continued)

| | | | |
|---|---|---|---|
| **13. AFF** Log into the Electronic Medical Record (EMR) using your username and secure password OR obtain the paper medical record from a secure location and assure it is kept away from public access. Record the procedure noting the date, time, specimen collected, and specimen processing procedure (i.e., sent to lab, tested using CLIA-waived test, etc.). Include your name and title according to office policy and procedure. | ❏ | ❏ | ❏ |

_____

_____

_____

_____

**CALCULATION**

Total Possible Points: _____

Total Points Earned: _____ Multiplied by 100 = _____ Divided by Total Possible Points = _____ %

**PASS    FAIL    COMMENTS:**
  ❏         ❏

Student's signature _____ Date _____

Partner's signature _____ Date _____

Instructor's signature _____ Date _____

**FSY** PROCEDURE 29-4 **Collect a Stool Specimen for Ova and Parasites**

Name: _____ Date: _____ Time: _____ Grade: _____

**EQUIPMENT/SUPPLIES:** Specimen container dependent on test ordered (sterile container or Para-Pak collection system for C&S or ova and parasites, tongue blade or wooden spatula, personal protective equipment, hand sanitizer, surface sanitizer, and biohazard transport bag

**STANDARDS:** Given the needed equipment and a place to work, the student will perform this skill with _____ % accuracy in a total of _____ minutes. *(Your instructor will tell you what the percentage and time limits will be before you begin practicing.)*

**KEY:** 4 = Satisfactory 0 = Unsatisfactory NA = This step is not counted

| PROCEDURE STEPS | SELF | PARTNER | INSTRUCTOR |
|---|---|---|---|
| **1.** Check the physician order. Wash your hands. | ❏ | ❏ | ❏ |
| **2.** Assemble the equipment and supplies. | ❏ | ❏ | ❏ |
| **3.** **AFF** Greet and identify the patient. Identify yourself including your title. Explain the procedure. | ❏ | ❏ | ❏ |
| **4.** **AFF** If you are in a significantly different generation than the patient, you will need to take extra precautions with communication. First, remember that collecting a stool specimen is embarrassing for most patients. Watch the patient's facial expressions to note if he or she is understanding your instructions. This is one of the times you may find that your patient does not understand professional terminology. | ❏ | ❏ | ❏ |
| **5.** When obtaining a stool specimen for C&S or ova and parasites, the patient should collect an amount of the first and last portion of the stool after the bowel movement with the wooden spatula or tongue blade and place it in the specimen container without contaminating the outside of the container. Fill Para-Pak until fluid reaches "fill" line, and recap the container. | ❏ | ❏ | ❏ |
| **6.** Upon receipt of the specimen, you should put on gloves and place the specimen into the biohazard bag for transport to the reference laboratory. Fill out a laboratory requisition slip to accompany the specimen. | ❏ | ❏ | ❏ |
| **7.** Label the specimen with the patient's name, the date and time of collection, and the origin of the specimen. | ❏ | ❏ | ❏ |
| **8.** Transport the specimen to the laboratory or store the specimen as directed. Refer to the laboratory procedure manual since some samples require refrigeration, others are kept at room temperature, and some must be placed in an incubator at a laboratory as soon as possible after collecting. | ❏ | ❏ | ❏ |

## PSY PROCEDURE 29-4 Collect a Stool Specimen for Ova and Parasites (continued)

| | | | |
|---|---|---|---|
| **9.** Properly dispose of the equipment and supplies in a biohazard waste container. Remove gloves and wash your hands. | ❑ | ❑ | ❑ |
| **10.** **AFF** Log into the Electronic Medical Record (EMR) using your username and secure password OR obtain the paper medical record from a secure location and assure it is kept away from public access. Record the procedure noting the date, time, specimen collected, and specimen processing procedure (i.e., sent to lab, tested using CLIA-waived test, etc.). Include your name and title according to office policy and procedure. | ❑ | ❑ | ❑ |

_____

_____

_____

_____

**CALCULATION**

Total Possible Points: _____

Total Points Earned: _____ Multiplied by 100 = _____ Divided by Total Possible Points = _____ %

**PASS    FAIL    COMMENTS:**
  ❑        ❑

Student's signature _____ Date _____

Partner's signature _____ Date _____

Instructor's signature _____ Date _____

## ᶠᴿˢʸ PROCEDURE 29-5 **Inoculating a Culture**

Name: _____ Date: _____ Time: _____ Grade: _____

**EQUIPMENT/SUPPLIES:** Specimen on a swab, permanent laboratory marker, Petri dish, gloves, hand sanitizer, surface sanitizer, biohazard waste container.

**STANDARDS:** Given the needed equipment and a place to work, the student will perform this skill with _____ % accuracy in a total of _____ minutes. *(Your instructor will tell you what the percentage and time limits will be before you begin practicing.)*

**KEY:**  4 = Satisfactory  0 = Unsatisfactory  NA = This step is not counted

| PROCEDURE STEPS | SELF | PARTNER | INSTRUCTOR |
|---|---|---|---|
| **1.** Check the physician order. Wash your hands. | ❏ | ❏ | ❏ |
| **2.** Assemble the equipment and supplies, checking expiration dates. | ❏ | ❏ | ❏ |
| **3.** Put on gloves. | ❏ | ❏ | ❏ |
| **4.** Label the medium side of the plate with the permanent marker. Include the patient's name, identification number, source of specimen, time collected, time inoculated, your initials, and date. | ❏ | ❏ | ❏ |
| **5.** Remove the Petri plate from the cover (the Petri plate is always stored with the cover down), and place the cover on the work surface with the opening up. Do not open the cover unnecessarily. | ❏ | ❏ | ❏ |
| **6.** Using a rolling and sliding motion, streak the specimen swab across one fourth of the plate, starting at the top and working to the center. Dispose of the swab in a biohazard container. The specimen will spread in gradually thinning colonies of bacteria. | ❏ | ❏ | ❏ |
| **7.** Use a disposable sterile loop and turn the plate a quarter turn from its previous position. Pass the loop a few times in the original inoculum, and then across the medium approximately a quarter of the surface of the plate. Do not enter the originally streaked area after the first few sweeps. | ❏ | ❏ | ❏ |
| **8.** Turn the plate another quarter turn so that now it is 180 degrees to the original smear. Working in the previous manner, draw the loop at right angles through the most recently streaked area. Again, do not enter the originally streaked area after the first few sweeps. | ❏ | ❏ | ❏ |
| **9.** Place the prepared culture with the lid on in an incubator per office policy and procedure. Properly dispose of the contaminated supplies in a biohazard waste container. Remove gloves and wash your hands. | ❏ | ❏ | ❏ |

## PSY PROCEDURE 29-5 Inoculating a Culture (continued)

| | | | |
|---|---|---|---|
| 10. **AFF** Log into the Electronic Medical Record (EMR) using your username and secure password OR obtain the paper medical record from a secure location and assure it is kept away from public access. Record the procedure noting the date, time, specimen collected, and specimen processing procedure (i.e., sent to lab, tested using CLIA-waived test, etc.). Include your name and title according to office policy and procedure. | ❑ | ❑ | ❑ |

_____

_____

_____

_____

**CALCULATION**

Total Possible Points: _____

Total Points Earned: _____ Multiplied by 100 = _____ Divided by Total Possible Points = _____ %

**PASS   FAIL   COMMENTS:**
❑        ❑

Student's signature _____ Date _____

Partner's signature _____ Date _____

Instructor's signature _____ Date _____

**PSY** PROCEDURE 29-6 **Mononucleosis Testing**

Name: _____ Date: _____ Time: _____ Grade: _____

**EQUIPMENT/SUPPLIES:** Patient's labeled specimen (whole blood, plasma, or serum, depending on the kit), CLIA-waived mononucleosis kit (slide or test strip) with instructions, stopwatch or timer, gloves, hand sanitizer, surface sanitizer, biohazard waste container

**STANDARDS:** Given the needed equipment and a place to work, the student will perform this skill with _____ % accuracy in a total of _____ minutes. *(Your instructor will tell you what the percentage and time limits will be before you begin practicing.)*

**KEY:**        4 = Satisfactory              0 = Unsatisfactory                NA = This step is not counted

| PROCEDURE STEPS | SELF | PARTNER | INSTRUCTOR |
|---|---|---|---|
| 1. Check the physician order. Wash your hands. | ❏ | ❏ | ❏ |
| 2. Assemble the equipment and ensure that the materials in the kit and the patient specimen are at room temperature. | ❏ | ❏ | ❏ |
| 3. Label the test pack or test strip (depending on type of kit) with the patient's name, positive control, and negative control. Use one test pack or strip per patient and control. | ❏ | ❏ | ❏ |
| 4. Put on gloves. Collect the blood specimen according to the test kit instructions. | ❏ | ❏ | ❏ |
| 5. Perform the test as directed. Also, perform the controls according to the kit instructions. | ❏ | ❏ | ❏ |
| 6. Set timer for the period indicated in package insert. | ❏ | ❏ | ❏ |
| 7. Read reaction results at the end of time period. | ❏ | ❏ | ❏ |
| 8. Verify the results of the controls before documenting the patient's results. Log the QC and patient information on any worksheet required per the office policy and procedure manual. | ❏ | ❏ | ❏ |
| 9. Properly dispose of the equipment and supplies in a biohazard waste container. | ❏ | ❏ | ❏ |
| 10. Remove your gloves and wash your hands | ❏ | ❏ | ❏ |
| 11. **AFF** Log into the Electronic Medical Record (EMR) using your username and secure password OR obtain the paper medical record from a secure location and assure it is kept away from public access. Record the procedure noting the date, time, specimen collected, and specimen processing procedure (i.e., sent to lab, tested using CLIA-waived test, etc.). Include your name and title according to office policy and procedure. | ❏ | ❏ | ❏ |

**PSY** PROCEDURE 29-6    **Mononucleosis Testing** (continued)

_____

_____

_____

_____

**CALCULATION**

Total Possible Points: _____

Total Points Earned: _____ Multiplied by 100 = _____ Divided by Total Possible Points = _____ %

**PASS    FAIL    COMMENTS:**
  ❏          ❏

Student's signature _____ Date _____

Partner's signature _____ Date _____

Instructor's signature _____ Date _____

**PSY** PROCEDURE 29-7 **Perform HCG Pregnancy Test**

Name: _____ Date: _____ Time: _____ Grade: _____

**EQUIPMENT/SUPPLIES:** Patient's labeled urine specimen, CLIA-waived HCG pregnancy kit, timer, gloves, hand sanitizer, surface sanitizer, biohazard waste container

**STANDARDS:** Given the needed equipment and a place to work, the student will perform this skill with _____ % accuracy in a total of _____ minutes. *(Your instructor will tell you what the percentage and time limits will be before you begin practicing.)*

**KEY:** 4 = Satisfactory 0 = Unsatisfactory NA = This step is not counted

| PROCEDURE STEPS | SELF | PARTNER | INSTRUCTOR |
|---|---|---|---|
| **1.** Check the physician order. Wash your hands. | ❏ | ❏ | ❏ |
| **2.** Assemble the equipment and supplies. | ❏ | ❏ | ❏ |
| **3.** Verify the urine specimen is for the correct patient. Verify the HCG test kit is not expired. | ❏ | ❏ | ❏ |
| **4.** Perform the test as indicated on the test kit package insert directions. | ❏ | ❏ | ❏ |
| **5.** Sample the positive and negative controls as directed for the test kit. | ❏ | ❏ | ❏ |
| **6.** Set the timer for running the test as indicated in package insert. | ❏ | ❏ | ❏ |
| **7.** Read reaction results at the end of prescribed period of time. | ❏ | ❏ | ❏ |
| **8.** Verify the results of the controls before documenting the patient's results. Log controls and patient information on the worksheet according to office policy and procedure. | ❏ | ❏ | ❏ |
| **9.** Properly dispose of the equipment and supplies in a biohazard waste container. | ❏ | ❏ | ❏ |
| **10.** Remove gloves and wash your hands. | ❏ | ❏ | ❏ |
| **11. AFF** Log into the Electronic Medical Record (EMR) using your username and secure password OR obtain the paper medical record from a secure location and assure it is kept away from public access. Record the procedure noting the date, time, specimen collected, and specimen processing procedure (i.e., sent to lab, tested using CLIA-waived test, etc.). Include your name and title according to office policy and procedure. | ❏ | ❏ | ❏ |

**PSY** PROCEDURE 29-7 **Perform HCG Pregnancy Test** (continued)

_____

_____

_____

_____

**CALCULATION**

Total Possible Points: _____

Total Points Earned: _____ Multiplied by 100 = _____ Divided by Total Possible Points = _____ %

**PASS** **FAIL** **COMMENTS**:
❏ ❏

Student's signature _____ Date _____

Partner's signature _____ Date _____

Instructor's signature _____ Date _____

## PSY PROCEDURE 29-8 Rapid Group A Strep Testing

Name: _____ Date: _____ Time: _____ Grade: _____

**EQUIPMENT/SUPPLIES:** CLIA-waived Group A strep kit (controls may be included, depending on the kit), timer, gloves, hand sanitizer, surface sanitizer, biohazard waste container

**STANDARDS:** Given the needed equipment and a place to work, the student will perform this skill with _____ % accuracy in a total of _____ minutes. *(Your instructor will tell you what the percentage and time limits will be before you begin practicing.)*

**KEY:**          4 = Satisfactory          0 = Unsatisfactory          NA = This step is not counted

| PROCEDURE STEPS | SELF | PARTNER | INSTRUCTOR |
|---|:---:|:---:|:---:|
| **1.** Check the physician order. Wash your hands. | ❑ | ❑ | ❑ |
| **2.** Assemble the equipment including the test kit. Familiarize yourself with the instructions before obtaining the specimen and performing the procedure. | ❑ | ❑ | ❑ |
| **3.** Apply gloves. Obtain the throat specimen from the patient after assuring you have the correct patient. Use the swabs that come with the testing kit. | ❑ | ❑ | ❑ |
| **4.** Follow the directions for the kit. Add the appropriate reagents and drops to each of the extraction appropriate test tubes. | ❑ | ❑ | ❑ |
| **5.** Insert the patient swab into the labeled extraction tube. | ❑ | ❑ | ❑ |
| **6.** Add the appropriate controls to each of the labeled extraction tubes. | ❑ | ❑ | ❑ |
| **7.** Set the timer for the appropriate time to ensure accuracy. | ❑ | ❑ | ❑ |
| **8.** Add the appropriate reagent and drops to each of the extraction tubes. | ❑ | ❑ | ❑ |
| **9.** Use the swab to mix the reagents. Then press out any excess fluid on the swab against the inside of the tube. | ❑ | ❑ | ❑ |
| **10.** Add the appropriate number of drops from the well-mixed extraction tube to the sample window of the strep A test unit. Do the same for each control. | ❑ | ❑ | ❑ |
| **11.** Set the timer for the time indicated in the kit package insert. | ❑ | ❑ | ❑ |
| **12.** Depending on the test kit used, a positive result may appear as a line in the result window within 5 minutes. The strep A test unit or strip has an internal control; if a line appears in the control window, the test is valid. | ❑ | ❑ | ❑ |
| **13.** Read a negative result at exactly 5 minutes or as per the test kit instructions to avoid a false negative. | ❑ | ❑ | ❑ |
| **14.** Verify results of the controls before recording or reporting test results. Log the controls and the patient's information on the worksheet according to office policy and procedure. | ❑ | ❑ | ❑ |

| **FSY** PROCEDURE 29-8 **Rapid Group A Strep Testing** (continued) | | | |
|---|---|---|---|
| **15.** Properly dispose of the equipment and supplies in a biohazard waste container. | ❑ | ❑ | ❑ |
| **16.** Remove your gloves and wash your hands. | ❑ | ❑ | ❑ |
| **17.** **AFF** Log into the Electronic Medical Record (EMR) using your username and secure password OR obtain the paper medical record from a secure location and assure it is kept away from public access. Record the procedure noting the date, time, specimen collected, and specimen processing procedure (i.e., sent to lab, tested using CLIA-waived test, etc.). Include your name and title according to office policy and procedure. | ❑ | ❑ | ❑ |

_____

_____

_____

_____

**CALCULATION**

Total Possible Points: _____

Total Points Earned: _____ Multiplied by 100 = _____ Divided by Total Possible Points = _____ %

**PASS   FAIL   COMMENTS:**
   ❑        ❑

Student's signature _____ Date _____

Partner's signature _____ Date _____

Instructor's signature _____ Date _____

# CHAPTER

# 30 Urinalysis

## Learning Outcomes

### COG Cognitive Domain

1. Spell key terms
2. Define medical terms and abbreviations related to all body systems
3. Identify CLIA-waived tests associated with common diseases
4. Analyze health care results as reported in graphs and tables
5. Describe the methods of urine collection
6. List and explain the physical and chemical properties of urine
7. Describe the components that can be found in urine sediment and describe their relationships to chemical findings
8. Explain the procedures included in urine drug testing including chain of custody.

### PSY Psychomotor Domain

1. Obtaining a clean-catch midstream urine specimen (Procedure 30-1)
2. Perform a physical and chemical urinalysis (Procedure 30-2)

### AFF Affective Domain

1. Incorporate critical thinking skills when performing patient assessment
2. Incorporate critical thinking skills when performing patient care
3. Show awareness of a patient's concerns related to the procedure being performed
4. Demonstrate empathy, active listening, nonverbal communication
5. Demonstrate respect for individual diversity including gender, race, religion, age, economic status, appearance
6. Explain to a patient the rationale for performance of a procedure
7. Demonstrate sensitivity to patient rights
8. Protect the integrity of the medical record

### ABHES Competencies

1. Use standard precautions
2. Screen and follow up patient test results
3. Perform selected CLIA-waived urinalysis testing that assist with diagnosis and treatment
4. Instruct patients in the collection of a clean-catch, midstream urine specimen

Name: _____   Date: _____   Grade: _____

## ⬤⬤⬤ MULTIPLE CHOICE

Circle the letter preceding the correct answer.

**1.** What color will be observed on the reagent pad if nitrites are present in urine?
   **a.** Blue
   **b.** Pink
   **c.** Red
   **d.** Yellow
   **e.** Green

**2.** Why is a 24-hour collection a better indicator of some values than a random specimen?
   **a.** Some substances are excreted with diurnal variation.
   **b.** Some bacteria do not develop fully for 24 hours.
   **c.** A 24-hour collection gives the physician a more accurate idea of the patient's diet.
   **d.** The higher the volume of urine tested, the more accurate the result.
   **e.** Some substances are excreted only at night.

**3.** The most common method of urine collection is:
   **a.** suprapubic aspiration.
   **b.** clean-catch midstream.
   **c.** random specimen.
   **d.** first morning void.
   **e.** postprandial specimen.

**4.** Which of these conditions may cause a patient's urine to smell sweet?
   **a.** Urinary tract infection
   **b.** Kidney infection
   **c.** Diabetes
   **d.** Dehydration
   **e.** Yeast infection

**5.** What is the specific gravity of a normal urine specimen?
   **a.** 0.900–1.000
   **b.** 1.001–1.035
   **c.** 1.100–1.135
   **d.** 1.500–1.635
   **e.** 2.000–2.001

**6.** What is the expected pH range for urine?
   **a.** 3.0–6.0
   **b.** 4.0–7.0
   **c.** 5.0–8.0
   **d.** 6.0–9.0
   **e.** 7.0–10.0

**7.** Increased numbers of epithelial cells in urine may indicate that:
   **a.** there is an irritation, such as inflammation, somewhere in the urinary system.
   **b.** the patient is overly hydrated.
   **c.** the patient is pregnant.
   **d.** the urine sample has sat for too long before examination.
   **e.** the testing was not performed correctly.

**8.** Which group of people is most at risk of developing galactosuria?
   **a.** Teenagers
   **b.** Newborns
   **c.** Pregnant women
   **d.** Older adult men
   **e.** Older adult women

**9.** A patient with uric acid crystals in his or her urine possibly has:
   **a.** osteoarthritis
   **b.** a urinary tract infection.
   **c.** hepatitis.
   **d.** gout.
   **e.** gallbladder cancer.

**10.** Which of these should be included on a chain-of-custody document?
   **a.** The results of the urine test.
   **b.** The reason for the chain of custody.
   **c.** Instructions for providing a specimen.
   **d.** The date the specimen was collected or transferred.
   **e.** The volume of urine in the specimen.

**11.** Which biological pigment gives urine its color?
   **a.** Melanin
   **b.** Hemoglobin
   **c.** Myoglobin
   **d.** Beta-carotene
   **e.** Urochrome

**12.** Why is a urine test preferable to a blood test for a routine drug test?
   **a.** It is less invasive and has national standards for testing.
   **b.** It is less expensive.
   **c.** There is less risk of contamination.
   **d.** It requires less equipment.
   **e.** A urine specimen will stay fresh longer than a blood sample.

**13.** Strenuous physical exercise may cause:
  **a.** increased protein in urine.
  **b.** decreased amounts of epithelial cells.
  **c.** increased quantities of ketones.
  **d.** increased glucose in urine.
  **e.** decreased concentration of phosphates.

**14.** Cast formation occurs in the:
  **a.** liver.
  **b.** small intestine.
  **c.** bladder.
  **d.** pathways of the digestive tract.
  **e.** tubules of the nephron.

## COG MATCHING

Grade: _____

Match each key term with the correct definition.

**Key Terms**

**15.** _____ bacteriuria
**16.** _____ bilirubinuria
**17.** _____ chain-of-custody procedure
**18.** _____ conjugated bilirubin
**19.** _____ diurnal variation
**20.** _____ glycosuria
**21.** _____ hematuria
**22.** _____ ketoacidosis
**23.** _____ ketones
**24.** _____ microhematuria
**25.** _____ proteinuria
**26.** _____ pyuria
**27.** _____ sediment
**28.** _____ specific gravity
**29.** _____ supernatant
**30.** _____ turbidity

**Definitions**

**a.** variation during a 24-hour period
**b.** presence of glucose in the urine
**c.** group of chemicals produced during fat and protein metabolism
**d.** blood in urine
**e.** bilirubin in the urine
**f.** the written policy for maintaining an accurate written record to track the possession, handling, and location of samples and data from collection through reporting
**g.** too much ketone in the blood and urine
**h.** type of bilirubin that does dissolve into the bloodstream
**i.** presence of bacteria in urine
**j.** cloudiness
**k.** reflects the ability of the kidney to concentrate or dilute the urine
**l.** increased amounts of protein in the urine
**m.** white cells in urine
**n.** the amount of blood in the urine is so small that the color of the specimen is not affected
**o.** the button of cells and other particulate matter that collects in the bottom of the tube when centrifuging a urine specimen
**p.** urine above the sediment when the tube of urine is centrifuged

## COG MATCHING

Grade: _____

Match each type of specimen collection method with the correct description.

**Collection Methods**

**31.** _____ Random specimen
**32.** _____ First morning void
**33.** _____ Postprandial specimen
**34.** _____ Clean-catch urine specimen
**35.** _____ Suprapubic aspiration
**36.** _____ 24-hour collection

**Descriptions**

**a.** A specimen that is collected 2 hours after a patient consumes a meal
**b.** A specimen that is voided into a sterile container after the urinary meatus and surrounding skin have been cleansed
**c.** A specimen that is formed over a 6- to 8-hour period
**d.** A specimen voided into a clean, dry container
**e.** A specimen consisting of all urine voided over a 24-hour period
**f.** A specimen that is taken directly from the bladder using a needle

## COG AFF MATCHING

_____ Grade: _____

Read the descriptions of five patients. From your knowledge of chemical and physical properties of urine, match each patient with Dr. Philbin's diagnosis.

**Patients**

37. _____ Mr. Himmel is a 45-year-old father who is suffering from a stomach upset. His urine sample has a high specific gravity and is a deep yellow color.
38. _____ Mrs. Lincoln is a 33-year-old receptionist. Her urine sample is alkaline and contains leukocytes and a small amount of blood.
39. _____ Mr. Ackton is a 60-year-old gardener. His urine sample is dark yellow and contains bilirubin.
40. _____ Mrs. Franklin is a 75-year-old widow. Her urine sample has a high specific gravity, contains a high level of glucose, and is very acidic.
41. _____ Mrs. Taylor is a 29-year-old surgeon who has little time to exercise. She has a large quantity of protein in her urine.
42. _____ Ms. Sheffield is a 20-year-old college student. She has a large quantity of ketones in her urine.
43. _____ Mrs. Kotizky is a 43-year-old homemaker. Her urine is cloudy with a positive nitrite reaction.
44. _____ Mr. Kubik is a 67-year-old retiree. He has been a heavy drinker for 30 years and has increased his intake of alcohol significantly since retirement. His urine has an elevated urobilinogen level.

**Diagnoses**

a. Urinary tract infection
b. Diabetes mellitus
c. Dieting until protein breakdown
d. Pregnancy
e. Cirrhosis
f. Dehydration
g. Hepatitis

## COG IDENTIFICATION

_____ Grade: _____

List and explain the physical and chemical properties of urine.

| PROPERTY | EXPLANATION |
| --- | --- |
| 45. | |
| 46. | |
| 47. | |
| 48. | |
| 49. | |
| 50. | |
| 51. | |
| 52. | |
| 53. | |
| 54. | |
| 55. | |

## COG MATCHING

Grade: _____

As a medical assistant, you'll probably be asked to assist in the urinalysis procedure. Study the list of tasks below and decide which duties are within the scope of practice for a medical assistant. Place a check in the "Yes" box for tasks you would complete yourself and in the "No" box for tasks that would be completed by another member of the team.

| Task | Yes | No |
| --- | --- | --- |
| **56.** Prepare urine sediment for microscopic examination. | | |
| **57.** Instruct patient on how to provide urine sample. | | |
| **58.** Perform microscopic examination of urine sediment. | | |
| **59.** Ensure that urine is tested or refrigerated within the correct time period. | | |
| **60.** Use suprapubic aspiration to collect a urine sample. | | |
| **61.** Perform confirmatory tests on urine samples. | | |
| **62.** Label specimens for clear identification. | | |
| **63.** Assemble equipment needed for urinalysis procedures. | | |

## COG AFF SHORT ANSWER

Grade: _____

**64.** A patient provides a sample of urine for testing. You know that everyone in the medical office is extremely busy and that it will not get tested for at least 3 hours. What should you do with the sample?

_____

_____

_____

_____

**65.** A patient gives a urine sample at 11 AM, and the physician asks you to perform a urinalysis on the specimen. Before you can analyze the sample, there is an emergency situation in the office, and you become distracted. At 2 PM you remember that the specimen has still not been analyzed, and it is in a container that is not refrigerated. What should you do? Explain your answer.

_____

_____

_____

**66.** A severely underweight 15-year-old girl comes into the physician's office to give a urine sample. The test reveals that there are ketones in the patient's urine. Explain why this may be the case.

_____

_____

_____

_____

**67.** A urine sample has tested positive for protein. What procedure would be used to confirm the reagent strip reaction? Explain how the procedure works.

_____

_____

_____

_____

**68.** You are instructing your female patient how to collect a clean-catch specimen. She says she has diarrhea and is concerned about contaminating the specimen. How do you instruct her to collect the specimen? How do you use this information to coach her about her ongoing general health?

_____

_____

_____

_____

## OOG IDENTIFICATION

Grade: _____

The chain-of-custody process is used to ensure that all urine specimens are identifiable and have not been tampered with. Read the scenarios in the table below and decide whether the correct chain-of-custody patient screening and procedure have taken place. Place a check mark in the appropriate box.

| Scenario | Correct Procedure Used | Possibility of Contamination |
|---|---|---|
| **69.** A patient faxes you her identification in advance to save time at the reception desk. | | |
| **70.** A patient enters the bathroom to give a urine sample wearing jeans and a T-shirt. | | |
| **71.** A patient selects his own sealed collection container from the cupboard. | | |
| **72.** A patient empties her pockets and enters the bathroom to give a urine sample while carrying a bottle of water. | | |
| **73.** A patient enters the bathroom to give a urine sample wearing cargo pants, a sweater, and a baseball cap. | | |
| **74.** A patient washes and dries his hands before entering the bathroom to give a urine sample. | | |
| **75.** A patient has forgotten her ID, but an employer representative verifies that she is the correct person. | | |

**COG PSY AFF CASE STUDIES** _____ Grade: _____

1. One of your patients needs to provide a 24-hour urine collection. She has never done it before and is unsure how to carry out the procedure. Write the patient a list of instructions, explaining what she should do in order to provide an accurate specimen. Why is it important that the patient thoroughly understands and complies with your instructions?

_____

_____

_____

_____

2. You instruct a patient how to perform a clean-catch midstream urine specimen. When you test the sample, you discover that the urine is cloudy, with a pH level of 7.5, and contains traces of red blood cells, nitrites, and leukocytes. How would you document this information on the patient's chart?

_____

_____

_____

_____

3. A patient asks you what types of drugs can be detected in urine. Two weeks later, the same patient comes into the office to provide a urine specimen. He appears to be acting suspiciously and you think you see him pick up a bottle before entering the bathroom. What should you do next?

_____

_____

_____

_____

4. Your patient, Sharon, has never collected a clean-catch midstream urine specimen before. As you describe the procedure, her facial expressions begin to change, and she becomes aloof. What are the possible reasons for her response? How do you adjust your behavior to support the patient's understanding of the procedure? How do you demonstrate empathy to this patient?

_____

_____

_____

_____

5. The results have come back from the testing laboratory on a drug screen test you collected. The medical assistant working in the front office comes to you asking about this patient's test results. She says the woman babysits her children after school, and she wants to know if the patient is taking drugs. How do you respond?

_____

_____

_____

| **PSY** PROCEDURE 30-1 | **Obtaining a Clean-Catch Midstream Urine Specimen** |
|---|---|

Name: _____  Date: _____  Time: _____  Grade: _____

**EQUIPMENT/SUPPLIES:** Sterile urine container labeled with patient's name, cleansing towelettes (two for males, three for females), gloves if you are to assist patient, hand sanitizer

**STANDARDS:** Given the needed equipment and a place to work, the student will perform this skill with _____ % accuracy in a total of _____ minutes. *(Your instructor will tell you what the percentage and time limits will be before you begin practicing.)*

**KEY:**          4 = Satisfactory              0 = Unsatisfactory              NA = This step is not counted

| PROCEDURE STEPS | SELF | PARTNER | INSTRUCTOR |
|---|---|---|---|
| **1.** Check the physician order. Wash your hands. | ❏ | ❏ | ❏ |
| **2.** Assemble the equipment and supplies. | ❏ | ❏ | ❏ |
| **3.** **AFF** Identify the patient and explain the procedure. Identify yourself including your title. Explain the rationale for performance of a procedure to the patient. | ❏ | ❏ | ❏ |
| **4.** **AFF** If the patient is hearing impaired, you may need to face the person and speak clearly, not loudly. You should have an easy-to-read instruction guide for the patient to follow and point out where there are questions. If the patient can sign and you cannot, have someone proficient in sign language assist you in instructing the patient. | ❏ | ❏ | ❏ |
| **5.** If the patient is to perform the procedure, provide the necessary supplies. | ❏ | ❏ | ❏ |
| **6.** Have the patient perform the procedure properly with the following instructions:<br>**A.** Male patients:<br>  **i.** If uncircumcised, expose the glans penis by retracting the foreskin, then clean the meatus with an antiseptic wipe. The glans should be cleaned in a circular motion away from the meatus. A new wipe should be used for each cleaning sweep.<br>  **ii.** Keeping the foreskin retracted, initially void a few seconds into the toilet or urinal.<br>  **iii.** Bring the sterile container into the urine stream and collect a sufficient amount (about 30 to 60 mL). Instruct the patient to avoid touching the inside of the container with the penis.<br>  **iv.** Finish voiding into the toilet or urinal.<br>**B.** Female patients:<br>  **i.** Kneel or squat over the toilet bowl. Spread the labia minora widely to expose the meatus. Using an antiseptic wipe, cleanse on either side of the meatus, and then cleanse the meatus itself. Use a wipe only once in a sweep from the anterior to the posterior surfaces, and then discard it.<br>  **ii.** Keeping the labia separated, initially void a few seconds into the toilet.<br>  **iii.** Bring the sterile container into the urine stream and collect a sufficient amount (about 30 to 60 mL).<br>  **iv.** Finish voiding into the toilet. | ❏ | ❏ | ❏ |

**PSY** P R O C E D U R E 3 0 - 1 **Obtaining a Clean-Catch Midstream Urine Specimen** (continued)

| | | | |
|---|---|---|---|
| **7.** Cap the filled container and place it in a designated area. | ❏ | ❏ | ❏ |
| **8.** Transport the specimen in a biohazard container for testing or test the urine specimen according to office policy and procedure. | ❏ | ❏ | ❏ |
| **9.** Properly care for or dispose of equipment and supplies. Clean the work area. Remove gloves and wash your hands. | ❏ | ❏ | ❏ |
| **10.** **AFF** Log into the Electronic Medical Record (EMR) using your username and secure password OR obtain the paper medical record from a secure location and assure it is kept away from public access. Record the procedure noting the date, time, specimen collected, and specimen processing procedure (i.e., sent to lab, tested using CLIA-waived test, etc.). Include your name and title according to office policy and procedure. | ❏ | ❏ | ❏ |

_____

_____

_____

_____

_____

**CALCULATION**

Total Possible Points: _____

Total Points Earned: _____ Multiplied by 100 = _____ Divided by Total Possible Points = _____ %

**PASS    FAIL    COMMENTS:**
  ❏        ❏

Student's signature _____ Date _____

Partner's signature _____ Date _____

Instructor's signature _____ Date _____

## FSY PROCEDURE 30-2 Perform a Physical and Chemical Urinalysis

Name: _____ Date: _____ Time: _____ Grade: _____

**EQUIPMENT/SUPPLIES:** Gloves, patient's labeled urine specimen, chemical reagent strips (such as Multistix™ or Chemstrip™), hand disinfectant, biohazard waste container

**STANDARDS:** Given the needed equipment and a place to work, the student will perform this skill with _____ % accuracy in a total of _____ minutes. *(Your instructor will tell you what the percentage and time limits will be before you begin practicing.)*

**KEY:** 4 = Satisfactory   0 = Unsatisfactory   NA = This step is not counted

| PROCEDURE STEPS | SELF | PARTNER | INSTRUCTOR |
|---|---|---|---|
| **1.** Check the physician order. Wash your hands. | ❏ | ❏ | ❏ |
| **2.** Assemble the equipment. | ❏ | ❏ | ❏ |
| **3.** Put on gloves. | ❏ | ❏ | ❏ |
| **4.** Verify the name on the specimen container and the physician order. | ❏ | ❏ | ❏ |
| **5.** In bright light against a white background, examine the color of the specimen. The most common colors are straw (very pale yellow), yellow, dark yellow, and amber (brown–yellow). | ❏ | ❏ | ❏ |
| **6.** Determine clarity. Hold the specimen container in front of a surface with print such as blank print. If you see the image or print clearly (not obscured), record as clear. If you see the image or print but they are not well delineated, record as hazy. If you cannot see the image or print at all, record as cloudy. | ❏ | ❏ | ❏ |
| **7.** Remove the reagent strip from its container and replace the lid to prevent deterioration of the strips by humidity. | ❏ | ❏ | ❏ |
| **8.** Immerse the reagent strip in the urine completely, immediately remove it, sliding the edge of the strip along the lip of the container to remove excess urine. Pooling of excess urine on the dipstick causes cross-contamination among the reactions, possibly obscuring accurate color detection. | ❏ | ❏ | ❏ |
| **9.** Start your stopwatch or timer immediately. | ❏ | ❏ | ❏ |
| **10.** Compare the reagent pads to the color chart, determining results at the intervals stated by the manufacturer. Example: Glucose is read at 30 seconds. To determine results, examine that pad 30 seconds after dipping and compare with color chart for glucose. | ❏ | ❏ | ❏ |
| **11.** Read all reactions at the times indicated and record the results. | ❏ | ❏ | ❏ |

**PSY** PROCEDURE 30-2 **Perform a Physical and Chemical Urinalysis** (continued)

| | | | |
|---|---|---|---|
| **12.** Discard the reagent strips in the biohazard receptacle. Discard urine. | ❏ | ❏ | ❏ |
| **13.** Remove your gloves and wash your hands. | ❏ | ❏ | ❏ |
| **14.** **AFF** Log into the Electronic Medical Record (EMR) using your username and secure password OR obtain the paper medical record from a secure location and assure it is kept away from public access. Record the procedure noting the date, time, specimen collected, and specimen processing procedure (i.e., sent to lab, tested using CLIA-waived test, etc.). Include your name and title according to office policy and procedure. | ❏ | ❏ | ❏ |

_____

_____

_____

_____

**CALCULATION**

Total Possible Points: _____

Total Points Earned: _____ Multiplied by 100 = _____ Divided by Total Possible Points = _____ %

**PASS**  **FAIL**   **COMMENTS**:
  ❏        ❏

Student's signature _____ Date _____

Partner's signature _____ Date _____

Instructor's signature _____ Date _____

# 3

## Career
## Strategies

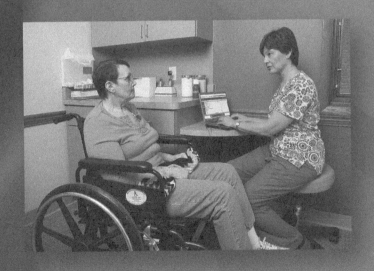

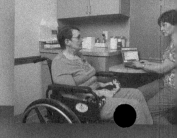

CHAPTER

# *31* Capstone Activities: Applying What You Have Learned

Working in a medical office means dealing with situations as they arise in a professional, nonjudgmental manner. Your education and training has provided you with the information and tools to give you the clinical skills necessary to function in the medical office, but you must also use professional judgment and critical thinking when making decisions and interacting with patients, families, and staff. This chapter will provide opportunities for you to practice using professional judgment and critical thinking skills as would a practicing medical assistant in the physician office. Each section, containing documentation and active learning exercises, provides real-life scenarios followed by questions for you to think about and respond to according to directions from your instructor. Be sure to read carefully and, as usual, have fun!

## COG PSY DOCUMENTATION

Grade: _____

## CHAPTER 1

A 40-year-old woman comes to talk to the physician because she would like to start a new exercise routine and change her diet to lose 15 pounds. She is currently 25 pounds overweight, so this is a great idea and a good move toward healthy living. The physician asks you to discuss exercise and diet changes with the patient. Write a narrative patient note describing your interaction with the patient to include in her chart.

_____

_____

_____

_____

## CHAPTER 2

Although you always take care to protect yourself from exposure to biohazardous materials, you spill a tube of a patient's blood while performing hematology testing. You have a fresh cut on your hand that came into contact with the blood. Following your office's exposure control plan, you clean up and then document the incident. What information will you make sure to include in your report?

_____

_____

_____

_____

## CHAPTER 3

You are interviewing a young patient during an assessment when you notice that he has three small burn marks on his arm. The burns are round and less than a centimeter in diameter. When you ask the patient about the burns, he suddenly turns solemn and avoids answering the question. You suspect that the patient has been abused. How should you document this interaction on the patient's chart?

_____

_____

_____

_____

## CHAPTER 4

How should you record an axillary temperature, and why is it important to record it differently from other temperatures?

_____

_____

_____

# CHAPTER 5

A 45-year-old patient comes into the office for a routine physical examination. He has high blood pressure and is considerably overweight. The patient asks you for advice on healthy eating, and you provide him with several pamphlets and advise him to cut down on fatty foods. How would you document this interaction in the patient's chart?

_____

_____

_____

_____

# CHAPTER 6

The autoclave in your office has not been working properly. It takes twice as long for the steam in the autoclave to reach an adequate temperature for sterilization. You realize that this may affect daily procedures within the office and could lead to bigger problems with the autoclave. You decide to have the autoclave serviced by a professional. What documentation will be needed in connection with this service request?

_____

_____

_____

_____

# CHAPTER 7

A patient is recovering from a Caesarian section and returns to the office to have her staples removed. The physician asks you to remove the staples and apply adhesive skin closures over the incision site. The patient asks you when the strips should be removed, and you tell her that they should fall off on their own within 10 days. How would you document this interaction in the patient's chart?

_____

_____

_____

_____

# CHAPTER 8

The physician has prescribed a patient 250 mg of amoxicillin for an ear infection. The patient should take this medication three times a day by mouth for 9 days. Write a note to document this in the patient's chart.

_____

_____

_____

_____

## CHAPTER 9

The physician has asked you to prepare an administration of gr iii Haldol IM for a patient. The dispenser is labeled in milligrams. How do you convert this dosage to the metric system, and how many milligrams of Haldol should you dispense? Write the preparation as a chart note.

_____

_____

_____

_____

## CHAPTER 10

You have just taken a chest x-ray to rule out pneumonia. Write a narrative note detailing this procedure to be included in the patient's chart.

_____

_____

_____

_____

## CHAPTER 11

A patient received penicillin for a sexually transmitted infection, and this was the last event documented in the patient's chart. Fifteen minutes later, the patient began wheezing and gasping and within 5 minutes was clearly suffering anaphylactic shock. A first injection of epinephrine administered SC at that time was ineffective, and the patient was in respiratory arrest when EMS arrived. Mask-to-mouth respirations were given with supplemental oxygen at 15 L per minute for 2 minutes before EMS assumed care of the patient. How would you document this interaction in the patient's chart?

_____

_____

_____

_____

## CHAPTER 12

A representative from the local fire department calls your office and informs you that there is a "natural gas leak" in the neighborhood where the office is located. You did notice a strong smell of propane gas as you came into the office this morning but did not notice the odor once you entered the building. Who should be notified in the office? If an evacuation is necessary, how would you proceed to safely remove everyone from the building?

_____

_____

# CHAPTER 13

Your patient is a 9-year-old girl who suffers from severe eczema. The physician has recommended that she wear bandages at night to protect against scratching. You demonstrate to the patient's mother how to apply the bandages. The patient's mother asks how often she should apply ointment to her daughter's skin, and you repeat the physician's instructions to use it twice a day. How would you document this interaction in the patient's chart?

_____

_____

_____

_____

# CHAPTER 14

Your patient is an older adult man. The physician has determined that the patient requires an ambulatory assist device. You first attempt to teach the patient to use a cane. The patient is unsteady while using the cane, so you instead teach the patient to use a walker. The patient successfully learns how to use the walker and demonstrates stability and control. You explain to the patient how to use the aid safely, including how to maintain the aid and what changes the patient should make at home to operate the aid safely. The patient verbalizes that he is comfortable using the walker and that he understands his maintenance responsibilities. How would you document this interaction on the patient's chart?

_____

_____

_____

_____

# CHAPTER 15

A patient has come in for ceruminosis treatment. Document the steps that were taken to complete this procedure as well as any complications that might have arisen during the procedure. Be sure to include any instructions that were given to the patient after the procedure.

_____

_____

_____

_____

# CHAPTER 16

Write a patient care note for a patient recovering from bacterial pneumonia. Explain what her symptoms are as well as what remedies the physician recommends/prescribes. Also, indicate how these remedies are intended to combat specific elements of the disease. You do not need to explain the details of how a remedy works, only what it is intended to do (i.e., a glucocorticoid is prescribed to reduce inflammation).

_____

_____

_____

_____

## CHAPTER 17

When interviewing a patient prior to a physical examination of the cardiovascular system, what should you ask the patient and document in his chart?

_____

_____

_____

_____

## CHAPTER 18

A patient is being scheduled for a colonoscopy. You explain the preparation to him. Document your actions for inclusion in the patient's chart.

_____

_____

_____

_____

## CHAPTER 19

A father brings in his 8-year-old daughter because she fell and hit her head while rollerblading. She was not wearing a helmet and seems to have lost consciousness for just a few seconds. The father is concerned about a possible traumatic brain injury. After a physical examination, the physician finds that the child has suffered a mild concussion. She is sent home, and you give her father instructions regarding her treatment. Write a narrative note documenting this visit for inclusion in the patient's chart.

_____

_____

_____

_____

## CHAPTER 20

You have just spoken with a 20-year-old patient about cystitis and have given her tips on how to avoid cystitis in the future. Record what you would write on the woman's chart, and make a note of any handout materials you might give the patient.

_____

_____

_____

_____

# CHAPTER 21

Ms. Molly Espinoza is a 43-year-old female patient. Dr. Cord ordered a routine screening mammogram for this patient. You confirm with her that she is not pregnant and explain the procedure. Then you prepare the patient, and two radiographs are taken of each breast, with repositioning the patient between each image. All four radiographs are developed and are readable and accurate. Record the incident in the chart.

_____

_____

_____

_____

# CHAPTER 22

John Suiker is an athletic 38-year-old man scheduled for a routine visit. He arrives disoriented and appears to be drunk and unsteady on his feet. He presents with pale, moist skin; rapid, bounding pulse; and shallow breathing. You notify the physician, Dr. Burns, of the patient's condition, and she orders an immediate blood glucose test. The patient's blood glucose is 48 mg/dL. The patient is still conscious, so you provide him with fruit juice, which he accepts. Recovery is immediate. Record the incident in the chart.

_____

_____

_____

_____

# CHAPTER 23

Rose Ryan is a 24-month-old girl visiting your office for a well-child visit. The physician directs you to obtain her length, weight, and head and chest circumference. You find the child measures 92 cm tall and weighs 15 kg. Her head circumference is 50 cm, and her chest circumference is 52 cm. Document these procedures. Use the space below to record the procedure in the chart. How would you document the above scenario on the child's chart? Be sure to document the interaction, as well as the education that was provided during her visit, and any scheduled follow-up appointments. How would you record the procedure in the chart?

_____

_____

_____

_____

# CHAPTER 24

A 78-year-old patient visits the physician's office to ask about treatment for arthritis in his knees. While you are talking to the patient, you notice that his hearing has decreased considerably since the last time he was in the physician's office. How would you document this information in the patient's chart?

_____

_____

_____

## CHAPTER 25

You have just completed maintenance on the glucose meter. Document this maintenance as you would in the laboratory instrument maintenance log.

_____

_____

_____

_____

## CHAPTER 26

Nicole Patton is a 35-year-old female inpatient receiving both a Lovenox injection and oral Coumadin. You are directed to obtain blood specimens by evacuated tube for platelet count, prothrombin time, and partial thromboplastin time tests. Document your collection as you would in the patient's chart. Include the type(s) of specimens you collected.

_____

_____

_____

_____

## CHAPTER 27

You perform an ESR test on an older adult male patient with rheumatoid arthritis. You measure a rate of 16 mL/hour. How would you document the results of this test in the patient's chart?

_____

_____

_____

_____

## CHAPTER 28

Dr. Ashanti asks you to perform a blood cholesterol test on a patient. The results are 282 mg/dL. Write a note to document this test and its results in the patient's chart as you would if your office does not use laboratory report forms.

_____

_____

_____

_____

## CHAPTER 29

The physician has ordered an influenza test on your patient. The influenza test requires a nasopharyngeal specimen. You collect the specimen. Document the collection as you would in a patient's chart.

_____

_____

_____

_____

## CHAPTER 30

You instruct a patient how to perform a clean-catch midstream urine specimen. When you test the sample, you discover that the urine is cloudy, with a pH level of 7.5, and contains traces of red blood cells, nitrites, and leukocytes. Your office does not use laboratory report forms. How would you document this information in the patient's chart?

_____

_____

_____

_____

## PSY ACTIVE LEARNING

## CHAPTER 1

The Centers for Disease Control (CDC) offers a body mass calculator on its Web site. Visit http://www.cdc.gov and search for the BMI calculator. Determine whether your BMI is within normal limits for your gender, age, and height. Describe at least three things you can do to either maintain your current weight or lose/gain weight if necessary.

## CHAPTER 2

You have been asked to select the best hand soap for use throughout the urgent care center where you work. Do Internet research to identify different types of antibacterial agents that are commonly used in hand soaps. Cite any evidence you can find as to the effectiveness of the agents. Determine which soap you believe is best. Write a letter to the office manager that gives your recommendation, clearly explaining why you chose that soap.

## CHAPTER 3

Conduct a patient interview with a family member or friend. Use a sample patient history form such as the one found in this chapter from your textbook. Be sure to perform the interview in person so that you can observe the physical and mental status of your patient. When you are finished, ask your patient for feedback, such as demeanor and professionalism or comfort level of the patient. Use his or her comments to set one goal for yourself regarding your skills conducting patient interviews.

## CHAPTER 4

With a partner, practice taking body temperature measurements with all the types of thermometers you have access to. For those you cannot access, mime the process so that you at least have the steps down the first time you are faced with the real thermometer. For all methods, go through all the steps from picking up the thermometer to returning it to the disinfectant or returning the unit to the charging base.

## CHAPTER 5

Even though the physician is the person who is responsible for using most of the instruments discussed in this chapter, you should still be familiar with how all the instruments are used. Working with a partner, access at least three of the following instruments: tongue depressor, percussion hammer, tuning fork, nasal speculum, otoscope, and stethoscope. If you do not have access to these instruments, ask your teacher if he or she can assist you. Once you have the instruments, identify the main use of those instruments during a physical exam.

# CHAPTER 6

Using the library and the Internet, research the instruments and equipment commonly used by the following medical specialties: endocrinology, rheumatology, palliative care, and radiology. Add to the list found in Chapter 6 of your text with the information you find. Include images of some of the instruments and equipment.

# CHAPTER 7

One of the most common minor surgeries performed in your office is the excision of skin lesions and moles, often related to the possibility of skin cancer. Skin cancer is prevalent today, and you feel that it's important to educate young people on the importance of taking proper precautions to protect skin from harmful sunrays. You have been asked to prepare a one-page patient education handout highlighting the dangers of skin cancer and prevention techniques designed especially for young adults.
- Do Internet research to identify the leading causes of skin cancer and the dangers associated with harmful sun exposure. Gather any statistics that are available from reputable Web sites.
- Outline steps that can be taken to protect the skin when outside.
- Highlight issues that are especially important to teens (e.g., summer jobs as lifeguards and outdoor sports practice during the day).
- Create a one-page handout to be given to teens in the office explaining how to protect their skin from the sun.

# CHAPTER 8

You have just begun working in a medical office and are getting yourself acquainted with the types of medications that the physician frequently prescribes. You know that many medications interact with food; however, you don't know a lot about specific food–drug interactions. Choose 10 common drugs from different therapeutic classifications in Table 8-1 and then research any possible food interactions. Make a chart for patients showing how common drugs and foods interact with one another.

# CHAPTER 9

Accidental needlesticks are one of the most frightening occupational hazards you will encounter as a medical assistant. The greatest fear is centered on human immunodeficiency virus (HIV) and hepatitis B (HBV). Research the incubation, signs and symptoms, treatment, and prognosis associated with these two diseases. Prepare a one-page handout on each.

# CHAPTER 10

Research the current recommendations by the American Cancer Society for mammography. At what age does the ACS recommend that women get their first mammogram? What other important information do women need to know about breast cancer?

# CHAPTER 11

Some medical professionals live on the front line of emergency medical care. Locate an EMT-Basic (EMT-B) textbook at a library, bookstore, or other source. Make a list of some basic emergency care that is expected of the EMT-B that may also be expected of the practicing medical assistant. Are there any skills that are similar? Different?

# CHAPTER 12

Research your local fire department or city website for resources related to disaster preparedness. Document these resources in a word processed document.

# CHAPTER 13

Use the Internet to research the major causes of fungal infections and find out how they can be prevented. Produce a poster to display in the office, educating patients about the main types of fungal infection, how they are spread, and how patients can protect their families from outbreaks.

# CHAPTER 14

School children, especially girls, are commonly screened for scoliosis. Research the methods used for this screening using the Internet or the library. Then, prepare a patient education pamphlet for school children who are about to undergo the screening. Explain the procedure in a way that will calm any anxieties. Include information about scoliosis as well as preventative measures the children can take and warning signs they should look for in the years following their school screening.

# CHAPTER 15

The composer Beethoven was afflicted with hearing loss that left him completely deaf. Many music lovers today suffer from hearing loss as well, and they rely on the technology available to help them enjoy the subtle tones that are written into compositions. Research the new programs and software that are being installed in hearing aids that are specifically aimed toward listening to music. List differences between listening to music and listening to speech, and make a note of tips for listening to music that physicians can give to patients with hearing aids.

# CHAPTER 16

Most people are aware of the dangers of smoking. However, it is still important to educate children about the long-term dangers of smoking. Create a pamphlet outlining the dangers of smoking to be presented to a group of middle school children.

# CHAPTER 17

Pretend you are a patient who is keeping a Holter monitor diary. Create a diary based on experiences a patient is likely to have. What kinds of activities do you participate in during the day? How are these activities influencing your symptoms?

# CHAPTER 18

One of the deadliest types of cancer is pancreatic cancer, which kills most patients within a year of diagnosis. Research the latest information about the suspected causes of pancreatic cancer on the Internet. Try to find out which treatments are proving the most effective and whether there have been any recent developments.
- Use the information you find to create an informational poster about pancreatic cancer, educating high-risk patients on how they can lower their chances of developing pancreatic cancer.
- Write a one-page leaflet for physicians, informing them of the latest treatments for pancreatic cancer.

# CHAPTER 19

Safe use of car seats can reduce brain and spinal cord injuries in infants and young children. Research the guidelines for car seat use. Then research car seat ratings and find five car seats that receive high safety ratings in each category. Create a handout for parents of young children to promote car seat safety awareness.

# CHAPTER 20

Prostate cancer is most common in men over age 50 years, and like many other cancers, it is best treated in the early stages. Testicular cancer is another form of cancer, but it occurs most often in younger men, ages 15 to 34 years. Go online and research more information about these diseases. Design a presentation to be educational for both your classmates and patients alike. Be sure to include information about the causes, the symptoms, the ways to diagnose them, and the treatments available.

# CHAPTER 21

With so many prenatal tests, procedures, and appointments at the physician's office, a pregnant patient can feel overwhelmed. Create a packet that can be distributed to a patient during the first prenatal visit. Include the schedule of prenatal visits and the procedures that will be done at each of these visits. Also include important information for the patient to consult throughout the duration of the pregnancy: especially include a list of signs and symptoms that may indicate a problematic condition.

# CHAPTER 22

Make a list of common foods for a diabetes sufferer to avoid. Then create a poster to display in the office highlighting your findings. Be sure to stress the importance of proper nutrition.

# CHAPTER 23

The physician has asked that you make a poster for the waiting room that shows important hygienic tips for children, such as washing hands, covering the mouth while sneezing, etc. Come up with a list of five hygienic tips that could be illustrated and design the poster. Use visuals so that children who are too young to read can understand the concepts being displayed.

# CHAPTER 24

Research the latest information about Alzheimer disease on the Internet. Produce an informative poster to display in a physician's waiting room, educating people about the early warning signs of Alzheimer disease. Include information about the stages of Alzheimer disease and what friends and families can expect if a loved one develops it.

# CHAPTER 25

You perform an HCG pregnancy test for your patient. She has a weak positive result, which fails the QC, so you must administer the test again. The second time, the test shows a positive result, and the QC is acceptable. Document the QC results as you would in the office QC log.

# CHAPTER 26

Familiarize yourself with phlebotomy equipment and draw a diagram of your blood-drawing station; detail on your diagram where supplies are kept. Think, in terms of safety, about where your blood station should be positioned in the office. Think about how the organization of your station will assist you in phlebotomy procedures and minimize the likelihood of accidents.

# CHAPTER 27

White blood cells are the body's defense against foreign substances and objects that enter the bloodstream. However, there are cancers, diseases, and other ailments that attack white blood cells and their production. Research one of these diseases. How many people are reported to have this disease? Is there current treatment or therapy? What are some of the cures that are being developed to stop these diseases and to rebuild the immune system? After you have gathered the information, prepare a report on this disease to present to the class.

# HAPTER 28

new patient says there is a history of heart attacks in his family, and he wants to know what can do to prevent it. He is middle aged and slightly overweight; however, he has a healthy and exercises regularly. Search the Internet and list Web sites that could contain credible information for the patient. Compile a brochure for the prevention of heart disease.

# C APTER 29

Many soaps and cleaning products today are antibacterial, meaning that they work to kill bacteria. People use these antibacterial products to wash and sanitize their hands as well as their homes, especially the kitchen and bathroom. Some studies have shown that the rise in popularity of antibacterial products may be creating strains of bacteria that are resistant to antibiotics. Perform research on this topic and present it to the class.

# CHAPTER 30

Identify common features that patients can take note of in their own urine (e.g., dark color = possible dehydration). Make a brochure to raise patients' awareness of how their physical health can be reflected in the color and clarity of their urine.